Recreation and Protected Land Resources in the United States

A Technical Document Supporting the Forest Service 2010 RPA Assessment

H. Ken Cordell, Carter J. Betz,
and Stanley J. Zarnoch

The Authors:

H. Ken Cordell, Pioneering Research Scientist;
Carter J. Betz, Outdoor Recreation Planner;
and **Stanley J. Zarnoch**, Mathematical
Statistician, U.S. Department of Agriculture,
Forest Service, Southern Research Station,
Asheville, NC 28804.

January 2013
Southern Research Station
200 W. T. Weaver Blvd.
Asheville, NC 28804

www.srs.fs.usda.gov

Recreation and Protected Land Resources in the United States: A Technical Document Supporting the Forest Service 2010 RPA Assessment

H. Ken Cordell, Carter J. Betz, and Stanley J. Zarnoch

Contents

List of Figures

List of Figures

List of Figures

List of Figures

List of Figures

Abstract

This report provides an overview of the public and private land and water resources of the United States. Described is use of natural and developed land as recreation resources with an emphasis on nature-based recreation. Also described is land protection through conservation organizations and public funding programs, with an emphasis on protecting private land through funding for purchase or for conservation easements. Outdoor recreation resources include land, water, snow and ice, scenery, developed sites, facilities, and user services. Protected land resources range from farm lands to remote wilderness, but mostly are the undeveloped lands in the United States with various forms of protection status.

The total U.S. land area is 2.43 billion acres, which contains 169 million acres of water, and consists of a diversity of land use and cover types. The United States loses about 2 million acres of forest, farm, and open space each year. In attempting to conserve such lands, land trusts and governments have instituted programs to obtain easements or purchase the land outright. The Federal Government holds in trust about 640 million acres of land (30 percent of the country's total land area). This includes national parks, national forests, national wildlife refuges, and other Federal agency ownerships. These lands, along with State and local government lands are important recreation resources serving the public interest. Private lands and recreation businesses are also important recreation resources. Projections to 2060 of per capita area of public and private land and water show a steady downward trend across all regions of the United States.

Keywords: Land conservation, private land, public land, recreation resources, trends and forecasts.

CHAPTER 1
Introduction

This assessment report is part of a series of national reports developed for the 2010 Renewable Resources Planning Act (RPA) National Assessment of Forest and Rangelands, hereafter referred to as the 2010 RPA Assessment. This report presents results of an analysis of outdoor recreation and protected land resources, both public and private, in the United States.

As required by the Forest and Rangeland Renewable Resources Planning Act of 1974, RPA assessments are completed every 10 years. Each RPA assessment reviews the status, current trends, and forecasts future trends of U.S. forests and rangelands on all ownerships. Each RPA assessment evaluates such renewable resources as fish, wildlife, water, forests, range, and wilderness, and assesses how well these resources support outdoor recreation opportunities, and since 1990, the effects of climate change on forest resources have been an additional focus of RPA assessment research. Results of RPA assessments are used by public and private land managers, nongovernmental organizations, and lawmakers to set a broad-scale context for evaluating future changes in renewable resources.

This report begins with an overview of public and private land and water resources of the United States, including trends. The rest of the report describes the use of natural and developed land as recreation resources, both rural and urban lands, with an emphasis on nature-based recreation. The report also describes conservation organizations and public funding programs that protect natural land resources, with emphasis on protecting private land through funding for purchase or for conservation easements. For the purposes of this report, outdoor recreation resources include land, water, snow and ice, scenery, developed sites, facilities, and user services.

This first chapter outlines the objectives and background for this assessment of recreation and protected land resources. The next chapters are generally in the order of those objectives. Chapter 8 revisits key findings noted in the chapter summaries.

Objectives

In the following chapters, information is provided on outdoor recreation lands, facilities, and management, as well as updated information on land and inland water protection at all levels of government and by the private sector. Examining trends is an opportunity to highlight both progress and setbacks in providing recreation opportunities and in protecting natural

land and water. To address the overall goals of this RPA assessment report, seven objectives were identified:

Objective 1—Define recreation resources such that their current status and trends can be examined (current chapter).

To achieve the first objective, measures of land, water, open space, services, and facilities are used consistent with previous RPA recreation assessments. These measures are expressed as total and per capita quantities summarized at the region and sub-region levels, with spatial analysis based on county-scale data. Reliable sources of quantitative data have been identified and documented.

Objective 2—Provide an overview of the land and water resources of the United States (chapter 2).

An overview of land and water is given as a context for assessing recreation and protected land resources. This overview covers public and private lands, including farm/agricultural lands, rangelands, and forest lands. The overview also looks at urban forests and water as key resources for outdoor recreation, as well as for protecting ecosystems.

Objective 3—Describe trends in private land protection and in protection through public ownership (chapter 3).

Chapter 3 examines the Nation's systems of protected private and public land, including land trusts (from the National Land Trust Alliance), government-sponsored conservation easements and fee-simple acquisition, and the most highly protected Federal land systems, namely, the National Park System, the National Wildlife Refuge System, and the National Wilderness Preservation System (the chapter includes an analysis of ecosystem types protected by these Federal land systems).

Objective 4—Analyze the status and trends of private sector recreation resources, including land, forests, businesses, and other resources (chapter 4).

Chapter 4 looks at the large role of privately owned and operated resources in outdoor recreation. The people of the United States use private lands for a wide variety of outdoor activities. Some of this private land, especially rural land, is forested and owned by individuals and families. Some of the rural private land is agricultural, but much of it is used for various forms of outdoor recreation. Increasingly, private land has been used for primary and second homes and as access to nearby or adjacent natural amenities (e.g., rivers, lakes, and public land). In addition to land, private commercial businesses provide a huge array of information, services, and equipment for outdoor recreation. A number of private businesses operate under contracts or through joint venture agreements on public land.

Objective 5—Describe the status and trends of local, State, and Federal public lands as a recreation resource (chapter 5).

Local governments at municipal, county, and special district levels are among the most important providers of outdoor recreation resources such as parks, athletic fields, rivers and lakes, greenways, zoos, and a wide variety of other outdoor venues. Some local resources are not highly developed and share some of the same backcountry characteristics as State and Federal lands. Local facilities, by definition, tend to be located either within or very near urban and rural communities. State governments provide State parks, recreation areas, historic sites, wildlife management areas, and various other public sites. Many of these parks and areas emphasize conservation of the natural resource along with recreation. The Federal Government owns the most extensive system of land and water in the United States. Most of these public lands are in natural cover (forests, range, and desert). An important trend over the last 30 years has been a huge increase in the development of homes, resorts, and other facilities on private lands adjacent to the public lands.

Objective 6—Map and describe the geospatial distribution of selected recreation resources as percent of land area and per capita supplies for counties in the United States (chapter 6).

The geographic distribution of recreation resources relative to the distribution of population of the United States is a very important dimension of the supply of recreation opportunities. For this objective, we consider nine basic resources that form a foundation for outdoor recreation supply. Resources analyzed include Federal land and State parks, water area, non-Federal forest area, non-Federal open range and pasture, ocean and Great Lakes coasts, mountains, snow cover, designated Federal lands, and privately owned recreation businesses. These resources are summarized in tables by region of the country and per capita quantities. Maps of the lower 48 States showing the distribution of these nine resources across all counties are also presented. An additional element of the analysis describes resources as they occur within three distance zones for each county. Resources are counted in zones including (1) within each "home" county, (2) within the home county along with all other counties within 75 miles, and (3) within counties that are 75 to 125 miles from each home county.

Objective 7—Tabulate and map projections of per capita future recreation resources for the 75-mile spatial zone (chapter 7).

An understanding of the possible future geographic distribution of recreation resources relative to the distribution of the population of the United States is needed to fully assess future outdoor recreation policy. With this objective, we consider forecasting per capita quantities of the nine categories of basic resources: Federal land and State parks, water, forest, open range and pasture, ocean and Great Lakes coasts, mountains, snow cover, specially designated Federal lands, and privately owned recreation businesses. Current and projected per capita quantities of the resources are summarized in tables by region and sub-region of the country. The expected proportional change in resources, which is measured as the ratio of the per capita quantity of resources in the projected year (2060) to that of the base year (2008) is included. Maps of the lower 48 States are presented, showing the distribution of these nine resources across all counties. These maps depict the amount of resource per capita only for the 75-mile distance zone, which is interpreted as the region within a 1- to 2-hour drive of an individual's residence, where the large majority of day-trip recreation occurs.

Background

Each RPA assessment provides a snapshot of current U.S. forest and rangeland conditions and trends on all ownerships, identifies drivers of change, and projects 50 years into the future. Analyses of the status and trends for recreation, water, timber, wildlife (biodiversity), urban forest, and range resources, as well as land use change and climate change, are included. The regions covered include the North, South, Rocky Mountains, and the Pacific Coast (see fig. 1.1).

For much of the 2010 RPA Assessment, analyses were completed across three future scenarios to characterize the common demographic, socioeconomic, and technological driving forces underlying changes in resource conditions. This use of scenarios links underlying assumptions of the individual analyses and frames the future uncertainty in these driving forces within the integrated modeling and analysis framework of the 2010 RPA Assessment. These three scenarios are described below as context for the overall RPA Assessment, but only the A1B scenario is used for the analysis reported in this assessment document.

Three scenarios, considered equally likely, were chosen for the Forest Service RPA Assessment such that they linked to globally consistent and well-documented scenarios used in the Fourth Assessment Report: Climate Change

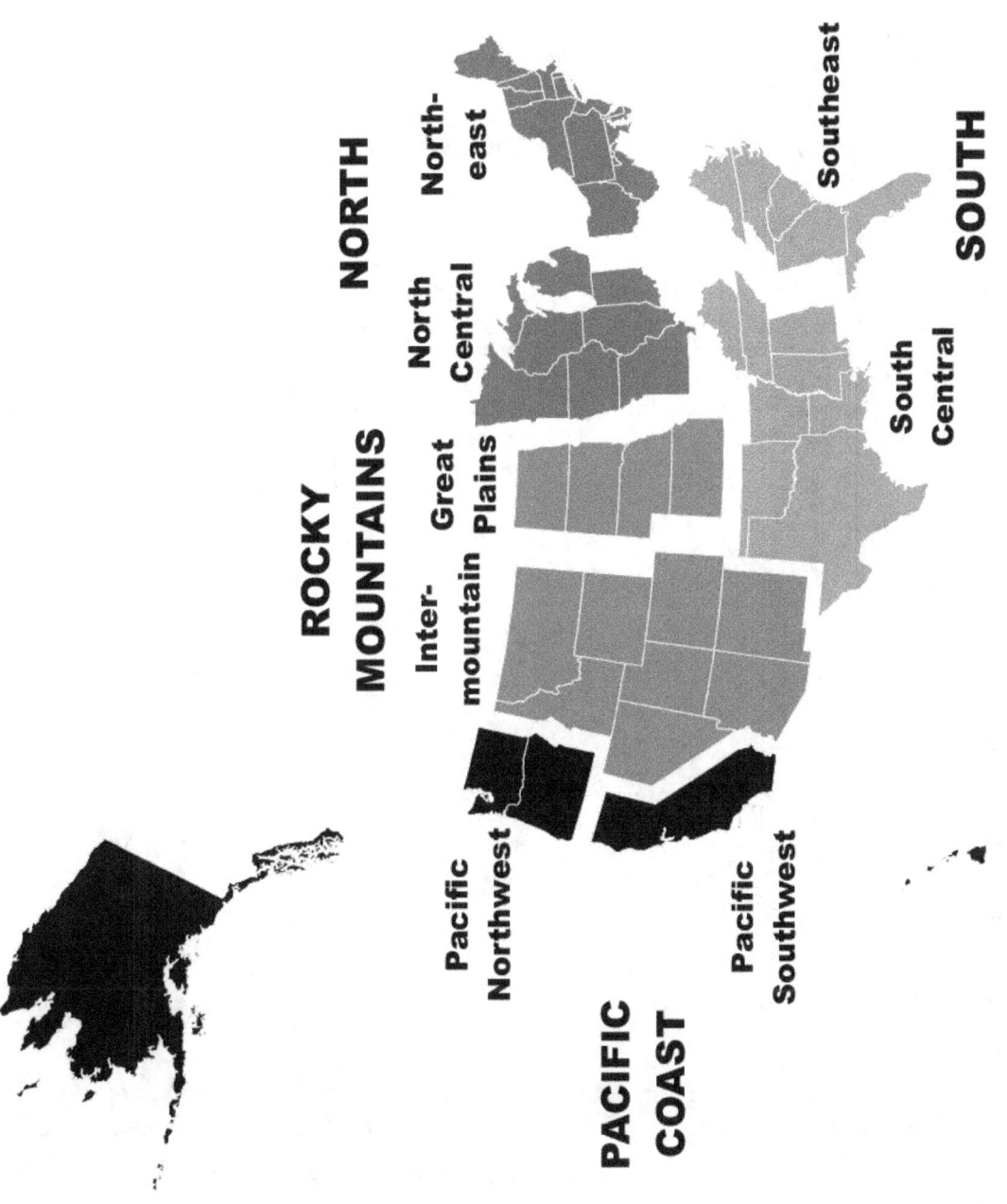

Figure 1 1—Regions and sub-regions for the 2010 Resources Planning Act Assessment of Forest and Rangeland Resources.

2007 by the Intergovernmental Panel on Climate Change (IPCC) (Intergovernmental Panel on Climate Change 2007). The scenarios include a range of future global and U.S. socioeconomic conditions with associated climate projections that are likely to have different effects on future U.S. resource conditions and trends (USDA Forest Service, in press). The IPCC scenario names A1B, A2, and B2 have been maintained in the RPA Assessment documentation for continuity. The IPCC global data were scaled to the U.S. national and subnational levels to facilitate the resource analyses for the 2010 RPA Assessment. U.S. gross domestic product (GDP) and population projections used in IPCC analyses were updated, and the updated U.S. population and disposable personal income data were then downscaled to the U.S. county level (USDA Forest Service, in press; Zarnoch and others 2010). In addition, the associated climate projections from several global circulation models (GCM) were downscaled to the county level.

As shown in figure 1.2, scenario A1B corresponds to mid-range population growth, closely following the national projections of the U.S. Census Bureau. This scenario is the primary basis for projections presented in chapter 7 of this report. Under this IPCC scenario, the United States can expect to see a population of about 447 million people (370 million adults age 16 and older) by 2060. Scenario A2 projects the highest population growth, reaching more than 505 million people (418 million adults) by 2060. Scenario B2 projects the

lowest population growth by 2060, predicting a population of 397 million people (329 million adults).

In accordance with the assessment scenarios A1B, A2, and B2, projected land use changes to 2060 were developed by Wear (2011). In general, Wear's projections indicate an increase in urban area and a decline in forest and cropland area. Wear also projects that about 90 percent of forecasted forest land losses are found in the eastern United States, with more than half of those losses in the South. Federal lands, water areas, weather conditions (snow days), and county elevations are assumed static throughout the projection period.

Recreation Resources Defined: A Land, Water, and Recreation Resources Framework

Natural resources in and of themselves do not guarantee that outdoor recreation will occur. Rather, resources are a critical "input" in the production of recreational use on both developed and undeveloped areas (Avery 1975). Natural resources in combination with management and user inputs determine the "supply" of outdoor recreation. Together, the decisions of managers (and/or policymakers) and the desires of users (constituents) determine whether a natural resource becomes a recreation resource. For example, the decision whether or not to open a particular area to public

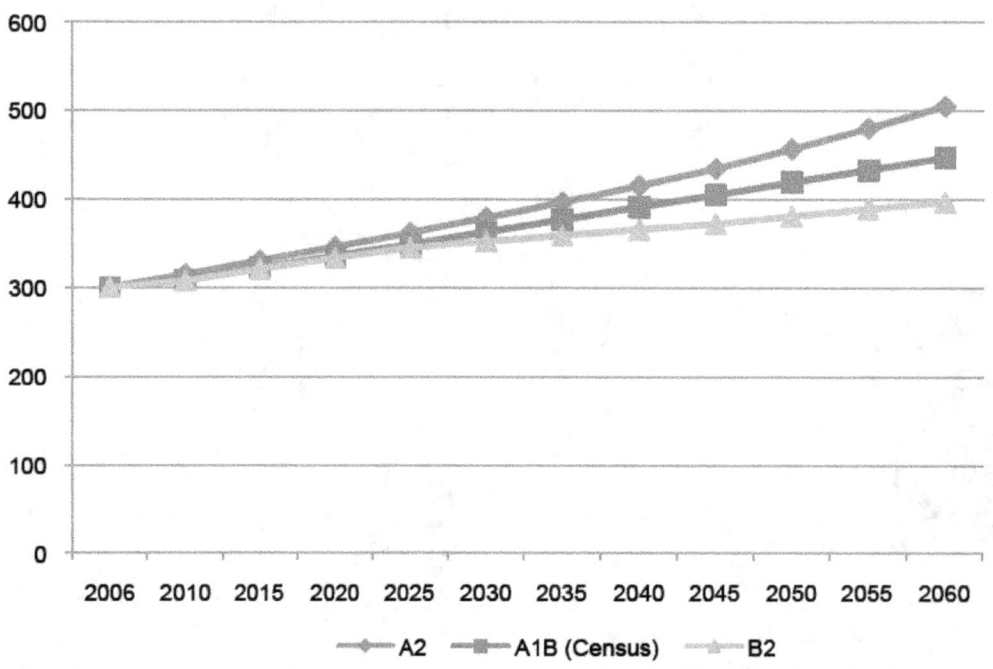

Figure 1.2—National population projections for the three scenarios used for the 2010 Resources Planning Act Assessment. The current population trend is the A1B (Census) scenario. A high population scenario is A2, while a low population scenario is B2.

use is a management input that may create a resource for recreational use. An area probably would not be opened to use, however, if there was no evidence of user demand for the site (i.e., user input). Jubenville (1978) cites these basic considerations of the resource/management/user interrelationship that help determine outdoor recreation supply: location and access, physical characteristics of the site, basic design considerations in proper planning for the anticipated recreational behavior, and good administration and maintenance of the site after development.

We draw the distinction here between resources and supply because not all resources contribute to recreation supply and, generally speaking, it is much easier and more practical to assess the status of resources for outdoor recreation than it is to attempt to assess outdoor recreation supply. Supply is usually referred to as "supply of opportunities for activity x" (e.g., fresh water lakes in the South for warm freshwater fishing). To speak about outdoor recreation supply in general is ambiguous; it could refer to any type of recreation opportunity. But water resources are a necessary condition for the supply of fishing and many other types of opportunities, so there is no ambiguity with respect to their role in recreation supply. To be able to describe recreation "supply," we would need information on the management and user inputs in combination with the resource inputs, which, obviously, is not practical for a national assessment. So, our description of the outdoor recreation resources in the United States is the rudiments or building blocks for a supply of recreation opportunities (see appendix table 1.1 for a list of the recreation resource datasets that were used in this assessment). The interaction of recreation supply with the demand for such opportunities results in recreational "use" (Avery 1975). In economic analysis, recreational use is identical to the quantity of the good or service consumed.

Previous Recreation Supply Assessments

National assessments of outdoor recreation are a relatively new phenomenon in the United States, at least compared to the whole of our Nation's history. Marion Clawson, with Resources for the Future, was an early and significant leader in developing economic analyses of outdoor recreation. His early assessments noted four "fueling factors" that drove outdoor recreation demand (Clawson and Harrington 1991): rapid increases in population, per capita real incomes, leisure time, and mobility. Development of the interstate highway system and lower transportation costs for the average American were also important driving factors. In light of burgeoning demand for outdoor recreation in 1958, the Federal Government commenced a broad-based national assessment of the outdoor recreation situation with the goal of evaluating the current demand and supply situation and planning for future needs.

The following is a brief description of the supply analyses associated with former national recreation assessments.

The Outdoor Recreation Resources Review Commission —The 85th Congress of the United States established the Outdoor Recreation Resources Review Commission (ORRRC) in 1958 with the charge to determine Americans' recreation wants and needs, the recreation resources available to satisfy those needs, and policies and programs that should be implemented. The ORRRC summary report, released in 1962 along with 29 related special study reports (Outdoor Recreation Resources Review Commission 1962), heightened public awareness and concern about outdoor recreation. This effort represented the first official acknowledgment that outdoor recreation was a legitimate concern of the Federal Government and it triggered unparalleled expansions of both public and private recreation resources (including Federal creation of the National Wilderness Preservation System, the National Trails System, the National Wild and Scenic Rivers System, and National Recreation Areas System, among others). Further, the Land and Water Conservation Fund (LWCF) of 1965 was passed in order to provide dedicated funding for outdoor recreation. Most of the LWCF funding has been targeted for matching grants to States and local governments.

As a part of this effort, the ORRRC conducted a nationwide inventory of non-urban public designated recreation areas. Information was obtained from surveys of the administering Federal and State officials of nearly 5,000 public areas larger than 40 acres. Based on those data, the ORRRC recommended that all agencies administering outdoor recreation resources adopt a standardized system of classifying recreation lands, ranging from high-density urban areas to primitive areas and also including historic and cultural sites.

The nationwide recreation plans—Another important outcome of the ORRRC was the passage of the Outdoor Recreation Act of 1963 (U.S. Public Law 88-29), which required that a nationwide outdoor recreation plan be presented to the Congress every 5 years. The purpose of the plan was to coordinate development of Federal outdoor recreation policy and programs; describe the public demands for outdoor recreation, and the current and future availability of resources to meet those needs; and identify outdoor recreation problems with suggested solutions and desirable actions. The Outdoor Recreation Act authorized the Bureau of Outdoor Recreation (BOR), created by the ORRRC in 1962 to formulate and implement the comprehensive nationwide plan.

The first nationwide plan, The Recreation Imperative, was completed in 1968 but never officially released; it was later published in draft form. The second plan was a reworking of the first plan and thus, the first official plan. Known as Outdoor Recreation: A Legacy For America and published in

1973, the second plan provided guidelines for coordinating actions of Federal and other public agencies and established roles for public and private sectors.

The third plan, called Third Nationwide Outdoor Recreation Plan, completed in 1979, focused on establishing a continuous planning process. In contrast to the first and second plans, the third plan sought broad public participation and addressed criticism that the earlier plans were unrealistic and hypothetical and that they tended to ignore non-Federal dimensions of recreation and park systems. By the time of the third plan, the BOR had been reorganized into the Heritage Conservation and Recreation Service (HCRS), which was later abolished in 1981. Most of the duties and responsibilities formerly assigned to BOR and HCRS were transferred to the National Park Service (NPS). However, the nationwide outdoor recreation planning process failed to survive the transition. The NPS assumed the technical assistance and LWCF grant-assistance duties, but the Third Plan represented the final direct and lead involvement of the U.S. Department of the Interior in national recreation assessments and planning.

The Third Nationwide Plan's Assessment (USDI Heritage Conservation and Recreation Service 1979) document was not geared as much as the previous plans toward presenting supply inventory statistics, but instead was careful to cover all aspects and providers of recreation supply. This was accomplished through three separate but related chapters: The Enablers; The Resource Base; and Facilities, Equipment, and Program Services. The Enablers chapter focused on the government and private institutions that act as providers of recreation opportunities and services. The Resource Base chapter examined all of the natural resources that become recreation resources for human leisure time use. The Facilities, Equipment, and Program Services chapter focused on recreation infrastructure, classifying recreation facilities into one of five basic categories and arranging them along a continuum from intensively developed to remotely located: neighborhood and/or private yard, community, citywide, regional, and dispersed facilities. A few of the most substantive findings in the Third Nationwide Plan with regard to outdoor recreation supply were (as directly quoted from the findings):

- The future of remaining open space in the United States is being rapidly determined.
- Recreation planning should be broadened from site-specific planning to include continuous and comprehensive evaluation of all components of the recreation/conservation system and the development of an action plan.
- Systematic efforts should be made to inventory remaining natural, cultural, and recreation resources.
- The private sector should be more heavily relied upon to assist government both on and off public lands in the provision of recreation services.

President's Commission on Americans Outdoors— The Reagan administration effectively ended national outdoor recreation planning with the abolishment of the HCRS, but established the President's Commission on Americans Outdoors (PCAO) by executive order in early 1985. The PCAO's course of study was not nearly as extensive as the ORRRC's, taking more of an issues-oriented and case study approach as opposed to quantitative analyses. The PCAO final report, issued in late 1986, is remembered for its call to "light a prairie fire of local action," imploring grassroots groups to take the initiative to develop new recreation resources and not wait for Federal or even State financial assistance (President's Commission on Americans Outdoors 1986). This charge had some notable influence, especially in the trails and greenways communities, where the stated goal was to one day have a trail located "within 15 minutes" of every American. The new unwritten Federal policy that emerged from the PCAO stressed the need for an outdoor recreation ethic, private property rights, landowner liability, cooperative partnerships, and environmental quality.

The PCAO held 18 public hearings to learn about Americans' preferences as well as the kinds of recreation resources and environments that comprise recreation supply. Further, the PCAO commissioned the advice of 20 senior advisors, and accepted contributed papers from more than 300 technical experts in addition to the work of its full-time staff and the 15 commission members. Seven key findings of the PCAO with respect to recreation supply are (as directly quoted from the findings):

- Outdoor recreation depends on healthy resources.
- Our greatest recreation needs are in urban areas, close to home.
- A vision for the future: a living network of greenways.
- We need initiatives to protect rivers all across America.
- We are losing wetlands and shorelines.
- We can enjoy scenic byways and thoroughfares.
- We must protect and enhance recreation opportunities on Federal lands and waters.

The Renewable Resources Planning Act—The Forest Service has been conducting assessments since Congress passed the Forest and Rangeland Renewable Resources Planning Act (RPA) in 1974 (U.S. Public Law 93-378), which directed the Secretary of Agriculture to prepare a renewable resources assessment by the end of 1975, with an update in 1979 (the first full-fledged report, given the short time frame before the first) and every 10 years thereafter. RPA objectives have remained the same since the first assessment. Forest Service scientists have conducted each assessment with assistance from university and other cooperators.

The RPA national recreation assessment is the information base for Forest Service planning and policy. It was never intended to become a national recreation plan or to prescribe a coordinating role among Federal, State, or other recreation providers. Rather, the intent of each RPA assessment is to gather unbiased, scientifically based information and report it in a factual, descriptive manner. Information from the assessment is used as an input for Forest Service long-range strategic planning. The following are brief descriptions of the supply portions of the three most recent RPA assessments.

The 1979 report included a substantial section on the role of private lands in meeting recreation demand (USDA Forest Service 1980). Information describing private lands and their recreational potential were derived through a nationwide survey during 1977–1978 of private, corporate, and government landowners and managers. Description of public outdoor recreation resources is brief, and almost all of the coverage is devoted to Federal recreation areas. The authors acknowledged the difficulty of assessing the role of State and locally owned recreation resources. Some of the report's findings about recreation supply are (as directly quoted from the findings):

- The greatest opportunity for realizing the recreation potential of lands already used for recreational purposes is the further development of such facilities as trails, campgrounds, picnic areas, and boat ramps.
- Equally important to providing new recreational developments is the provision for the proper maintenance of existing ones.
- Cooperative effort by government agencies, private interests, and individuals—whether in technical assistance or coordinated planning—is one means by which a greater abundance of recreational opportunities can be provided.
- Effective planning and rational decision-making regarding proper resource allocation and facility development is a necessity if the Nation's demands for outdoor recreation are to be met.

The 1989 RPA Assessment represented the first time each individual resource area published a separate, stand-alone report as opposed to a chapter in an overall Forest Service report (USDA Forest Service 1990). An important development in the recreation assessment report was the use of a resource/use paradigm that evaluated recreational use and supply along a continuum within the three major resource categories of land, water, and snow/ice. The supply chapter was based on data and information compiled in a database called the National Outdoor Recreation Supply Information System (NORSIS). Data were acquired from a variety of Federal, State, local, and private sources and summarized by the county geographic unit. The local government and private sectors were considerably weaker in coverage than the Federal

and State sectors. Recreation supply assessment findings included (as directly quoted from the findings):

- Despite increased wilderness designation, road developments on public lands have significantly reduced total remote backcountry acreage. New acreage made accessible by road developments has been offset by closures of private lands.
- The number and capacities of developed land resources such as picnic areas, campgrounds, resorts, nature centers, and golf courses have increased.
- Remote and wild water resources available for recreation have increased slightly in recent years. The number of intensively developed water sites has grown rapidly in recent years.
- Snow and ice resource changes parallel those for undeveloped land resources in general. Private land closure has especially limited resource availabilities for snow and ice recreation.

The fourth national outdoor recreation and wilderness assessment was published as a book in 1999 titled "Outdoor Recreation in American Life: A National Assessment of Demand and Supply Trends" (Cordell 1999). In addition to the then-current situation, the book also considered recent trends and likely futures in outdoor recreation. The scale of the earlier outdoor recreation assessments was primarily national, with some regional comparisons where data was available. The 2000 assessment placed much more emphasis on identifying regional differences in demand and supply and, where possible, examined geographic patterns of recreation resources and uses at the county level. A number of agency, conservation, and recreation industry representatives contributed short papers, primarily in the chapters describing resources and participation.

Federal, State, and local government recreation systems were covered in depth, and the private sector was represented by information on both commercial recreation enterprises and not-for-profit organizations. Data on private land accessibility for outdoor recreation, the focus of one of the assessment chapters, was reported from the Forest Service-sponsored 1995 National Private Land Owners Survey. The NORSIS database (begun for the 1989 RPA Assessment) was revised and updated, resulting in more than 400 separate measures of recreation opportunities. Findings from the 2000 supply assessment include (as directly quoted from the findings):

- Growth in acreage of the Federal estate has been very limited, but special designations such as wilderness and national rivers have increased appreciably.
- State park systems grew significantly in the number of areas managed during the 1990s, but much slower in total acreage.

- Local park and recreation systems continue to supply more sites, facilities, and programs than any other provider.
- About 14 percent of the Nation's 1.3 billion acres of rural private land is available for public recreation under various conditions—permission, usage fees, leasing, or open access. The amount of available private land has decreased 35 percent since 1985.
- Greenways, scenic byways, and "watchable wildlife" programs and sites have grown since the late 1980s, largely through public-private partnerships.

National reports on sustainable forests: 2003 and 2010 (Montreal Process)—The Sustainable Forests reports, better known as the Montreal Process, originated in a 1992 United Nations Conference on Environment and Development initiative to develop a standardized set of criteria and indicators (C&I) for nations worldwide to define and measure progress towards sustainable development of forests. A working group of member countries developed the internationally agreed upon set of C&I in 1994. Seven broad criteria for sustainability were further defined in terms of 65 identifiable and measurable indicators. Criterion number 6, "Maintenance and enhancement of long-term multiple socioeconomic benefits to meet the needs of societies," included three indicators that are directly related to outdoor recreation:

- 6.35) Area and percent of forest land managed for general recreation and tourism, in relation to the total area of forest land
- 6.36) Number and type of facilities available for general recreation and tourism, in relation to population and forest area
- 6.37) Number of visitor days attributed to recreation and tourism, in relation to population and forest area.

The indicators were renumbered for the 2010 report—6.35 became 6.41—and the latter two were revised to:

- 6.42) Number, type, and geographic distribution of visits attributed to recreation and tourism and related to facilities available
- 6.43) Area and percent of forests managed primarily to protect the range of cultural, social, and spiritual needs and values.

Measurements and descriptions of these indicators appear in both reports as well as in two-page briefs produced by the Forest Service. Indicator 6.41 measures the extent to which forests are managed to provide opportunities for recreation and tourism as a specific objective in management plans of public agencies and private landowners. An important change since 2003 involved the reduction in the amount of private nonindustrial forest land made available to the public for recreation. In 1995, about 14.5 percent of owners permitted

some general public access, compared to about 11 percent in 2000-2001. Indicator 6.42 provides a measure of recreation and tourism use of forests. Since the 2003 report, the trend has been increased use (i.e., visits) to forest recreation sites, by about 4.4 percent in terms of number of participants and roughly 25 percent in total annual activity days summed across all participants. Indicator 6.43 measures the area of forest land managed primarily to protect cultural, social, and spiritual values. Since the 2003 report, there has been a considerable, though not precisely known, increase in the amount of forest lands protected in experimental forests through land trusts; other conservation easement programs, such as the Forest Legacy Program; as well as land protected by means of Federal, State, and local government ownership. The World Commission on Protected Areas classification system was used in the report to categorize the protected natural areas.

Outdoor Resources Review Group—In 2008, U.S. Senators Lamar Alexander and Jeff Bingaman convened (and served as honorary co-chair) of the Outdoor Resources Review Group (ORRG), a bipartisan, nongovernmental effort to assess conservation and recreation resources in the United States. The ORRG was designed to follow up on the work of the PCAO, the last independent national commission that studied outdoor recreation more than 20 years earlier, and was also chaired by Alexander, then-Governor of Tennessee. Further, the release of the ORRG report was scheduled to coincide with the first year of the new Presidential administration following the 2008 election with the intent of informing, if not influencing, the new president's recreation and conservation policy. A major impetus behind formation of the ORRG was the continuing concern over the lack of consistent funding for the LWCF which has been the primary source of funding for recreation resource acquisitions by all levels of government since its passage in 1964. Not coincidentally, a "consistent and reliable source of conservation funding" was a primary recommendation of the PCAO's report in 1986.

Comprised of 17 conservation, recreation, and government leaders, the ORRG had professional support from scientists at the non-partisan research organization Resources For the Future (RFF), as well as contributions from the National Geographic Society. The objective of the ORRG was to assess the "priorities, challenges, and opportunities in outdoor resources" for the purpose of making recommendations that will keep "outdoor resources high on the national agenda." Public input was sought in a series of meetings and workshops held in 2008 throughout the country. Many of the same issues which have informed public debate about recreation, conservation, and public health in recent years came to the forefront: national concerns about physical inactivity, obesity, convenient and affordable access to places for recreation—especially in urban areas, the declining connection between youths and nature, time use pressures, decreasing leisure time, and others.

After its report in July 2009 (Outdoor Resources Review Group 2009), the ORRG followed up with a separate, but related final and more detailed report from RFF in September 2009 (Walls and others 2009). The RFF report was compiled from a series of 14 supporting documents that it calls "Backgrounders" and "Discussion Papers," which can be accessed at http://www.rff.org/News/Features/Pages/ OutdoorResourcesReviewGroup-Pubs.aspx. The RFF report discussed two linked trends that emerged from the ORRG assessment process. First has been the shift away from Federal spending specifically for recreation purposes, and directed instead toward farmland, wetlands, and wildlife habitat conservation. Second was the trend toward private land conservation, especially the proliferation of land trusts and land protection through conservation easements, where public access is often limited. While these efforts are laudable, RFF comments that the extent to which these programs and initiatives connect American citizens to nature is debatable.

The ORRG report offers eight recommendations toward its stated goal of "protecting and improving the country's outdoor resources for the benefit of all Americans" (Outdoor Resources Review Group 2009) (as directly quoted from the recommendations):

- Congress should permanently dedicate funding for the LWCF at the highest historical authorized level ($900 million a year) adjusted for inflation—that is, no less than $3.2 billion annually—with a share guaranteed to the States and, in turn, to urban areas.
- To overcome fragmentation among multiple programs at multiple levels, geospatial planning tools should be fully utilized to improve the efficiency, effectiveness, and transparency with which the LWCF and other public and private funds are spent.

- Public and private organizations should aggressively promote recreation and nature education for America's youth so as to engage them early in realizing the lifelong health and other benefits from participating in outdoor activities.
- Federal, State, and local agencies should continue to promote and support private-sector stewardship through public-private partnerships, joint funding, extended tax benefits for conservation easements, and other incentives.
- Federal and other public agencies, as the U.S. Forest Service and the Bureau of Land Management are doing, should elevate the priority for regional- or landscape-level conservation in their own initiatives and through partnerships across levels of government, and with land trusts, other nonprofit groups, and private landowners to conserve America's treasured landscapes.
- A new nationwide network of Blueways and water trails along rivers and coastal waterways should be established through public-private partnerships among Federal, State, and local agencies, nonprofits and private landowners.
- Any national program to reduce greenhouse gases should include funding to adapt resource lands and waters to the ecological impacts of climate change. As climate change increases the pressure on the public lands to develop renewable and conventional energy resources and transmission capacity, funding also will be needed to reconcile growing conflicts over resource use and mitigate impacts where they cannot be avoided in project design.
- Current structures and funding for outdoor resources are insufficient to meet the needs of a growing population.

To make optimal use of limited financial resources, the ORRG further suggests "elevating the priority and promoting the value" of outdoor resources in the U.S. Department of the Interior, creating an interagency council to ensure coordination across Federal agencies, and finally, creating a new, independent Federal conservation trust fund at the level of $5 billion annually.

CHAPTER 2
An Overview of Land and Water Resources in the United States

This chapter addresses objective 2 of this assessment report on outdoor recreation and protected land resources: to provide an overview of the land and water resources of the United States. This assessment report is part of a series of national reports developed for the 2010 RPA Assessment. As context for the chapters that follow it, this chapter describes public and private lands (including ownership and use of private lands in the invited paper by White, Alig, and Marzillo) as well as farm and agricultural lands, rangelands (in the invited paper by Reeves), forest lands, and urban land and urban forest.

Overview of the Land and Water Resources

Land, water, mountains, and other natural resources of the United States are essential resources for outdoor recreation, especially nature-based outdoor recreation. These same natural resources are critical for production of ecosystem and amenity services (e.g., water and scenery). The land area across the 50 States covers approximately 2.3 billion acres (not including water area). Both private and public land is important as recreation resources and for ecosystem services. Sixty percent (1.4 billion acres) of U.S. land is in private ownership (see the paper by White and others in this chapter), 29 percent is in Federal ownership, 9 percent is State and local government owned, and 2 percent is in Indian reservations (Lubowski and others 2006). In 2002, about 20 percent of land area was cropland, 26 percent was permanent grassland, pasture, or rangeland, and 29 percent was forest. Approximately 3 percent of the Nation's total land area in 2002 was urban land.

Water is especially important as a recreation and ecological resource. The recreational importance of water was clearly pointed out in 1960 by the Outdoor Recreation Resources Review Commission (Outdoor Recreation Resources Review Commission 1962). The ecological importance and the demand for water were pointed out by Brown (1999). According to the 2000 Census Typologically Integrated Geographic Encoding and Referencing System (TIGER) geographic data (U.S. Census Bureau 2000), total water area of the United States is about 164 million acres, which is around 7 percent of total surface area of the country. Census water is classified as inland, coastal, Great Lakes, and territorial. Inland water includes rivers, streams, lakes, and impoundments. An update of the Census/TIGER data in 2008 showed a decrease of 3.6 million land acres, but an increase in water area of about 4.8 million making the 2008 total about 169 million acres (U.S. Census Bureau 2010a), which is a gain of just under 3 percent (table 2.1). Most of this growth was due to additions of inland water area, which increased nearly 10 percent nationally.

Not only is the primary use of land important to recreation, but also important is the type of land cover (e.g., whether it is forest, wetlands, or other cover). The National Land Cover Database (NLCD) is the product of a group of Federal agencies working collaboratively through the Multi-Resolution Land Characteristics Consortium (www.mrlc.gov/). Results from the 2001 data describing the cover characteristics of the surface area of the United States are presented in table 2.2.

The NLCD estimate of total water cover area is almost 180 million acres (table 2.2). Wetlands cover over 124 million

Table 2.1—U.S. land and water area by RPA region, 2008, and percent change from 2000

Type of resource 2008	North Area	North Percent Change	South Area	South Percent Change	Rocky Mountains Area	Rocky Mountains Percent Change	Pacific Coast Area	Pacific Coast Percent Change	United States Area	United States Percent Change
					- - - - thousand acres - - - -					
Land area	412,621	-0.2	532,887	-0.3	741,872	0.0	572,987	-0.2	2,260,367	-0.2
Total water area	57,649	1.4	30,868	5.4	7,572	3.9	72,955	3.0	169,044	2.9
Inland water	12,692	8.4	18,641	9.7	7,572	3.9	16,396	13.6	55,301	9.7
Coastal water	3,676	0.2	4,125	-2.5	0	na	19,836	3.7	27,637	2.3
Great Lakes	38,373	-0.5	0	na	0	na	0	na	38,373	-0.5
Territorial water	2,907	0.2	8,100	0.6	0	na	36,722	-1.5	47,729	-1.1
Total land and water area	470,269	0.0	563,753	0.0	749,443	0.0	645,941	0.2	2,429,406	0.0

na = Not applicable; RPA = Resources Planning Act.
Sources: U.S. Census Bureau (2000, 2010a).

acres, almost half of which are in the South. Land with natural cover makes up the greatest national area, composed of forest, shrublands, and grasslands (herbaceous vegetation). Forest and shrublands together compose almost 1.2 billion acres.

The North, South, and Pacific Coast regions have the greatest areas of forest at between 161 and 169 million acres each (table 2.2). The Rocky Mountains and Pacific Coast regions have the greatest areas of shrubland, 254 and 242 million acres, respectively. The Rocky Mountains lead all other regions in grassland cover by a wide margin with almost 64 percent of the Nation's total. Planted and cultivated area is the third highest land cover with almost 450 million acres nationally.

The highest regional area of planted and cultivated land is in the North; the lowest area is in the Pacific Coast region.

Figure 2.1 shows the geospatial pattern of land cover across the United States. Large areas classified as cultivated crops include the Midwest, the massive wheat fields of southwest Washington, the extensive agriculture of the central valley of California, and farming down the Mississippi valley. Deciduous forests are most evident in the eastern half of the country, whereas coniferous (evergreen) forests are most evident in the West. Open water is found in the Great Lakes, The Great Salt Lake, and in coastal waters where there are bays and estuaries. Shrublands (shrub/scrub) are abundant

Table 2.2—General land cover classes and area in each class across the United States by RPA region

Land cover class	North		South		Rocky Mountains		Pacific Coast		United States
	Area	Percent	Area	Percent	Area	Percent	Area	Percent	Totals
	- - - - - - - - - - - - - - - - - thousand acres - - - - - - - - - - - - - - - - - -								
Water areas	52,778	29.4	29,116	16.2	8,525	4.7	89,374	49.7	179,793
Developed areas	38,200	36.7	38,595	37.1	15,782	15.2	11,446	11.0	104,023
Barren land	1,197	2.1	2,399	4.2	13,925	24.2	39,963	69.5	57,484
Forest	161,207	26.3	169,216	27.7	116,996	19.1	164,560	26.9	611,979
Shrubland	4,936	0.8	82,639	14.2	253,717	43.5	241,725	41.5	583,016
Herbaceous vegetation	8,498	2.7	59,466	18.6	204,171	63.9	47,358	14.8	319,492
Planted or cultivated areas	174,186	38.8	127,318	28.3	126,176	28.1	21,574	4.8	449,254
Wetlands	29,223	23.5	55,005	44.2	10,152	8.2	29,943	24.1	124,323
Total land and water area	470,224	19.4	563,755	23.2	749,444	30.8	645,942	26.6	2,429,365

RPA = Resources Planning Act.
Note: There are differences in class definitions between Census TIGER and National Land Cover Data (NLCD), for example, water. Thus, estimates of total acres differ somewhat between these sources. Percents sum across to 100.
Source: Barnes (2010).

The highlands of the Big Island in Hawaii. (Photograph by Ken Cordell 2010)

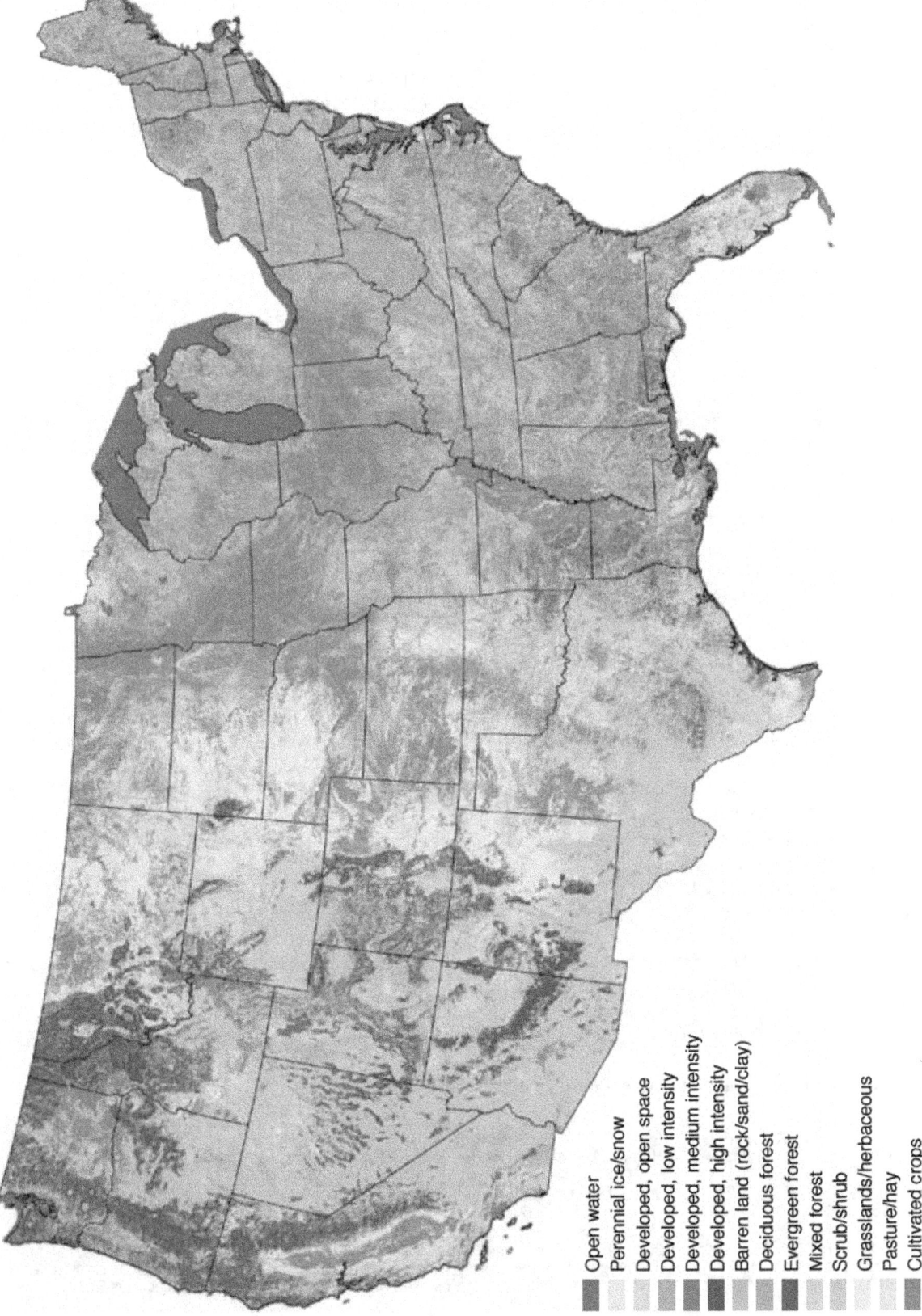

Open water
Perennial ice/snow
Developed, open space
Developed, low intensity
Developed, medium intensity
Developed, high intensity
Barren land (rock/sand/clay)
Deciduous forest
Evergreen forest
Mixed forest
Scrub/shrub
Grasslands/herbaceous
Pasture/hay
Cultivated crops
Woody wetlands
Emergent herbaceous wetlands

Figure 2 1—The geospatial pattern of land cover across the surface area of the United States, 2001. Source: Multi-resolution Land Characteristics Consortium (2001).

in the Southwest from Texas to western Oregon. Wetlands (woody wetlands) are easily recognizable along the Gulf Coast, along the Atlantic Coast, and in the upper portions of the Lakes States.

Public Lands in the United States

Public lands held in trust by local, State, and Federal Governments are critical resources for nature-based outdoor recreation and as a means to conserve open land. Below are brief descriptions of these public lands. More detail is provided in chapter 3, which covers protection of private lands and the most protected of Federal lands.

Local government lands—Approximately 9,000 local government units in the United States provide recreation and park areas and services. While the total land area owned by local governments is modest relative to State and Federal Governments, these local lands are highly important because they are close to and sometimes a part of local neighborhoods. Across local governments, parks and recreation departments are most prevalent in county governments (41 percent of counties), followed by municipalities, townships, and special districts. For all jurisdictions, the region with the highest proportion of local governments providing recreation services and parks was the South and the lowest was the Rocky Mountains (U.S. Census Bureau 2007a—see chapter 7 for more detail.)

State lands—Every State has one or more divisions or agencies responsible for management of State-owned land and water resources. A prime example is the State park systems, which are managed for both resident and tourist use. Two other categories of State agencies that are charged with management of substantial land systems are State forestry and State wildlife and fish divisions or commissions. A fourth type of State government lands are those called State trust lands, which are limited to the States west of the Mississippi River.

State park systems encompass a total of 6,548 individual park, recreation, historic, or other areas covering nearly 14 million acres (table 2.3). This total represents a 16 percent increase in number of areas and a 6 percent increase in total acreage

between 2002 and 2009. Regional statistics from the 2006 National Association of State Foresters reported that there are approximately 66.4 million acres of State-owned forest land, 25.3 million acres of which are managed by State forestry agencies. The amount of State-owned forest increased almost 8 percent between 2002 and 2006.

The Wildlife Management Institute (1997)—the most recent report available—reported that 30.3 million acres of land was either owned or managed by the 50 State wildlife and fish agencies. About 11.5 million of these acres (38 percent) were leased from other owners. Leasing is a practical means of managing wildlife and fish resources whose habitats are not contained within jurisdictional boundaries. In addition to State wildlife and fish agency management, almost 57 million acres nationwide are available for public use under cooperative agreements with other State and Federal agencies, industry, or individual landowners. Nationwide, State wildlife and fish agencies manage or cooperatively manage more than 3 million lake acres and nearly 4,000 river miles.

State trust lands were granted by Congress following the Revolutionary War to support public institutions in Western States entering the Union. Each State was left to decide how to use or sell their State trust lands. Most States have chosen to sell these lands into private ownership. The remaining 48 million acres of these trust lands include forests, grasslands, and arid desert lands of the Southwest. The 23 States which still have some trust lands include Alaska, Arizona, Arkansas, California, Colorado, Hawaii, Idaho, Louisiana, Minnesota, Mississippi, Montana, Nebraska, New Mexico, Nevada, North Dakota, Oklahoma, Oregon, South Dakota, Texas, Utah, Washington, Wisconsin, and Wyoming. In the lower 48 States, Arizona, Colorado, Idaho, Montana, New Mexico, Oregon, Utah, Washington, and Wyoming together still own almost 40 million acres.

Federal land—There are almost 640 million acres of Federal land in the United States, which is about 28 percent of the total U.S. land area (fig. 2.2). These lands are managed by seven different Federal agencies, Indian tribes, and other Federal entities. With the exception of some national wildlife refuges, areas reserved for science and research, and other

Table 2.3—Number and acres of State park system units by type of area, 2009

State	State Parks		Recreation Areas		Natural Areas		Historic Sites		Other Areas		All Areas		% change, 2002–09	
	#	Acres	#	Acres	#	Acres	#	Acres	#	Acres	#	Acres	#	Acres
U.S. Total	2,156	8,894,131	786	1,213,286	711	1,118,574	609	116,018	2,286	2,642,064	6,548	13,973,344	15.8	6.2

Source: National Association of State Park Directors. 2009 Annual Information Exchange. The 2009 AIX reports data from July 1, 2008, to June 30, 2009. Percent change is from Annual Information Exchange for the period July 1, 2001, to June 30, 2002. Natural areas include environmental education sites and areas classified as scientific sites. Other areas include forests, fish and wildlife areas, and other miscellaneous State park system sites.

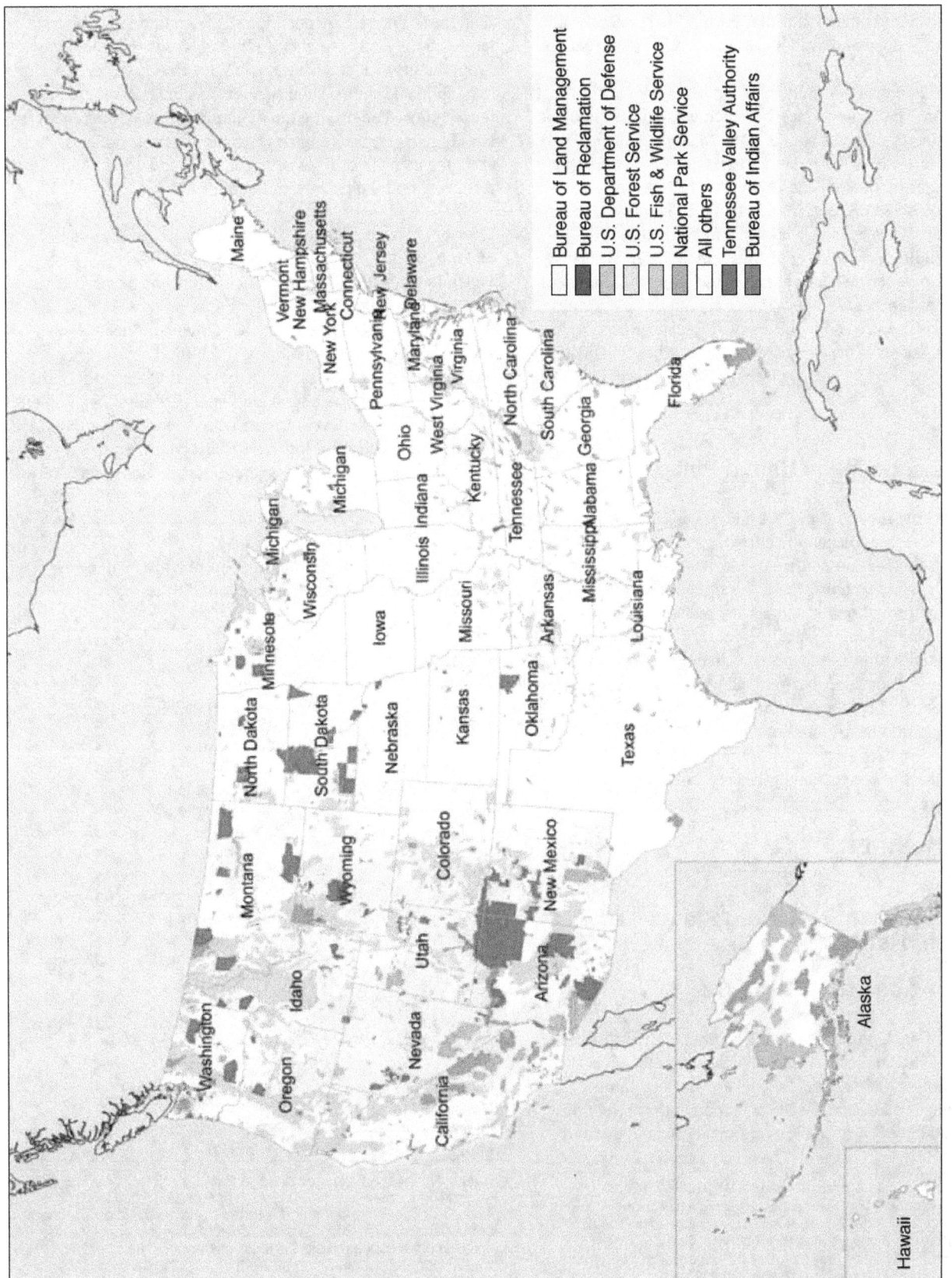

Figure 2.2—Federal lands and Indian reservations in the United States. Source: U.S. Geological Service (2005a, 2005b).

administrative and operational sites such as dams, nearly all Federal land is open and available to the public for recreation.

More than 92 percent of U.S. Federal land is located in the West, 36 percent in Alaska alone. Nearly 70 percent of all Federal land is either property of the Bureau of Land Management or the Forest Service, U.S. Department of Agriculture. Not counting Alaska, the proportion of Federal land that belongs to these two agencies rises to 84 percent. An additional 27 percent of Federal land in all 50 States is in the National Park Service and U.S. Fish and Wildlife Service. About 3 percent of Federal property is managed by water-resource agencies including the Bureau of Reclamation, Tennessee Valley Authority, and the U.S. Army Corps of Engineers. Nearly all Bureau of Reclamation land is in the West, but all of the Tennessee Valley Authority land and about 70 percent of U.S. Army Corps of Engineer areas are in the East.

Private Lands in the United States

In the following invited paper, the authors use the results of existing research to examine current patterns of land ownership as well as past, current, and projected future patterns of private land use. First, the authors examine the spatial pattern of public and private ownership in the contiguous United States. Next, they describe the uses of private land within U.S. regions, with emphasis on the distribution of undeveloped rural land uses (i.e., forest, crop, and rangeland). Then, they identify trends in non-Federal rural land area and past transitions among rural land uses. Finally, the authors discuss past patterns of urbanization of rural lands and projections of conversion in the coming decades.

INVITED PAPER

Private Lands in the United States—Their Ownership and Use

Eric M. White, Ralph J. Alig, and Anita T. Morzillo[1]

The lands of the United States are a combination of differing ownerships and land uses. Generally, the uses (e.g., forests, development) and area of public land are stable with only minor changes over time. However, although the area of the private land base is also stable over time, both land use and

[1] Eric M. White, Faculty Research Associate, Department of Forest Engineering, Resources and Management, Oregon State University, Corvallis, OR 97331; Ralph J. Alig, Research Forester with the Pacific Northwest Research Station, USDA Forest Service, Corvallis, OR 97331; Anita T. Morzillo, Assistant Professor, Department of Forest Ecosystems and Society, Oregon State University, Corvallis, OR 97331.

the types of private ownership (e.g., commercially owned lands versus land owned by individuals) change frequently. From the private land base, society receives a variety of goods (e.g., food and timber) and services (e.g., clean water and recreation). Recognizing the dynamic nature of the private land base is important in considering the uses, policies, and management of forests, rangelands, and other natural resources on both private and public land.

Ownership patterns—The land area of the contiguous 48 United States is approximately 1.9 billion acres. The Federal Government owns about 400 million of these acres. A mixture of private individuals, other private entities, State and local governments, and Native American tribal governments own the remaining 1.5 billion acres. Private lands account for the vast majority (about 85 percent) of the contiguous U.S. non-Federal land base (Lubowski and others 2006). At the State level, private lands are most common in Kansas, Nebraska, and Iowa, and least common in Nevada and Arizona (table 2.4). On average across the country, private lands constitute about 77 percent of State land area.

Table 2.4—Percent of land area in private ownership by State for the 48 contiguous United States

State	Percent	State	Percent
Alabama	97	Nebraska	98
Arizona	17	Nevada	13
Arkansas	90	New Hampshire	72
California	47	New Jersey	74
Colorado	57	New Mexico	44
Connecticut	87	New York	84
Delaware	90	North Carolina	90
Florida	74	North Dakota	89
Georgia	93	Ohio	96
Idaho	28	Oklahoma	94
Illinois	97	Oregon	44
Indiana	95	Pennsylvania	84
Iowa	98	Rhode Island	81
Kansas	99	South Carolina	91
Kentucky	94	South Dakota	69
Louisiana	92	Tennessee	92
Maine	82	Texas	96
Maryland	82	Utah	22
Massachusetts	81	Vermont	85
Michigan	78	Virginia	86
Minnesota	75	Washington	54
Mississippi	95	West Virginia	90
Missouri	93	Wisconsin	90
Montana	59	Wyoming	57

Source: National Association of State Park Directors. 2009 Annual Information Exchange. The 2009 AIX reports data from July 1, 2008, to June 30, 2009. Percent change is from Annual Information Exchange for the period July 1, 2001, to June 30, 2002. Natural areas include environmental education sites and areas classified as scientific sites. Other areas include forests, fish and wildlife areas, and other miscellaneous State park system sites.

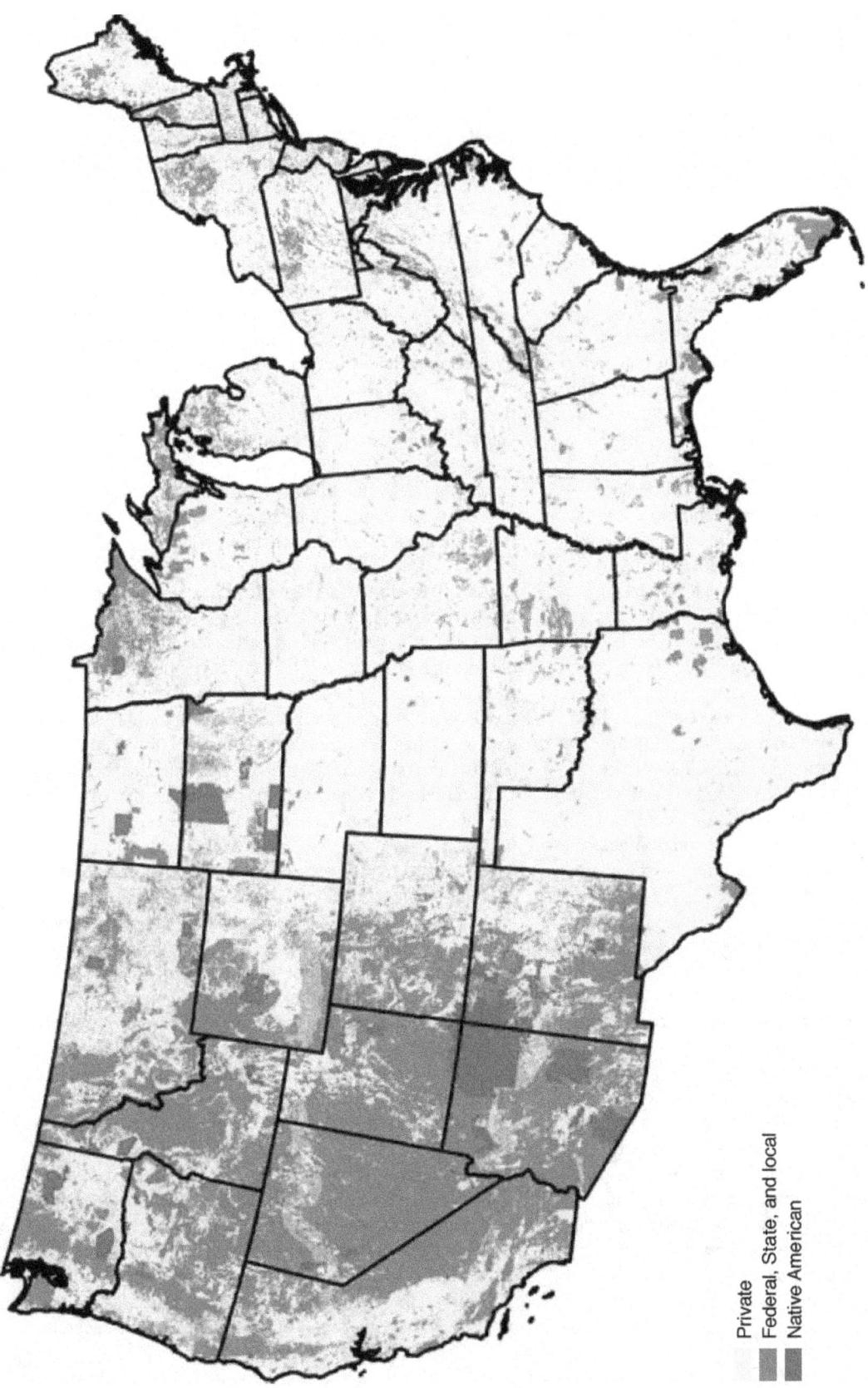

Private

Federal, State, and local

Native American

Figure 2.3—Land ownership in the contiguous United States. Data source: Protected lands of the continental U.S. (CUS_UPPT_100). Unpublished dataset, 2007. On file with D.M. Theobald, Forestry 245, Colorado State University, Ft. Collins, CO 80523.

Because of settlement patterns, Eastern U.S. lands are primarily privately owned (fig. 2.3). Publicly owned lands (primarily in Federal ownership) are a prominent fixture of the Western States. The contiguous Western States contain about 8.5 times the Federal land of the Eastern States (White and others 2010). The West also contains the majority of the American Indian tribal lands. Many of the western Federal lands are remnants of land settlements gained by treaty from foreign governments. The aggregate areas of land in both Federal and non-Federal ownership have remained stable since 1982 (USDA Natural Resources Conservation Service 2007).

Private land use—Approximately 7 percent of the non-Federal land base of the United States is used for urban and developed land uses (USDA Natural Resources Conservation Service 2007). In this research, developed land includes large and small urban and built-up lands as well as rural transportation lands (USDA Natural Resources Conservation Service and Iowa State University Statistical Laboratory 2000). Urban and developed lands are most common in the South and North regions—15 and 14 percent of non-Federal lands, respectively. New Jersey is the most developed State (42 percent of the non-Federal land base) and Montana is the least developed (2 percent of non-Federal land area).

Although developed land is common, crops, rangeland, and forest account for the vast majority of non-Federal land area in each U.S. region. These undeveloped rural land uses are most common on non-Federal land in the Great Plains, Intermountain, and South Central regions (fig. 2.4). In the Great Plains and North Central regions, crop land is the most common land use. In the Intermountain region, rangeland is the most prevalent land use. In the Northeast and Southeast, the regions with the smallest non-Federal rural land base, the majority of undeveloped rural land is forest.

Rural land use transitions—The national area of non-Federal rangeland and forest has remained relatively stable since 1982 at a little more than 400 million acres each (fig. 2.5). Even though private forest area has increased in recent decades, that increase has been slight (Smith 2009). Since 1982, the area of crop and pasture land has declined from about 550 million to about 509 million acres in 2007. The decline in crop and pasture land has remained fairly steady. For the most recent periods for which we can quantify region-level trends in rural land area, the Southeast, Northeast, South Central, and North Central regions have experienced the greatest aggregate reductions in land in crops and pasture (table 2.5). The area of land in range declined most precipitously in the Great Plains and Intermountain regions. Forest area gained in aggregate in the North Central and South Central regions, but remained generally steady or declined elsewhere.

Knowing the acreage of aggregate trends in rural land uses (e.g., fig. 2.5) is useful, but it masks underlying land use transitions involving forests, crop, pasture, and rangeland. For example, although total forest area has remained stable, some forest has been lost to urbanization, while some new forest has been gained from other rural land uses. These underlying transitions are important because many of the goods and services provided by rural lands are location specific. The addition of forest in one location may not offset the goods and services lost when forest in another location is converted to other land uses. In the Eastern States, between 1982 and 1997 (the latest year for which sub-national land conversion data are available), nearly 3 percent of forest area was converted to developed land uses and about 1 percent of forest area was converted to pasture (White and others 2010). At the same time, new forests were added from former pasture and crop lands. In the Western States, about 3 percent of forest area was converted to rangeland, and 1 percent of forest area was converted to developed uses (White and others 2010). Forests in the Western United States gained some acreage from pasture land during the same time period.

Loss of rural land to development—Between 1982 and 2003, developed land in the contiguous United States increased by nearly 57 percent. This expansion resulted in the conversion of more than 40 million acres of undeveloped non-Federal rural lands to developed uses. Between 1982 and 2007, forests provided the greatest number of acres for new development with more than 17 million acres converted, followed by crops, pasture, and range land (fig. 2.6). More than one million acres of other rural lands, which includes farmsteads, barren land, and marshland, were converted to developed uses.

Projections of developed land area expansion—The expansion of developed land is spurred in large part from demands for new housing and commercial space from increasing populations, from the desire of many to live in natural amenity-rich environments, and from many other factors. A projected population increase to more than 360 million individuals by 2030 is projected to require about 44 million more housing units (White and others 2009). Previous modeling efforts have estimated that each additional housing unit equates to about 1.2 acres of newly developed land for residential, commercial, transportation, and industrial purposes. Based on a simulation model of rural land development in the United States (White and others 2009), a projected 4 percent of the current non-Federal rural land base will be converted for developed uses by 2030. The Southeast region is projected to have the greatest percentage of non-Federal rural lands converted to developed uses, followed by the Northeast region (table 2.6). The Great Plains and Rocky Mountains regions are projected to have the smallest percentages of non-Federal

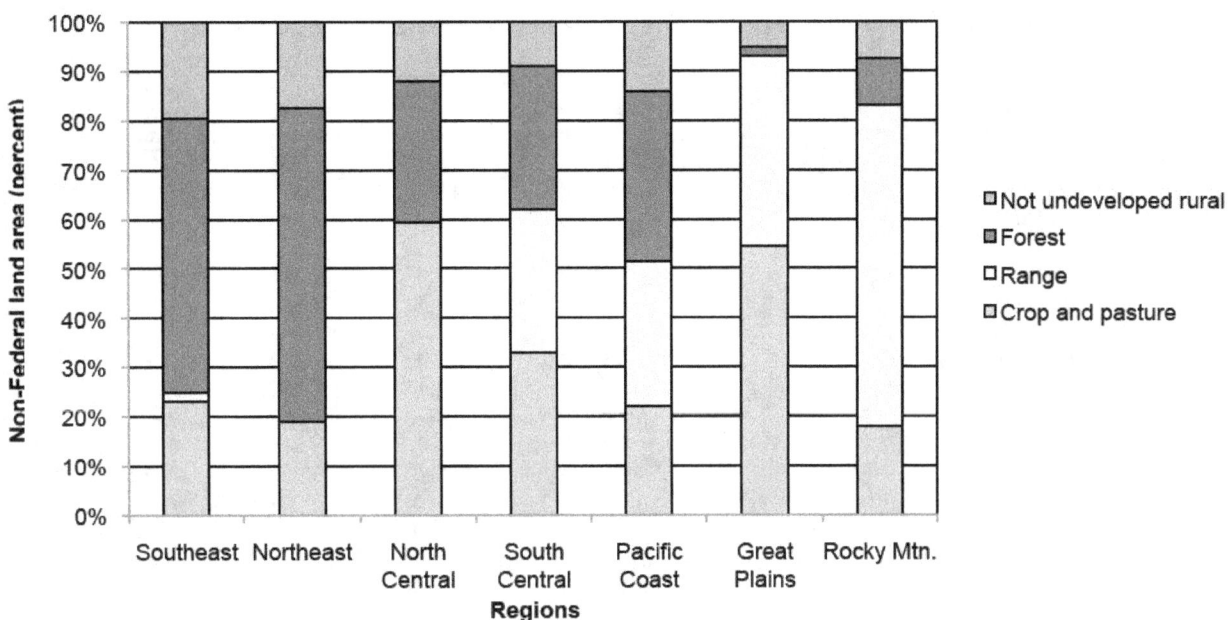

Figure 2.4—Undeveloped rural land use on non-Federal lands by U.S. region. Data source: USDA Natural Resources Conservation Service (2007).

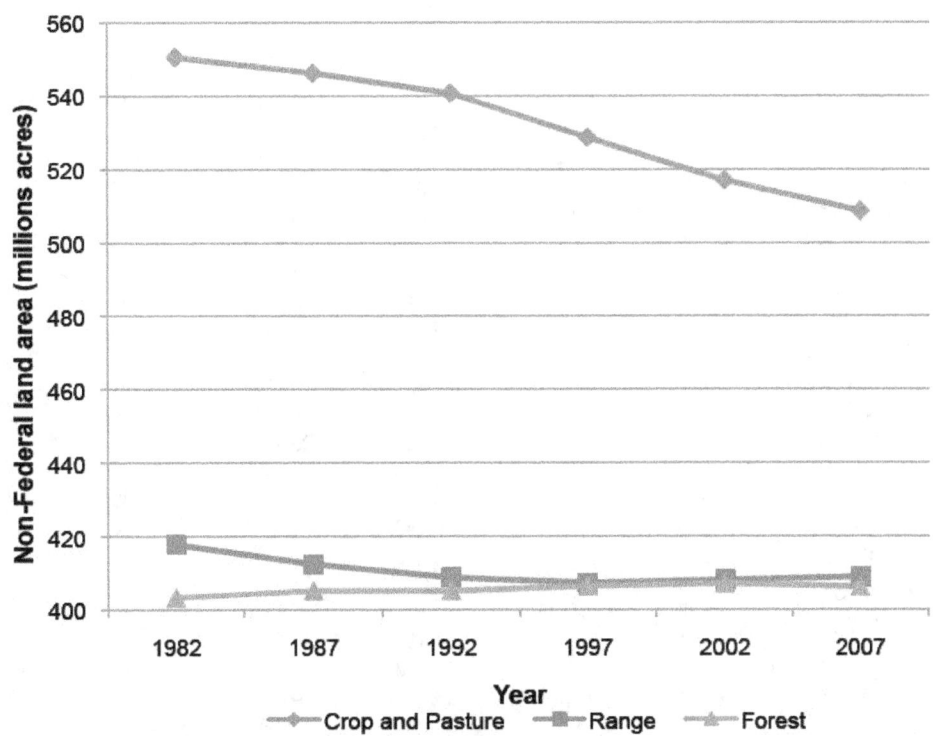

Figure 2.5—Area of non-Federal rural land in crop and pasture, range, and forest land uses, 1982–2007. Note: Crop and pasture includes Conservation Reserve Program land. Source: USDA Natural Resources Conservation Service (2009).

Table 2.5—Acreage trends for non-Federal rural land by U.S. subregion, 1982-2007 (thousands of acres)

Region	Year	Cropland	CRP land	Pasture	Range	Forest	Other rural land	Total rural land
Southeast	1982	23,830	na	13,666	4,388	77,195	5,453	124,533
	1987	21,983	550	13,890	4,060	77,001	5,431	122,915
	1992	20,113	1,210	13,967	3,524	76,333	5,420	120,567
	1997	18,695	1,179	13,470	3,212	75,656	5,650	117,861
	2002	18,106	719	12,604	2,881	75,381	5,637	115,327
	2007	17,103	683	12,331	2,636	74,908	5,794	113,455
South Central	1982	82,892	na	51,178	112,766	103,613	7,556	358,005
	1987	77,912	3,201	50,713	111,635	104,802	7,753	356,017
	1992	71,052	7,689	51,056	110,906	105,506	7,809	354,016
	1997	68,232	7,439	49,654	111,484	106,683	7,938	351,430
	2002	65,010	7,226	49,175	111,748	107,330	8,041	348,528
	2007	61,517	7,240	49,309	112,596	107,321	8,372	346,355
Northeast	1982	30,206	na	13,211	0	85,239	4,884	133,540
	1987	29,498	95	11,938	0	85,759	4,965	132,255
	1992	28,469	522	11,010	0	85,697	4,955	130,653
	1997	27,592	517	9,637	0	85,712	4,825	128,283
	2002	26,395	408	9,807	0	85,544	4,607	126,760
	2007	25,523	364	9,923	0	85,242	4,662	125,713
North Central	1982	123,630	na	32,777	129	67,363	9,351	233,250
	1987	121,530	3,120	30,334	92	67,999	9,269	232,344
	1992	116,956	7,550	29,027	88	68,526	9,223	231,369
	1997	116,836	6,975	27,240	78	69,497	9,173	229,797
	2002	115,866	6,189	27,048	78	70,251	9,159	228,592
	2007	114,423	5,955	27,566	83	70,258	9,315	227,600
Great Plains	1982	93,324	na	7,931	74,720	3,290	4,400	183,665
	1987	93,023	2,109	7,481	73,221	3,309	4,396	183,538
	1992	86,860	8,904	7,528	72,098	3,384	4,417	183,190
	1997	87,669	8,581	7,185	71,592	3,385	4,467	182,879
	2002	87,106	8,267	7,272	72,036	3,431	4,566	182,679
	2007	85,878	8,917	7,556	72,103	3,500	4,591	182,544
Intermountain	1982	43,126	na	7,453	191,146	25,984	10,405	278,113
	1987	40,240	3,762	7,561	189,299	25,843	10,523	277,228
	1992	37,413	6,484	7,962	188,687	25,605	10,943	277,094
	1997	37,069	6,328	8,323	187,677	25,794	11,157	276,348
	2002	34,815	7,319	7,937	188,407	25,521	11,225	275,222
	2007	33,023	7,631	8,197	188,862	25,465	11,205	274,382
Pacific Northwest	1982	12,108	na	3,324	15,619	25,843	1,403	58,296
	1987	11,185	860	3,359	15,424	25,756	1,385	57,970
	1992	10,513	1,556	3,355	15,340	25,619	1,390	57,772
	1997	10,387	1,500	3,201	15,215	25,441	1,521	57,265
	2002	10,229	1,689	2,783	15,302	25,398	1,563	56,965
	2007	10,067	1,887	2,615	15,308	25,326	1,584	56,788
Pacific Southwest	1982	10,431	na	1,357	19,132	14,854	3,791	49,564
	1987	10,174	118	1,447	18,843	14,867	3,822	49,270
	1992	10,066	181	1,115	18,275	14,625	3,909	48,171
	1997	9,659	173	1,072	18,285	14,428	4,018	47,635
	2002	9,573	174	1,156	17,757	14,402	4,134	47,196
	2007	9,489	174	1,120	17,532	14,390	4,118	46,823

na = Not available.
Note: The Conservation Reserve Program (CRP) was established by Congress in 1985. Because of methodological differences, the forest area estimates in this table after 1997 may differ substantially from forest area estimated by another USDA source of data, the Forest Inventory and Analysis Program of the U.S. Department of Agriculture, Forest Service.
Source: USDA Natural Resources Conservation Service (2009).

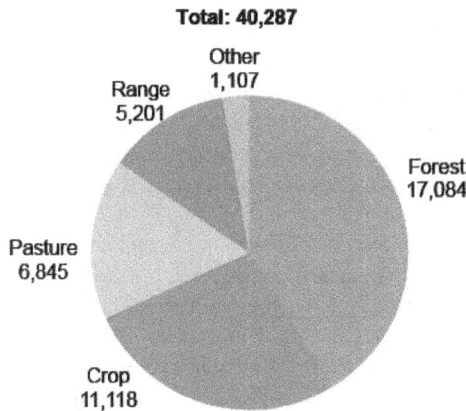

Total: 40,287

Other 1,107
Range 5,201
Forest 17,084
Pasture 6,845
Crop 11,118

Figure 2.6—Area of non-Federal rural land in the contiguous United States converted to developed uses, 1982–2007 (thousands of acres). Note: The land use subtotals do not add to the national total of converted acres because about 1.07 million acres of developed land in 1982 were converted to other uses. Source: USDA Natural Resources Conservation Service (2009).

Table 2.6—Percent of rural land projected to be developed between 2000 and 2030 by U.S. region

Region	Percent
Southeast	15.1
Northeast	6.3
North Central	3.6
South Central	4.5
Pacific Coast	2.9
Great Plains	0.5
Rocky Mountains	1.8
Contiguous United States	4.0

Source: White and others (2009).

Scattered new houses are visible as development begins on a mountain side as seen from the Raggeds Wilderness Area on the White River National Forest in Colorado. (Photograph by Ken Cordell)

rural lands converted to developed uses. In the East, all else being equal, forest is projected to be the greatest provider of newly developed land. In the West, rangeland and cropland are projected to be the greatest providers of land for development.

In addition to reducing the area of undeveloped rural land, increases in developed land area can place remaining natural resource lands under increased pressure for provision of goods and services, such as timber production and recreation opportunities. The Southeast and South Central regions are projected to experience the greatest percentage increases in developed land area (fig. 2.7). In the West, projected percentage increases in developed land area are greatest in the Rocky Mountains region. Large projected increases in developed area in many Western States reflect both significant projected increases in population and the small relative amounts of existing developed land area.

End Invited Paper

Farm and Agricultural Land

Substantial acreages of rural land are privately owned and in use as farms and agricultural land (table 2.7). By the definitions used for the Census of Agriculture, agricultural land is that which is used mostly for crops, pasture, or grazing (USDA National Agricultural Statistics Service 2007). Also included are associated woodlands and wastelands not actually in cultivation, pasture, or grazing, but part of a farm operation. All grazing land, except government land, is included. Recreational access to these properties is typically limited to owners, their families, friends, or lessees. Table 2.7 shows that the number of farms has increased slightly since 1990, but that the average acreage per farm and total farm acreage of the United States have decreased substantially.

One of the most important uses of farm land is growing crops—occupying about 39 percent of total farm land (USDA Natural Resources Conservation Service 2009).

Table 2.7—Number and acreage of farms in 1990, 2000, and 2008

Item	Unit	1990	2000	2008
Number of farms	Thousands of farms	2,146	2,167	2,200
Land in farms	Millions of acres	987	945	920
Average per farm	Acres	460	436	418

Source: U.S. Census Bureau (2010b).

Hillside strawberry farming in 2000 in Monterey County, CA. (Photograph by Lynn Betts, USDA Natural Resources Conservation Service)

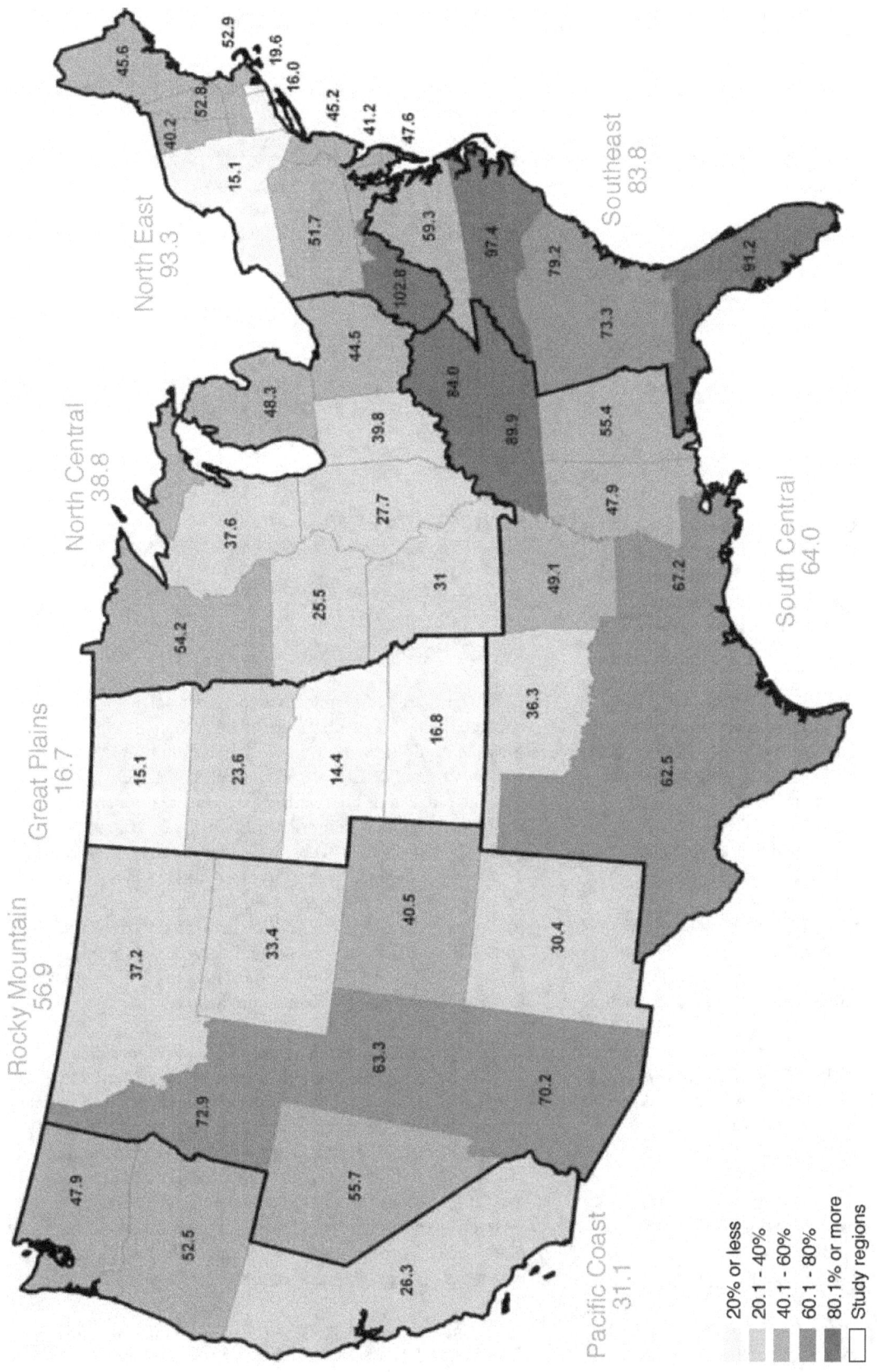

Figure 2.7—Percentage increase in developed land area projected for States and regions, 2000 to 2030. Source: White and others (2009).

20% or less
20.1 - 40%
40.1 - 60%
60.1 - 80%
80.1% or more
Study regions

Table 2.8—Acres of land in farms in the United States by type of agricultural use and RPA region, 2007

Type of agricultural use	North Acres	North Percent	South Acres	South Percent	Rocky Mountains Acres	Rocky Mountains Percent	Pacific Coast Acres	Pacific Coast Percent	United States Total Acres
Cropland	143,851,909	35.4	99,549,664	24.5	140,675,207	34.6	22,348,129	5.5	406,424,909
Woodland	22,606,724	30.1	37,523,483	50.0	9,858,854	13.1	5,109,542	6.8	75,098,603
Permanent pasture and rangeland	17,257,624	4.2	127,498,795	31.2	235,401,232	57.6	28,674,465	7.0	408,832,116
Farmsteads, buildings, livestock, ponds, roads, etc.	9,724,442	30.6	9,199,658	29.0	10,208,203	32.2	2,607,909	8.2	31,740,212
Total land in farms	193,440,699	21.0	273,771,600	29.7	396,143,496	43.0	58,740,045	6.4	922,095,840

RPA = Resources Planning Act.
Note: Percentages sum across to 100.0.
Source: USDA National Agricultural Statistics Service (2007).

According to the National Resources Inventory by the U.S. Department of Agriculture, cropland acreage has declined from about 420 million acres in 1982 to 357 million acres in 2007. About half of this reduction is the result of enrollments of environmentally sensitive cropland in the Conservation Reserve Program of the U. S. Department of Agriculture.

Total land area in farms, based on the Census of Agriculture, is shown by region in table 2.8. The greatest acreage is in the Rocky Mountains, followed by the South and North regions. The Rocky Mountains region also has the greatest acreage of permanent pasture and rangeland, nearly 58 percent of the U.S. total. The North and Rocky Mountains regions each have about one third of the Nation's cropland, and the South has about half of the Nation's farm woodland.

Unlike cropland, virtually all (99 percent) of which is in private ownership, rangeland has a substantial presence on public lands, especially on U.S. Forest Service and Bureau of Land Management lands. Almost 61 percent of "grassland pasture and range" is privately owned, with about one-fourth on Federal lands and the remainder on other public and American Indian lands (Lubowski and others 2006). The following invited paper by Reeves describes range land uses, ownership, ecosystem services, and benefits, among other concerns.

INVITED PAPER

Rangelands

Matt C. Reeves[2]

Rangelands are found in many ecoregions and are characterized by a diverse suite of vegetation. Shrublands; grasslands; alpine communities; oak, mesquite, and juniper woodlands; and deserts are all examples of rangeland. In general, rangelands are relatively remote areas where potential natural vegetation is comprised principally of grasses, forbs, grass-like plants, and shrubs, which are suitable for browsing or grazing, although the presence of herbivory is not a requisite for rangeland status. Though estimates vary, rangelands occupy approximately 662 million acres in the contiguous United States when defined using the Natural Resources Inventory definition (USDA Natural Resources Conservation Service 2009) (fig. 2.8) (Reeves and Mitchell, in press).

The majority of rangelands lie west of the 95th meridian (fig. 2.8). In the contiguous United States, roughly 662 million acres of rangelands occupy approximately 50 percent of the vegetated area, with 224 million rangeland acres occurring on Federal lands (table 2.9). The Bureau of Land Management administers roughly 139 million acres, the majority of Federal rangelands (fig. 2.9). The majority of U.S. rangelands overall, however, are privately owned (table 2.9). The U.S. rangeland base is currently quite stable, though roughly 33 percent of the historic rangeland extent has been permanently modified by human influence

[2] Matt C. Reeves, Research Ecologist, U.S. Department of Agriculture, Forest Service, Rocky Mountains Research Station, Missoula, MT 59801.

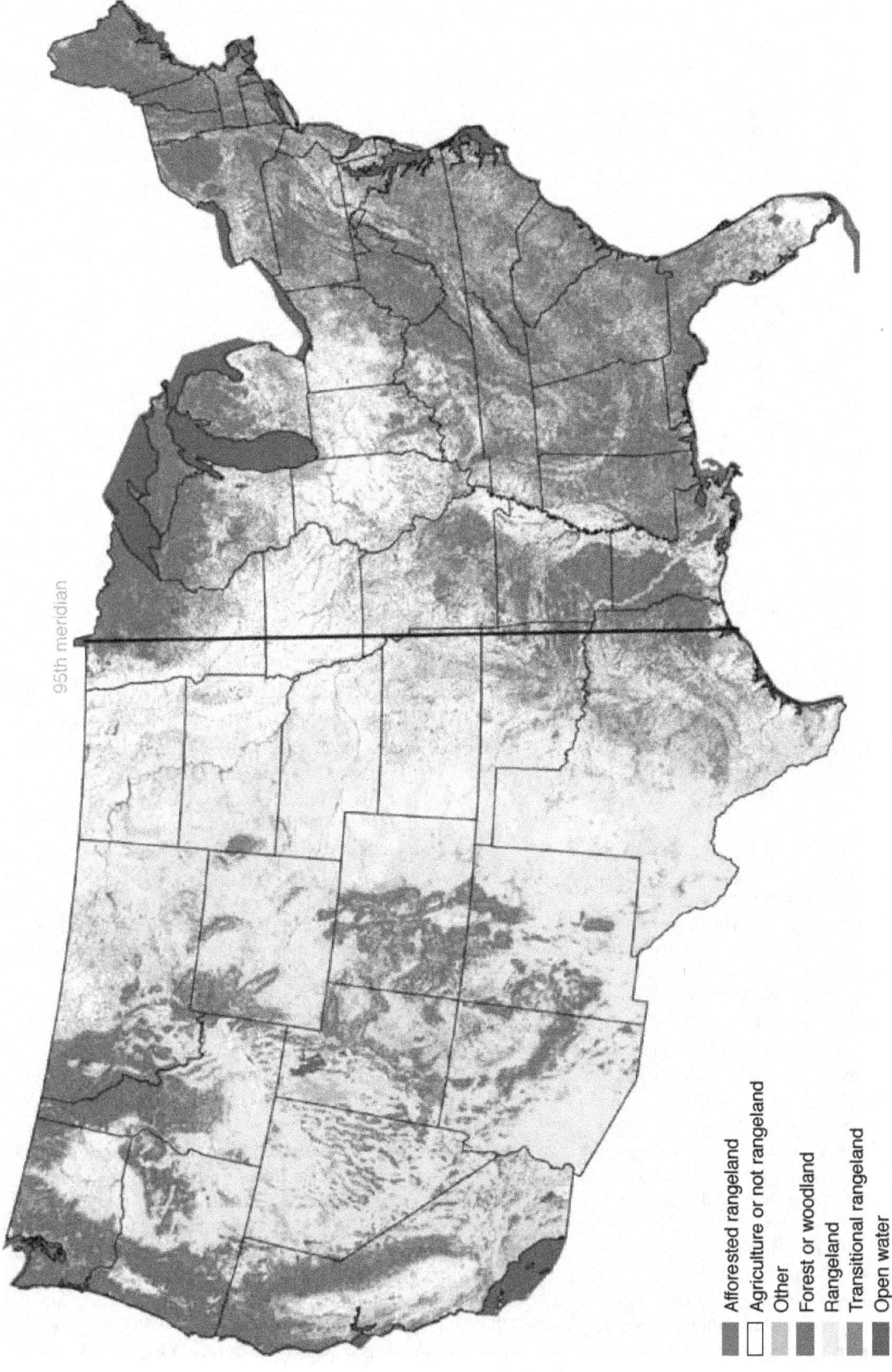

Afforested rangeland
Agriculture or not rangeland
Other
Forest or woodland
Rangeland
Transitional rangeland
Open water

95th meridian

Figure 2.8—Estimated distribution of rangelands occurring in the contiguous United States (Reeves and Mitchell, in press). The estimated distribution is based on the rangeland definition used by the Natural Resources Inventory (USDA Natural Resources Conservation Service 2009).

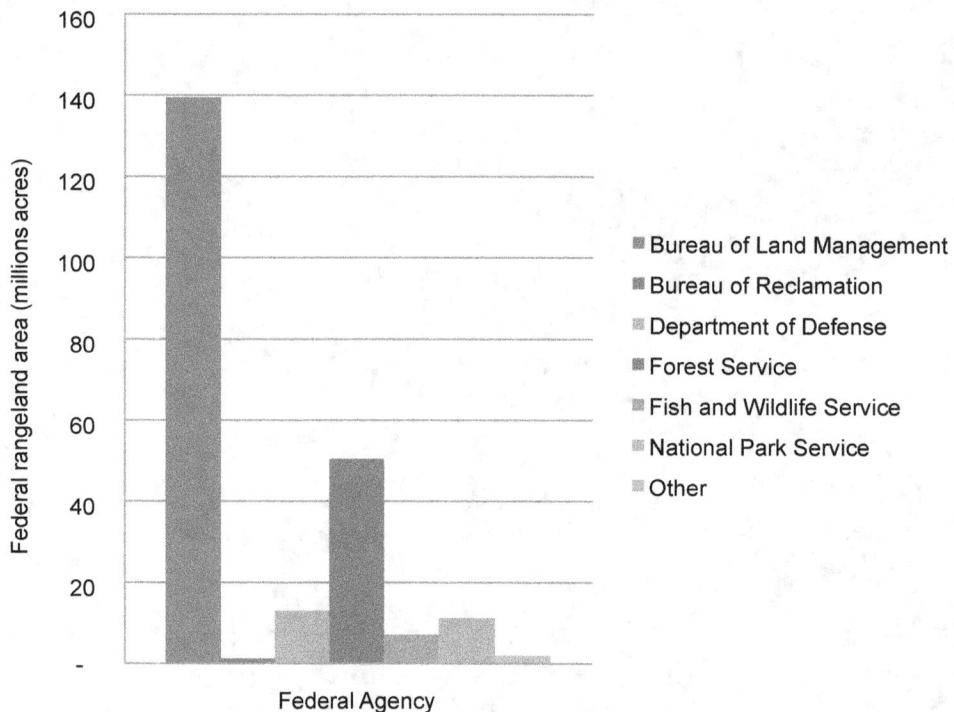

Figure 2.9—Estimated rangeland area managed by Federal agencies (Reeves and Mitchell, in press). The total area managed by Federal agencies is approximately 224 million acres. The estimated area is based on the rangeland definition used by the National Resources Inventory (USDA Natural Resources Conservation Service 2009).

(Reeves and Mitchell, in press) (fig. 2.10). Between 1982 and 2007, nearly 430,000 acres of non-Federal rangelands were lost annually to various land use changes, though the rate of loss over the last decade is less than in previous decades (USDA Natural Resources Conservation Service 2009).

Though estimates vary, rangelands occupy approximately 47 percent of the global land base, excluding Antarctica (Reeves and Mitchell, in press). These lands provide livelihood to millions of people (Papanastasis 2009) and provide a multitude of biological and social benefits. Cattle alone provide tens of billions of dollars to the world economy. In 2009 the United States generated roughly $32 billion worth of beef cattle production. Since many beef cattle raised in the contiguous United States spend all or part of their grazing cycle on rangelands (i.e., where cattle are not dependent on feedlots or crop residues to provide sufficient daily forage intake), much of the revenue generated through sales of cattle is attributable to forage from rangelands. Though forage production is perhaps the most visible and ubiquitous rangeland resource, it is not, by any means, the only one.

Public perception and associated issues with rangelands have undergone transformation in the last decade. Chief among these changes is an increased focus on ecosystem goods and services other than those associated with the production of red meat. The recent focus on ecosystems should help communicate the importance of not only extractable goods, but also tangible and intangible benefits from rangelands and their unique contributions to the Nation's well-being. A comprehensive evaluation of goods and services derived from rangelands is beyond the scope of this paper. Here, only selected sets are mentioned as examples, though more complete works exist (e.g., Maczko and Hidinger 2008).

Rangelands offer significant prospects for the development of renewable energy (such as power generated from wind and solar sources) in addition to recreational opportunities, seeds and plant materials, and carbon sequestration. The juxtaposition and aridity of many rangelands enable reasonably consistent power generation potential. In addition, the remoteness, abundance of open space, and natural beauty of rangelands make them prime candidates for recreational activities such as hiking, bird watching, and hunting. A more recently recognized service is the ability of rangelands to sequester carbon. Even though rangelands store and process far less carbon than forests (Negra and others 2008), nonetheless, they cumulatively have the potential to sequester a significant quantity of carbon because of their broad expanse. In addition, rangelands contain approximately 10 percent of terrestrial biomass and 10 to 30 percent of soil organic carbon (Schlesinger 1997, Scurlock and Hall 1998). Finally, the value of all goods and services derived from rangelands is not easily quantified. Despite this fact,

Table 2.9—Estimated area of rangelands in the contiguous United States under Federal and non-Federal jurisdictions

State and RPA Assessment Region	Rangeland area	Vegetated area[a]	Federal rangeland area	Proportion of vegetated land that is rangeland
	------------- acres -----------------			percent
California	52,133,586	82,224,879	28,693,031	63
Oregon	27,374,132	54,309,410	16,152,613	50
Washington	9,620,070	32,447,736	1,966,833	30
Pacific Northwest total	89,127,788	168,982,025	46,812,477	53
Nevada	58,515,548	67,016,472	19,357,393	87
Arizona	57,110,317	69,509,330	24,435,602	82
New Mexico	55,754,605	74,455,901	48,364,457	75
Montana	47,850,531	74,044,430	9,902,821	65
Wyoming	46,267,568	59,056,765	20,727,210	78
Colorado	31,223,942	53,140,886	8,610,193	59
Nebraska	28,506,430	28,922,685	18,942,567	99
Utah	27,971,126	44,062,149	655,626	63
South Dakota	26,547,944	28,282,097	2,574,907	94
Idaho	23,414,143	44,713,552	16,116,770	52
Kansas	18,605,013	22,400,674	278,596	83
North Dakota	14,623,902	15,166,814	2,164,985	96
Rocky Mountains total	436,391,069	580,771,755	172,131,127	75
Minnesota	3,491,414	24,782,883	78,043	14
Wisconsin	3,431,506	19,063,093	207,035	18
Missouri	3,177,941	18,410,205	80,054	17
Iowa	1,602,247	3,952,303	11,454	41
Illinois	1,264,260	6,332,458	32,286	20
North total	12,967,368	72,540,942	408,872	18
Texas	90,805,931	125,375,997	1,930,404	72
Oklahoma	15,601,518	28,030,408	531,361	56
Florida	6,707,664	22,890,659	1,001,674	29
Louisiana	3,172,729	18,567,372	204,482	17
Georgia	1,348,008	26,579,024	130,189	5
South Carolina	1,321,778	14,112,990	162,904	9
North Carolina	1,317,001	20,690,943	161,548	6
South total	120,274,629	256,247,393	4,122,562	51
U.S. total	662,337,819	1,318,358,448	224,115,815	50

RPA = Resources Planning Act.
[a]Vegetated estimates include all land cover types except agriculture. Some States are missing, especially in the North and South Assessment regions, because they contain < 1 million acres of rangeland. U.S. totals given represent all area in all States, and is not limited to those States listed here.
Note: Rangeland area is expressed as a proportion of vegetated land that is classified as rangeland (Reeves and Mitchell, in press).

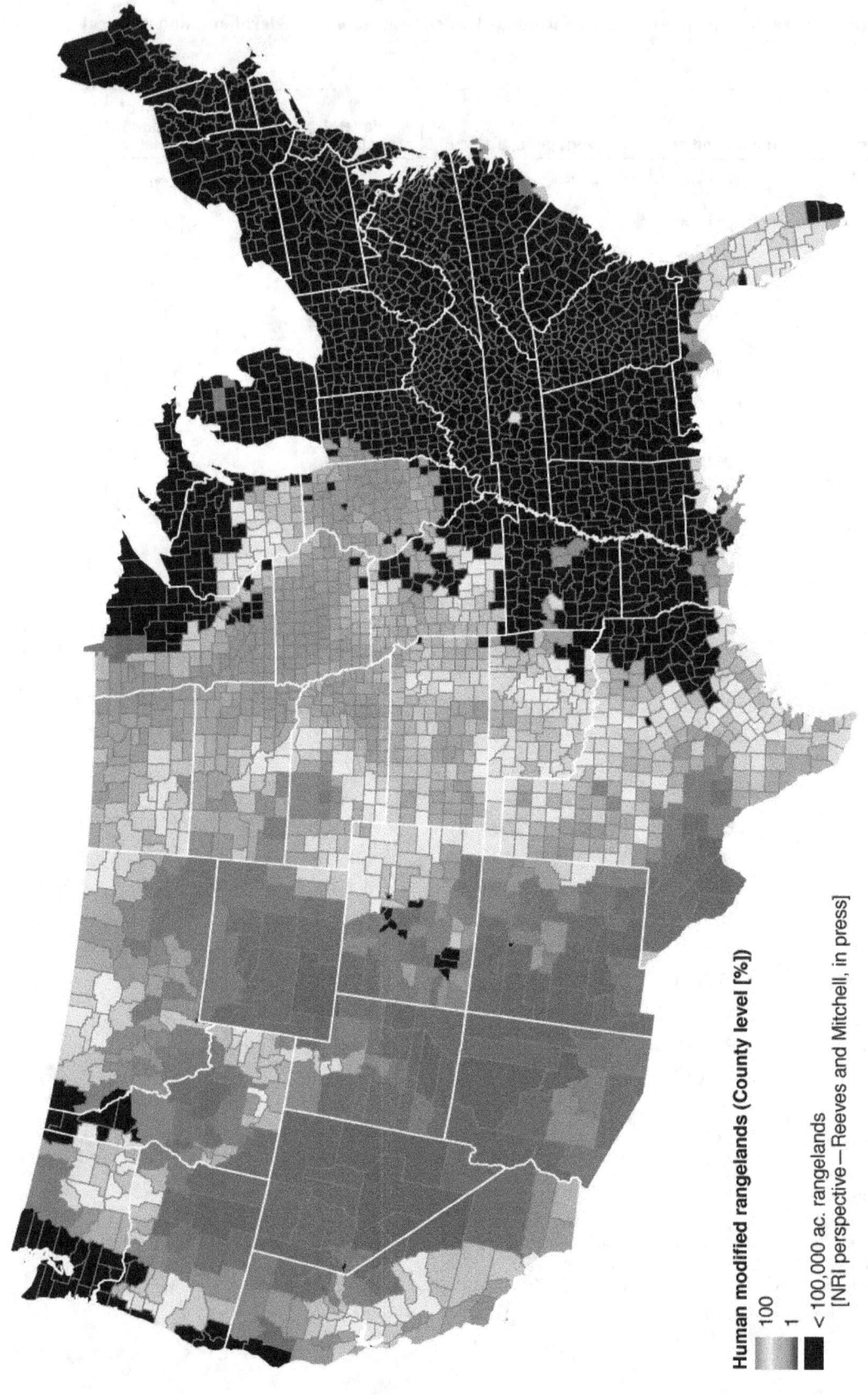

Human modified rangelands (County level [%])

100

1

< 100,000 ac. rangelands

[NRI perspective—Reeves and Mitchell, in press]

Figure 2 10—Estimated area of human modified rangeland expressed as a percent of historic rangeland area for the conterminous United States. This analysis is based on unpublished data.

rangelands are a unique and valuable land type critical for the maintenance of ecological function and economic sustainability of the United States.

End Invited Paper

Forest Lands

The Forest Inventory and Analysis (FIA) Program of the Forest Service, U.S. Department of Agriculture, defines forest land as "...land at least 120 feet wide and 1 acre in size with at least 10 percent cover by live trees of any size" (Smith and others 2009). According to FIA program estimates, just over 33 percent of the Nation's land area, about 751 million acres, is in forest cover meeting this definition. While about 300 million acres less than it was before European settlement in the early 1600s, the size of the Nation's forest cover has been relatively stable for the last 100 years. The proportion of land in forest cover is for about the same among the North (42 percent), South (40 percent), and Pacific Coast regions (without Alaska) (42 percent). With Alaska included, forest cover in the Pacific Coast region is somewhat less than the other regions, at 37 percent. The Rocky Mountains (20 percent) has about half as much forest land cover as the other three regions. The four Great Plains States of Kansas, Nebraska, South Dakota, and North Dakota have just under 3 percent of total land area in forest.

Almost 44 percent of the current U.S. forest land area is publicly owned (Federal, State, local), over 18 percent is owned by private corporations, and almost 38 percent is privately owned by non-corporate entities (fig. 2.11) (Smith and others 2009). Of the non-corporate private forest land, over 92 percent is family or individually owned.

The national distribution of forest lands shows that eastern forests are predominantly in private ownership, while western forests are predominantly public (fig. 2.12). Industrial forests are concentrated in Maine, the Lake States, the lower South, and the Pacific Northwest regions.

Private forest lands include forest-industry lands, other corporation forest lands, individual and family lands, and other non-corporation private lands. Over half of the forest industry forests are in the South. Large portions of corporation lands not owned by the forest industry are located in the Pacific Coast and South regions. Almost half of the family and individually owned private forest land is in the South region; nearly 36 percent is in the North region. The National Woodland Ownership Survey estimated that about 54 percent of family forest land was open only to family or friends for recreational uses (Butler 2008).

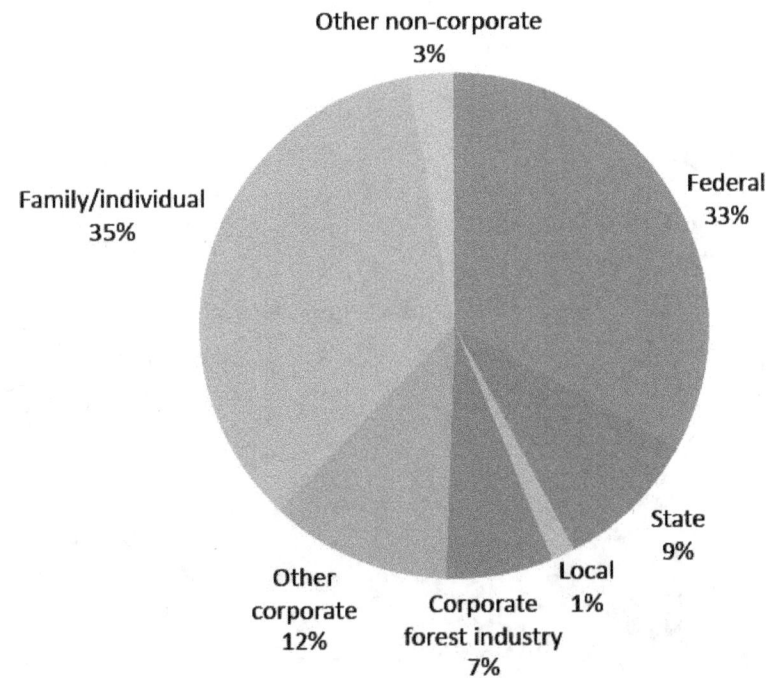

Figure 2.11—Percent of forest land in the United States by ownership, 2007 (1000s of acres, percentages sum to 100s). (Reproduced from 2010 United States Sustainable Forest Management Report.)

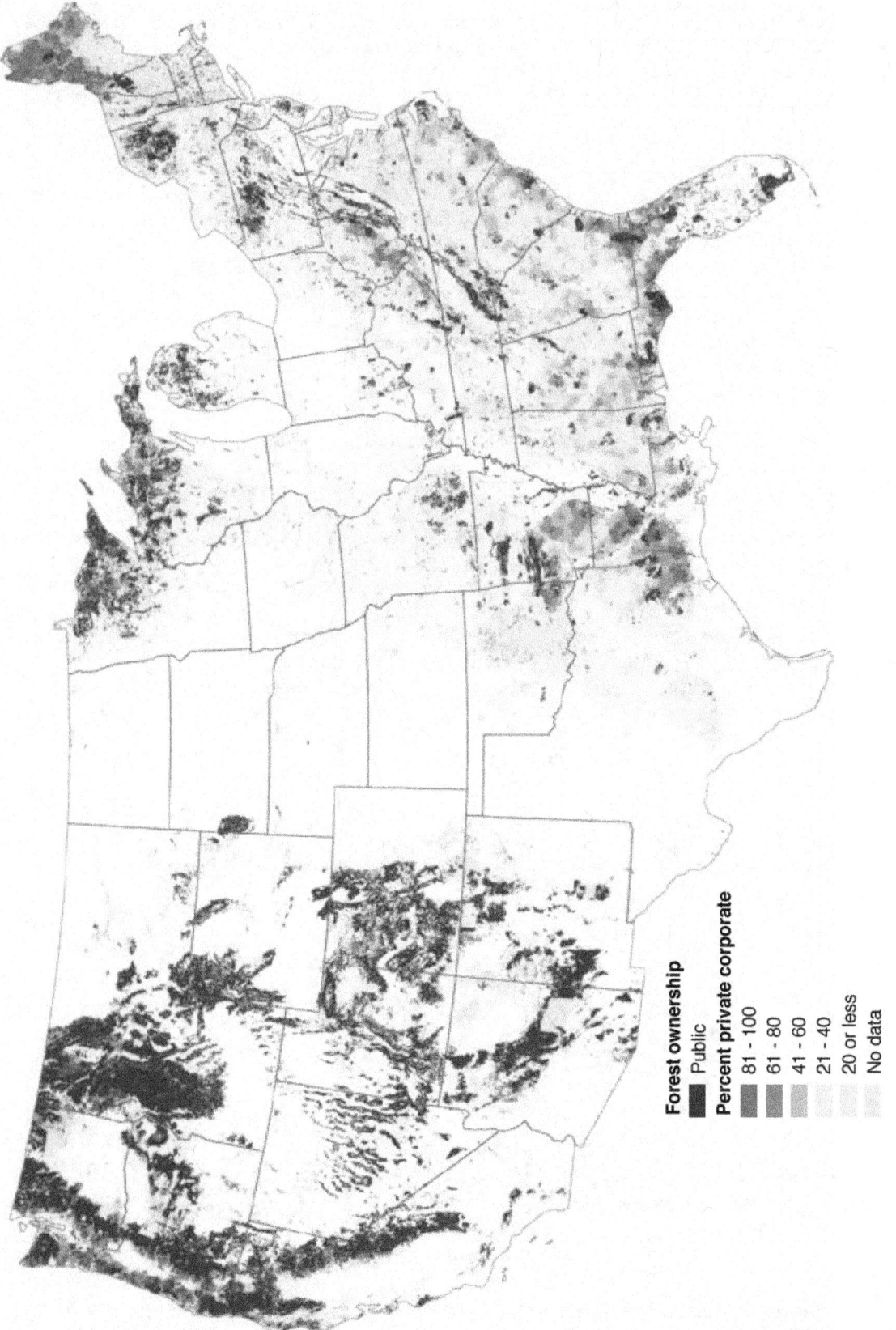

Forest ownership

Public

Percent private corporate

81 - 100
61 - 80
41 - 60
21 - 40
20 or less
No data

Figure 2 12—Public and private forest land in the United States and percent of private forest that is industrial. Source: USDA Forest Service (2010)

Ownership has a profound effect on forest management policies and allowed uses. Federal forest lands include those on national forests, national parks, Bureau of Land Management lands, wildlife refuges, and any other Federally managed public land. State forest lands mostly occur on State forestry commission areas, in State parks, and in other State management areas. Local forests include municipal watersheds, local parks, local forest preserves, greenways, and other local government forests. Some public lands have heightened protection status. An estimated 106 million acres of these protected lands are forested, representing 14 percent of all forest land.

Urban Land

Urban land in the contiguous United States increased from 2.5 percent of the Nation's total land area in 1990 to 3.1 percent in 2000. This expansion of total urban land area is approximately equal to the combined acreage of Vermont and New Hampshire (Nowak and others 2005). Figure 2.13 highlights counties across the country classified by the Census Bureau as urban (500 or more people per square mile). Most of these more heavily populated counties are along the coast of the Atlantic, in Florida, along the Piedmont Crescent (from Virginia to Alabama), in the upper Great Lakes, up through the northern Mississippi River Valley and along the Pacific Coast.

As table 2.10 indicates, average of total surface area that is in non-Federal forest cover across urban counties of the United States is just over 17 percent. The average percent of urban county area that is forest is greatest in the Pacific Coast region, at almost 23 percent, followed by about 18 in the North and 16 percent in the South. Mean county area that is in forest cover is greatest for counties with a population density of 50 to 249 people per square mile.

Table 2.10—Mean percent of county total surface area that is non-Federal forest, by population density and RPA region, 2010

Persons per square mile	North Mean percent	n	South Mean percent	n	Rocky Mountains Mean percent	n	Pacific Coast Mean percent	n	United States Mean percent	n
< 50	31.6	419	37.7	628	3.7	534	24.6	66	24.6	1,647
50-99	32.5	230	44.2	306	4.1	30	33.7	19	37.2	585
100-249	30.9	185	39.6	212	8.0	9	21.1	19	34.3	425
250-499	30.3	97	33.1	87	4.8	14	24.8	12	29.4	210
500+ (urban)	17.6	104	16.4	73	8.4	9	22.9	16	17.2	202

RPA = Resources Planning Act. Note: The "n" columns are the number of counties in the population density by region cells. Non-Federal forest land forecasts were not completed for Alaska and Hawaii or these cities/counties: Washington, DC; Denver, CO; Baltimore (city), MD; St. Louis (city), MO. Source: Wear (2011).

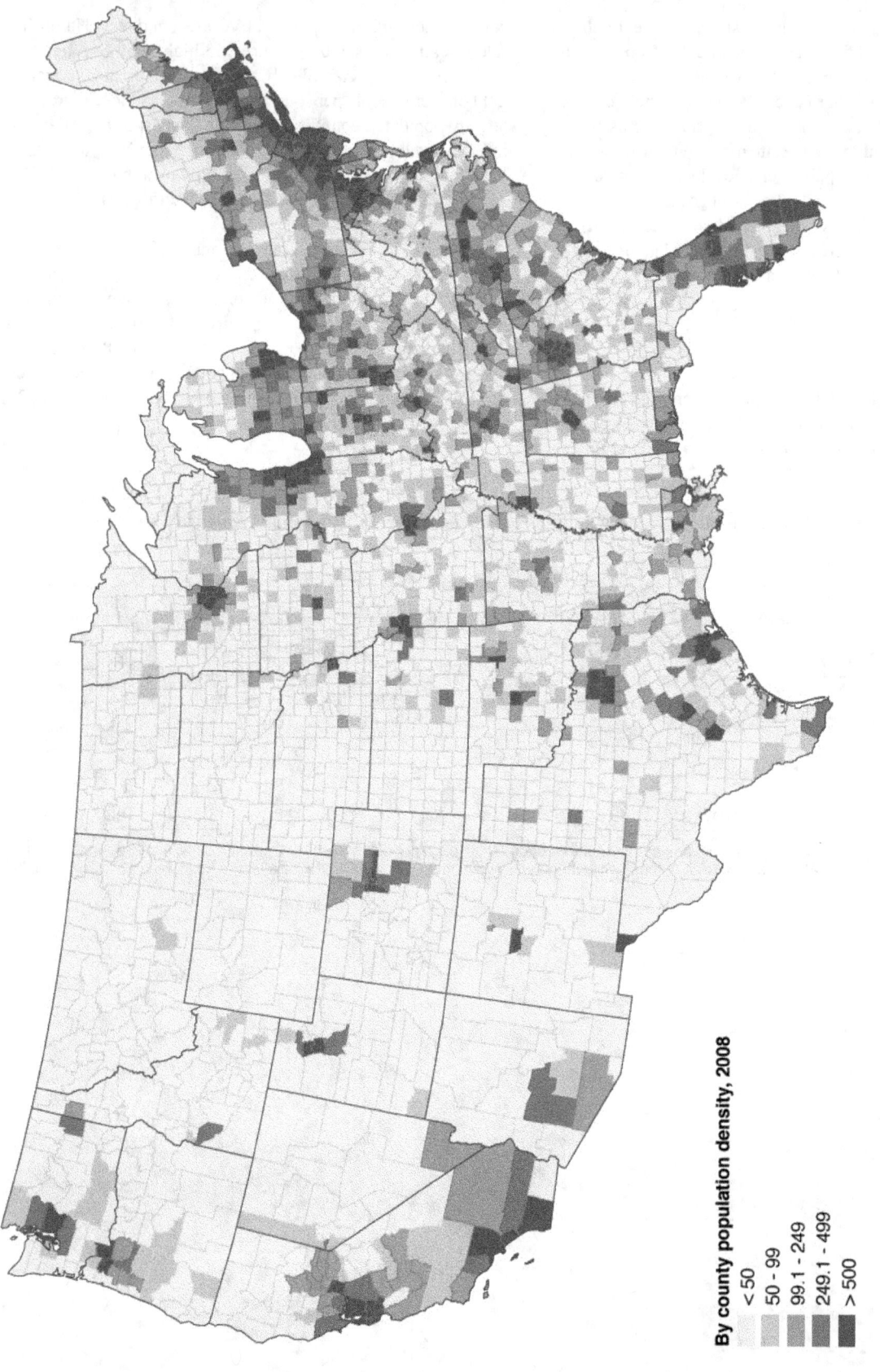

By county population density, 2008

< 50
50 - 99
99.1 - 249
249.1 - 499
> 500

Figure 2.13—Counties of the United States by level of population density, 2008. (A density equal to or greater than 500 persons per square mile meets the U.S. Bureau of Census definition of "urban.")

CHAPTER 3
Protecting Rural Land

This chapter addresses objective 3 of this assessment report on outdoor recreation and protected land resources: to describe trends in natural land protection. The importance of protecting rural land is underscored in invited papers that examine pressures to develop private forest land and private land near designated Federal wilderness. This chapter examines the land protection systems in place across the country, including the land trusts, conservation easements, fee simple acquisition (an invited paper from duMoulin and Alford of The Trust for Public Land), and Federal land protection including the National Park System, the National Wildlife Refuge System, and the National Wilderness Preservation System. The results from a Geographic Information Systems (GIS) spatial analysis of the location of these protected Federal lands are presented to show which types of ecosystems are being protected.

An Overview of Protected Lands in the United States

Increasingly important in continuing efforts to protect land and water systems are programs such as the Protected Areas Database, PAD (http://gapanalysis.usgs.gov/data/padus-data/). PAD-US data covers the Nation's protected areas with standardized spatial geometry and resource attributes including ownership, management, and conservation status (based on U.S. national GAP and International Union for Conservation of Nature (IUCN) codings). Included is voluntarily protected, fee simple private land. Types of conservation measures employed to protect ecological functions and natural, recreational, and cultural uses are encoded. Underpinning the PAD-US effort is the U.S. Geological Survey (USGS) GAP Program, which assesses the conservation status of native vertebrate species and natural land cover types. The primary objective of the GAP Program is to help assure adequate representation of common species on conservation lands.

According to the PAD-US, the current national total acreage of land protected is approximately 715 million acres, including Federal, State, and local government ownerships, as well protected lands owned (in fee simple)

by nongovernmental organizations. This number is roughly one-third of all U.S. land area. Not included in this 715 million is around 40 million acres of private land protected through easements.

The map in figure 3.1 shows public and fee simple privately owned protected lands included in the current PAD database. Some of the protected public lands in the East are obvious, such as the Everglades National Park, the Okefenokee National Wildlife Refuge, the Nantahala National Forest in the Southern Appalachian Mountains, and U.S. protected areas bordering the Great Lakes (such as the Boundary Waters Canoe Area). Overall, protected lands in the East are not as extensive as in the West. For example, there are nearly 600 million Federal acres in the West compared to < 50 million in the East.

Development Pressures on Rural Land Resources

Protection of natural lands, such as forest and range, public and private, has increased in importance in recent decades as pressures for residential, tourism, commercial, industrial, agricultural, and other development have grown. About 1.5 billion acres of the land area of the contiguous United States are non-Federal and owned by private individuals and other private entities, or by State and local governments, or tribal governments. Approximately 7 percent of this non-Federal land base is already in urban and other developed uses (USDA Natural Resources Conservation Service 2007). Private lands account for the large majority (about 85 percent) of the U.S. non-Federal land base (Lubowski and others 2006).

The two papers that follow are designed to help the reader better understand the rising pressures for development on both private and public lands. The first paper, by Stein and others, describes development pressures on private forest lands. Similar pressures are occurring on rangelands, croplands, and other rural lands. The second paper, by Ginn and others, presents an analysis of development pressures on private lands near designated Federal wilderness.

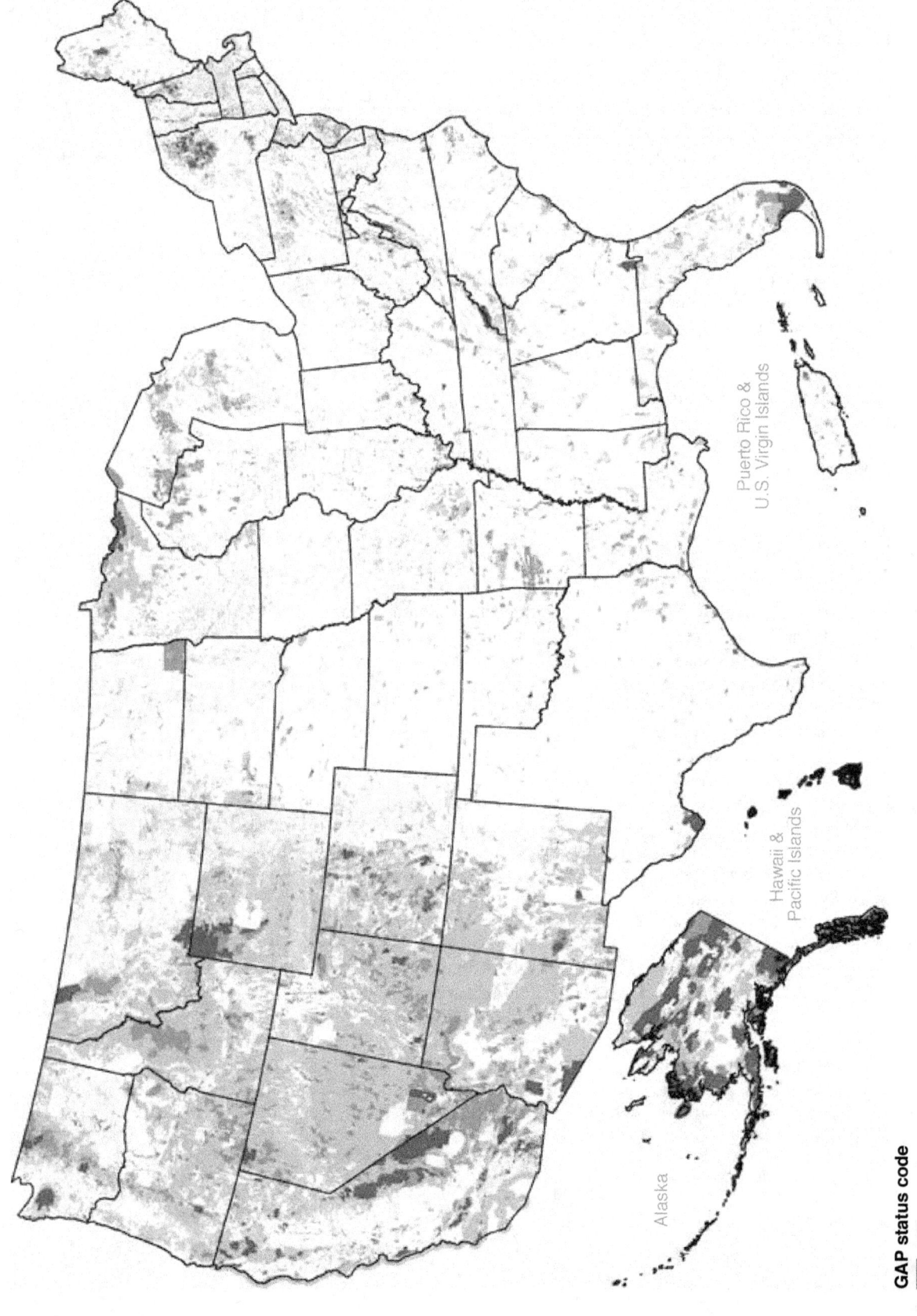

GAP status code

1 Permanent Protection – disturbance events allowed to proceed

2 Permanent Protection – disturbance events suppressed

3 Permanent Protection – subject to extractive uses such as mining or logging

4 Private lands – no known mandate for protection

Figure 3 1—Map based on PAD-US data showing location of public and private protected land and water in the United States by GAP level of protection http://gapanalysis.usgs.gov/gallery/. Note: Explanation of GAP levels: Status 1—lands managed solely for biodiversity conservation in perpetuity; Status 2—lands managed primarily for biodiversity conservation, but with some management, (e.g., suppression of wildfire or activities designed to mimic natural disturbances); Status 3— lands having permanent protection, but subject to extractive uses (e.g., logging or mining) or motorized recreation (Duarte 2010).

INVITED PAPER

Development Pressures on the Private Forests

Susan Stein, Ronald E. McRoberts, Lisa G. Mahal, and Sara Comas[1]

More than 420 million acres (56 percent) of U.S. forests are privately owned (Smith and others 2009) and provide critical benefits and services to people, as well as to wildlife and ecosystems. Most of our private forests are in the eastern United States—up to 85 percent of some watersheds in the East are covered by private forest (fig. 3.2). Private forests in the West also play many important roles, including providing critical wildlife habitat (Robles and others 2008). Benefits and services from forests include a diverse array of recreational activities including fishing, hunting, hiking, and biking; habitat for over 60 percent of at-risk wildlife species in the United States (Robles and others 2008) in addition to deer, pheasants, squirrels, and many other animal and plant species not at-risk; the provision of clean air and water; timber; and carbon sequestration.

As urban development expands into rural places, and as more people choose to live near our national forests and other beautiful, rural places, housing density will likely continue to increase on nearby private forests. And, it is possible that, as current landowners become older, more private forest lands will be available for development. Currently, about 264 million acres of private forest land are owned by people age 55 or older (Butler 2008). Additionally, many private industrial timberlands have been sold over the past decade, including 23 million acres between 2000 and 2004 (Clutter and others 2005). While the majority of these lands are retained for timber management purposes, some are sold for development (Weinberg and Larsen 2008).

Impacts of housing development and other pressures on private forests—Many factors can affect the health of private forests and, hence, the benefits and services they provide. Factors range from the clearing, fragmentation, and disturbance that accompany the development of new homes and associated infrastructure; to the damage to roots, leaves, and stems caused by an associated influx of native and exotic pests and diseases; and to the soil erosion and tree mortality that follows intense wildfires. Each

[1] Forests on the Edge Coordinator, Cooperative Forestry Staff, State and Private Forestry, U.S. Department of Agriculture, Forest Service, Washington, DC 20250; Mathematical Statistician, Northern Research Station, U.S. Department of Agriculture, Forest Service, St. Paul, MN 55108; Computer Systems Analyst, University of Minnesota, St. Paul, MN 55104; and Natural Resource Specialist, Cooperative Forestry Staff, State and Private Forestry, U.S. Department of Agriculture, Forest Service, Washington, DC 20250 .

Private forest factoids

- There are 423 million acres (56 percent) privately owned forests in the United States (Smith and others 2009).
- More than 60 percent of private forest landowners are at least 55 years old (Butler 2008).
- Between 2000 and 2004, there were 23 million acres of private industrial timberland sold in the United States (Clutter and others 2005).
- About 53 percent of U.S. water supplies originate on forest land, and more than half of this water supply comes from land on private forests (Brown and others 2005).
- Private forests supplied 91 percent of all timber harvested in the United States in 2007 (Smith and others 2009).
- About 60 percent of all at-risk animal and plant species are associated with private forests (Robles and others 2008).
- More than 57 million acres of rural private forest is projected to experience a substantial increase in housing density between 2000 and 2030; more than 70 percent of private forests in some watersheds could experience this change (Stein and others 2009).

of these pressures can increase the potential for or exacerbate the impacts of the others.

To understand where private forests in the United States provide the greatest benefits and where these benefits are most likely to decrease due to increased housing density, fire, or insect pests and diseases, the Forests on the Edge project of the Forest Service, U.S. Department of Agriculture, undertook an assessment, based on readily available, nationally consistent GIS data. This paper provides a snapshot of the assessment as it pertains to housing density, fire, and insect pests and diseases. A complete overview of the study is presented in Stein and others (2009).

Increased housing density in rural forest lands—
An assessment of projected future increases in housing density can help to understand where in the United States private forest might change as a result of future housing development. Although recent economic conditions may have led to a downturn in the housing market, given that the U.S. population is expected to increase by another 80 million people between 2000 and 2030 (U.S. Census Bureau 2004a), it is likely that housing density will continue to increase in many areas, including private forests across the country and especially in the Southeast.

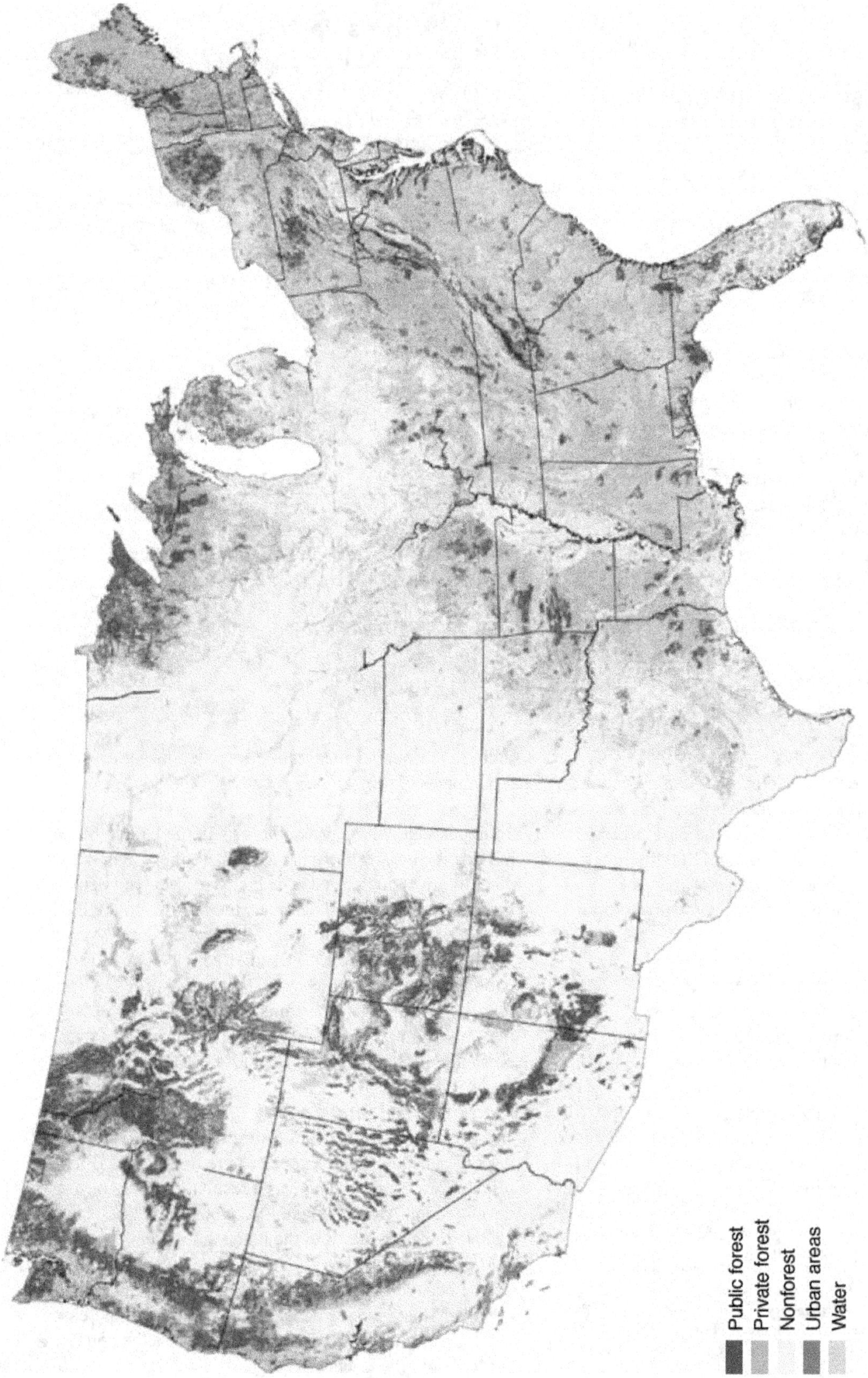

Public forest
Private forest
Nonforest
Urban areas
Water

Figure 3.2—Ownership of forest lands in the United States, 2007 (Stein and others 2009).

A broad range of impacts has been associated with increased housing density and increased urbanization in and around forests (Stein and others 2009). These include decreased water quality and quantity, as well as increased volume and peak rate of runoff (Im and others 2003), higher rates of soil erosion and water pollution (Houlahan and Findlay 2004, Stein and Butler 2004), reduced carbon sequestration, and an increase in fire risk (Syphard and others 2007). Impacts to wildlife include the loss and degradation of habitat, an increase in predation, parasitism, and reproductive failures (Stein and others 2009). Studies in some areas of the country have noted that, as housing density increases, landowners are less likely to invest in timber production and active forest management (Munn and others 2002, Thorne and Sundquist 2001, Wear and others 1999).

Areas where private, rural forest lands might be most affected by substantial increases in housing density were identified by combining several GIS data layers, summarizing the results by eight-digit hydrological unit code, or watershed, and ranking each watershed by the resulting value. Layers used for this analysis included data on projected future housing density, forest cover, and land ownership. Forests were projected to experience a substantial increase in housing density if they were projected to shift from one of the following three categories into a higher-density category:

Rural I: fewer than 16 housing units per square mile
Rural II: 16 to 64 housing units per square mile
Exurban/urban: more than 64 housing units per square mile.

A detailed methodological description for these analyses can be found in Stein and others (2009).

As depicted in figure 3.3, up to 72 percent of private forests in some watersheds are estimated to experience a substantial increase in housing density between 2000 and 2030. Watersheds in the 90th percentile are found throughout the East as well as parts of the West. Many high-ranking eastern watersheds are located in or near coastal areas as well as along the Appalachian Mountain range, and include much of North Carolina and Florida, as well as an area surrounding Atlanta. High-ranking watersheds are also found in Michigan, the California Sierra Nevada Mountain range, along the Washington and Oregon Cascade Mountain range, and near major population centers in the Southwest.

Insect pests and diseases—Both native and exotic forest insects and diseases have caused substantial damage to U.S. forests. Tree defoliation and damage to roots and stems have resulted in decreased tree growth and mortality (Tkacz and others 2007). Over 5 million acres of tree mortality was caused by insects and diseases in 2006 (USDA Forest Service 2007).

Data collected and analyzed by the Forest Health Monitoring Program of the Forest Service (Krist and others 2007), when combined with data on forest ownership, allows identification of watersheds where future damage from insect pests and diseases is likely to affect tree growth on private forests. Damage by forest insects and diseases can result in decreased growth, as measured by basal area (the cross section of a tree stem in square feet, commonly measured at breast height).

Watersheds in the 90th percentile, as depicted in figure 3.4, contain private forest that could potentially experience, on average, from 16 percent to as high as 41 percent basal area loss due to forest insects and diseases. These watersheds are most numerous in western Oregon and Washington, along California's northern Sierra Nevada range, as well as in the Southwest, the vicinity of the Great Lakes, and along a section of the Appalachian highlands running from Pennsylvania through Virginia.

Wildfire—Uncontrolled, intense wildfires can threaten forests as well as the increasing number of people and structures in forested areas. Wildfire impacts can include increased soil erosion; reduced carbon sequestration; death or displacement of wildlife; alterations to stream temperature, chemistry, and sediment levels; and increased activity by off-road vehicles (Carr 2005, Donovan and Brown 2007, Hurteau and others 2009, Kalabokidis 2000). Economic repercussions of wildfire include high suppression expenditures (wildfire expenditures by the Federal Government surpassed $1 billion for the first time ever, in 2000), the loss of timberland, and a loss of tourism revenues.

Data on wildland fire potential collected by the Fire Modeling Institute of the Forest Service (http:www fs fed.us/fmi) were combined with data on forest ownership to identify watersheds across the country with the greatest risk of private forest damage due to wildfire under extreme conditions (Menakis 2008). As displayed in figure 3.5, up to 100 percent of the private forests located in watersheds in the 90th percentile have a high wildfire potential. A large proportion of the western watersheds included in this analysis are found in the 90th percentile category, including most of the watersheds in Arizona and New Mexico as well as watersheds in southern Colorado, northern California, and southwestern Montana. The watersheds with the highest wildland fire potential in the eastern half of the United States are all located in the South, including a band of watersheds stretching from southern Virginia through Georgia, as well as watersheds in Florida, along the border of Mississippi and Arkansas, in Texas, and in southeastern Oklahoma.

End Invited Paper

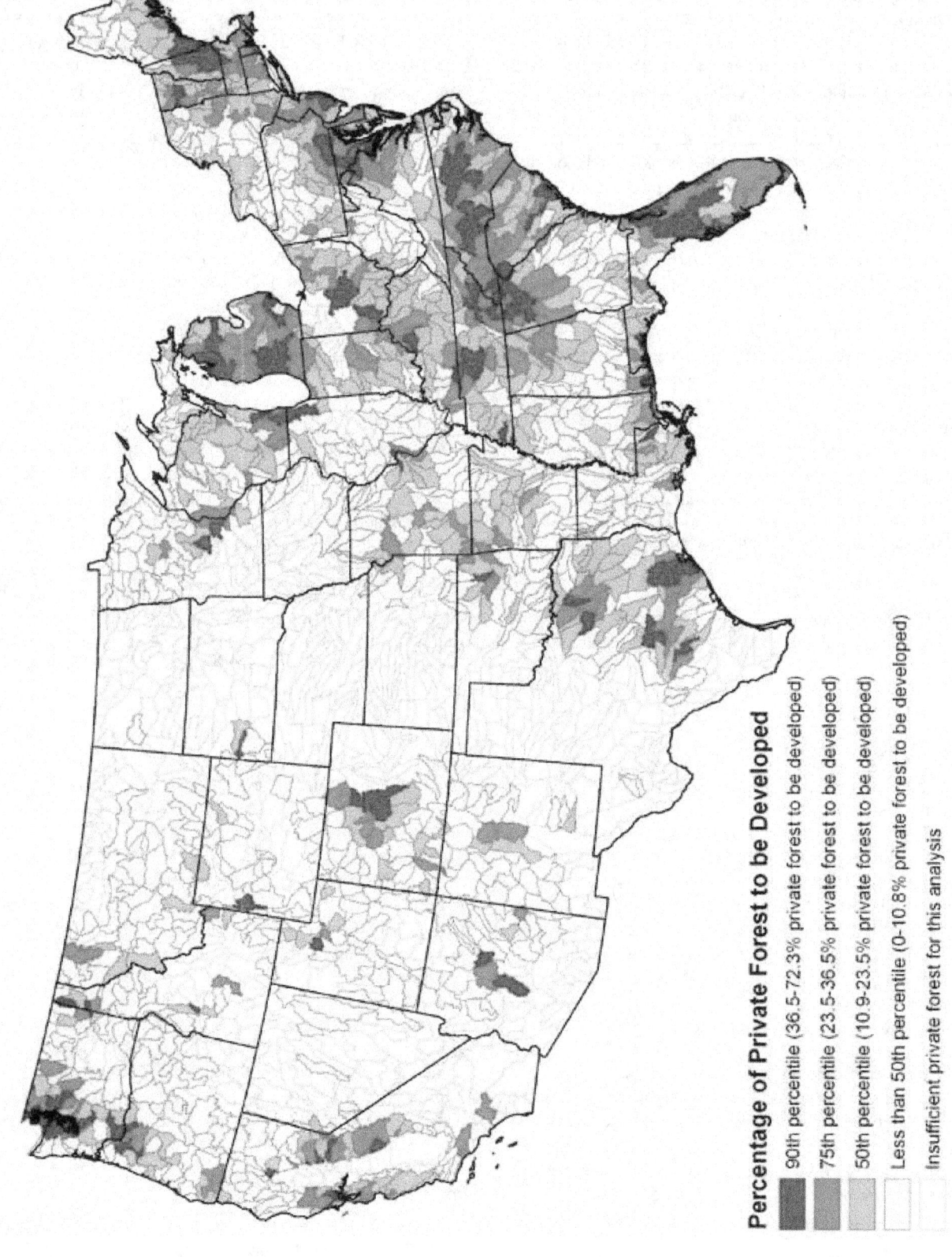

Percentage of Private Forest to be Developed

■ 90th percentile (36.5-72.3% private forest to be developed)

■ 75th percentile (23.5-36.5% private forest to be developed)

■ 50th percentile (10.9-23.5% private forest to be developed)

□ Less than 50th percentile (0-10.8% private forest to be developed)

□ Insufficient private forest for this analysis

Figure 3.3—Watersheds by percentage of private forest projected to experience increased housing density.

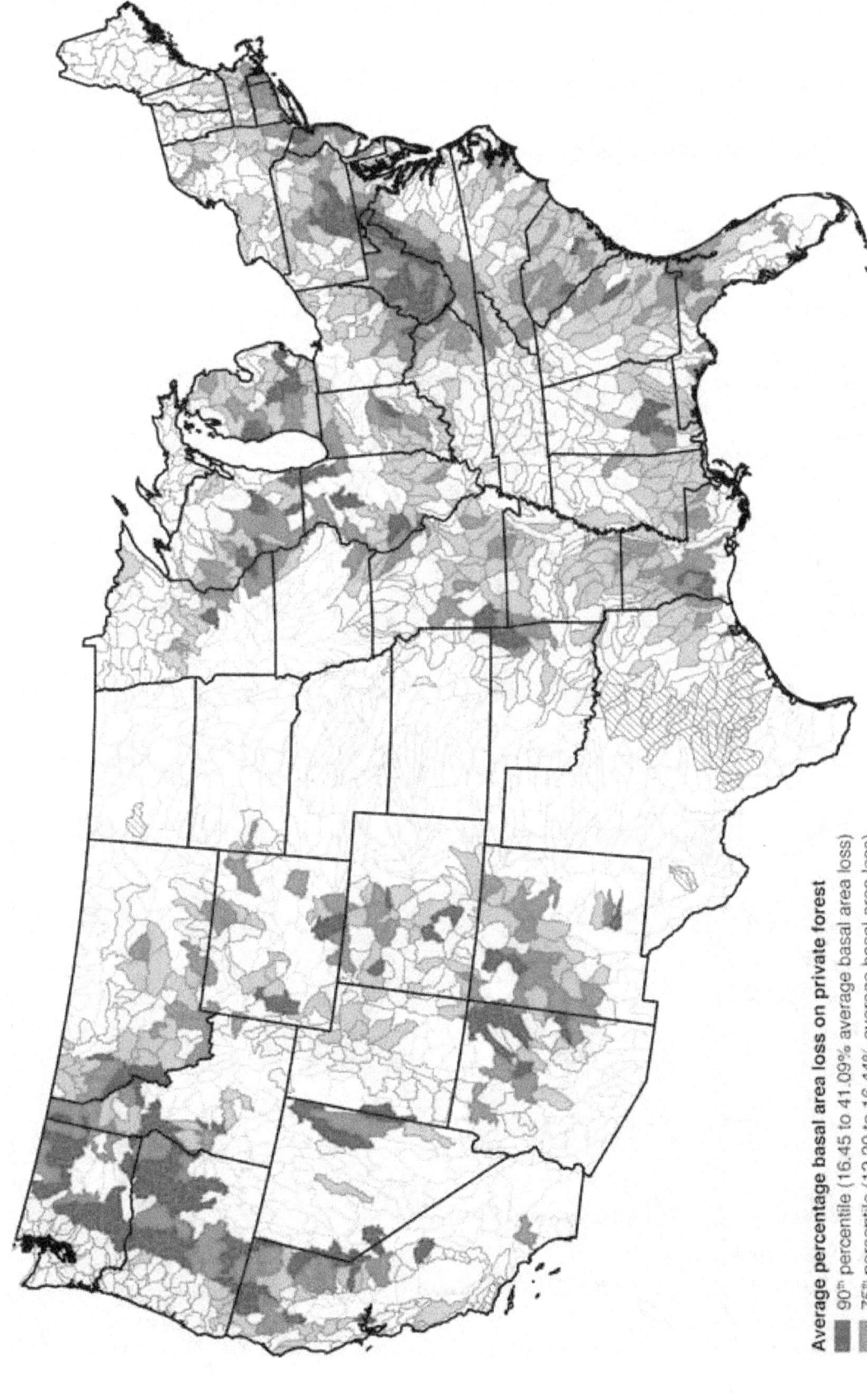

Average percentage basal area loss on private forest

90th percentile (16.45 to 41.09% average basal area loss)
75th percentile (12.20 to 16.44% average basal area loss)
50th percentile (8.21 to 12.19% average basal area loss)
50th percentile (0 to 8.20% average basal area loss)
No insect and disease data
Insufficient private forest for this analysis

Figure 3.4—Watersheds by potential for basal area loss due to insect pests and diseases.

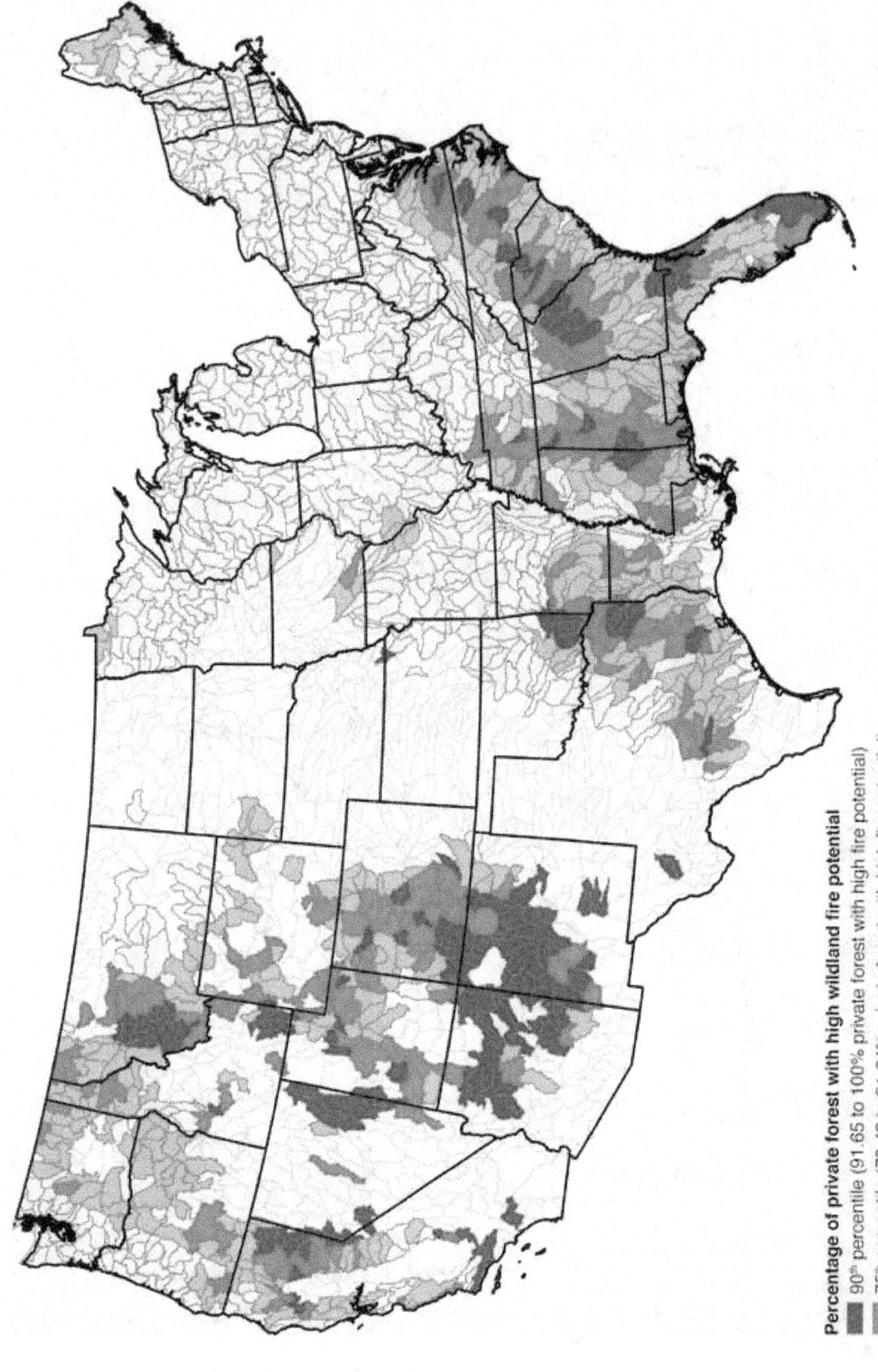

Percentage of private forest with high wildland fire potential

90th percentile (91.65 to 100% private forest with high fire potential)

75th percentile (73.42 to 91.64% private forest with high fire potential)

50th percentile (27.10 to 73.41% private forest with high fire potential)

50th percentile (0.00 to 27.09% private forest with high fire potential)

Insufficient private forest for this analysis

Figure 3.5—Watersheds by susceptibility and vulnerability of private forests to wildfire.

INVITED PAPER

Threatened Wilderness Areas in the National Wilderness Preservation System

Allison Ginn Barnes, Gary T. Green, Nathan P. Nibbelink, and H. Ken Cordell[2]

Continued residential development in the United States threatens the boundaries of most of America's valuable public lands (Radeloff and others 2010, see sidebar). Many Americans are relocating to wilderness areas or retiring to areas high in natural or recreational amenities in a movement referred to as "amenity migration" (Cordell and others, 2012; Price and others 1997). The term "backcountry sprawl" describes housing development increases within and near national forests and parks. Population growth between 1970 and 1988 near Federal public land (23 percent) was more than double the average growth nationwide (11 percent). However, national parks and forests are not the only protected lands at risk from development along their borders. It is also highly likely that housing density will increase significantly in and around Federal Wilderness Areas (Cordell and Overdevest 2001).

Federal Wilderness Areas are particularly vulnerable to exurban and rural sprawl. The land within areas designated as Wilderness is meant to be protected in its natural state, thus land development is highly inconsistent with this protection designation and with the associated values ascribed by the public (Cordell and others 2005). The pressures of human development and private land ownership around and within protected Wilderness landscapes create challenging issues for managers as they strive to protect natural and cultural assets and maintain access for recreation. Development within and around protected lands can significantly affect their ecological condition by increasing habitat fragmentation and reducing air and water quality. This development can also reduce recreational opportunities through denial of access. Even though most of it is low-density and residential, development nonetheless poses a threat to these sensitive and uniquely valuable wild lands which are defined by law as Wilderness Areas.

Problem statement—Being able to monitor and perhaps predict increases of housing density near Wilderness boundaries is essential if there is to be early detection of threats. Without this capability, land managers cannot effectively plan for and implement appropriate management

[2] Outdoor Recreation Specialist, Bureau of Land Management, U.S. Department of the Interior, Newcastle and Buffalo Field Offices, WY 82834; Associate Professor, University of Georgia, Warnell School of Forestry and Natural Resources, Athens, GA 30602; Associate Professor, University of Georgia, Warnell School of Forestry and Natural Resources, Athens, GA 30602; and Pioneering Scientist, Southern Research Station, U.S. Department of Agriculture, Forest Service, Athens, GA 30602.

In a study of protected Federal lands, Radeloff and others (2010) found that designated wilderness encountered greater growth (366 percent) between 1940 and 2000 in development of housing units in surrounding areas within 50 km of boundaries than either that of national parks or national forests. Growth of housing units was even greater within 1 kilometer of wilderness boundaries (474 percent between 1940 and 2000). As well, housing unit growth within 1 kilometer was projected to be faster near wilderness (64 percent) than near either national parks or forests from 2000 to 2030. This research pointed out that housing units within or near administrative boundaries can greatly influence the condition of protected areas (e.g., habitat disruption, noise and light pollution, and increased pressure on wildlife from pets). From as far away as 50 km housing development can result in increased recreational pressures from residents, most of whom are within a 1-hour drive of the protected land.

Number and growth in housing units (in millions) within 50 kilometers of U.S. protected areas from 1940 to 2000, with projections to 2030, by type of protected area

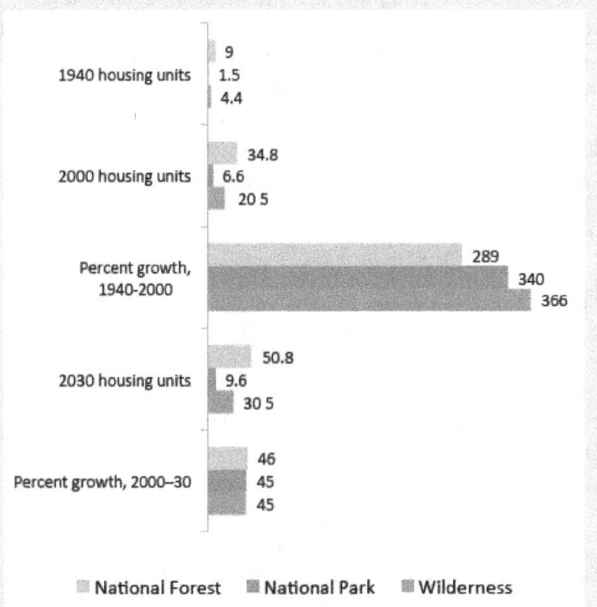

Note: Numbers of housing units are not additive because many wilderness areas are embedded in a national forest or national park, and similarly, many national forests are adjacent to each other, which would result in double-counting. Percent growth is based on unrounded numbers of housing units. Source: Radeloff and others (2010).

options. Similarly, overall management of the National Wilderness Preservation System (NWPS) will not be as effective if a general assessment of development pressure is not provided. Though research regarding amenity migration, exurban sprawl, human use impact, and the wildland-urban interface is plentiful, research examining nearby rural and exurban land development is, for the most part, lacking.

Purpose statement—This research assumes a close correlation between the likelihood of nearby development, and the proximity of Wilderness to urban areas, areas of high road density, and private land. By employing this assumption of correlation, this study will attempt to identify how many and which NWPS Areas are most likely to face development pressures nearby and within their boundaries. This research was done to provide the Forest Service with a report on the development pressures facing the National Wilderness Preservation System for inclusion in the 2010 Renewable Resources Planning Act Assessment.

Selecting areas for the study—At the time of this study, the NWPS consisted of nearly 800 Federal designated areas. Of these, our study was limited to screening the 600 that had geographic data (boundary files) in order to identify those meeting development potential criteria (described below). At the time of this study, the only areas that had the necessary boundary data were those that were more than 640 acres in size and were designated prior to 2004. From this pool of 600 designated areas, 71 met the selection criteria of proximity to urban areas, road systems, and private land.

Methodology—In examining the 71 selected areas, several buffer distances were chosen to mimic the approach used in a similar study quantifying development risks surrounding national forests (Stein and others 2005). These buffers were based on the fundamental assumption that impacts to public lands and their natural characteristics vary depending on the distance of existing development and human settlement from those lands. The analysis was focused on the land within individual Wilderness Areas and the development potential within three buffers ranging from zero to one-half, one-half

to three, and three to ten miles from the borders of each selected Wilderness Area. These buffers represent straight-line distances perpendicular to the NWPS borders and are analogous to a circular radius if Areas were a perfect circle. NWPS Areas are not circular but irregularly shaped. Thus, the buffers represent an outward expansion of this irregular shape. An additional buffer zone was analyzed consisting of all land within 10 miles of NWPS Area boundaries. As earlier described, Wilderness Areas with the greatest likelihood of development pressures are predicted to be positively related to existing exurban housing densities, the presence of nearby private land, and proximity to roads and metropolitan areas.

Table 3.1 specifies the calculation method for each of six metrics used to compare and rank the selected 71 Wilderness Areas by likelihood or potential for development. This comparison identified which Wilderness Areas were most likely to experience housing density increases along or near their borders. Metrics used included the following:

- Percent of nearby land protected by Wilderness managing agencies
- Percent of land protected by other Federal, tribal, State or local entities
- Housing density
- Distance to the nearest road
- The transformed value of the sum of passengers boarding at airports within 50 miles of the NWPS unit
- Area of water features within each buffer distance.

Each metric in table 3.1 was normalized to a zero-to-one scale, assigning a zero to the minimum value in the range and a one to the maximum value for each metric in each buffer distance zone. Thus, for each metric, a zero indicates the least likelihood of contributing to development, whereas a value of one indicates the highest likelihood of contributing to a housing density increase.

Current literature does not quantify the relative degree to which each of the above comparison metrics contributes to likelihood of development. Thus, an index was created that

Table 3.1—Calculation method for six metrics used to assess likelihood of nearby development

Metric	Unit	Calculation method
Non-Protected Land Tier 1	Percent	((Area of Buffer—Area of Land Protected by BLM, FS, FWS, or NPS)/Area of Buffer)*100
Non-Protected Land Tier 2	Percent	((Area of Buffer—Area of Land Protected by any entity)/Area of Buffer)*100
Housing density	Units/square mile	Housing Units/Total Land Area for Buffer
Mean distance to roads	Mile	Distance to Nearest Road for 30-meter Cell
Enplanements for airports within 50 miles	Persons	Sum of Number of Boarded Passengers for All Airports Intersecting a 50-Mile Buffer of NWPS
Presence of water features	Square mile	Area of all Lakes, Reservoirs, or Oceans Within Each Buffer Zone

assumes that the six metrics affect development equally. The values across metrics were averaged for each Wilderness Area, resulting in a comprehensive index score for comparison across the selected 71 NWPS units for each of the buffer zones. For each Wilderness Area, this comprehensive index score for each of three buffer zones (zero to half, half to three, and three to ten miles) was used to rank order Areas. Rank was then multiplied by the total distance to the outer perimeter of each particular buffer zone, then divided by that result by the number of zones included in the analysis. A lower score indicated a higher propensity for development.

By use of a comprehensive index score (i.e., Composite Potential Development Index = PDIc), Wilderness Areas were rank ordered to show relative risk of development for each buffer zone. This method assigns each Wilderness Area a rank that denotes its risk of exurban development relative to the other 70 units at the same buffer distance. In addition, to test the relative sensitivity of the PDIc to each metric, scores for each metric were doubled, then the composite score was re-calculated and Wilderness Areas were re-ranked.

Results—The weighted mean rank indicated which Wilderness Areas face the highest risk of borderland development (see table 3.2). The sensitivity analysis indicated that at least 8 of the 10 Wilderness Areas remained in the top 10 for risk of borderland development, despite a doubling of each metric (table 3.2). These results indicate that the PDIc is relatively robust, and assuming that the metrics chosen are in fact predicting risk of development, as the literature suggested, the Wilderness Areas remaining at the top of the list are priorities for further investigation into potential development risks.

Discussion and conclusions—This research represents a national analysis of development risk to designated Federal Wilderness. Based on available geographic data, this study identified that 71 of 600 Wilderness Areas are likely to face significant development threats near their borders. Wilderness has usually been thought of as remote lands located within a landscape of other natural lands. This increasingly is not the case. In selecting and ranking Wilderness Areas for this national study, metrics more sensitive at the local or regional levels may have been overlooked. Ultimately, it may be desirable to expand use of the PDIc approach to enable comparison of NWPS units across multiple spatial and temporal scales.

Spatial or temporal patterns may exist for Wilderness Areas experiencing a relatively high risk of development. More than one-third of the top 25 most threatened Wilderness Areas are located in the Pacific Coast region (table 3.2), a region often characterized as the interface of wild lands and urban areas. Future research may shed further light on these patterns and

quantify threshold values for each metric that prove useful in refining projections of the risk of future housing density increases. Future research may also lead to differential weighting of metrics for computing the development potential index.

The methods used in this research have provided a solid advancement of methods for identifying areas with relatively high or low risk at various local scales. However, more translation of the data, methodology, and results is needed before using index scores for establishing conservation goals. Inclusion of other disciplines, such as landscape ecology, is encouraged. The ability to link or connect Wilderness Areas with critical fish or wildlife habitat is also needed. Identification of stakeholders in land preservation, such as nongovernment organizations, and State and local governments, as well as programs such as the Conservation Reserve Program will increase the ability to plan for and execute landscape level protection of the NWPS. Nonprofit organizations such as The Nature Conservancy, Sierra Club, and the Campaign for America's Wilderness may find this study of use in prioritizing lands for conservation, or acquisition of buffer lands adjoining Wilderness.

End Invited Paper

Private Land Conservation

Land trusts—Increasingly important to private land conservation throughout the United States are conservation easements. Conservation easements keep land in private ownership, but with development restrictions. The incentive is lower taxes to landowners. Conservation easements are most often administered through a land trust, which is a special type of private, nonprofit organization with a mission to preserve undeveloped land. Land trusts may be national or regional organizations, but they are noted for being active at the local or community level. Land trusts have emerged as one of the more popular and successful of conservation movements in the country.

The Land Trust Census—The Land Trust Alliance conducts a census of land trust organizations at 5-year intervals. As estimated in its 2005 Land Trust Census, the United States loses about 2 million acres of farm, forest, and open space land each year (Land Trust Alliance 2006). Thus, conservation of private land through trusts or other mechanisms is of growing importance.

As noted in the executive summary of the 2005 Land Trust Census, rural landscapes are increasingly being converted to developed uses including shopping malls, subdivisions, and highways. These conversions impact more than 100,000 acres of wetlands each year. Such conversion of wetlands leads to degradation of water quality and unnatural flooding.

Table 3.2—National Wilderness Preservation System units as ranked by the Composite Potential Development Index (PDIc), followed by the ranking of each unit using the PDI for each buffer alone and then the ranking of the PDIc for a doubling of each contributing variable

Name	Agency	State	PDIc Rank	0–0.5 Rank	0.5–3 Rank	3–10 Rank	LO1x2	LO2x2	H2Ox2	MRDx2	ENPx2
Juniper Dunes	BLM	WA	1	9	4	1	1	1	2	1	1
Mingo	FWS	MO	2	15	3	2	4	4	4	3	6
Ishi	BLM/FS	CA	3	6	5	3	2	2	3	2	3
Soldier Creek	FS	NE	4	2	1	6	3	3	5	4	8
Kisatchie Hills	FS	LA	5	5	9	4	5	5	6	5	5
Hells Canyon	BLM	AZ	6	1	8	5	6	6	7	7	2
Table Rock	BLM	OR	7	4	2	7	7	7	9	6	4
Blackbeard Island	FWS	GA	8	3	6	9	24	22	8	40	14
Greenhorn Mountain	FS	CO	9	34	14	8	8	8	10	8	15
Glacier View	FS	WA	10	18	10	12	15	12	17	17	7
Wambaw Creek	FS	SC	11	30	16	11	14	17	13	12	9
Mount Sneffels	FS	CO	12	27	12	13	10	10	12	10	11
Devils Backbone	FS	MO	13	14	17	15	9	9	16	9	43
Swanquarter	FWS	NC	14	10	11	18	19	16	1	26	10
Mountain Lakes	BLM/FS	NV	15	22	18	17	28	25	11	13	17
Sylvania	FS	MI	16	8	7	22	20	14	14	11	18
Badlands	NPS	SD	17	24	23	16	11	15	15	14	12
Menagerie	FS	OR	18	11	21	19	23	20	18	15	16
Jacumba	BLM	CA	19	17	19	21	18	23	25	25	28
Chanchelulla	FS	CA	20	12	15	23	21	18	21	16	20
Mill Creek	FS	OR	21	45	53	10	26	26	23	18	19
Juniper Mesa	FS	AZ	22	13	22	25	17	13	20	20	27
Capitan Mountains	FS	NM	23	55	45	14	12	19	19	19	26
Black Mountain	BLM	CA	24	7	13	31	22	24	24	21	22
Tamarac	FWS	MN	25	16	24	28	13	41	22	23	24
Hell Hole Bay	FS	SC	26	39	34	24	31	29	31	22	21
North Maricopa Mountains	BLM	AZ	27	31	20	30	34	30	29	29	13
Caribou-Speckled Mountain	FS	ME	28	62	42	20	25	21	26	28	38
Yolla Bolly-Middle Eel	BLM/FS	CA	29	58	28	26	29	27	27	24	23
Welcome Creek	FS	MT	30	49	36	29	32	28	32	36	25
Seney	FWS	MI	31	21	35	33	16	11	30	27	54
Sky Lakes	FS	OR	32	54	47	27	39	37	28	30	29
Upper Kiamichi River	FS	OK	33	29	38	32	35	32	34	31	30
Cache La Poudre	FS	CO	34	33	30	37	36	35	39	37	35
East Fork	FS	AR	35	37	39	34	33	31	36	33	41
Trinity Alps	BLM/FS	CA	36	44	32	36	40	40	33	32	31
Rodman Mountains	BLM	CA	37	26	25	40	30	33	35	34	33
Strawberry Crater	FS	AZ	38	32	31	41	37	34	38	35	36
Lizard Head	FS	CO	39	46	26	43	44	39	40	42	34

continued

44

Table 3.2—(continued) National Wilderness Preservation System units as ranked by the Composite Potential Development Index (PDIc), followed by the ranking of each unit using the PDI for each buffer alone and then the ranking of the PDIc for a doubling of each contributing variable

Name	Agency	State	PDIc Rank	0–0.5 Rank	0.5–3 Rank	3–10 Rank	LO1x2	LO2x2	H2Ox2	MRDx2	ENPx2
Laurel Fork South	FS	WV	40	23	27	45	47	42	41	38	42
Uncompahgre	BLM/FS	CO	41	41	33	42	42	36	42	41	32
Big Island Lake	FS	MI	42	38	56	35	48	44	44	39	45
Fish Creek Mountains	BLM	CA	43	20	29	46	27	46	37	45	39
Apache Creek	FS	AZ	44	47	50	38	41	38	43	44	48
San Pedro Parks	FS	NM	45	48	48	44	51	49	46	43	47
Trigo Mountain	BLM	AZ	46	42	37	51	46	50	47	53	44
Coyote Mountains	BLM	CA	47	40	41	50	45	57	54	54	51
Anaconda Pintler	FS	MT	48	68	67	39	43	45	45	48	40
Strawberry Mountain	FS	OR	49	50	46	49	49	43	51	47	67
Cebolla	BLM	NM	50	28	57	48	38	48	50	49	65
Mount Jefferson	FS	OR	51	53	44	52	52	51	48	46	46
Mount Skokomish	FS	WA	52	25	40	56	58	55	56	65	37
Cloud Peak	FS	WY	53	64	62	47	56	54	52	50	52
Goat Rocks	FS	WA	54	51	49	55	54	53	53	52	50
Bosque del Apache	FWS	NM	55	56	55	53	50	47	55	51	66
Imperial Refuge	FWS	AZ/CA	56	35	43	59	53	52	49	56	49
Riverside Mountains	BLM	CA	57	43	51	58	55	59	57	55	58
Picacho Peak	BLM	CA	58	36	54	60	60	60	60	58	53
William O. Douglas	FS	WA	59	59	59	57	59	58	61	59	55
Salmo-Priest	FS	WA	60	66	68	54	57	56	62	57	69
Glacier Peak	FS	WA	61	70	58	61	63	63	59	67	57
Swansea	BLM	AZ	62	19	52	67	61	62	63	61	60
Lake Chelan-Sawtooth	FS	WA	63	52	65	63	62	61	58	62	56
Rice Valley	BLM	CA	64	60	61	64	66	65	66	60	64
Death Valley	NPS	CA/NV	65	65	60	65	65	67	67	66	62
Bob Marshall	FS	MT	66	69	70	62	64	64	68	71	61
Salome	FS	AZ	67	63	66	66	69	69	65	64	68
East Cactus Plain	BLM	AZ	68	61	64	68	67	66	64	63	63
Jennie Lakes	FS	CA	69	57	63	69	68	68	69	69	59
Sierra Ancha	FS	AZ	70	67	71	70	70	70	70	68	70
Tatoosh	FS	WA	71	71	69	71	71	71	71	70	71

LO1 and LO2 = Land Ownership Tiers; H2O = Area of Water Features; MRD = Mean Road Distance; ENP = Enplanements; BLM = Bureau of Land Management; FWS = U.S. Fish and Wildlife Service; FS = U.S. Forest Service; NPS = National Park Service.

As of the 2005 Land Trust Census, there had been a promising wave of growth in land conservation through land trusts. At the time of that Census, there were 1,667 private land conservation trusts across the country. Lands being protected through trusts included, for example, ranches, urban undeveloped lands, wetlands, forests, riparian areas, and mountainous sites. Land trusts rely heavily on volunteer labor and on land owners' participation with their organization. Trusts work with land owners to conserve land through acquisition of conservation easements, and will sometimes manage the conserved land and/or the associated easement.

Results from the 2005 National Land Trust Census report—The 2005 Census (released November 30, 2006) described national trends in private land conservation over the last several decades. Each 5-year interval showed dramatically more land protected than during the preceding interval. The following key findings were highlighted in the report (Land Trust Alliance 2006):

- Total acreage conserved through private means in 2005 was 37 million acres, a 54 percent increase from the previous 24-million-acre level in 2000. This included local, State, and large national land conservation groups such as The Nature Conservancy, Ducks Unlimited, The Conservation Fund, and The Trust for Public Land.
- The pace of private land conservation by local and State land trusts had tripled. From 1995 to 2000, land trusts conserved an average of 337,937 acres per year. That pace rose to 1,166,697 acres on average per year from 2000 to 2005.
- Land trusts moved to enhance their professionalism and their numbers grew from 1,263 in 2000 to 1,667 in 2005.
- Acres conserved by local and State land trusts doubled to 11.9 million acres in 2005—an area twice the size of the State of New Hampshire. This was an increase of 5.8 million acres since 2000.
- The States with the highest total acres conserved through land trusts were California, Maine, Colorado, Montana, Virginia, New York, Vermont, New Mexico, Pennsylvania, and Massachusetts. At that time, only Colorado and Virginia were offering State tax incentives for conservation.
- Local and State land trusts increased the acres under conservation easements by 148 percent. These private, voluntary agreements saved 6,245,969 acres as of 2005, versus 2,514,566 in 2000.
- Easements, on the rise for more than a decade, allow landowners to take advantage of Internal Revenue Service-approved tax incentives. Easements are sometimes the only way family farmers can afford to conserve their working farm, ranch, or timber lands.
- The land type reported as being the primary focus of land trust efforts was protecting natural areas and wildlife habitat (39 percent), followed by open space (38 percent), and water resources (26 percent), especially wetlands. Other protected areas include farms, coastal shores, prairies, deserts, urban gardens, and local parks.
- The West was the fastest growing region in both the number of acres conserved and in the number of land trusts, especially for protection of rangeland in many Western States. The second fastest growing region, by percentage of acres conserved, is the Southeast, an area that historically has had fewer land trusts.
- The highest number of land trusts is found in California (198), followed by Massachusetts, Connecticut, Pennsylvania, New York, and Maine. The large number of land trusts in the Northeast reflects the birth of land trusts there over 100 years ago.
- Land trusts numbers and financial status have grown strongly over the last 5 years. Land trusts grew 32 percent in number and by over $1 billion in endowments for long-term stewardship of protected land.
- Rangeland protection is rising. As of December 31, 2005, the Partnership of Rangeland Trusts held 786 conservation easements on 1,061,969 acres in the States of California, Colorado, Nevada, Oregon, Montana, Kansas, and Wyoming.

In addition to land trusts, which are nonprofit, nongovernmental organizations, another strategy to achieve private land conservation is to pursue ballot measures. Local and State governments may bring conservation issues to their citizens via referendum votes, typically to fund land and water conservation programs or grants to be administered by those governing bodies. The use of this democracy-in-action tactic for conservation purposes is promoted and monitored closely by The Trust for Public Land.

INVITED PAPER

State and Local Government Financing for Land Conservation

Andrew du Moulin and Mary Bruce Alford[3]

Between 1998 and 2005 State governments demonstrated significant commitments to support land conservation. During this period, State governments conserved 8.6 million acres and spent $13 billion to protect land from development. The East outspent other regions of the country.

Over the past two decades voters approved more than 75 percent of conservation ballot measures put before them, with approval rates in some States topping the 80–90 percent

---

[3] Director, Center for Conservation Finance Research, The Trust for Public Land, Boston, MA 02108; and Senior Research Associate, Conservation Finance Program, The Trust for Public Land, Jackson, MS 39201.

level. This support cuts across political parties and regions and is evidence that land and water conservation is a core value of the citizenry. Between 1990 and 2010, counties passed 343 ballot measures involving general obligation bonds, sales taxes, and property taxes. This represents over $17 billion for open space, parks, watersheds, recreational lands, wildlife preserves, forests, and farmlands. In some States, local governments have been the primary and occasionally the only source of conservation funding. Voting results from 2010 confirmed that this trend of support is continuing, as voters in 19 States approved local conservation finance ballot measures of almost $424 million to protect open space. Furthermore, voters in 4 States approved statewide conservation finance ballot measures in 2010 for almost $2 billion to protect open space.

The Trust for Public Land has developed two primary data sources to track funding for land conservation in the United States, LandVote (www.landvote.org) and the Conservation Almanac (www.conservationalmanac.org). In the 2009 Trust for Public Land annual report, the recession was listed as a contributing factor to a decrease in contributions for land and water conservation. However, at the same time, new opportunities arose because of falling land prices for prime woodlands, waterfronts, and urban lands. Illustrating the overall effort of conservation organizations and State and local governments, The Trust for Public Land completed over 200 conservation transactions in 2009, adding 312,000 new acres under protection.

The LandVote database reported 2009 and 2010 as very good years for State and local government conservation funding. In 2009, the State of Minnesota approved $5.5 billion, the Nation's largest ever single State or local conservation finance measure. In 2010, voters across the country approved a variety of measures for land conservation, generating over $2 billion, including statewide financing measures in Oregon, Rhode Island, Maine, and Iowa.

Trends in State spending on land conservation: National activity and trends

—Between 1998 and 2005, 8.6 million acres of land were conserved in the United States by State governments. Well over half (61 percent) of these acres were purchased in fee title, while the remainder was protected through conservation easements. States spent more than $13 billion to protect these lands, or an average of $1.6 billion annually. The average cost was $1,500 per acre. Spending peaked in 2003, outpacing other years, largely due to a spike in Florida, which accounted for approximately one-third of State conservation spending nationally that year (fig. 3.6). The Conservation Almanac, The Trust for Public Land online database, covers conservation activity across the United States. This activity involves removing lands from the inventory of lands that can be developed or used for commercial and/or other intensive uses.

Between 1998 and 2005 States had, on average, protected 1.1 million acres per year, the most in 2002 (1.3 million acres) and the least in 1998 (816,000 acres) (fig. 3.7).

Trends summarized by region—There have been significantly different levels of spending between the North and South regions and those of the West. Several Eastern States—notably New Jersey and Massachusetts—adopted new enabling authority during this period which resulted in several hundred local governments adopting new ballot measures. Table 3.3 shows higher spending in the South and North regions relative to the Pacific and Rocky Mountains regions between 1998 and 2005. On a per-capita basis, States in the Pacific Coast region outspent the rest of the country at $8 per capita annually. The North followed at $6 per capita per year, then the South ($4 per capita), and then the Rocky Mountains ($2 per capita).

During 1998–2005, for which spending data are available, some trends can be noted. The South outspent other regions in 5 of 8 years (fig. 3.8). Much of this regional difference (70 percent) was attributable to Florida's State program, Florida Forever. On average, the South spent $644 million per year. The North consistently spent the next highest amount with an average of $568 million per year. Following next was the Pacific region ($381 million) and then the Rocky Mountains region ($86 million).

Levels of funding for States across the United States are illustrated in figure 3.9. States with the greatest funding include Florida, California, North Carolina, and New Jersey (see also table 3.4). Each of these States spent over $800 million, which is a result of voter and legislative approval of long-term dedicated funding for conservation. The next highest spending levels were by the States of New York, Pennsylvania, Maryland, Colorado, Ohio, Washington, Massachusetts, Virginia, Connecticut, Wisconsin, and Minnesota. The average across all States was approximately $268 million.

As a result of State financing for land conservation, an average of nearly 172,000 acres per State were protected between 1998 and 2005. States conserving the most acreage (greater than 250,000 acres) included California, Colorado, Minnesota, New York, New Jersey, Pennsylvania, Maryland, Virginia, North Carolina, and Florida (fig. 3.10 and also table 3.4). Next highest States (between 99,000 and 250,000 acres) were Washington, Montana, Wisconsin, Maine, New Hampshire, Massachusetts, and Alabama.[4]

Local and State government ballot measures

—Voters have continued to support conservation funding measures, even during the current economic recession.

---

[4] The Trust for Public Land Conservation Almanac, www.conservationalmanac.org. Data includes conservation activity from 1998 to 2005.

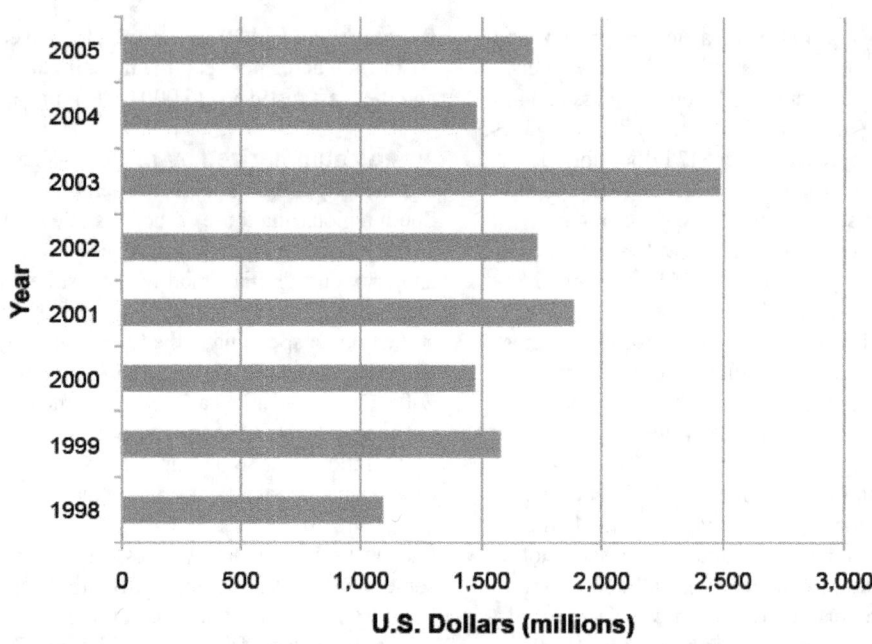

Figure 3.6—Trend in land conservation spending using State government funding by year, 1998–2005. Source: The Trust for Public Land (2010). Note: The acreage and cost data included in the Conservation Almanac is through the end of 2005. The Trust for Public Land is currently in the process of updating the Conservation Almanac data through 2008. As of December 2010, almost half the country was completed or in the process of being updated, and the Almanac also includes conservation information at the local level of government as well as spatial data.

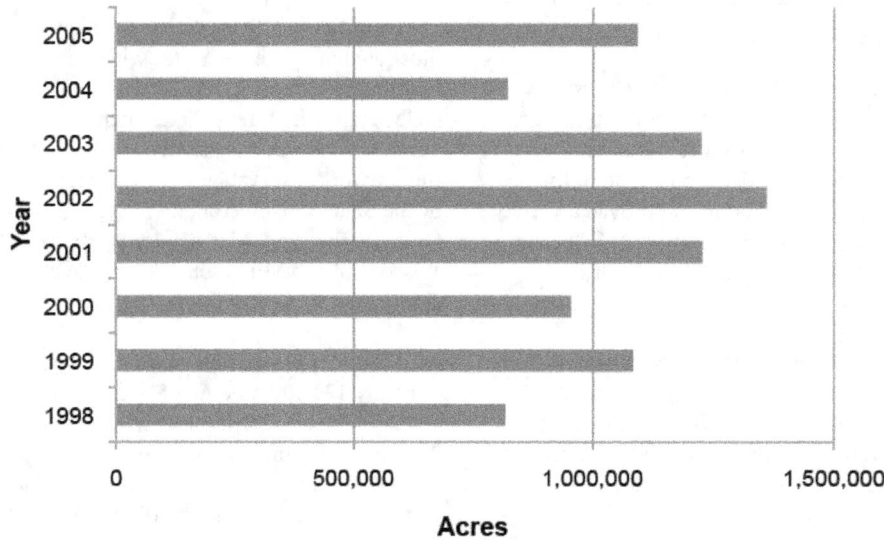

Figure 3.7—Total acres protected using State government funding in the United States, 1998–2005. Source: The Trust for Public Land (2010).

Table 3.3—Total State funds spent for conservation per capita spending and acres protected from 1998 to 2005[a]

Region	Dollars spent (in millions)	Annual average dollars per capita	Average acres per year	Total acres acquired
Pacific	$3,050	$8	38,208	1,528,332
North	$4,561	$6	19,738	3,158,157
South	$5,152	$4	27,096	2,817,953
Rocky Mountains	$753	$2	1,223	117,454

[a] Data represents land conservation conducted through State programs and agencies.
Source: Trust For Public Land's Conservation Almanac (2010).

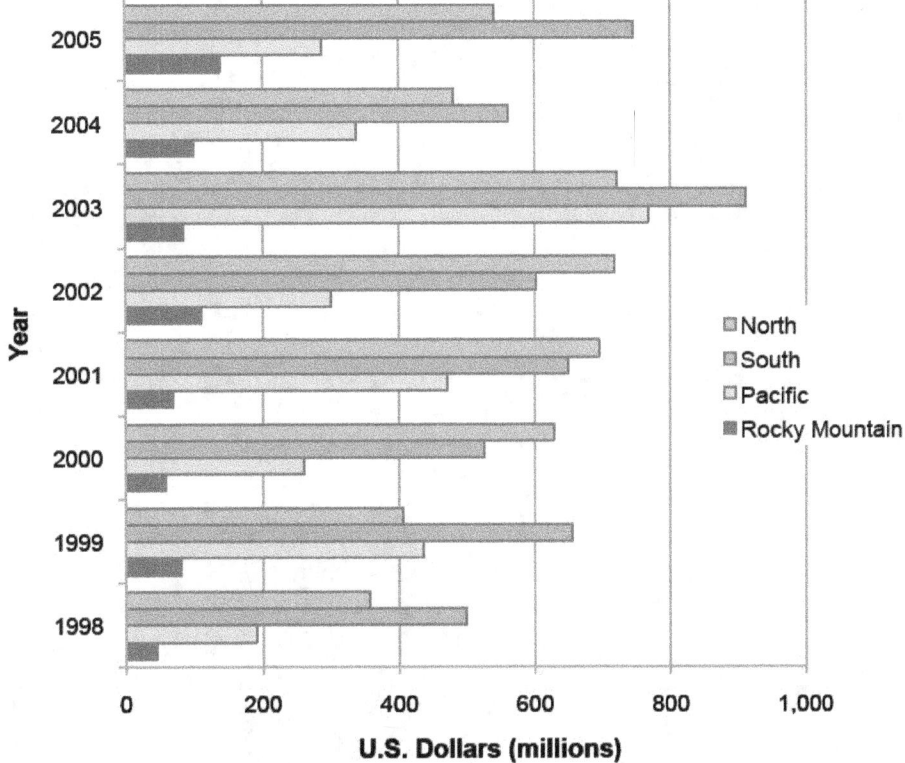

Figure 3.8—Trend in total State funds spent by region and year, 1998–2005. Source: The Trust for Public Land (2010).

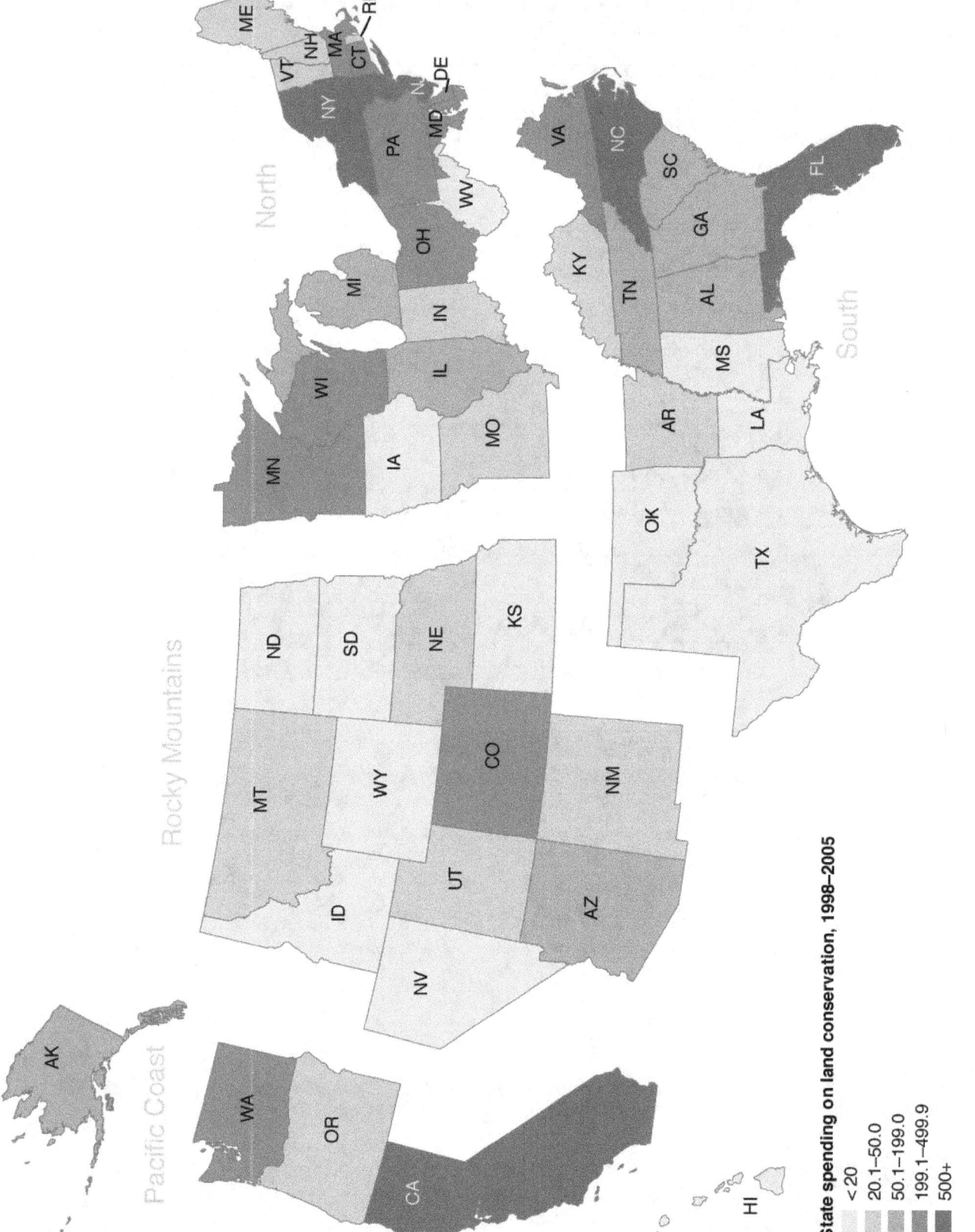

State spending on land conservation, 1998–2005

<20
20.1–50.0
50.1–199.0
199.1–499.9
500+

Figure 3 9—Conservation funding level (millions of dollars) by State for the period 1998–2005.

Table 3.4—List of State government dollars spent, annual average dollars per capita, and acres acquired from 1998 to 2005

	U.S. State Land Conservation Activity 1998–2005		
State	State dollars spent	Annual average dollars spent per capita	Acres acquired
1 Florida	$3,567,559,516	$24.33	1,671,784.29
2 California	$2,552,568,280	$8.68	1,221,303.85
3 North Carolina	$851,733,148	$11.54	467,492.18
4 New Jersey	$821,390,608	$11.83	251,822.12
5 New York	$742,645,658	$4.76	432,253.34
6 Pennsylvania	$454,806,480	$4.57	372,082.25
7 Maryland	$413,048,657	$9.16	370,329.18
8 Colorado	$409,099,361	$10.35	658,511.76
9 Ohio	$354,926,417	$3.86	76,881.39
10 Washington	$325,041,643	$6.20	132,934.96
11 Massachusetts	$308,132,263	$5.93	145,297.00
12 Virginia	$285,041,067	$4.59	259,472.44
13 Connecticut	$263,885,427	$9.42	64,573.62
14 Wisconsin	$235,781,026	$5.24	216,499.44
15 Minnesota	$221,668,874	$5.31	440,481.15
16 Delaware	$204,374,534	$29.26	80,405.89
17 Georgia	$163,470,548	$2.11	68,211.87
18 Michigan	$163,320,671	$2.04	96,085.69
19 Alaska	$133,056,808	$24.23	132,315.90
20 Illinois	$122,091,450	$1.18	27,395.38
21 Arizona	$101,382,607	$1.95	41,797.18
22 Alabama	$61,604,202	$1.65	104,661.43
23 Tennessee	$60,085,004	$1.21	42,782.55
24 South Carolina	$51,792,018	$1.45	40,305.30
25 Indiana	$50,000,000	$0.98	64,940.81
26 Maine	$40,294,050	$3.83	117,751.30
27 New Hampshire	$39,948,752	$3.80	215,029.01
28 Montana	$38,891,863	$5.03	165,952.00
29 Vermont	$37,201,772	$7.49	68,844.70
30 Missouri	$35,456,930	$0.75	42,078.39
31 Kentucky	$33,145,796	$0.97	38,927.61
32 Utah	$29,023,991	$1.33	79,776.28
33 Rhode Island	$26,257,273	$3.12	10,406.81
34 Oregon	$25,469,490	$0.84	41,451.66
35 Arkansas	$23,966,049	$1.05	29,299.37
36 New Mexico	$23,041,501	$1.45	6,965.10
37 Nebraska	$22,203,269	$1.56	62,512.18
38 Louisiana	$19,657,931	$0.56	21,714.07
39 Nevada	$19,247,614	$0.93	14,194.06
40 Mississippi	$17,849,115	$0.76	12,084.52
41 Iowa	$17,357,650	$0.72	23,997.30
42 Texas	$13,486,362	$0.07	56,132.33
43 Hawaii	$13,450,000	$1.31	325.25
44 South Dakota	$11,997,287	$1.86	27,376.04
45 Idaho	$9,268,002	$0.76	12,980.45
46 West Virginia	$8,378,518	$0.58	41,002.31
47 Kansas	$4,806,085	$0.21	6,247.34
48 Oklahoma	$2,764,892	$0.09	5,084.61
49 Wyoming	$383,000	$0.09	1,799.35
50 North Dakota	$12,000	$0.00	80
U.S. average	$268,641,309	$4.62	171,652.66

Source: The Trust for Public Land (2010).

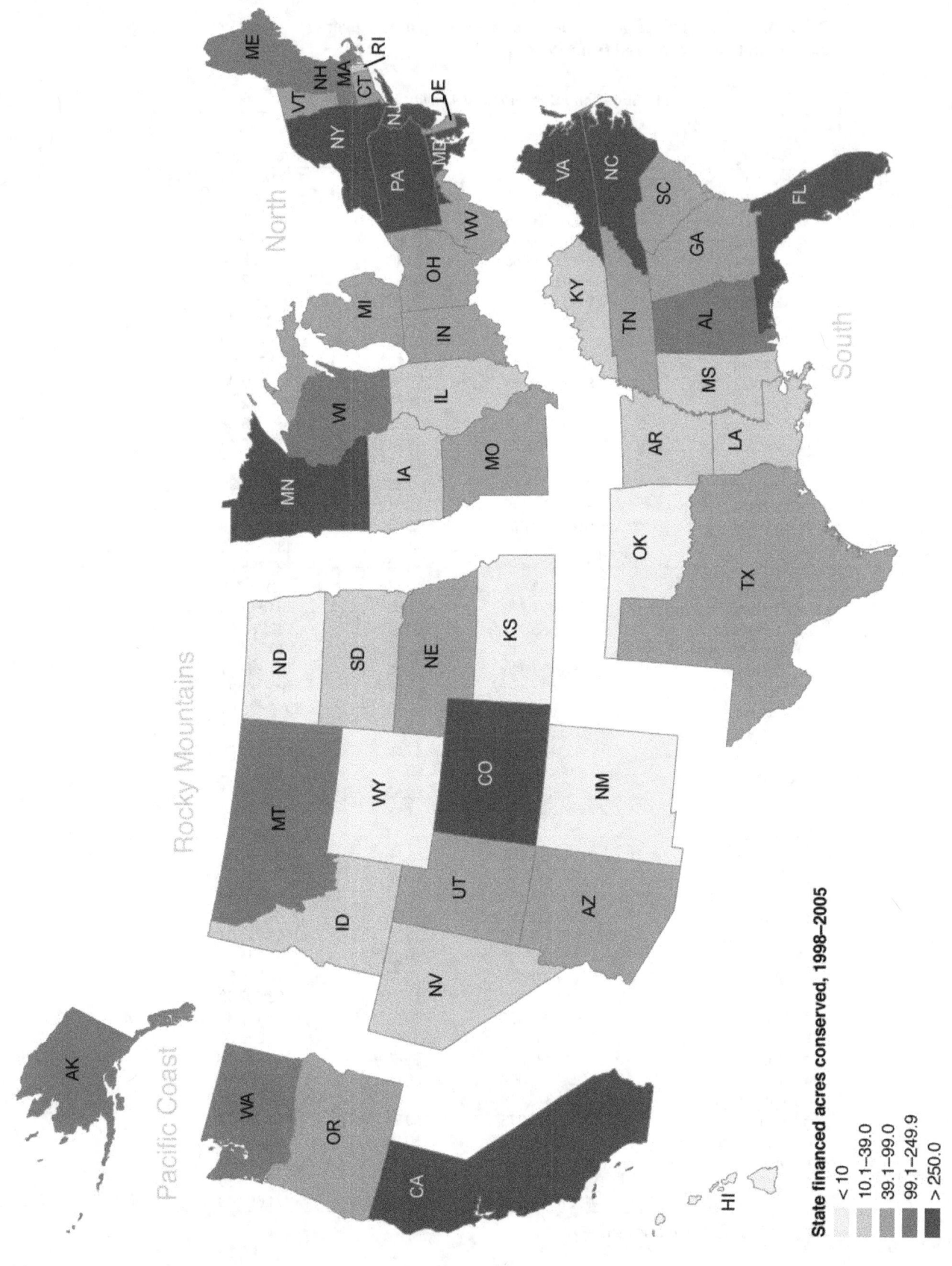

State financed acres conserved, 1998–2005

- <10
- 10.1–39.0
- 39.1–99.0
- 99.1–249.9
- >250.0

Figure 3 10—Acres of land protected (1,000 acres) through State financing of conservation easements or fee simple purchase, 1998–2005. Source: Trust for Public Land, 2010.

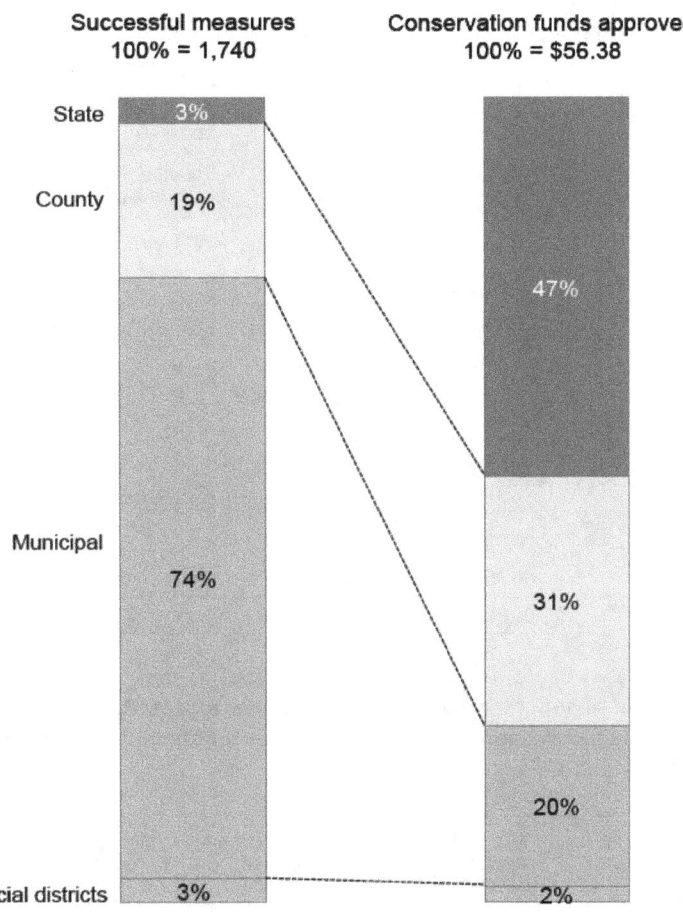

Successful measures
100% = 1,740

Conservation funds approved
100% = $56.38

State   3%

County   19%

47%

Municipal   74%

31%

20%

Special districts   3%   2%

Figure 3.11—Successful ballot measures for land conservation and conservation funds approved by level of government, 1990–2010.

Local governments (county and municipal) in particular have had sustained support for public funding of land conservation. This includes traditionally supportive States such as New Jersey and Massachusetts, as well as less traditionally supportive States, such as Iowa, Idaho, and Montana. Figure 3.11 shows the percentage of successfully approved voter ballots by level of government since 1990. By far, municipal governments have been most successful, accounting for 74 percent of approved measures. State governments, however, represent the highest percentage of total funds approved at 47 percent, followed by county governments (31 percent) and then municipal governments at 20 percent (fig. 3.11).

County conservation finance—Between 1990 and 2010, 172 counties in 30 States passed a total of 343 ballot measures for land conservation. In a number of counties, there have been multiple measures. These measures, supported primarily by general obligation bonds, property taxes, and sales taxes (as well as real estate transfer taxes and income taxes in selected States), generated over $17 billion for open space, parks, watersheds, recreational lands, wildlife preserves, forests, and

farmland. Almost 75 percent of all county conservation ballot measures in the last two decades have won voter approval.

Dozens of counties, particularly in Maryland, Virginia, Pennsylvania, and New York, have approved county programs for land conservation through the legislative process. State constitutions and statutes do not always provide enabling legislation to allow residents to vote on conservation funding. Instead, it is often left to local officials to decide on conservation funding.

The North region has the best passage rate at 79 percent, and this region generated the most funding for open space, farmland, forest land, wildlife habitat, and other natural areas at over $7 billion. Nationally, over $1 billion was generated through county ballot measures where forest land conservation was among the prime purposes (table 3.5). Leading States for county conservation measures that included funding for forest land were Arizona, Illinois, Georgia, and Florida. Almost $5 billion were approved where farmland was among the prime purposes of the conservation finance measure. The counties most successful were in the States of New Jersey, New York,

Table 3.5—Forest related county ballot measures, 1990–2010

State	Total ballot measures	Total funds approved	Conservation funds approved	Measures passed	Passage rate
	number	----- -*dollars*- ------ -		*number*	*percent*
AZ	2	207,300,000	194,100,000	2	100
FL	1	55,000,000	55,000,000	1	100
GA	1	100,000,000	71,400,000	1	100
IA	1	20,000,000	20,000,000	1	100
IL	10	625,000,000	615,000,000	10	100
KY	1	0	0	0	0
MT	2	10,000,000	10,000,000	1	50
OH	4	37,000,000	8,325,000	2	50
SC	2	5,000,000	5,000,000	1	50
VA	1	20,000,000	20,000,000	1	100
WI	1	30,000,000	30,000,000	1	100
Total	26	1,109,300,000	1,028,825,000	21	81

Table 3.6—Number of ballot measures proposed, funds approved, conservation funds approved, measures passed, and passage rate through county ballot initiatives for farmland conservation, 1990–2010

State	Total ballot measures	Total funds approved	Conservation funds approved	Measures passed	Passage rate
	number	----- - *dollars* - -----		*number*	*percent*
CA	5	611,000,000	611,000,000	2	40
CO	8	232,880,000	224,380,000	4	50
FL	2	150,000,000	150,000,000	1	50
IA	1	20,000,000	20,000,000	1	100
ID	1	0	0	0	0
MD	5	78,000,000	78,000,000	5	100
MI	5	35,563,230	35,563,230	2	40
MN	1	20,000,000	20,000,000	1	100
MT	4	30,000,000	30,000,000	3	75
NC	1	0	0	0	0
NJ	35	2,850,510,223	2,614,789,763	32	91
NV	1	0	0	0	0
NY	4	732,000,000	729,400,000	3	75
OH	4	0	0	1	25
PA	6	312,500,000	275,000,000	6	100
SC	2	50,000,000	50,000,000	1	50
UT	1	0	0	0	0
VA	1	20,000,000	20,000,000	1	100
WA	2	5,000,000	5,000,000	1	50
WI	1	0	0	0	0
Total	90	5,147,453,453	4,863,132,993	64	71

Table 3.7—Approved county ballot measures by region, 1990–2010

Region	Total ballot measures	Total funds approved	Conservation funds approved	Measures passed	Passage rate
	number	------ *dollars* ------		*number*	*percent*
North	151	7,882,226,375	6,807,050,082	118	78
Pacific Coast	41	32,870,334,820	2,759,944,820	20	49
Rocky Mountains	84	2,458,116,303	2,357,159,511	63	75
South	157	13,124,771,220	4,969,651,280	120	76
Total	433	56,335,448,718	16,893,805,693	321	74

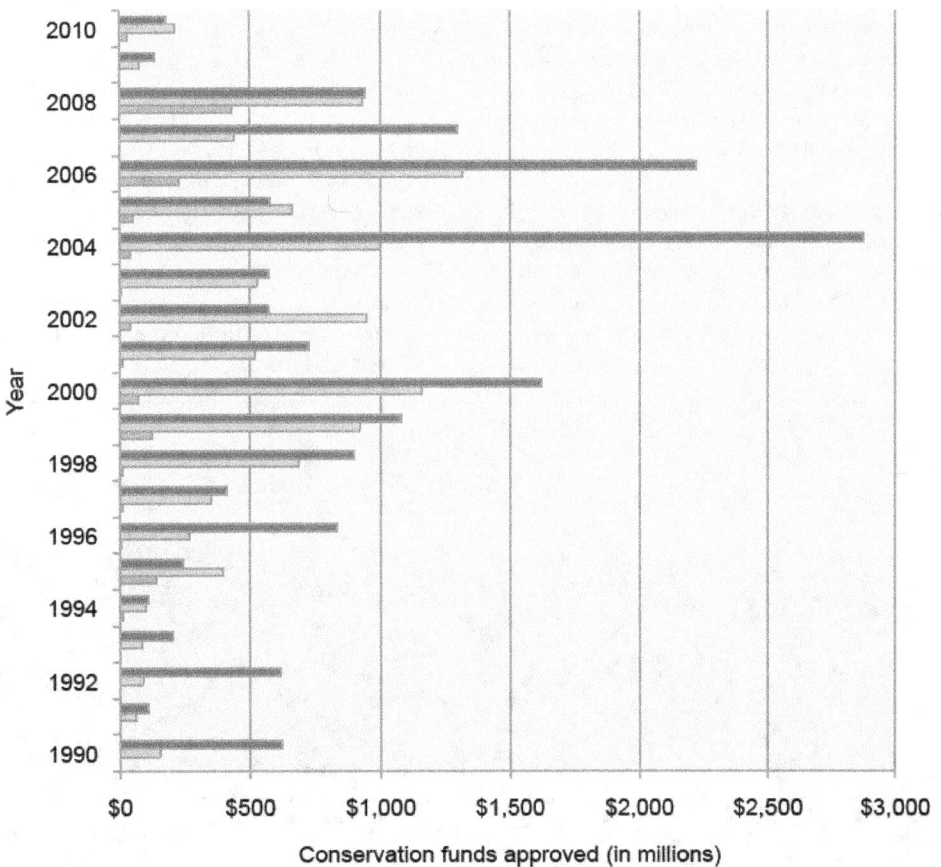

■County ▢Municipal ▢Special District

Figure 3.12—Trends in local government spending by level of government from 1990 to 2010.

California, Pennsylvania, Colorado, Florida, Maryland, South Carolina, and Michigan (table 3.6).

Table 3.7 shows county ballot measures for each of the four regions of the United States defined by the Renewable Resources Planning Act (RPA) National Assessment of the Forest Service, U.S. Department of Agriculture. Leading counties in the North region were in the States of Illinois, New Jersey (where all 21 counties have passed a dedicated funding source for conservation), and New York (where funding initiatives were passed primarily in Suffolk and Nassau counties). Total conservation funds approved for the North region were just over $7 billion. For counties in the Pacific Coast region, far and away California led, accounting for 88 percent of that region's conservation funds. Alaska had no funds approved. In the Rocky Mountains region, counties in Colorado accounted for over 79 percent of the region's conservation funds. In the South, Florida stood out from the other States accounting for almost 59 percent of conservation funds. Georgia followed as a distant second.

The growth of local conservation funding—Figure 3.12 illustrates the trend of local government (county and municipal) conservation funding over the past two decades. In some cases, local funding has been either the largest or the only source of conservation funding in many States. Across the country, local government is the fastest growing source of government funding (see New Jersey case example in side bar on the following page). This may be due to a number of reasons:

- Greater public confidence in local governments
- Funds can be used to manage land use, a local government role
- There are opportunities to leverage funds from other sources
- There is opportunity for a "domino effect" whereby other local governments act to create new conservation funding sources as well.

Ballot measures in 2010—On Election Day 2010, voters across the United States once again demonstrated their commitment to supporting public investments in parks and natural areas. Voters in 23 States approved conservation finance ballot measures that will generate almost $2.2 billion to protect open space. Of the 49 measures on the ballot, 84 percent were successful. As documented in the LandVote database (www.landvote.org), since 1988 voters have approved more than 1,700 measures yielding more than $56 billion in conservation funding. This support has remained strong even during prior economic slowdowns. The 2010 results confirm that conservation remains a cause voters will support.

- In Iowa, voters gave 63 percent approval to an amendment to the State constitution creating a permanent trust fund to protect and restore the State's natural resources.

Pololu coast line on the north side of the Big Island in Hawaii. Most of the land in the Pololu Valley area is privately owned. (Photograph by Ken Cordell 2010)

New Jersey land conservation facts

- Municipal open space taxes brought in over $94.5 million in 2009
- County open space taxes brought in over $261 million in 2009
- Since 1998, in New Jersey, 316 out of 411 municipal open space measures have passed. The 316 measures passed in New Jersey represented almost one-third of all municipal open space ballot successes nationally over the past decade.
- Over $1.1 billion in municipal conservation funds were generated during the decade from 2000 to 2010.
- During the period from 1998 to 2009, some 240 different municipalities went to the ballot to establish, renew, or increase their open space tax.
- Since 1998, 27 of 30 county measures have passed, generating over $2.2 billion—the highest conservation dollar amount generated by any county in the Nation.
- New Jersey is one of only two States to have all counties approve dedicated conservation funding. Hawaii is the other.

- In Oregon, 69 percent of voters approved a measure that will indefinitely set aside 15 percent of revenue generated by the Oregon Lottery for protection of water, parks, and wildlife habitat in the State. The provision has generated more than $800 million in the past decade for conservation.
- In Maine, voters gave 59 percent approval to a statewide bond providing for investments in land conservation, the preservation of working waterfronts, and State parks.
- Voters in Dorchester County, SC, gave 71–29 percent approval to issuing $5 million in bonds to buy parkland, trails, and wildlife habitat.

The economic arguments for land conservation are likely to increase in importance in future years. As highlighted in a January 1, 2010, front-page article in The New York Times, the current economic downturn also has led to a new window of opportunity for land conservation—sometimes referred to as the recession's "green lining." Because of the decline in the real estate market, conservation has become a more attractive alternative to development for some landowners. This has made many properties more affordable and provided once-in-a-generation opportunities to conserve land once destined for development.

End Invited Paper

Federal Financing

There are a number of Federal programs aimed at land and water conservation. Some of these specifically focus on conservation easements or fee simple purchase of land and water areas. Perhaps most prominent among these is the Land and Water Conservation Fund administered by the National Park Service and the Conservation Reserve Program administered by the Natural Resources Conservation Service. Selected Federal conservation programs are highlighted below to represent Federal land conservation incentive programs.

Land and Water Conservation Fund—The Federal Land and Water Conservation Fund (LWCF) was established by law in 1965 to use revenues from offshore oil and gas leasing for financing U.S. land and water conservation. Often, these finances have been used to purchase land and easements, some of which had been originally acquired by land trusts.

Though the LWCF receives $900 million a year from energy royalties, Congress has not authorized spending all of those funds on an annual basis. The current Administration seems to be moving to increase LWCF funding from $172 million in fiscal year (FY) 2009 and $318 million in FY2010, to a proposed $432 million for FY2011. Authorization for FY2011 and beyond is very much uncertain at this time.

The Federal portion of the LWCF is used to purchase lands significant to the management of national parks, refuges, forests, and BLM lands (http://wilderness.org/content/lwcf-projects-2010). As human activities have increased, it has become more important to connect land and water ecosystems and habitats to better assure their long-term ecological health. LWCF funding for Federal acquisition of inholdings, buffer areas, and wildlife migration corridors by agency in FY2010 is listed below:

Bureau of Land Management	$ 24,650,000
U.S. Fish and Wildlife Service	$ 86,340,000
National Park Service	$ 86,266,000
U.S. Forest Service	$ 63,522,000

Forest Legacy Program—There are a number of Federal conservation fund programs in addition to LWCF, such as the Forest Legacy Program, a voluntary program of the Forest Service. This program provides grants to States through their forestry agencies for the purchase of conservation easements and fee simple purchase of sensitive or threatened forest lands. The Forest Legacy Program provides an alternative to selling forest land by allowing voluntary conservation to private owners. In FY2010, Forest Legacy Program funding was projected to grow by 60 percent to nearly $80 million. As of November 2010, the program passed the milestone of 2 million acres protected (http://www.fs fed.us/spf/coop/

programs/loa/flp.shtml). These protected lands are located in 42 States and Territories (fig. 3.13). Currently 48 States and Territories are enrolled in the program. For FY2012, a total of $87 million has been proposed in the President's budget.

Federal Highway Bill Funding—The 2005 Federal Highway Bill provides funding for scenic and historic conservation such as conversion of abandoned railway corridors to trails and environmental mitigation of highway projects. In 2009 a total of $370 million was provided for recreational trails for pedestrian, equestrian, bicycling, non-motorized snow, and off-road motorized vehicle activities. The same year, additional funding was granted for land purchase or leasing. The Federal Highway Bill funded $175 million in 2009 for scenic byways programs involving highways with outstanding scenic, historic, cultural, natural, recreational, and archaeological qualities. The Federal Highway Bill also funds national historic covered bridge preservation for those eligible for listing on the National Register of Historic Places. Often an easement or purchase of associated land is a part of these projects. A new program to fund pilot projects aimed at creating a network of non-motorized transportation modes was started in 2009 to demonstrate the benefits of walking and bicycling transportation.

State Wildlife Grants—The Federal State Wildlife Grants Program is aimed at protecting wildlife. It requires participating States to develop wildlife action plans and then provides annual funding for implementation of these plans. Many States place some of these funds with partners such as land trusts. The wildlife action plans themselves are a useful tool for land trusts to prioritize acquisition and stewardship decisions. This program is administered by the U.S. Fish and Wildlife Service.

Conservation Reserve Program—The Conservation Reserve Program was established to provide technical and financial assistance to farmers and ranchers for the conservation of soil, water, and other natural resources. The program assists farmers and ranchers with Federal, State, and other environmental laws and provides incentives for environmental protection. The Conservation Reserve Program is administered by the Natural Resources Conservation Service, which evaluates assistance eligibility and manages assistance financing.

The Conservation Reserve Program is aimed at addressing soil erosion, managing land for food and fiber production, reducing sedimentation in streams and lakes, improving water quality, assuring habitat for wildlife, and protecting forest and wetland resources. The program encourages landowners to manage vegetative cover, such as grasses, wildlife plantings, trees, or riparian buffers, on erodible land. Farmers who sign the multi-year contract are paid to establish and sustain vegetative cover.

Between 1990 and 2008, the program enrolled an average of about 33 million acres per year, with a high of 36.8 million acres in 2007 (fig. 3.14) (Hellerstein 2010). After a period of relative stability in acreage enrolled in the program, the Conservation Reserve Program seems to be declining, possibly due to the 2008 Farm Bill which reduced the maximum enrollment to 32 million acres. As of February 2010, the program enrollment was at 31.2 million acres.

Protected Federal Land

Federal lands are covered in this chapter and also later in chapter 5. Federal lands are included in both chapters for different reasons. In this chapter, the emphasis is on Federal lands designated primarily to protect their natural condition. In chapter 5, the emphasis is on Federal properties as recreation resources, where access and facilities are the key attributes.

The Federal Government holds about 640 million acres in trust. This is about 30 percent of the country's total land area. Federally owned and managed public lands include national parks, national forests, national wildlife refuges, and other Federal agency ownerships. Each Federal agency is charged through specific laws to manage their lands responsibly and to enhance their contributions to the national economy. The primary land-management agencies include the Bureau of Land Management, the Bureau of Reclamation, the Forest Service, the U.S. Fish and Wildlife Service, the National Park Service, the U.S. Army Corps of Engineers, and the Tennessee Valley Authority.

Resource protection is the primary mission of two of these agencies, the National Park Service and the U.S. Fish and Wildlife Service. The National Wilderness Preservation System is a specially designated Federal system established to preserve natural resource character. Four agencies share in management of the National Wilderness Preservation System. Provided below are descriptions of these three systems.[5] Following these descriptions, we provide an overview of the ecosystem representation provided by these three Federal land protection systems.

The National Park System—National parks and other categories of protected areas within the National Park System are among the most protected of lands in the United States. As figure 3.15 later shows, units of the National Park System protect a number of natural ecosystems across the country.

---

[5] The U.S. Forest Service and Bureau of Land Management are not included here because those agencies manage for multiple uses. Also not covered in this section are the other Federal agencies—the Bureau of Reclamation, the U.S. Army Corps of Engineers, and the Tennessee Valley Authority—that manage natural resources primarily for flood control, navigation, and hydropower production.

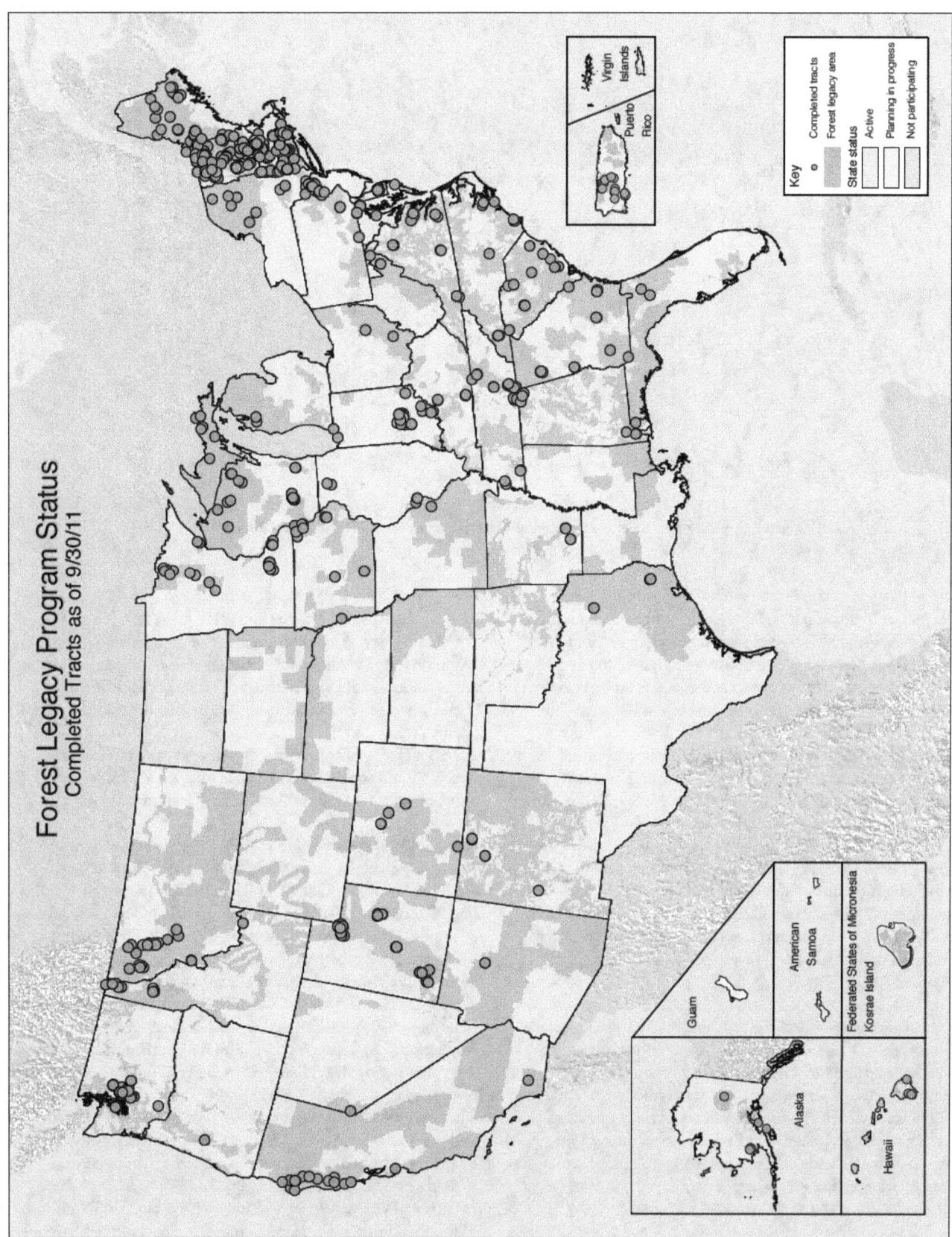

Figure 3 13—State enrollment status, Legacy areas, and completed tracts in the USDA Forest Service Forest Legacy Program, 2010.

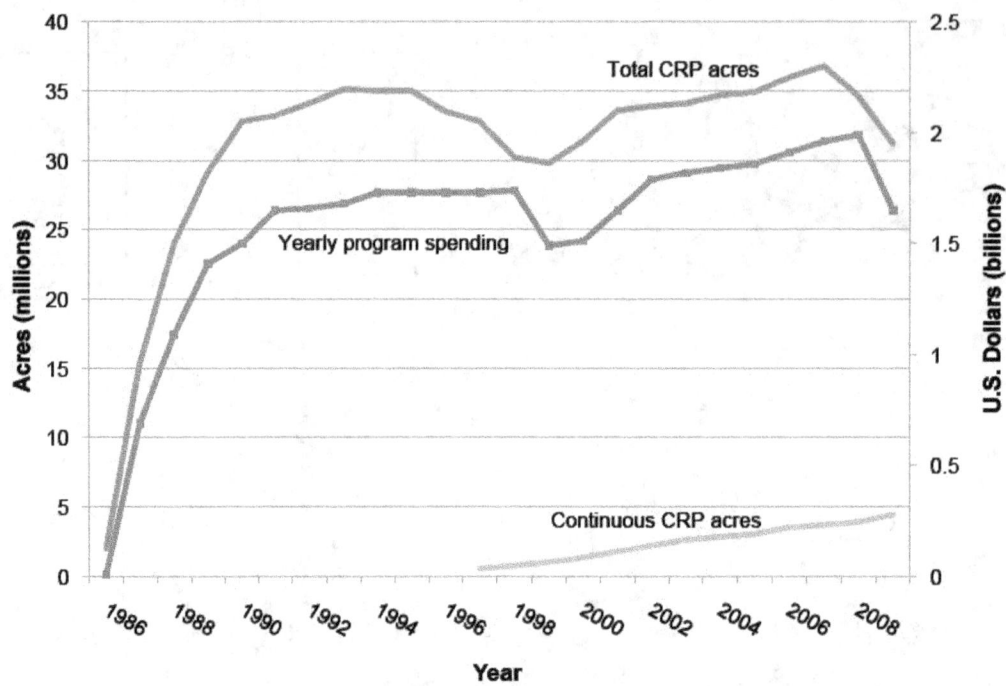

Figure 3.14—Long-term trend in acreage enrolled and program costs, 1986–2008 (Hellerstein 2010).

The origin of national parks, large-scale natural land areas for public enjoyment, is traced to artist George Catlin, who traveled throughout the Western United States in the early 1830s. Thirty years after his travels, Federal land in Yosemite Valley was ceded to the State of California to "...be used and preserved for the benefit of mankind." In 1872, the same preservation motives resulted in the establishment of the Yellowstone region as a public park. However, since it was located in two territories that were not yet States, Yellowstone was kept under Federal control. It was another 44 years until the 1916 Organic Act established the National Park Service, placing all existing parks, including Yellowstone, within the Department of the Interior and under National Park Service management. The act also included historic, prehistoric, and other structures and landmarks of scientific interest, known as "national monuments," that were protected under the Antiquities Act of 1906.

The protection purposes of the National Park Organic Act are well-known: "...to conserve the scenery and the natural and historic objects and the wild life therein and to provide for the enjoyment of the same in such manner and by such means as will leave them unimpaired for the enjoyment of future generations." Later, in 1933, all Federal Government parks, monuments, battlefields, and memorials were placed under the National Park Service's jurisdiction.

The National Park Service ultimately grew into the system we know today. It includes an array of different types of areas having somewhat different purposes. Designations include parks, monuments, battlefields, military parks, historical parks, historic sites, lakeshores, seashores, recreation areas, scenic rivers, and trails. As of December 2008, the National Park Service was comprised of 388 areas or units covering nearly 79 million acres. The types of areas which protect large acreages of intact natural lands are shown in table 3.8.

Alaska dominates the National Park Service system total acreage, especially since the 1980 passage of the Alaska National Interest Lands Conservation Act. Excluding Alaska, the National Park Service is much more balanced in terms of regional distribution of protected acreage. The North has by far the least protected land of any region. Not counting national preserves, which are almost entirely in Alaska, national recreation areas (3.4 million acres) and national monuments (2.3 million acres) are a distant second and third, respectively, to national parks (almost 50 million acres) in total area nationally. There are 59 national parks in the United States, 14 of which are in the East. By contrast, the two eastern regions lead the west by a wide margin in both acreage and units of the following NPS designated areas: National Seashore, National River, National Scenic Trail, National Wild and Scenic River, Parkways, and National Lakeshore. In terms of wilderness protection on NPS lands, 43.9 million of the 78.8 million acres (56 percent) are part of the National

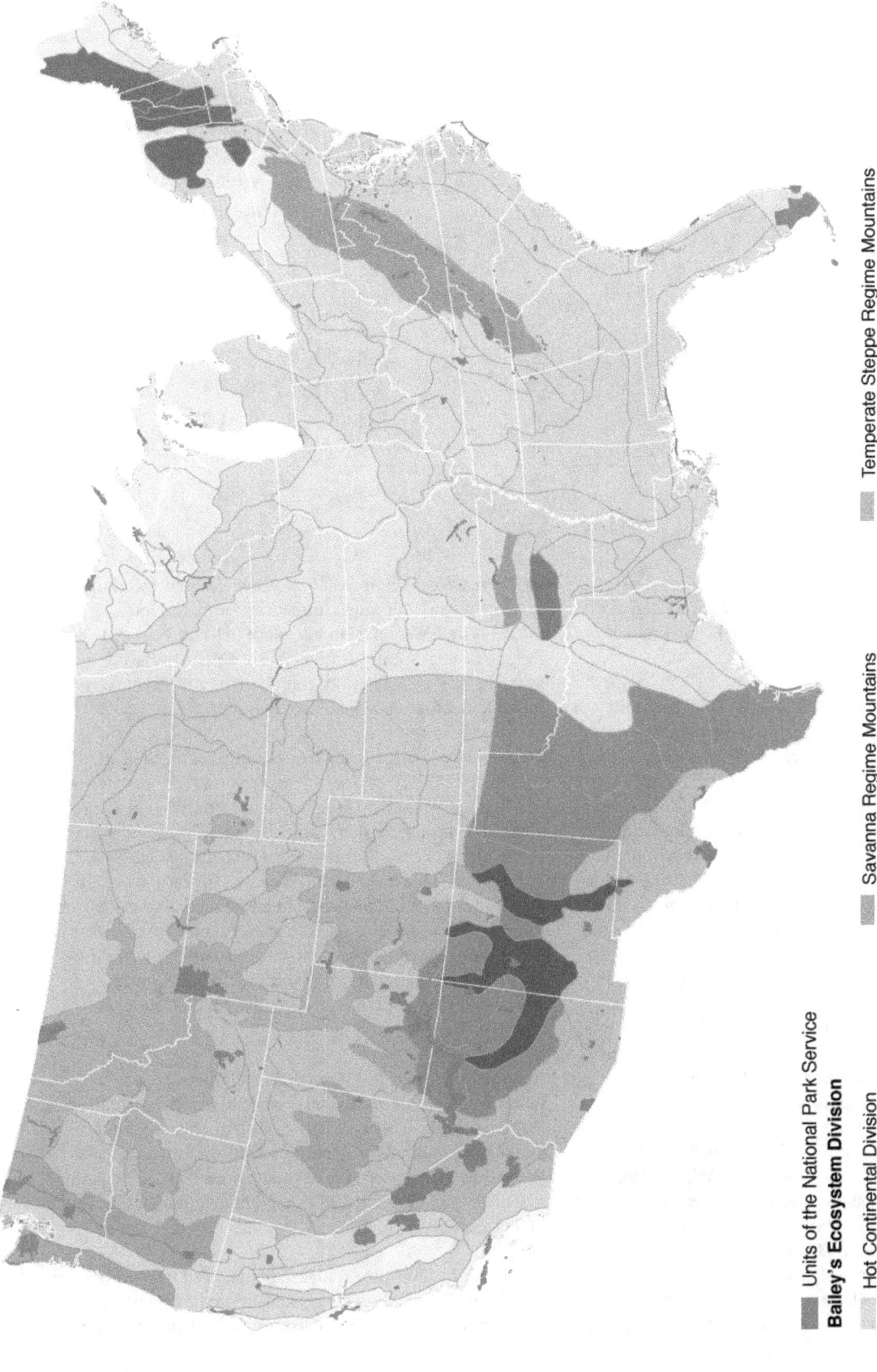

Units of the National Park Service

Bailey's Ecosystem Division

Hot Continental Division
Hot Continental Regime Mountains
Marine Division
Marine Regime Mountains
Mediterranean Division
Mediterranean Regime Mountains
Prairie Division
Rainforest Regime Mountains
Savanna Division

Savanna Regime Mountains
Subarctic Division
Subarctic Regime Mountains
Subtropical Division
Subtropical Regime Mountains
Temperate Desert Division
Temperate Desert Regime Mountains
Temperate Steppe Division

Temperate Steppe Regime Mountains
Tropical/Subtropical Desert Division
Tropical/Subtropical Regime Mountains
Tropical/Subtropical Steppe Division
Tundra Division
Tundra Regime Mountains
Warm Continental Division
Warm Continental Regime Mountains

Figure 3 15—National Park System coverage of ecosystem types in the contiguous United States.

Tale 3.8—Number and acres of National Park Service (NPS) natural land protected type of designation and RPA region, 2008

NPS designation	North Units	North Acres	South Units	South Acres	Rocky Mountains Units	Rocky Mountains Acres	Pacific Coast Units	Pacific Coast Acres	United States Units	United States Acres
		thousand		thousand		thousand		thousand		thousand
National Park	4	738.5	10	3,378.6	23	6,751.6	22	39,052.0	59	49,920.8
National Preserve	0	0.0	5	763.3	0	0.0	11	20,835.4	16	21,598.7
National Recreation Area	4	81.4	4	117.1	4	2,820.6	6	394.4	18	3,413.4
National Monument	10	3.9	12	33.4	43	1,413.1	9	814.0	74	2,264.4
National Seashore	3	41.1	7	373.2	0	0.0	1	65.1	11	479.4
National River	4	114.6	1	116.3	1	0.2	0	0.0	6	231.1
National Scenic Trail	2	110.6	2	60.6	0	0.0	0	0.0	4	171.2
National Wild and Scenic River	5	43.6	3	95.5	1	0.0	1	28.4	10	167.6
Parkways	1	2.8	3	140.3	1	23.8	0	0.0	5	166.9
National Lakeshore	4	146.1	0	0.0	0	0.0	0	0.0	4	146.1

RPA = Resources Planning Act.
Source: USDI National Park Service (2008).

Wilderness Preservation System, most of which is in Alaska. Excluding Alaska, about 10.9 million acres are protected as Federal wilderness, about 84 percent of which is in the two western regions.

The National Wildlife Refuge System—The U.S. Fish and Wildlife Service was formally created in 1940 as the "Fish and Wildlife Service" when the Bureaus of Fisheries and of Biological Survey were merged after their respective moves to the Department of the Interior. The Fish and Wildlife Act of 1956 established a comprehensive national policy for wildlife and fish, as well as reorganizing the U.S. Fish and Wildlife Service into the bureaus of Sport Fisheries and Wildlife and Commercial Fisheries. It also added "U.S." to the agency's name. The Bureau of Sport Fisheries and Wildlife included the Division of Wildlife Refuges and is still a part of the U.S. Fish and Wildlife Service. The Bureau of Commercial Fisheries became the National Marine Fisheries Service and was transferred to the Commerce Department in 1970.

The Federal role in wildlife protection began much earlier than these administrative and legislative actions of the mid-20th century. U.S. President Theodore Roosevelt established Florida's Pelican Island National Wildlife Refuge by executive order in 1903, which was the beginning of the National Wildlife Refuge System. Much like the National Park System, the origins of Federal wildlife protection date back to the mid-19th century with actions to safeguard the Yosemite Valley and Greater Yellowstone areas, as well as legislation in 1869 to set aside the Pribilof Islands in Alaska as a reserve for the northern fur seal. Despite the enabling Fish and Wildlife Act of 1956 and

the Refuge Recreation Act of l962, which authorized limited recreational use of refuges, directives for management of the refuge system were not put into place until the National Wildlife Refuge System Administration Act of l966. This law defined a standard of "compatibility" between the defined purposes of individual refuges and their actual uses.

Some have observed that a true organic act for the U.S. Fish and Wildlife Service did not exist until the passage of the National Wildlife Refuge System Improvement Act of 1997. This law strengthened the compatibility standard and clarified which wildlife-dependent recreational uses are appropriate. This law also directed that the refuge system be managed as a national system based on the biological integrity of ecosystems and the conservation of wildlife. The Improvement Act recognized six compatible wildlife-dependent recreational uses, which included wildlife observation, photography, environmental education, and interpretation.

According to the U.S. Fish and Wildlife Service, national wildlife refuges generally are "...special places where the U.S. Fish and Wildlife Service and its partners restore, protect, and manage habitat for America's wildlife." Included are Waterfowl Production Areas, small natural wetlands, and associated uplands in the Prairie Pothole region of the United States, especially the Dakotas, Minnesota, and Montana.

By September 2008, the refuge system totaled 94.5 million acres in 530 national wildlife refuges and 206 waterfowl production areas (table 3.9). A number of natural ecosystems are protected

Table 3.9—Number of acres and areas in the National Wildlife Refuge System by RPA region, 2008

Region	National Wildlife Refuges		Waterfowl Production Areas		Total system
	Number	Acres	Number	Acres	Acres
		thousand		*thousand*	*thousand*
North	110	1,388.8	87	322.0	1,710.9
South	162	4,356.9	0	0.0	4,356.9
Rocky Mountains	154	6,843.1	119	3,049.4	9,892.5
Pacific Coast	104	78,544.1	0	0.0	78,544.1
Total	530	91,133.0	206	3,371.4	94,504.4

RPA = Resources Planning Act.
Source: USDI Fish and Wildlife Service (2009).

Waterfowl flying over wetland on Chincoteague National Wildlife Refuge in Virginia. (Photograph courtesy of U.S. Fish and Wildlife Service)

by refuge designation as shown later by figure 3.16. About 96 percent of the system is in national wildlife refuges, dominated by the West region, especially by Alaska. Excluding Alaska, the system is much more balanced regionally. Nevada, Arizona, Montana, and the Dakotas account for a large proportion of the Rocky Mountains region habitat acreage, which is more than 1.5 times that of the East. Refuges are also located in Puerto Rico, the U.S. Virgin Islands, and in American Samoa, Guam, and some U.S. minor outlying islands in the Pacific.

In January 2009, the George W. Bush Administration added over 50 million acres to the National Wildlife Refuge System by creating three island refuges in the Pacific Ocean for protection under the Antiquities Act. More than 95 percent of this territory is in the Mariana Trench National Wildlife Refuge.

About 20.7 million acres (22 percent of the National Wildlife Refuge System) are protected as Federal designated wilderness. This area, which represents nearly 19 percent of all Federal wilderness, is administered in more than 70 separate units in 26 States. Approximately 90 percent of refuge system wilderness is in Alaska, with most of the remaining being in Arizona, Florida, and the Okefenokee National Wildlife Refuge in Georgia.

The National Wilderness Preservation System—The National Wilderness Preservation System consists of specially designated Federal lands identified by an act of Congress to protect wild character as outlined in the Wilderness Act of 1964. The National Wilderness Preservation System represents the most pristine and protected of Federal natural

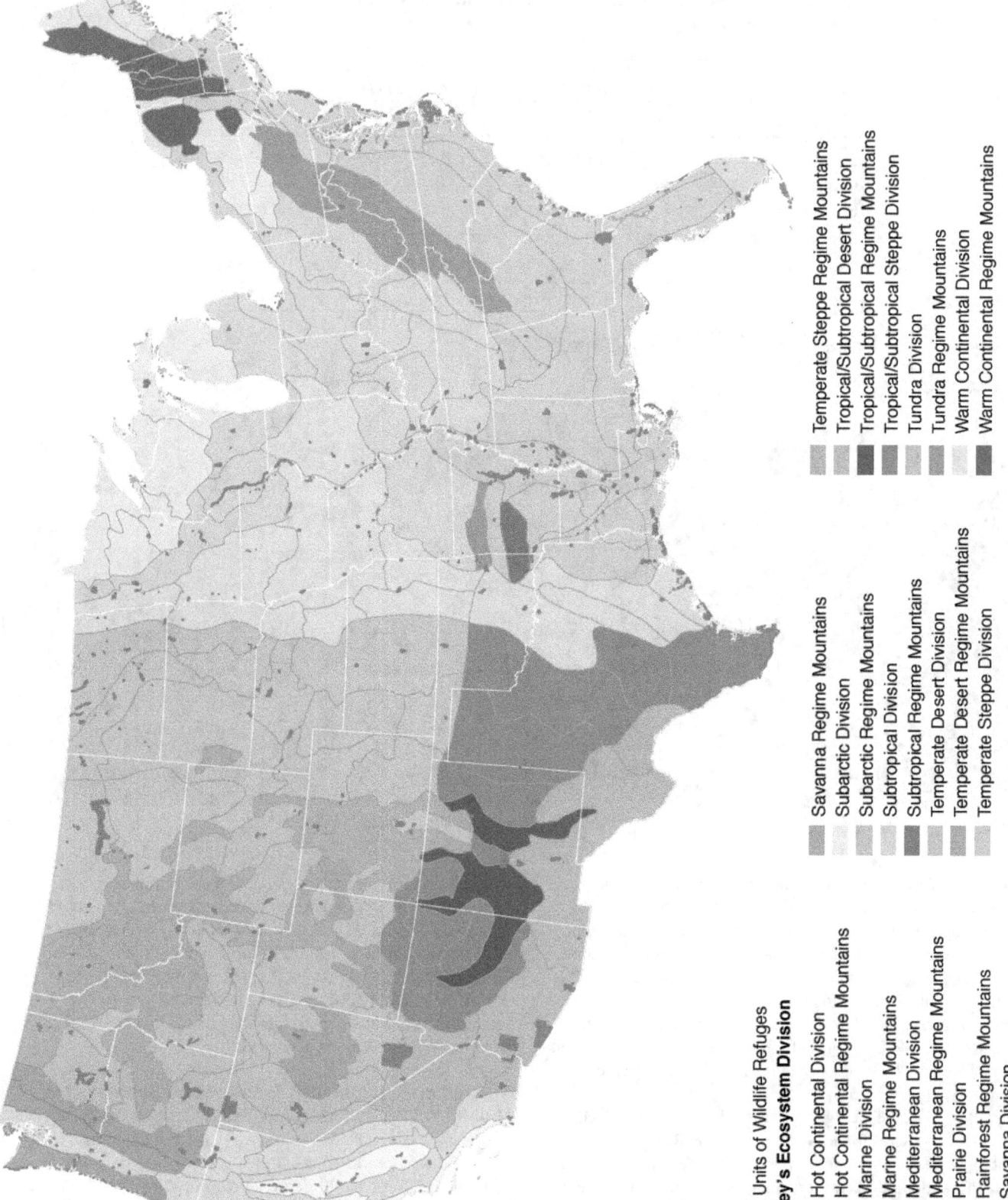

Units of Wildlife Refuges

Bailey's Ecosystem Division

Hot Continental Division
Hot Continental Regime Mountains
Marine Division
Marine Regime Mountains
Mediterranean Division
Mediterranean Regime Mountains
Prairie Division
Rainforest Regime Mountains
Savanna Division

Savanna Regime Mountains
Subarctic Division
Subarctic Regime Mountains
Subtropical Division
Subtropical Regime Mountains
Temperate Desert Division
Temperate Desert Regime Mountains
Temperate Steppe Division

Temperate Steppe Regime Mountains
Tropical/Subtropical Desert Division
Tropical/Subtropical Regime Mountains
Tropical/Subtropical Steppe Division
Tundra Division
Tundra Regime Mountains
Warm Continental Division
Warm Continental Regime Mountains

Figure 3.16—National Wildlife Refuge System coverage of ecosystem types in the continental United States.

lands that include over 109 million acres.[6] Four Federal agencies share administration of the National Wilderness Preservation System: the National Park Service (U.S. Department of the Interior), the Bureau of Land Management (U.S. Department of the Interior), and the U.S. Fish and Wildlife Service (U.S. Department of the Interior), and the U.S. Forest Service (U.S. Department of Agriculture). The National Wilderness Preservation System is predominately in the western regions, particularly in Alaska, which alone contains more than 52 percent of Wilderness acreage which is largely managed by the National Park Service and U.S. Fish and Wildlife Service. Including Alaska, about 96 percent of the National Wilderness Preservation System is located in the West. Without Alaska, the proportion drops only slightly to 92 percent of total area.

The invited papers that follow below cover a number of important aspects of the National Wilderness Preservation System. The first was written by two of the world's foremost experts on wilderness as the premier land protection system in the United States. One section of this paper that focuses on wilderness recreation opportunities is included in chapter 5. A second paper emphasizes the broad public appeal of wilderness resource protection based on the values people see and appreciate in it. There are numerous dimensions of wilderness values. These values are the reasons for protection of Wilderness Areas.

INVITED PAPER

The National Wilderness Preservation System and Its Stewardship

Chad P. Dawson and John C. Hendee[7]

Humans are thought to have deep historical and cultural connections with "wild nature." These connections can come about through direct experiences in wilderness, through art and photography, or through reading about the adventures of others. While there is widespread public support for wilderness, there are divergent and polarized viewpoints on how to define it. These viewpoints range from extreme protectionists who believe that humans have no place in wilderness to utilitarian interests who view wilderness as a backdrop for economic development and for recreation and tourism activities.

The United States has a legal definition of wilderness. This legal definition is in the form of legislation passed in 1964 to create the National Wilderness Preservation System (U.S. Public Law 88-577). Based on this legal definition, by 2010, the National Wilderness Preservation System included over 790 management units and more than 109 million acres of public lands managed by four Federal agencies.

The term wilderness was historically used to describe places that were untamed and not under the control of humans. Areas of civilization that were cultivated and heavily influenced by human activities often bordered or were surrounded by areas that had little human influence. As the population has grown and the majority of land area has come under human influence, wilderness has now become scarce. There are few places that are not now, or have not been at one time, under human control, habitation, cultivation, or other direct influence. A gradient of human influence and impact exists from wilderness to urban centers and rural areas with population growth, road building, food production, power generation, industrialization, and human habitation.

The early history of the United States (and of the rest of the world) during European immigration was one of cultivating and "taming" the wild places and taking dominion over the land. Wilderness was seen as a place for exploration, and was often feared and avoided. As the amount of land with wild conditions began to diminish, it became more appreciated. The public's interest in wild places grew larger as wild places became scarcer. Special places were first set aside as national parks, such as Yellowstone, Yosemite, and the Grand Tetons. These areas were at first seen as park destinations for the development of recreation and tourism, rather than as preserves.

After World War II, greater public interest began to emerge to save wild areas. Some of that concern was due to interest in wilderness recreation experiences, but also due to concern about rapid industrialization and population growth. Some would argue that there are few places in the world that are wilderness in the strictest sense of the word. Thus, the more common usage of the term wilderness is in relation to our perception of areas that are little known or predominantly under the influence of natural forces. Although the term had been commonly applied to any large, remote area with natural characteristics, conditions, and processes, by 1964 it gained a new legal definition.

[6] The Wilderness Institute at the University of Montana maintains www.wilderness.net, which includes a database of National Wilderness Preservation System statistics. Congress designates land from four Federal agencies for inclusion in the NWPS, with those designated areas staying within the home agency, but with altered management priorities.

[7] Professor, Department of Forest and Natural Resources Management, College of Environmental Science and Forestry, State University of New York, Syracuse, NY 13210. Professor Emeritus, Resource, Recreation and Tourism, and former Dean, College of Natural Resources, University of Idaho, Moscow, ID 83844 .

Okefenokee National Wildlife Refuge and Wilderness Area is enjoyed by many thousands of visitors each year while at the same time managed to protect its wilderness character. (Photograph by Ken Cordell)

Wilderness legislation and policy in the United States

The Forest Service and the National Park Service did not begin to set Agency policies to protect primitive and roadless areas from development until the 1920s. During the following decades, roadless area inventories and administrative designations of wilderness occurred with increasing public interest. As recreational use and interest in these lands increased, concerns were raised by professionals in the agencies and the public that administrative regulation: (1) allowed too many development activities, such as mining, grazing, motorized access, and water resource development; (2) shifted boundaries or removed designation to permit resource development; (3) promulgated different regulations and management in different areas; and (4) had neither a clear policy for wilderness preservation nor a national system with coordinated management.

Eventually it became clear that legislative protection was needed to create a permanent and coordinated national system for wilderness preservation. From 1956 to 1964, more than 50 wilderness bills were introduced in the U.S. Congress. These bills were heavily debated by different interest groups. Political compromises were necessary to finally get wilderness legislation, thus some human activities were permitted in some areas, even though they would not be consistent with the intent of the wilderness legislation. These included activities such as mining, grazing, aircraft landings, and water resources development.

In 1964, the U.S. Congress passed The Wilderness Act (U.S. Public Law 88-577), thus creating the National Wilderness Preservation System. The Wilderness Act broadly states policy for designating Wilderness and recognizes the need to protect significant natural areas because of the rapid loss of such resources:

In order to assure that an increasing population, accompanied by expanding settlement and growing mechanization, does not occupy and modify all areas within the United States and its possessions, leaving no lands designated for preservation and protection in their natural condition, it is hereby declared to be the policy of the Congress to secure for the American people of present and future generations the benefits of an enduring resource of wilderness. For this purpose there is hereby established a National Wilderness Preservation System to be composed of Federally owned areas designated by Congress as "wilderness areas," and these shall be administered for the use and enjoyment of the American people in such manner as will leave them unimpaired for future use and enjoyment as wilderness, and so as to provide for the protection of these areas, the preservation of their wilderness character, and for the gathering and dissemination of information regarding their use and enjoyment as wilderness. (U.S. Public Law 88-577, section 2a).

The language above is referred to as the "guiding management intent" because it specifically refers to "use and enjoyment," provided that areas remain "unimpaired" and ensured "preservation of their wilderness character."

Section 2c of The Wilderness Act includes an important and often-quoted definition of Wilderness:

A wilderness, in contrast with those areas where man and his own works dominate the landscape, is hereby recognized as an area where the earth and its community of life are untrammeled by man, where man himself is a visitor who does not remain. An area of wilderness is further defined to mean...an area of underdeveloped Federal land retaining its primeval character and influence, without permanent improvements or human habitation, which is protected and managed so as to preserve its natural conditions and which (1) generally appears to have been affected primarily by the forces of nature, with the imprint of man's work substantially unnoticeable; (2) has outstanding opportunities for solitude or a primitive and unconfined type of recreation; (3) has at least five thousand acres of land or is of sufficient size as to make practicable its preservation and use in an unimpaired condition; and (4) may also contain ecological, geological, or other features of scientific, educational, scenic, or historical value (U.S. Public Law 88-577, section 2c).

This definition is an ideal tempered by four conditions to make it practical. One of those four conditions refers to "outstanding opportunities for solitude or a primitive and unconfined type of recreation," a phrase often referred to as the guiding principle for recreation management. Certain types and amounts of recreation are permitted, provided the area is "protected and managed so as to preserve its natural conditions." This principle is especially important regarding primitive facilities, trails, backcountry travel, recreational equipment (e.g., removable climbing gear, backpacking stoves), and management activities.

Creation of the National Wilderness Preservation System in 1964 was just the beginning of legislative designations. By 2009, there were more than 170 different laws passed by the U.S. Congress designating new areas or adding acreage to existing ones. The initial designation of 9.1 million acres was followed by congressional designations in 32 of the 45 years between 1964 and 2009 to add acres and units to the National Wilderness Preservation System (table 3.10). The largest single increase was the addition of approximately 56 million acres in Alaska under The Alaska National Interest Lands Conservation Act of 1980 (U.S. Public Law 96-487). Proposals for additional acreage are continuing to be brought before Congress and its committees.

Potential threats to Wilderness—Designating areas as Wilderness is just the first step and must be followed by stewardship to maintain those areas. Numerous types of internal and external conditions, influences, and changes threaten Wilderness resources and values, now and in the future [8] One example of a threat is that Wilderness Areas in many States are increasingly isolated remnants of historic ecosystems. As the surrounding landscape becomes more developed, Wilderness Areas become ecologic islands that can continue with various processes, provided they are large enough or are not disconnected from other natural areas. This concern is most pronounced in the Eastern United States, with its smaller Wilderness Areas. Most threats to Wilderness are projected to increase in the coming decades. Land managers will need to monitor potential threats and to prepare management plans to minimize, mitigate, or remove them.

Wilderness stewardship and management—Some level of Wilderness management is necessary because of increasing visitor use and changing uses of surrounding lands. The idea of management of an area intended to be free

---

[8] Dawson and Hendee (2009) identified 19 categories of internal and external threats as the change agents that affect wilderness conditions and values: Fragmentation and isolation of wilderness areas as ecologic islands; Impacts on threatened and endangered species; Increasing commercial and public recreation use; Permitted livestock grazing; Invasion of exotic and non-native species; Administrative access, facilities, and intrusive management; Adjacent land management and use; Private and public land inholdings within wilderness; Established mining claims; Wildland fire suppression activities; Reduced air quality; Reconstruction and maintenance of water projects and reduced water quality; Advanced communication and navigation technology that reduces solitude; Motorized and mechanical equipment trespass and legal use; Aircraft noise and air space reservations; Urbanization and encroaching development; Global climate change; Legislation designating new wilderness areas with compromised wilderness conditions; and Lack of political and financial support for wilderness protection and management.

Table 3.10—Acreage of Wilderness designated in 1964 at the creation of the National Wilderness Preservation System and in subsequent 5-year intervals through 2010

Year	Acreage
1964	9,139,721
1966–70	1,153,382
1971–75	2,612,902
1976–80	68,027,642
1981–85	8,563,271
1986–90	5,560,032
1991–95	8,772,384
1996–2000	1,119,621
2001–05	1,353,607
2006–10	3,199,777
Total	109,502,248

Source: wilderness.net (N.d.).

of the influences of modern human activities may appear paradoxical. However, Wilderness management has evolved to become the control of human uses and of the internal and external influences to protect and preserve an area's solitude and naturalness, including natural processes and conditions. Hendee and Dawson (2004) highlight the Wilderness stewardship philosophy for managers:

> Wilderness management should not mold nature to suit people. Rather, it should manage human use and influences so as not to alter natural processes. Managers should do only what is necessary to meet wilderness objectives and use only the minimum tools, regulations, and enforcement required to meet those objectives. In wilderness, people adapt to nature, to naturalness and solitude, and that is the source of human benefits from wilderness experience, as well as the ecological and non-use benefits.

This stewardship philosophy is based on the Wilderness Act and is balanced between protection of Wilderness naturalness and human use and enjoyment. The stewardship philosophy favors the natural integrity, but allows accommodation of some primitive styles of recreation and opportunity for solitude. Wilderness should be managed as a pristine extreme in the landscape (over 4 percent of U.S. land area) to maintain the distinctive qualities that define and separate it from other land uses (over 95 percent of U.S. land area). Wilderness is managed from a biological perspective where environmental integrity and primeval conditions are the basis for human enjoyment, values, and benefits. Wilderness is managed as an ecosystem and not as a separate set of resource types (e.g., water, forests, or wildlife) since this focuses managers on a comprehensive perspective across resource types.

If Wilderness is to be managed to maintain or improve natural conditions and not allow degradation at particular sites or across the area, then an understanding of the carrying capacity of the area is essential. One of the major components in managing Wilderness recreation is to manage in favor of activities that depend on natural conditions. This requires acknowledgment that there are other places for recreational experiences that do not require natural conditions. An implication of this management philosophy is that Wilderness is not primarily a place for recreation nor any associated activities. All management activities, including search and rescue operations, should have as light an impact on the land and on Wilderness experiences as possible. Required are minimum tools and regulations to allow naturalness and solitude. Examples are using hand tools instead of gas-powered tools in maintenance activities, using educational materials in place of direct trip management, or using minimal directional trail signs and not mileage markers.

Concluding remarks—The National Wilderness Preservation System is the ultimate in an attempt to protect natural land and preserve its natural functioning in perpetuity. Recreation is accommodated, but it should be compatible with the primary purpose of Wilderness, which is preservation of naturalness. In today's world of increasing population and expanding development, preserving wild lands requires some level of management. While management and Wilderness may seem paradoxical, management and stewardship is essential. The Wilderness Act acknowledged that some areas of the United States should stay wild and provide solitude and wild land experiences. The long-term results are that the natural forces and processes that shaped and formed the lands in the NWPS will be evident in the Wilderness Areas that we leave for future generations.

End Invited Paper

INVITED PAPER

Values of the Urban Wilderness

Patricia L. Winter[9]

Introduction—Wilderness is widely supported by the American public (Campaign for America's Wilderness 2003) and provides myriad ecosystem services and other benefits (Schuster and others 2005, Williams and Watson 2007). Wilderness services and benefits deemed important to the public include use (such as recreation) and non-use

values (such as scenery appreciation) (Brown and Alessa 2005). Protecting wilderness and its values as population and environmental changes evolve is a significant challenge (Hill 1994). Wilderness Areas near urban places (urban-proximate wilderness) are under elevated threat from human impacts, including encroaching development and spillover of ambient air pollution (Cordell and others 2005). It is hoped that this discussion will help broaden recognition of environmental issues with wilderness beyond the traditional biospheric focus to incorporate other values (Schultz and Zelezny 2003). Recognizing the broader variety of values invites a holistic consideration of wilderness protection efforts.

This paper examines values through the experiences of visitors to urban-proximate wilderness areas. Experiences are grouped according to types of values, considering direct reports from visitors both during and after their wilderness visits. In each case, the discussion surrounds direct-use values (Schuster and others 2005). Some of these benefits extend beyond the immediate wilderness visit. Focusing on visitor experiences can inform management of wilderness (Cole 2004), help broaden the consideration of wilderness benefits, and facilitate wilderness preservation efforts (Hill 1994). Findings may help illuminate the broad array of values represented in an urban-proximate wilderness, including the value of the recreational experience to a diverse urban public.

Methods—Through a series of four studies conducted by the author, experiences of the urban wilderness visitor are examined. These studies were oriented to urban-proximate wildernesses on the San Bernardino and Angeles National Forests in southern California. Urban-proximate wildernesses in other geographic areas may demonstrate their own unique use and resource character and thus conclusions from this paper may not apply.

Results—Evidence is provided for wilderness values linked to the following:

- physical (including exercise, physical challenge, and preparation for more challenging trips)
- psychological and spiritual (such as solitude, self-definition, self-affirmation, and renewal of soul)
- social (by fostering and maintaining social connections including spending time with family and/or friends, and serving as the basis of some relationships)
- transactional by fostering connection to nature (including being close to nature, observing wildlife, visiting a natural and unspoiled area, fostering environmental identity, and enhancing personal environmental responsibility).

Not all questions were worded in the same way across the four studies, presented in the same order, nor asked in the same wilderness areas.

[9] U.S. Department of Agriculture Forest Service, Pacific Southwest Research Station, 4955 Canyon Crest Drive, Riverside, CA 92507.

Physical Benefits—In studies two and four, respondents provided reasons for visiting wilderness areas. Among the top reasons were the physical benefits of wilderness visits. "I want to exercise" was indicated by 80.9 percent of respondents in study two, and 94.1 percent in study four. "I want to be physically challenged" was also a reason for wilderness visits (62.5 percent in study two and 82.4 percent in study four). Another physically oriented set of motivations involved preparation for more challenging back country trips (40.9 percent of respondents in study two and 58.8 percent of respondents in study four). In keeping with the continuing emphasis on improvement of public health and on getting people into the outdoors, urban-proximate wilderness represents a place for activities that provide physical exercise and challenge.

Psychological and Spiritual Benefits—Psychological and spiritual benefits can be derived by any wilderness visitor, whether visiting alone, with others, or through a facilitated experience. Solitude is one element of such benefits. In study one, the importance of solitude varied for respondents based on which aspect of the visit was in question. Solitude was least important while picnicking, somewhat important while in camp. Evidence suggests that high-use wilderness areas offer solitude as individuals adjust their expectations (see Cole and Hall 2008 for a discussion of "adapters").

Study three explored a set of outcomes linked to wilderness hiking (derived from Shamir's Leisure Identity Salience scale and an activity importance scale based on Schneider and Winter 1998). Results indicate that aspects of self-identity and self-affirmation may be expressed through the wilderness experience, with a larger effect for the more frequent wilderness hiker (see table).

The Vivian Creek Trail, San Gorgonio Wilderness, San Bernardino National Forest. (Photo by Deanne McCollum)

Spiritual value was represented in two studies. In study two almost half (46.5 percent) and in study four the majority (61.8 percent) indicated "I want to renew my soul" as a reason to visit wilderness (for further discussion see Clayton and Myers 2009).

Fostering and Maintaining Social Connections—Social identity and social connections also seem to be associated with wilderness visits. For example, although most visitors in study one sought solitude in their visit, for most it was sought in the company of others. In both studies two (51.2 percent) and four (72.5 percent), the majority chose "I want to be with friends or family who also visit the wilderness" as reasons for visiting wilderness. Wilderness hiking is an opportunity to share and foster a common bond with others (see table), an effect stronger among more frequent hikers in study three compared to those who hiked less often.

Comparison of psychological benefits for study three respondents (all t-tests significant at p < 0.01)

Benefit	Low[c]	High	Value of t
Says a lot about who I am[a]	3.56(n=107)	4.22(n=101)	5.03
Important for myself definition[b]	4.12(n=106)	5.19(n=95)	4.94
Helps me realize my aspirations[b]	4.11(n=106)	5.18(n=99)	4.90
One of the most satisfying things I do[a]	3.89(n=107)	4.39(n=101)	4.07

[a] Scale from 1 to 5; 1=strongly disagree, 5=strongly agree.
[b] Likert scale from 1 to 7; 1=not important, 7=important and 1=does not help, 7=helps.
[c] Low and high groups based on number of days hiked where low was equal to 10 or less days in the past year and high was more than 10 days.

Comparison of social benefits for study three respondents (all t-tests significant at p < 0.01)

Benefit	Low[b]	High	Value of t
I talk frequently about this activity with my friends[a]	3.18 (n=106)	3.81 (n=101)	4.95
I try to find other people who share my interest in this activity[a]	3.41 (n=106)	3.91 (n=101)	3.66

[a] Scale from 1 to 5; 1=strongly disagree, 5=strongly agree.
[b] Low and high groups based on number of days hiked where low was equal to 10 or less days in the past year and high was more than 10 days.

Fostering a Connection to Nature—Wilderness visitors also appear to be drawn to connect with nature. In studies two and four, nature-based motives were high among reasons to visit wilderness. "To be close to nature" was chosen by 76.6 percent in study two and by 83.3 percent in study four. Along similar lines, most respondents in both studies chose "visit a natural, unspoiled area" (84.7 percent in study two and 93.1 percent in study four), and "observe wildlife" (67.6 percent in study two and 79.4 percent in study four) as reasons for visiting wilderness.

A measure of connection to nature was included in study four through Clayton's environmental identity (EID) scale (Clayton 2003). In this study the number of days spent in wilderness was associated with EID as well as attitudes about wilderness management. Those with low EID showed less support for environmental protection (for example protection of plants), while those with high EID believed more natural resource areas were needed for environmental protection. (For further discussion see Winter and Chavez 2008).

Factors that Mitigate Value—The degree of wilderness experience (frequency and history of visitation) is an important consideration in weighing the values of a visit. As discussed earlier, frequent wilderness visitors report a greater level of values derived (examined through effects on identity and self) than less frequent visitors. In fact, it may be that more frequent visitors are gaining and recognizing benefits for reasons other than multiple visits.

A number of other influences beyond degree of experience weigh into the benefits of a wilderness visit, for example overall receptivity to the experience (Schuster and others 2005).

Discussion—This paper has presented four studies demonstrating mutual value of wilderness visits to nature and visitor. This mutual value goes beyond the immediate experience to include an array of benefits such as physical, psychological, spiritual, social, and transactive between the environment and individual. Physical, psychological, spiritual, and social benefits may represent important information in efforts to encourage outdoor activity and increase public health.

Managers serve as stewards of a diverse range of opportunities. Considering a larger array of values will likely be helpful in the ongoing mission to protect wilderness, while providing for recreational experiences. Discovering that urban-proximate wilderness visitors report many of the same values expected in more remote wilderness areas is enlightening. It appears that expectations, such as for solitude, are also met by urban-proximate wilderness (Cole and Hall 2008).

Management of wilderness can continue to benefit from knowing more about urban-proximate wilderness visitor perspectives. It might be valuable to continue to study whether and how the type of visitor and visitor values varies by trailhead and trails used. This may result in management strategies involving use limits and communication approaches that become place-specific. It might also be important to study visitors with longer visitation histories to capture their unique views on changing wilderness character over time. Values drawn from the wilderness experience may shift, or visitors may move to other "favorite" locations to preserve their wilderness recreation experience.

End Invited Paper

Ecosystems Represented in National Parks, Refuges, and Wilderness Areas

An analysis of ecosystem coverage was conducted across areas of the National Park, National Wildlife Refuge, and National Wilderness Preservation Systems. The analysis used digital spatial data to estimate land area coverage of different ecosystems at division levels (Bailey 1995). Results are shown using GIS-derived maps (figures 3.15, 3.16, and 3.17) to show the spatial distribution of units of these three protected Federal land systems relative to 25 ecosystem divisions across the continental United States. Alaska and Hawaii are not shown in these maps, but their ecosystem and protected land areas were included and are tabulated in tables 3.11, 3.12, and 3.13.

Tables 3.11 through 3.13 show ecosystem area in acres, percentage of each Federal land system in each ecoregion division, and percentage of each division in the protected land system. Because Wilderness Areas are designated from other Federal land, the Wilderness System area table and map somewhat overlap with the maps and tables covering the National Park and National Wildlife Refuge Systems. In other words, some of the land in these two systems has been designated as Wilderness, but it retains also its status with the original land management agency. Thus, some Wilderness System land statistics are also included in the National Park and National Refuge tables. Other agencies managing land in the National Wilderness Preservation System include the Forest Service and the Bureau of Land Management. The Wilderness lands of these two agencies are represented in the National Wilderness Preservation System table.

As defined in the National Atlas (www.nationalatlas.gov), ecoregions are large-scale areas that share common climatic and vegetation characteristics. This four-level hierarchy originated from and was defined by Bailey (1995) to differentiate between types of ecoregions. The broadest classification is the domain, which is a grouping of areas with similar climates that are differentiated by precipitation and temperature. There are four domains in the United States: (1) polar, (2) humid temperate, (3) dry, and (4) humid tropical.

Next in the hierarchy are divisions, which represent climates within domains with varying precipitation levels and patterns and temperatures. Divisions are subdivided into provinces based on vegetation or other natural land covers. Mountainous area provinces are differentiated by elevation, which is a primary determinant of vegetation and other natural cover. The finest level of ecosystem classification is a section, which is a subdivision of provinces that is based on terrain. This analysis focused on divisions.

The data and spatial analysis for generating the ecosystem maps, acreages, and percentages of area for National Parks, National Wildlife Refuges, and National Wilderness Areas relied on ecosystem boundary data. The Bailey's Ecosystem (Bailey 1995) boundary data was downloaded from the U.S. Geological Survey Web site at http://nationalatlas.gov/atlasftp. html#ecoregp. The Environmental Systems Research Institute (LESRI) ArcMap 9.2 was used to calculate the area covered by each ecoregion division. The general approach was to calculate the decimal degree total land area for each county in the United States. Next, the ESRI tool, Intersect Analysis, was used to find the Bailey's Ecosystem Division (BED) decimal degree area within each county. Intersect computes the geometric intersection of features or portions of features. The percentage of each county's area within each BED was then calculated and multiplied by the square mile area provided by ESRI for each county. This product was multiplied by 640 (acres per square mile) to derive acres of BED within each county. Acres were then summed across counties for each division.

National Park Service acres by Bailey's Ecosystem Division—Federal lands boundary data were downloaded from the U.S. Geological Survey Web site at http://nationalatlas.gov/atlasftp html#fedlanp. The National Park System boundary data was isolated from all other Federal land boundary data. The ESRI tool, Intersect, was used to overlay the National Park System boundary files over the BED boundary files by within each county to define the portions of National Park System area within each BED by county. Next, the ESRI tool, calculate, was used to find the decimal degree area of each National Park System unit within BEDs by county. Transferring these data to an Excel spreadsheet, the decimal degree area of National Park System land by BED was divided by the county decimal degree area and multiplied by county total acres. National Park System acres were then summed for each division.

Figure 3.15 and table 3.11 show the location and tabulated acreages of protected national park lands over the ecosystem types (divisions) they protect through National Park Service management. Much of the National Park System acreage is in Alaska, which dominates the System's national total acreage. This is especially true since the 1980 passage of the Alaska National Interest Lands Conservation Act. Excluding Alaska,

the National Park System is much more balanced in terms of acreage across regions of the United States. The North has by far the least acreage but the most units of any region. This is largely due to the presence of national historic sites, historical parks, and memorials. Not counting national preserves (which are almost entirely in Alaska), national recreation areas (3.4 million acres) and national monuments (2.3 million acres) are a distant second and third, respectively, to national park land area (50 million acres).

As figure 3.15 shows, in terms of percentage of the National Park System, national parks are especially important in protecting the Tundra and Subarctic Mountain Divisions, which have 26 and 23 percent of the System acreage in these Alaska divisions, respectively. The next greatest national park coverage of ecosystems is in the Marine Regime Mountains of the Northwest, Tropical/Subtropical Division of the Southwest, and Temperate Steppe Regime Mountains of the Rocky Mountains. In terms of percentage of divisions protected as national parks, the Savanna Division of southern Florida has the highest percentage protected at 34 percent. Next highest percentages are the mountain divisions of Alaska, followed by the Tropical/Subtropical Desert Division of the Southwest. Special note should be made of Bailey Divisions not well represented in the National Park System as seen by the column labeled "percentage of division in National Parks" in table 3.11. Almost all divisions are represented with at least some acreage in the National Park System, though some divisions, such as Prairie, Subtropical, Subtropical Regime Mountains, Warm Continental, and Warm Continental Regime Mountains, each comprise < 1 percent of the system.

Wildlife Refuge acres by Bailey's Ecosystem Division—The U.S. Fish and Wildlife Service Refuge boundary file was downloaded from http://www.fws.gov/GIS/data/CadastralDB/index htm. The ESRI tool, intersect, was used to lay refuge boundaries over the BED boundaries for each county to calculate proportions of Refuge area within each BED by county. Next, the ESRI tool, calculate, was used to find the decimal degree refuge area by BED by county. Transferring these data to an Excel spreadsheet, decimal degree area of refuge by BED was divided by the county decimal degree area and multiplied by the county total acres. Acres were then summed across counties of the United States for each division.

Figure 3.16 and table 3.12 describe ecosystem coverage by the National Wildlife Refuge System. The units of the refuge system are much more widely distributed across the continental United States than those in the National Park Service. However, like the National Park System, well over one half of the refuge system acreage is in Alaska. The Arctic and Yukon Delta National Wildlife Refuges make up a large proportion of this Alaska area, each occupying more than 19 million acres,

Table 3.11—Acreage of U.S. surface area by ecosystem division, acres of the National Park System in each division, percentage of division in national parks, and percentage of the National Park System area in each division

Ecosystem division	Total surface acres in ecosystem division	National Park Service acres	Percentage of division in national parks	Percentage of National Park System acres in division
Temperate Desert Division	172,248,684.85	1,356,983.79	0.79	1.68
Temperate Desert Regime Mountains	27,947,708.91	351,801.87	1.26	0.44
Temperate Steppe Division	272,098,505.57	497,464.56	0.18	0.62
Temperate Steppe Regime Mountains	144,647,151.35	4,341,184.94	3.00	5.38
Tropical/Subtropical Desert Division	110,639,680.87	7,808,610.28	7.06	9.68
Tropical/Subtropical Mountains	32,098,786.00	216,528.98	0.67	0.27
Tropical/Subtropical Steppe Division	162,959,706.07	2,827,337.05	1.73	3.51
Hot Continental Division	239,053,212.08	749,279.82	0.31	0.93
Hot Continental Regime Mountains	47,724,559.90	776,019.31	1.63	0.96
Marine Division	9,342,863.97	14,704.86	0.16	0.02
Marine Regime Mountains	73,362,234.04	10,019,581.86	13.66	12.43
Mediterranean Division	21,744,181.55	464,955.63	2.14	0.58
Mediterranean Regime Mountains	59,769,195.27	2,048,962.78	3.43	2.54
Prairie Division	191,037,877.41	56,482.41	0.03	0.07
Subtropical Division	262,963,235.27	367,575.18	0.14	0.46
Subtropical Regime Mountains	5,629,893.82	5,575.11	0.10	0.01
Warm Continental Division	93,922,951.74	565,484.92	0.60	0.70
Warm Continental Regime Mountains	28,035,272.84	638.62	0.00	0.00
Rainforest Regime Mountains	3,979,085.21	250,832.29	6.30	0.31
Savanna Division	5,019,943.39	1,721,136.44	34.29	2.13
Subarctic Division	53,796,334.71	3,112,716.89	5.79	3.86
Subarctic Regime Mountains	118,467,154.38	18,866,085.16	15.93	23.40
Tundra Division	55,724,043.44	3,506,394.12	6.29	4.35
Tundra Regime Mountains	99,859,410.16	20,705,332.22	20.73	25.68
Total	2,292,071,672.80	80,631,669.09		100.00

Note: Ecosystem divisions based on Bailey (1995).

Table 3.12—Acreage of U.S. surface area by ecosystem division, acres of the National Wildlife Refuge System in each division, percentage of division in national refuges, and percentage of the National Wildlife Refuge System area in each division

Ecosystem division	Total surface acres in ecosystem division	National Wildlife Refuge acres	Percentage of division in national refuges	Percentage of National Refuge acres in division
Temperate Desert Division	172,248,684.85	2,413,767.06	1.40	2.72
Temperate Desert Regime Mountains	27,947,708.91	39,762.33	0.14	0.04
Temperate Steppe Division	272,098,505.57	1,602,148.60	0.59	1.81
Temperate Steppe Regime Mountains	144,647,151.35	232,855.42	0.16	0.26
Tropical/Subtropical Desert Division	110,639,680.87	2,697,385.32	2.44	3.04
Tropical/Subtropical Regime Mountains	32,098,786.00	64,781.91	0.20	0.07
Tropical/Subtropical Steppe Division	162,959,706.07	412,410.14	0.25	0.46
Hot Continental Division	239,053,212.08	735,195.77	0.31	0.83
Hot Continental Regime Mountains	47,724,559.90	21,293.34	0.04	0.02
Marine Division	9,342,863.97	21,374.50	0.23	0.02
Marine Regime Mountains	73,362,234.04	1,146,665.75	1.56	1.29
Mediterranean Division	21,744,181.55	114,052.36	0.52	0.13
Mediterranean Regime Mountains	59,769,195.27	147,638.64	0.25	0.17
Prairie Division	191,037,877.41	426,456.64	0.22	0.48
Subtropical Division	262,963,235.27	2,643,382.19	1.01	2.98
Subtropical Regime Mountains	5,629,893.82	0.00	0.00	0.00
Warm Continental Division	93,922,951.74	181,082.61	0.19	0.20
Warm Continental Regime Mountains	28,035,272.84	55,696.77	0.20	0.06
Rainforest Regime Mountains	3,979,085.21	43,924.59	1.10	0.05
Savanna Division	5,019,943.39	51,582.17	1.03	0.06
Subarctic Division	53,796,334.71	15,880,057.88	29.52	17.90
Subarctic Regime Mountains	118,467,154.38	15,372,370.59	12.98	17.33
Tundra Division	55,724,043.44	18,991,033.75	34.08	21.41
Tundra Regime Mountains	99,859,410.16	25,410,226.40	25.45	28.65
Total	2,292,071,672.80	88,705,144.73		100.00

Note: Ecosystem divisions based on Bailey (1995).

Table 3.13—Acreage of U.S. surface area by ecosystem division, acres of the National Wilderness Preservation System in each division, percentage of division in National Wilderness Areas, and percentage of the National Wilderness Preservation System area in each division

Ecosystem division	Total surface acres in ecosystem division	National Wilderness Area acres	Percentage of division in Wilderness Areas	Percentage of National Wilderness acres in division
Temperate Desert Division	172,248,684.85	3,835,089.38	2.23	3.51
Temperate Desert Regime Mountains	27,947,708.91	1,181,970.32	4.23	1.08
Temperate Steppe Division	272,098,505.57	537,483.44	0.20	0.49
Temperate Steppe Regime Mountains	144,647,151.35	15,312,414.12	10.59	14.02
Tropical/Subtropical Desert Division	110,639,680.87	11,274,415.98	10.19	10.32
Tropical/Subtropical Regime Mountains	32,098,786.00	1,306,489.64	4.07	1.20
Tropical/Subtropical Steppe Division	162,959,706.07	1,364,195.94	0.84	1.25
Hot Continental Division	239,053,212.08	194,845.72	0.08	0.18
Hot Continental Regime Mountains	47,724,559.90	642,125.14	1.35	0.59
Marine Division	9,342,863.97	53,407.47	0.57	0.05
Marine Regime Mountains	73,362,234.04	18,849,390.07	25.69	17.26
Mediterranean Division	21,744,181.55	311,088.51	1.43	0.28
Mediterranean Regime Mountains	59,769,195.27	7,398,887.11	12.38	6.77
Prairie Division	191,037,877.41	2,241.62	0.00	0.00
Subtropical Division	262,963,235.27	684,972.56	0.26	0.63
Subtropical Regime Mountains	5,629,893.82	47,986.71	0.85	0.04
Warm Continental Division	93,922,951.74	1,399,270.13	1.49	1.28
Warm Continental Regime Mountains	28,035,272.84	247,296.91	0.88	0.23
Rainforest Regime Mountains	3,979,085.21	155,779.09	3.91	0.14
Savanna Division	5,019,943.39	764,990.48	15.24	0.70
Subarctic Division	53,796,334.71	2,011,315.40	3.74	1.84
Subarctic Regime Mountains	118,467,154.38	12,372,708.01	10.44	11.33
Tundra Division	55,724,043.44	2,511,180.27	4.51	2.30
Tundra Regime Mountains	99,859,410.16	26,761,277.54	26.80	24.50
Total	2,292,071,672.80	109,220,821.56		100.00

Note: Ecosystem divisions based on Bailey (1995).

which together make up more than 40 percent of the refuge system lands in the 50 States. The Arctic National Wildlife Refuge was established in 1960 and added onto when Congress passed the Alaska National Interest Lands Conservation Act in 1980, which more than doubled its size. Within the 20 million acres of the Arctic National Wildlife Refuge (an area greater than the size of South Carolina) are three Wild Rivers and 8 million acres of designated Wilderness. Created by the Alaska National Interest Lands Conservation Act of 1980 (ANILCA), The Yukon Delta National Wildlife Refuge consolidated existing refuges and added other lands. Thus over 85 percent of the refuge system is in the Subarctic and Tundra Divisions. The next largest refuge system acreages, though much smaller, are those in temperate and subtropical desert divisions. In terms of the percentage of ecosystem divisions represented in the refuge system, the picture is much the same as is the case with national parks. And, like national parks, it is important to note which Bailey's Divisions are not represented in the National Wildlife Refuge System. For example, the Tropical/ Subtropical Steppe, Hot Continental, Mediterranean, Prairie, Warm Continental, and Savanna each make up < 1 percent of the National Wildlife Refuge System, though these proportions are skewed somewhat by the vast acreages in Alaska.

Wilderness acres by Bailey's Ecosystem Division—
The Wilderness boundary file was downloaded from http:// www.wilderness net/index.cfm?fuse=NWPS&sec=geography. As with National Parks and Wildlife Refuges, the ESRI tool, Intersect, was used to lay Wilderness Area boundaries over Bailey's Ecosystem Division boundaries for each county to define the proportions of Wilderness within each BED by county. Next, the ESRI tool, calculate, was used to find the decimal degree area of each Wilderness within the BED by

county. Transferring these data to an Excel spreadsheet, the decimal degree area of the Wilderness was divided by the county decimal degree area and multiplied by county total acreage to estimate number of acres of Wilderness in each BED. Acres were then summed nationally for each division. Figure 3.17 and table 3.13 show ecosystem representation across areas in the National Wilderness Preservation System. The NWPS is found mostly in the western regions, particularly in Alaska. Alaska alone contains more than 52 percent of the NWPS, most of which is under the management of the National Park Service and U.S. Fish and Wildlife Service. Including Alaska, about 96 percent of the NWPS is located in the West; without Alaska, the proportion drops only to 92 percent.

In terms of percentage of the National Wilderness Preservation System among ecosystem divisions (table 3.13), the greatest portions are Tundra Division and Subartic Division in Alaska, Marine Regime Mountains in Washington and Oregon, and Temperate Steppe Regime Mountains, mostly in Montana, Idaho, Wyoming, and Utah. Also represented is the Tropical/Subtropical Desert Division of the Southwest. In terms of the percentage of divisions designated as Wilderness, Alaskan Tundra and Subarctic Divisions, Marine Division, Temperate Steppe Division, and Tropical/ Subtropical Desert are among the highest. As a percentage of divisions, significant percentages of the Savanna of southern Florida and the Mediterranean Mountains of California can be seen (fig. 3.17). Some of the Divisions not well represented include the Temperate Steppe, Tropical/Subtropical Steppe, Hot Continental, Marine (non-mountainous), Prairie, Subtropical, and Warm Continental Division.

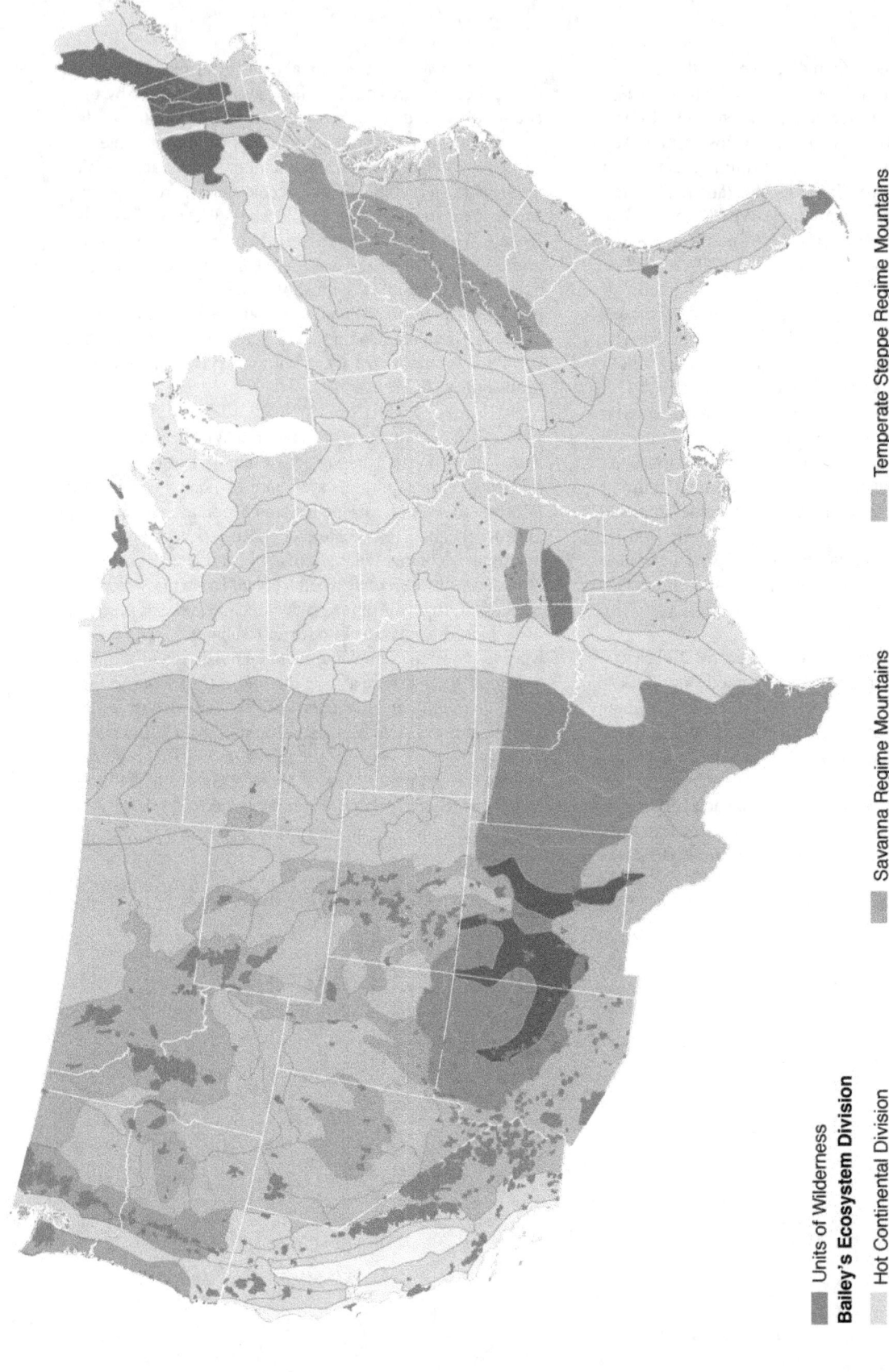

■ Units of Wilderness
Bailey's Ecosystem Division

Hot Continental Division
Hot Continental Regime Mountains
Marine Division
Marine Regime Mountains
Mediterranean Division
Mediterranean Regime Mountains
Prairie Division
Rainforest Regime Mountains

Savanna Regime Mountains
Subarctic Division
Subarctic Regime Mountains
Subtropical Division
Subtropical Regime Mountains
Temperate Desert Division
Temperate Desert Regime Mountains
Temperate Steppe Division

Temperate Steppe Regime Mountains
Tropical/Subtropical Desert Division
Tropical/Subtropical Regime Mountains
Tropical/Subtropical Steppe Division
Tundra Division
Tundra Regime Mountains
Warm Continental Division
Warm Continental Regime Mountains

Figure 3 17—National Wilderness Preservation System coverage of ecosystem types in the continental United States.

CHAPTER 4
Recreation Through the Private Sector

This chapter addresses objective 4 of this assessment report on outdoor recreation and protected land resources: to analyze the status and trends of private sector recreation resources including land, forests, businesses, and other resources. Covered are a number of dimensions of outdoor recreation through private ownerships and operations. Included are estimates of the number of recreation days supplied on private forest lands based on original data collected through the National Survey on Recreation and the Environment (NSRE). Included also is an analysis of the relationship between public lands and the private properties adjacent to them, access to individual and family-owned private forest lands, the supply role of farm and agricultural lands, and the supply role of individuals and households in providing recreation opportunities for themselves through ownership of second or vacation homes. Finally, a description is provided of the number and types of private businesses which provide outdoor recreation services and of private business operations on public land (Federal and State).

Recreational Access to Forest Lands

The NSRE is a random-digit-dial phone survey of people in the United States 16 years of age or older used to obtain data on outdoor recreation. Respondents were asked about their outdoor recreation activities and whether they had occurred primarily in forested settings. If activity had occurred in forested settings, the respondents were then asked if the land where they typically went for that activity was publicly or privately owned. NSRE respondents were also asked if

they used public or private access facilities for a number of water activities, such as fishing. All the percentages and total annual days were calculated on the basis of what the activity participant understood about the settings and ownership of places where the recreation occurred.

Private lands, as referenced in the NSRE, included any privately owned forest lands. These could be corporation, nongovernmental organization, or family ownerships. For the six activity groups examined, the percentage of total annual activity days in the United States that were produced on private lands ranged from a low of 26 percent for backcountry activities to a high of 55 percent for hunting (table 4.1). Due to much larger population numbers in the East, the majority of activity days occur in this region, but the proportional difference between East and West days is much greater for hunting and motorized activities than for the other activity groups. Backcountry activities had the largest relative share of days produced on private lands in the West.

Total days of forest land-based activities produced across the Nation at private recreation and historic sites (sites for family gatherings, picnicking, visiting historic or prehistoric remains, and camping) are relatively small compared with viewing and photographing nature (e.g., scenery, birds, and wildlife). Viewing and photographing nature dominates the other activity groups in terms of total annual days. Land-based activities making up viewing and photographing nature include viewing and photographing birds, natural scenery, other wildlife, wildflowers, and trees. About 43 percent of the nearly 36 billion total national activity days in this activity

Table 4.1—Number and percent of annual recreation activity days produced on private properties by activity group and region, 2005–2009

Activity group	East		West		United States		
	Annual days	Percent	Annual days	Percent	Total private annual days	Percent of all days	All annual days
	millions		millions		millions		millions
Visiting recreation and historic sites	834	28	262	9	1,096	37	2,960
Viewing/photographing nature	12,175	34	3,332	9	15,507	43	35,865
Backcountry activities	580	19	237	8	817	26	3,119
Motorized activities	488	43	91	8	579	51	1,126
Hunting	242	47	38	8	280	55	512
Cross-country skiing	11	30	4	10	14	40	36

Note: Days and percentages may not sum across exactly to national totals because of rounding. Cross-country skiing was the only winter activity with sufficient annual days data in forested settings. All annual days are the sum of days that occur on private and public lands. Source: USDA Forest Service (2009b).

group were produced on private lands. (One reason this activity group is so large is because it consists of 4 activities, each of which is counted as a single day, so multiple counting can result if an individual participated in more than one of these activities per day.)

The total 3.1 billion backcountry activity days (backpacking, day hiking, horseback riding on trails, mountain climbing, and visiting a wilderness or primitive area) were less than one-tenth those of viewing and photographing nature. Nationally, just over one-fourth of the backcountry activity days occurred on private lands.

Motorized land activities include off-road vehicle driving and snowmobiling. Nationally there is an estimated 1.1 billion activity days of motorized land activities on public and private land. Just over one-half of these days occur on private land, the second highest proportion of any activity group. The large majority of private motorized land activities occurred in the East.

The hunting activity group estimate for activity days (big-game and small-game) is about 512 million, which is < 2 percent of the total number of activity days of viewing and photographing nature. About 55 percent of hunting days were produced on private land with the largest share of any activity (47 percent) occurring in the East.

Finally, cross-country skiing is quite small in number of activity days relative to other groups of activities. It was the only snow-based activity in the NSRE with sufficient data on forest settings and land ownership. But like most of the other activity groups, the estimated days of participation indicate the importance of private lands as a resource for recreation activity with 40 percent of total national days occurring there. Three out of four cross-country skiing days on private lands took place in the East.

Nearby Private Land as Access to Public Land

Private lands have increasingly played an important role in enabling people to relocate near public lands that are rich in natural amenities such as whitewater rivers, natural scenery, snow areas, and mountains. In a study of net rural county migration, Santos (2010) examined the role of natural amenities as an influence on people's choice of residence location. Findings pointed to a positive effect of the existence of Federal lands on net migration rates. This result confirmed Rudzitis and Johansen's (1991) findings from a survey in the western United States that showed 53 percent of respondents

felt that presence of designated wilderness was a motivation to relocate or remain in a county. The implication of this finding is that private residential lands are important in providing access to natural public lands.

In a study by Radeloff and others (2010), U.S. Census data were analyzed to examine housing growth from 1940 to 2030 within about 30 miles of wilderness areas, national parks, and national forests. It was found that between 1940 and 2000, 28 million housing units were built within 50 km of these three categories of protected areas, and that another 940,000 were built within the proclamation boundaries of national forests. Housing growth rates during the 1990s within 1 km of these protected lands were 20 percent per decade, higher than the national average of 13 percent. With continuation of these trends, the authors project that another 17 million housing units will be built within 50 km by 2030. Development of these primary and secondary homes on nearby private land are a major means for gaining access to public lands, or at least enjoying the views those private lands afford.

The top frame of figure 4.1 shows the population density of U.S. counties with lands managed by four Federal agencies superimposed. Almost all residences (with the exception of military bases) are privately owned and are on private land. The Federal lands shown are highly important for outdoor recreation. For example, public lands in the Rocky Mountains are primary sources of opportunities for snowboarding and downhill skiing. In addition, residence locations near water, backcountry areas, and developed recreation sites are attractive to people locating in these communities. Often, access to public lands for recreation is near, which is one of the primary components of recreation supply. Close access reduces travel costs and provides more time for outdoor activities. While close access to Federal lands is only one of the factors determining population density patterns across the United States, it is clear that there is a relationship, as was found by Santos (2010). This relationship is seen in areas such as the Southern Appalachian Mountains, Front Range of the Rocky Mountains, Desert Southwest, and the Pacific Northwest.

Location of private residential communities and individual rural residences are also important in providing more convenient access to State parks (bottom frame of fig. 4.1). Residence locations throughout the East, especially in New England, Florida, and the Great Lakes, afford population access to a large number of State parks. Further, many private residence locations in Washington, Oregon, and California afford access to State parks. The importance of the role of private residence locations contributing to accessibility of Federal and State recreation lands is often overlooked.

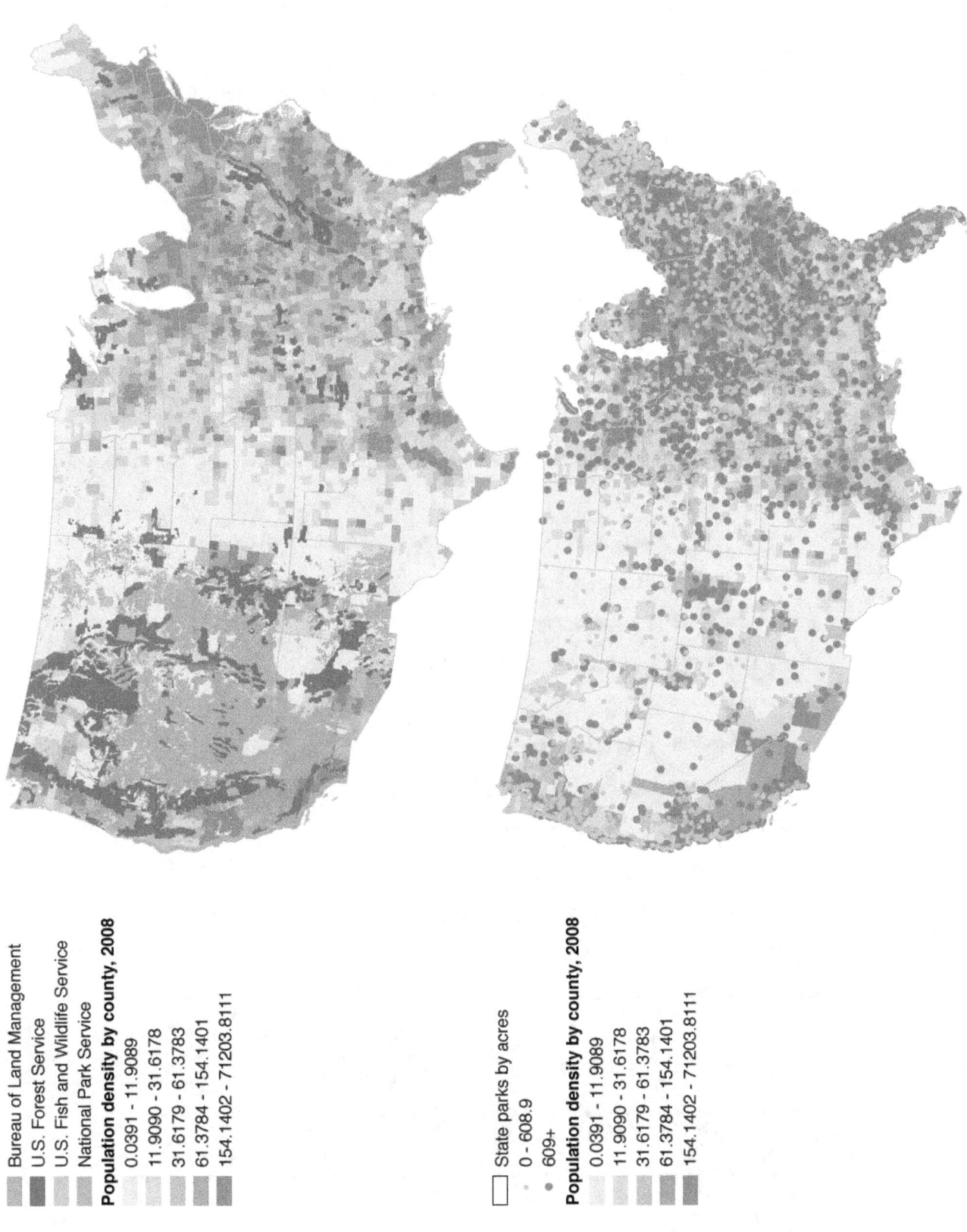

Bureau of Land Management
U.S. Forest Service
U.S. Fish and Wildlife Service
National Park Service

Population density by county, 2008

0.0391 - 11.9089
11.9090 - 31.6178
31.6179 - 61.3783
61.3784 - 154.1401
154.1402 - 71203.8111

State parks by acres
0 - 608.9
609+

Population density by county, 2008

0.0391 - 11.9089
11.9090 - 31.6178
31.6179 - 61.3783
61.3784 - 154.1401
154.1402 - 71203.8111

Figure 4.1.—Federal lands (top frame) and State parks (bottom frame) superimposed on conterminous U.S. counties, showing different levels of population density (person per square mile) in 2008.
Source: U.S. Census Bureau (2008), U.S. Geological Service (2005a), USDA Forest Service (2009b).

Recreation on Individually and Family Owned Forest Lands

The 2006 National Woodland Owner Survey by the Forest Service, U.S. Department of Agriculture, drew a sample from an estimated 10 million family forest owners who were reported to hold 264 million acres (35 percent) of forest land in the United States. Individual owners account for an estimated 10 of the 11 million private forest owners and 62 percent of private forest land (Butler 2008). Thirty-nine percent of individual and family forest owners across the country own more than 10 acres of forest land. Tract size is a factor determining the recreational importance of private forest land. Issues most commonly rated as major concerns by family forest owners are insects and plant diseases, keeping land intact for heirs, fire, trespassing, and property taxes.

Most of the private forest land is in the southern and northern regions (Butler 2008). Forty-four percent of the Nation's private forest land and 44 percent of the private forest owners are in the South. The North has 30 percent of the Nation's private forest land and 44 percent of the private

forest owners. Nationally, the average size of family forest holdings is 25 acres with the average land tenure being 26 years.

The reasons for owning forest land vary, but most have multiple objectives (fig. 4.2). Well over half of the land is owned primarily for its beauty and scenery, but also for nature protection, and other reasons. Among secondary reasons are for a vacation home or cabin and recreation, primarily for the landowner, their family, and friends. While only 15 percent of family forest land is open to the general public for recreation, all private forest land tracts may be considered available to be used by someone for recreation.

Recreation on Agricultural Lands

There were approximately 2.2 million U.S. farms totaling 922 million acres in 2007, a slight increase in farms but a decline in farm land from 2002. Nearly 40 percent of farms are less than 50 acres but these properties account for < 2 percent of the total U.S. farm land area (table 4.2). Of the land in farms,

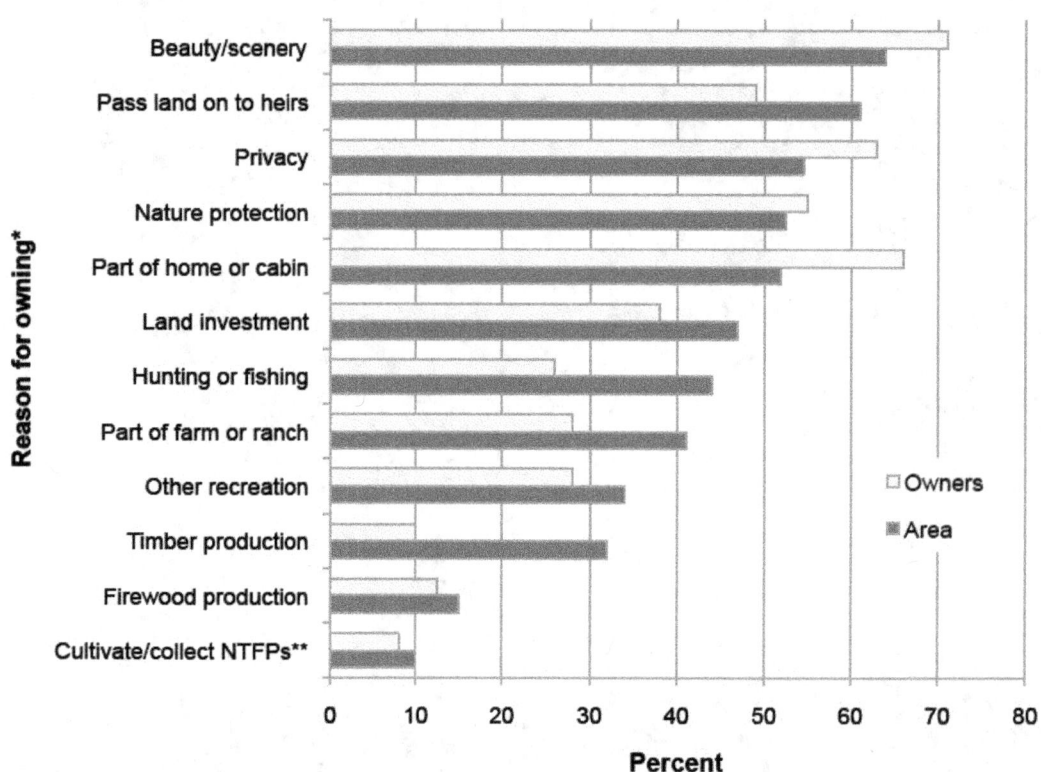

* Includes owners who rated the specific objective as very important (rating=1) or important (rating=2) on a seven point Likert scale with one defined as very important and seven as not important.
** Nontimber forest products

Figure 4.2—Reasons for individual or family ownership of private forest. Note: Green bars represent the percent of total family forest area owned by respondents. Source: Butler (2008).

Table 4.2—Number and acreage by size of farms in the United States in 2002 and 2007

Size of farm	2002	2007	2002	2007	2002	2007	Number of farms	All land in farms	Cropland harvested
	Number of farms		Land in farms		Cropland harvested		Percent distribution, 2007		
	thousand		million acres		million acres				
Under 10 acres	179	233	0.8	1.1	0.2	0.3	10.6	0.1	0.1
10 to 49 acres	564	620	14.7	15.9	4.1	4.3	28.1	1.7	1.4
50 to 69 acres	152	154	8.8	8.9	2.5	2.5	7.0	1.0	0.8
50 to 69 acres	191	192	15.7	15.8	4.7	4.5	8.7	1.7	1.5
100 to 139 acres	175	175	20.2	20.3	6.1	5.8	7.9	2.2	1.9
140 to 179 acres	142	139	22.3	22.0	7.3	6.6	6.3	2.4	2.1
180 to 219 acres	91	88	18.0	17.3	6.2	5.6	4.0	1.9	1.8
220 to 259 acres	72	68	17.1	16.3	6.5	5.7	3.1	1.8	1.9
260 to 499 acres	226	213	80.6	75.9	34.1	30.4	9.6	8.2	9.8
500 to 999 acres	162	150	112.4	104.1	56.7	51.6	6.8	11.3	16.7
1,000 to 1,999 acres	99	93	135.7	127.6	72.8	69.8	4.2	13.8	22.6
2,000 acres or more	78	80	491.9	496.9	101.6	122.5	3.6	53.9	39.6
Total	2,129	2,205	938.3	922.1	302.7	309.6	100.0	100.0	100.0

Source: U.S. Census Bureau (2011).

Table 4.3—Acres of land in farms in the United States by type of agricultural use and RPA region, 2007

Type of agricultural use	North		South		Rocky Mountains		Pacific Coast		United States
	Acres	Percent	Acres	Percent	Acres	Percent	Acres	Percent	Acres
	thousand		thousand		thousand		thousand		thousand
Cropland	143,852	35.4	99,550	24.5	140,675	34.6	22,348	5.5	406,425
Woodland	22,607	30.1	37,523	50.0	9,859	13.1	5,110	6.8	75,099
Permanent pasture and rangeland	17,258	4.2	127,499	31.2	235,401	57.6	28,674	7.0	408,832
Land in farmsteads, buildings, livestock facilities, ponds, roads, etc.	9,724	30.6	9,200	29.0	10,208	32.2	2,608	8.2	31,740
Total land in farms	193,441	21.0	273,772	29.7	396,143	43.0	58,740	6.4	922,096

RPA = Resources Planning Act.
Note: Percentages sum across to 100.0.
Source: USDA National Agricultural Statistics Service (2007).

less than one-half, 406 million acres, is cropland (table 4.3). Just over 75 million farm acres are woodland and around 409 million acres are permanent pasture and rangeland. Over two-thirds of farm land is in farms of over 1,000 acres.

The greatest acreage of farmland is in the Rocky Mountains region (which includes the Great Plains), amounting to over 396 million acres (table 4.3). Second highest is in the South followed by the North and Pacific Coast. Farm woodlands are important sources for outdoor recreation. The South has the greatest proportion of its farm land in woodland at 14 percent with the North next highest at 12 percent. Almost exactly one-half of U.S. woodland is located in the South. Farm pasture and rangeland are also important as recreation resources and in table 4.3 it is shown that over 59 percent of Rocky Mountains region farm land is in pasture and range. Just under 58 percent of all U.S. pasture and range is located in the Rocky Mountains region.

Recreation is an important use of farm and agricultural land as is indicated by the income that it generates. Estimates from the Census of Agriculture, which includes only operations with annual incomes of $1,000 or more, revealed that in 2002 just over 28 thousand farms earned a little over $200 million from "agritourism" and recreational services. Although the 2007 Census showed a drop to somewhat over 23 thousand farms participating, the receipts from agritourism and recreation went up to almost $567 million. This income pertains to recreational services such as hunting, fishing, farm or wine tours, and hay rides.

In another study of U.S. farms based on the Agricultural Resources Management Survey (ARMS), Brown and Reeder (2007) reported that farm-based recreation, or agritourism,[1] which includes hunting, fishing, horseback riding, and other on-farm activities, provided income to approximately 52 thousand owners (2.5 percent of total U.S. farms) in 2004. Brown and Reeder defined agritourism to include a number of farm and farm-related activities:

- Outdoor recreation (fishing, hunting, wildlife study, horseback riding)
- Educational experiences (cannery tours, cooking classes, wine tasting, on-farm museums)
- Entertainment (harvest festivals, barn dances, "petting" farms)
- Hospitality services (overnight farm or ranch stays, guided tours)
- On-farm direct sales ("pick-your-own" operations, roadside stands, farmers' markets).

---

[1] Broadly defined as any agriculturally based operation or activity that brings visitors to a farm or ranch.

The farms providing agritourism earned approximately $955 million from providing recreation activities. (The ARMS estimate of the number of farms involved and their income from farm-based recreation is much higher than the numbers reported in the Census of Agriculture because it excludes smaller operations. The Census of Agriculture definition of agritourism was also less specific than the one used in the ARMS, thus possibly excluding some farm-based enterprises.) Significant variation was found between regions of the country with the South accounting for over half of all farms receiving recreational income followed by the Midwest, which accounted for about one-fourth. They found that more recreational farm operations were located in rural counties and that the economies in these counties were more dependent on recreation.

The 2004 ARMS indicated that around 60 percent of farms providing recreation services actually specialized in raising cattle, horses, ponies, or mules (Brown and Reeder 2007). Cattle and calf operations accounted for a smaller share of farms with recreation income than their share of all farms (fig. 4.3). Farms specializing in horses, ponies, and mules were found to be disproportionately better represented among recreation farms, accounting for more than one-fourth of all farms with recreation incomes (about 10 percent of all farms). Other farm types with significant recreation included those growing grains, oilseeds, dry beans, and dry peas.

In a study by Bastian and others (2002), the researchers reported that rural farm lands in Wyoming that provide wildlife habitat, angling opportunities, and scenic vistas were valued higher than lands that were largely in agricultural production. GIS data were used to quantify recreational and scenic amenities. Using a hedonic price model, the impact of amenity and agricultural production land characteristics on price per acre for a sample of Wyoming agricultural parcels was estimated. Both recreational amenities, as well as agricultural production attributes were important in explaining land values. Significant recreational amenity variables included scenic view, elk habitat, sport fishery productivity, and distance to town. The researchers concluded that demand for amenities, such as outdoor recreation, scenery, and open space is expected to grow in the future which increases competition for different uses of agricultural lands (Cordell 2008). The researchers saw these findings as important for consideration of policies for preserving environmental amenities and improving valuation of agricultural land for conservation easements.

A study by the Economic Research Service (Barry and Hellerstein 2004) of the U.S. Department of Agriculture estimated that American farms produced recreational experiences for 62.4 million people in 2001, nearly 30 percent of the U.S. population age 16 and older in that year. They

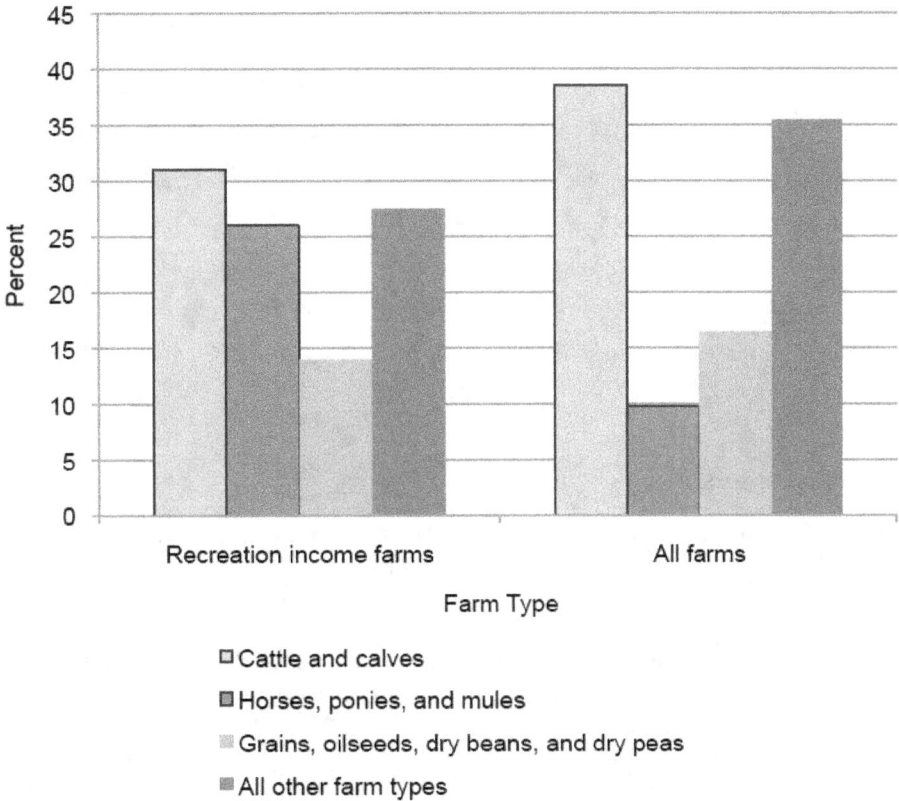

☐ Cattle and calves

◩ Horses, ponies, and mules

▨ Grains, oilseeds, dry beans, and dry peas

▨ All other farm types

Figure 4.3—Percentage of recreation and of all farms by primary agricultural production. Source: Brown and Reeder (2007).

Table 4.4—Number and percentage for each reason for visiting farms

Reason for visiting a farm	Important	Somewhat Important	Not at all Important	Don't know/ refused
To enjoy the rural scenery around the farm	43,361 70%	9,899 16%	8,475 13%	401 1%
To visit family or friends	33,415 53%	6,697 10%	21,528 34%	1,510 3%
To learn about or to appreciate where our food comes from	32,506 53%	11,378 18%	17,736 29%	468 0.5%
To watch and participate in farm activities	25,537 39%	15,593 25%	20,467 33%	1,650 4%
To purchase agricultural products	19,126 28%	7,499 11%	34,895 51%	1,620 10%
To pick fruit or produce	18,100 29%	8,863 14%	34,392 55%	1,700 2%
To spend the night	13,897 27%	5,539 11%	30,396 60%	757 0.4%
To hunt or fish	10,904 18%	5,319 9%	45,250 72%	640 1%

Note: National estimates in thousands. Percent are percent of the row. Because a separate question is used for each reason, each respondent could report that all, or none, of these reasons were "Important." Due to rounding, row totals may not sum to 62.4 million. Differences have not been tested for statistical significance.
Source: Barry and Hellerstein (2004).

Table 4.5—Number and percentage of farm visits by type of landscape feature desired along the way

Landscape feature	Like to see more	About the same	Like to see less	Don't know/ refused
Woodlands	31,640 50%	23,440 38%	4,719 7%	2,843 5%
Grazing animals	30,605 49%	24,526 39%	4,188 7%	3,338 5%
Land in orchards and vines	30,540 48%	23,744 37%	4,835 8%	4,522 7%
Land in pasture or range	22,770 37%	32,185 51%	4,343 7%	3,351 5%
Farmsteads	21,945 35%	31,391 50%	6,006 10%	3,262 5%
Croplands	18,874 30%	33,777 54%	6,318 10%	3,638 6%
Nonfarm business and residential development	6,410 10%	15,839 25%	37,434 60%	2,925 5%

Note: National estimates in thousands. Percent are percent of the row. Because a separate question is used for each reason, each respondent could report that all, or none, of these features are in the "Like to see more" category. Due to rounding row totals may not sum to 62.4 million. Differences have not been tested for statistical significance.
Source: Barry and Hellerstein (2004).

further estimated that nearly two-thirds of visitors had taken between one and five trips to a farm in the prior year.

Visits were made to farms for a number of reasons which varied in importance (table 4.4). Over 43 million Americans were estimated to place enjoyment of the rural scenery around the farm as important. About 34 million indicated that seeing family or friends at their farms also was important. An estimated 33 million indicated that learning about and better appreciating farms as a primary food source was important. Among farm visitors, about 86 percent rated "enjoying rural scenery" as important or somewhat important, and 39 percent felt it was important to "watch and participate in farm activities."

As shown in table 4.5, seeing woodlands, grazing animals, orchards and vineyards, pasture or range, and farmsteads were rated as desirable to the experience of visiting a farm. Between 85 and 88 percent of farm visitors indicated they would like to continue to see or see more of these landscape features during farm visits. Approximately 60 percent indicated they would like to see less non-farm business and residential development.

Second and Vacation Homes in the United States

A highly important and growing resource supporting recreation is that of vacation homes. The U.S. Census of Housing defines vacation homes as "units that are classified as vacant for seasonal, recreational, or occasional use...." (http://www.census.gov/hhes/www/housing/census/historic/vacation.

html). Included in this definition are homes ranging from "large summer estates on Long Island, time-sharing condos in Fort Lauderdale, or simple fishing cabins in northern Michigan." The "occasional use" category was not used prior to the 1960 Census. Counts of seasonal and occasional use vacant units were provided separately from 1960 to 1980, but they were combined beginning in 1990 because respondents had difficulty determining the difference.

The U.S. Census Bureau reported that Florida had the largest number of vacation homes over the last three U.S. censuses. Before 1980 New York had the greatest total number. Since the first housing census in 1940, Maine, New Hampshire, and Vermont led all States in percentage of the national total number of vacation homes. Figure 4.4 shows the spatial pattern of vacation housing across counties expressed as a percent of vacant housing units. It is clear that many vacation residences are in the cooler northern areas, along coasts, associated with mountains or water bodies, and are in dry western areas with significant public lands.

Table 4.6 shows the trend in number of all housing units and of vacation (seasonal or occasional) units by decade from 1960 to 2000. From the 1960 count of vacation homes, the number increased by almost 770 thousand, a 38 percent increase in 20 years up to 1980. From 1980 to 2000, the number increased by another 785 thousand. The number of vacation homes in 2000 was 29 percent larger than in 1980 and 77 percent larger than in 1960. The 10 States with the largest number of vacation housing units (each with over 100 thousand) included Arizona, California, Florida, Maine, Michigan, Minnesota, New Jersey, Pennsylvania, Texas, and Wisconsin. Florida led all States in 2000 with almost 485 thousand.

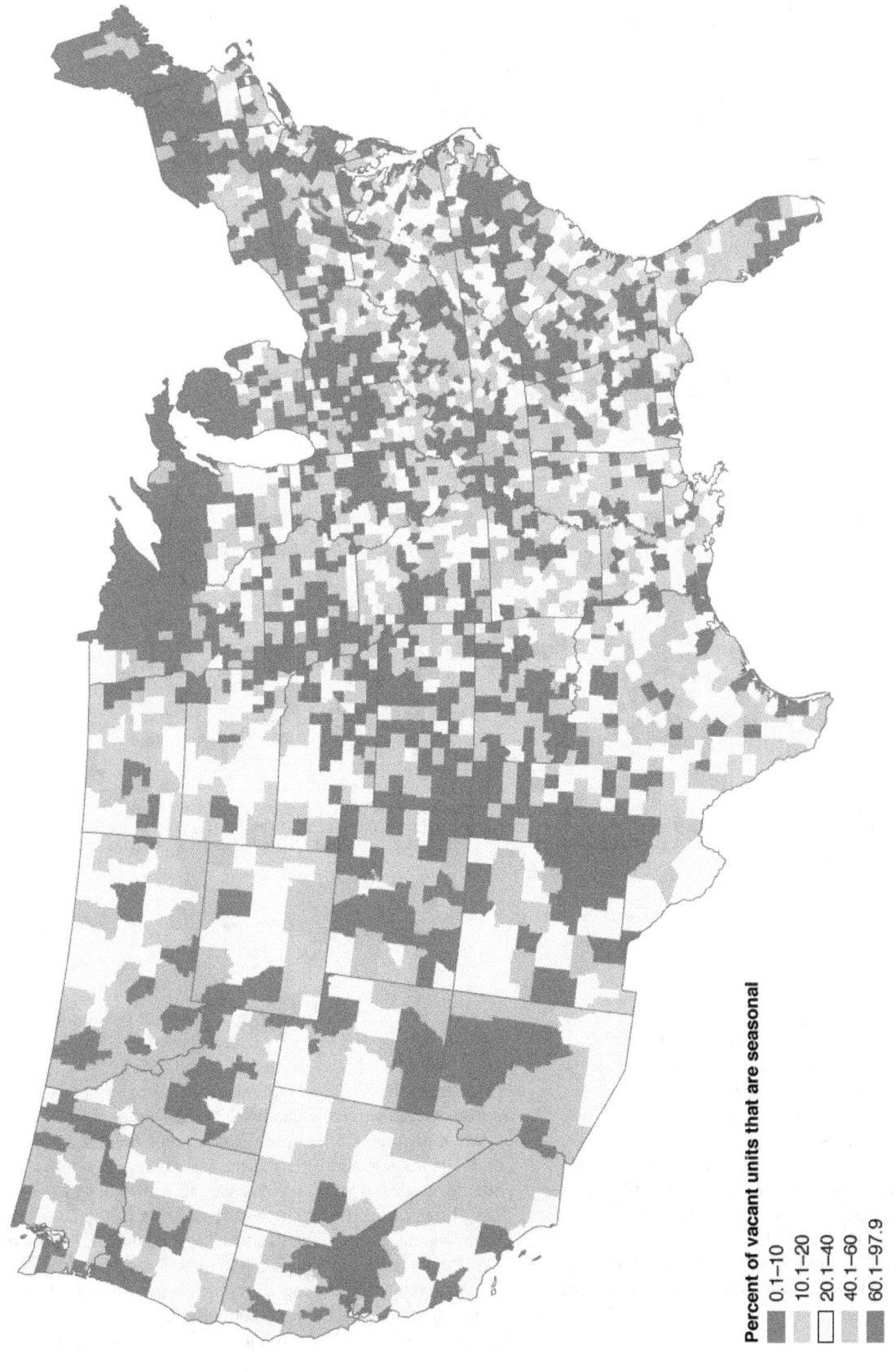

Percent of vacant units that are seasonal

0.1–10
10.1–20
20.1–40
40.1–60
60.1–97.9

Figure 4.4—Percent of vacant housing units in counties in the United States that are seasonal or recreational, 2000.

Table 4.6—Estimated number and percent of vacation housing units (for seasonal, recreational, or occasional use) in the United States by type and year for 1960, 1970, 1980, 1990, and 2000

Year	All housing Number	Seasonal, recreational, or occasional use Number	Percent	Seasonal use Number	Percent	Occasional use Number	Percent
1960	58,326,357	2,024,381	3.5	1,742,465	3.0	281,916	0.5
1970	68,679,030	2,020,087	2.9	1,022,464	1.5	997,623	1.5
1980	88,411,263	2,794,054	3.2	1,718,440	1.9	1,075,614	1.2
1990	102,263,678	3,116,867	3.0				
2000	115,904,641	3,604,216	3.1				

Note: Counts of seasonal and occasional use units were separately provided from 1960 to 1980, but these categories were combined in 1990 (and the language "recreational use" was added) because responding households had difficulty determining the difference.
Source: U.S. Census Bureau (2004b).

Table 4.7—Estimated number of vacation housing units (for seasonal, recreational, or occasional use) and total and mean annual days of use by region in 2009

Homes or days	North Number	Percent	South Number	Percent	Rocky Mountains Number	Percent	Pacific Coast Number	Percent	United States Number
Vacation homes	1,574,636	44.0	1,077,194	30.1	397,238	11.1	529,650	14.8	3,578,718
Total days used per year	188,866,730	43.2	125,826,268	28.8	54,678,339	12.5	66,390,727	15.2	437,021,079
Mean annual days	45.3	na	44.2	na	52.1	na	47.4	na	46.2

na = Not applicable.
Note: Region percentages sum across to 100. May not equal 100.0 exactly due to rounding. Estimates of number of second homes or condominiums by region and nationally were adjusted to sum to the 2000 Census estimate presented in table 4.6.The U.S. total does not match exactly because 25,498 housing units for migrant workers were included in table 4.6. Migratory units were classified as seasonal units before 1990.
Source: USDA Forest Service (2009b).

Based on original data collected by the authors in 2009 through the National Survey on Recreation and the Environment, data were analyzed to estimate proportions of the U.S. population of adults owning a second home or condominium. Questions were limited to ownership for the purposes of enjoying natural scenery and accessing land for outdoor recreation. In addition, respondents indicating ownership were asked to estimate how many days during the past year they had spent at their second home or condominium. Results are reported in table 4.7. The base number of recreational second homes or condominiums used is the number estimated by the Census of Housing as shown in table 4.6.

The estimated proportions of second homes or condominiums nationally vary considerably across regions (table 4.7). The high is 44 percent in the North region and the low is 11 percent in the Rocky Mountains region. The South had just over 30 percent while the Pacific Coast had almost 15 percent of the national total. There was a similar regional distribution of total days spent at privately owned recreation residences with the North and South regions leading with about 189 and 126 million, respectively. There were about 66 million days in recreation residences in the Pacific Coast and under 55 million in the Rocky Mountains region. Mean number of days spent at recreation residences ranged from a low of just over 44 days (about 6 weeks) in the South to about 52 days (roughly 7½ weeks) in the Rocky Mountains region. It is anticipated that the second home or condominium means of self-supply of outdoor recreation participation will continue to grow into the future. A key concern regarding this growth will be location relative to public lands and sensitive ecosystems.

Private Commercial Businesses

Business enterprises are a major, and perhaps the most significant, provider and facilitator of outdoor recreation opportunities. Across the spectrum of public recreation interests, recreation-related businesses contribute by providing services, equipment, instruction, transportation, and frequently access to privately owned land and water. Most of the time, these goods and services are sold for profit, which sets private providers apart from the public sector. Private sector recreation operations occur in all types of recreation settings, from primitive, wilderness-like environments to the most developed, urbanized areas.

The diversity of recreation businesses makes their classification by economic sector difficult. Many provide a combination of instruction and leadership, equipment rentals and/or sales, and access to land and water resources. Data covering recreation businesses, especially trend data on a national scale is scarce because of the dynamic nature of the recreation and tourism industry. Multiple business start-ups and closures occur daily. Further, the competitive nature of business is an impediment to information sharing, especially for smaller businesses. The most reliable source for recreation business trends, though limited in extent, is the annual U.S. Census Bureau's *County Business Patterns* (CBP).

Since 1998, the CBP has classified businesses according to the North American Industry Classification System (NAICS). Not included in the economic information covered by the CBP are data on self-employed individuals, employees of private households, railroad employees, agricultural production employees, and most government employees. Many of the individual NAICS industries correspond directly to the former classification system, but for recreation-related business categories, most do not correspond closely enough to allow long-term trend comparisons. We limit the presentation of recreation business data in this report to the number of establishments and do not describe amounts and trends in sales revenues. An establishment is defined as "...a single physical location at which business is conducted or services or industrial operations are performed" (U.S. Census Bureau 2007b).

Table 4.8 lists the number of establishments for nine categories of outdoor recreation and tourism industries. These are listed in descending order according to the total number nationally. Golf courses and country clubs far outnumber all other categories, with almost 12,000 across the United States in 2007. The greatest proportion was in the North, followed by the South, together accounting for 80 percent of the national total, which had remained almost stable between 2002 and 2007. Next in total national number were recreational vehicle (RV) parks and campgrounds, with more than 4,400. Together, the North and South accounted for almost two-thirds of the national number, which had grown over 8 percent since 2002. There were over 4,000 marinas in the United States in 2007, which represented a slight increase since 2002. Recreation and vacation camps (sometimes called group camps) numbered over 3,000 in 2007, representing a decline of over 6 percent since 2002. Almost one-half of the currently existing camps were in the North region. Privately operated historical sites, for example a restored Appalachian homestead, numbered over one thousand in 2007. Nearly 56 percent of these businesses were in the North and another 27 percent were in the South. Historic sites increased by almost 5 percent between 2002 and 2007.

Nature parks and similar institutions are private establishments primarily engaged in the preservation and exhibition of natural areas or settings. Nationally there were 746 of these businesses, almost 70 percent of which were in the North and South regions, with an expansion of over 16 percent between 2002 and 2007. Amusement and theme parks saw great expansion in the 1960s through the 1980s, but had declined almost 18 percent in the period 2002 to 2007, when there were 634 such establishments. There were 595 zoos and botanical gardens in 2007, representing 13 percent growth between 2002 and 2007. Skiing facilities include establishments operating downhill, cross-country, or related skiing areas and/or operating equipment, such as ski lifts and tows. These establishments sometimes also provide food and beverage, equipment rental, and ski instruction services (see description at the North American Industry Classification System 2007 Web site, http://www.census.gov/naics/2007/NAICOD07.HTM, search for NAICS code 713920). The total of 402 skiing facilities in 2007 represented a 5-year growth rate of 6 percent. Fifty-two percent of these facilities were in the North region; almost 28 percent were in the Rocky Mountains.

When expressed as number of recreation business establishments per million people (table 4.9), a somewhat different trend is shown. Per million people, golf courses and country clubs, marinas, recreation and vacation camps, and amusement and theme parks decreased nationally between 2002 and 2007. Greatest growth was in nature parks and in zoos and botanical gardens. Greatest per million population percentage declines regionally were in recreational and vacation camps and marinas in the Rocky Mountains, amusement and theme parks in the North and South, and in the limited number of skiing facilities in the South.

Table 4.8—Number of selected private recreation business establishments by region in 2007

Recreation business	North		South		Rocky Mountains		Pacific Coast		U.S. total	
	Number	Percent	Number	Percent	Number	Percent	Number	Percent	Number	Percent change 2002–2007
Golf courses and country clubs	5,902	49.8	3,589	30.3	1,211	10.2	1,149	9.7	11,851	0.1
Recreational vehicle (RV) parks and campgrounds	1,714	38.8	1,162	26.3	726	16.5	811	18.4	4,413	8.6
Marinas	2,119	51.9	1,361	33.3	153	3.7	452	11.1	4,085	1.6
Recreational and vacation camps (not campgrounds)	1,417	46.9	684	22.6	440	14.6	480	15.9	3,021	-6.1
Historical sites	586	55.8	289	27.5	87	8.3	89	8.5	1,051	4.9
Nature parks and similar Institutions	309	41.4	205	27.5	94	12.6	138	18.5	746	16.2
Amusement and theme parks	238	37.5	228	36.0	66	10.4	102	16.1	634	-17.9
Zoos and botanical gardens	235	39.5	197	33.1	53	8.9	110	18.5	595	13.3
Skiing facilities	210	52.2	22	5.5	111	27.6	59	14.7	402	6.1

Note: Percentages sum across to 100. May not equal 100.0 exactly due to rounding.
Sources: U.S. Census Bureau (2002, 2007b).

Table 4.9—Number of selected private recreation business establishments per million population by region and percent change, 2002–2007

Recreation business	North		South		Rocky Mountains		Pacific Coast		United States	
	Number per 1 million people, 2007	Percent change, 2002–2007	Number per 1 million people, 2007	Percent change, 2002–2007	Number per 1 million people, 2007	Percent change, 2002–2007	Number per 1 million people, 2007	Percent change, 2002–2007	Number per 1 million people, 2007	Percent change, 2002–2007
Golf courses and country clubs	47.6	-3.8	35.4	-5.9	44.3	-3.1	23.7	-1.6	39.3	-4.4
Recreational vehicle (RV) parks and campgrounds	13.8	6.2	11.5	5.0	26.6	-0.8	16.7	-0.5	14.7	3.8
Marinas	17.1	1.7	13.4	-7.6	5.6	-18.0	9.3	0.4	13.6	-3.0
Recreational and vacation camps (not campgrounds)	11.4	-10.6	6.7	-6.4	16.1	-18.8	9.9	-5.4	10.0	-10.3
Historical sites	4.7	-1.9	2.9	13.1	3.2	-3.6	1.8	-9.9	3.5	0.3
Nature parks and similar institutions	2.5	12.7	2.0	11.0	3.4	8.2	2.8	8.8	2.5	11.2
Amusement and theme parks	1.9	-27.5	2.3	-23.7	2.4	0.0	2.1	-11.4	2.1	-21.6
Zoos and botanical gardens	1.9	6.1	1.9	6.6	1.9	14.8	2.3	12.9	2.0	8.2
Skiing facilities	1.7	7.6	0.2	-15.4	4.1	-1.9	1.2	-3.9	1.3	0.8

Note: U.S. population estimates are 287.73 million (2002) and 301.29 million (2007).
Sources: U.S. Census Bureau (2002, 2007b).

Private Concession Operations on Public Lands

The invited paper by Margaret Bailey, of CHM (Capital Hotel Management, LLC)–Government Services Division, focuses on concession operations on public lands using three Federal agencies as examples. Bailey, who specializes in advising public sector clients regarding recreational real estate holdings, has developed policy guidance and implementation support on concessions, pricing, and other operational practices for public land management agencies. Bailey advises municipal, State, and Federal land management agencies, including the Forest Service, the National Park Service, and State and municipal park and recreation agencies.

Following Bailey's paper is a short report on concession operations on Bureau of Land Management properties. This short report was written by Phil Walker, the National Recreation Concessions Program Manager, in the Business Practices and Visitor Services Branch of the Bureau of Land Management, Washington Office.

INVITED PAPER

Private Partnerships on Federal Lands

Margaret Bailey[2]

The private sector has been a partner with Federal agencies in planning and operation of visitor services on Federal lands for over a century. This tradition began at the time of founding the U.S. Forest Service and the National Park Service, and continued with water-based and other types of recreation opportunities, such as at U.S. Army Corps of Engineers projects. The following article provides an overview of the following:

- Scope of private sector operations on Federal land
- Overview of how contract structures, terms, and conditions have evolved over time between Federal agencies and private operators
- Discussion of the business elements important to enticing private sector operators to Federal lands
- Outline of typical business structure elements included in visitor service contracts.

The article concludes with observations about Federal land management and providing visitor services through private sector partners.

[2] Senior Vice President, Capital Hotel Management, LLC–Government Services, Beverly, MA 01915 .

Scope of private sector managed visitor services on Federal land—Gross revenue generated by private sector partners operating on Forest Service, National Park Service, and U.S. Army Corps of Engineers lands equates to a multi-billion dollar industry. Private sector partners operate under permits, concession contracts, and leases. Currently, the primary categories of assets and activities provided by private sector partners include overnight accommodations (e.g., lodging, camping), food and beverage, retail, marina, transportation, day use activities (e.g., outfitting and guides), and ski areas. Each Federal agency has a different mix of these recreation opportunities based on the nature of their land and on how their private sector partner relationships have evolved over time. For example, many ski areas are located on Forest Service land while many of the Nation's marina operations are located on U.S. Army Corps of Engineers and National Park Service lakes.

Evolution of public agency contract structures—

Forest Service—In 1897, the Organic Act was passed and provided the main statutory basis for management of forest reserves in the United States. In 1915, the Forest Service officially recognized recreation as a viable use of its land with a corresponding need to manage use through requirements of the Term Permit Act of 1915. This act authorized special permits for residences, stores, and resorts on national forest land. Recreation was further confirmed as a viable land use in 1960 with the development and approval of the Multiple Use and Sustained Yield Act. From 1915 until the 1950s, the Organic Act and Term Permit Act were the primary tools used to oversee private recreational use and development. During this period, the Forest Service developed recreational facilities without private sector operator involvement to include campgrounds, trails, and visitor centers. During the early 1970s, the Forest Service began to face a trend of decreasing appropriated funds, which materially affected operating budgets. This forced a different line of thinking about operating funding. In an effort to offset this trend, the Forest Service began to issue more special use permits for new development and outsourcing of management of several of their own facilities under the Grainger-Thye authority.

The Granger-Thye authority allows private sector operators the use of government-owned buildings. It also allows use of a portion of the fees collected from recreational facilities for maintenance of facilities under special use permits. However, these fees cannot be used for management compensation or new development. In 1986, the Ski Area Permit Act was passed which provided for "a unified and modern permitting process for nordic and alpine ski areas on national forest lands; ski area permits more closely reflecting the acreage and other physical requirements of modern ski area development; and a permit system which will be more commensurate with the long-term construction, financing, and operation needs of ski areas on national forest lands." This act was designed to replace authorizations of ski areas operating under the Organic Act of 1897 or the Term Permit Act of 1915.

National Park Service—The National Park Service, established in 1916, recognized early the need for accommodating visitors. The National Park Service Act established the National Park Service and gave the Secretary of the Interior the responsibility to "grant privileges, leases, and permits for the use of land for the accommodation of visitors...." Within the first decade of existence, leaders of the National Park Service pondered the best method for handling visitor facilities. In its early years, park service leadership seemed to consider it unrealistic to allocate funds for the development of visitor facilities. This led to a philosophy of "regulated monopoly" regarding facility development. As a result, most of the commercial recreational facilities in national parks were privately developed and managed.

The National Park Service Act guided oversight on recreational asset development and operations until U.S. Public Law 89-249 was enacted in 1965. Congress established a Concession Program in the National Park Service through the passage of the 1965 Concession Policy Act (U.S. Public Law 89-249). On November 13, 1998, the Concessions Policy Act was reformed with the passage of the National Parks Omnibus Management Act of 1998, U.S. Public Law 105-391, Title IV. U.S. Public Law 105-391 provided a change in several key components of the 1965 law including, but not limited to the following:

- Creation of a new method of determining compensable private interest in real property; establishment of a maximum contract term length of 20 years
- Creation of new proposal selection factors focused on environmental stewardship
- Retention of franchise fees
- Change in the preferential right of renewal from all existing concessioners to only those grossing no more than $500,000 annually, and outfitters and guides.

U.S. Army Corps of Engineers—The U.S. Army Corps of Engineers officially recognized recreation as part of its mission beginning in 1944, with the passage of the Flood Control Act. This act gave the U.S. Army Corps of Engineers authority to "construct, maintain, and operate public park and recreation facilities in reservoir areas under control of the Department of the Army and to permit the construction, maintenance, and operation of such facilities." This act also allowed the Corps to facilitate commercial developments for public use via leases with concessionaires.

In 1965, the Federal Water Project Recreation Act of 1965 (U.S. Public Law 89-72) required that the true potential of recreation be evaluated and developed, all other conditions considered. The law also required that, from 1965 forward, recreation assets could only be constructed if there was a non-Federal partner share in the project costs. Additionally, it was required that the non-Federal partner be responsible for the costs of facility operation and maintenance. This legislation further indicated that if a non-Federal partner could not be found then development of recreational facilities should be limited to the minimum facilities required for public health and safety.

U.S. Public Law 102-575, passed in 1992, allowed the Corps to cost share with non-Federal agencies for operations, maintenance, and repair of recreation assets. However, based upon the complexity of operations, the requirement for maintenance and asset recapitalization, and the increasing pressure of the non-Federal agency to fund these requirements, the Corps developed policies and guidelines to better outline the requirements of the parties. Additionally, if non-Federal agencies are unable to maintain their facilities and wanted to return them to the Corps, Corps policy required the operator to shutter the facilities and return the land to its natural condition. Both this law and supporting Corps policies limit the methods that could be considered for new development, as well as operations, maintenance, and rehabilitation of recreation facilities.

Business structure elements desired by private sector partners—Private sector investors operating on public land seek to the greatest degree possible the ability to create agreement structures that mirror those they are able to find in the private sector. Key elements desired are:

- Predicable and manageable revenue streams
- Predicable and manageable expense profiles
- Opportunity to make investments that are additive to revenue and assist with managing expenses while still meeting internal return on investment expectations
- Opportunity to amortize investments over contract/lease/permit term
- Qualifiable risk profile.

As private sector operators consider entering into visitor service business relationships with public agencies, they evaluate their ability to achieve and manage each of these elements. Absence of an element (e.g., predictable and manageable expense profile) affects the overall risk profile of a particular opportunity. The risks and respective returns are constantly being compared to those that are available in the private sector. Ultimately, the business decisions of the private sector are based on which business opportunity is more financially attractive.

Each of the three agencies covered in this article have approaches for entering into relationships with private sector partners. The structures are guided by statutory, regulatory, and policy frameworks, and visitor service needs. In most cases, historical precedents or political priorities created the statutory foundations that continue to affect policies today. The business structure elements affect the private sector's interest in each type of business opportunity. For many agencies the statutory frameworks upon which a contract or permits are structured have not changed for over half a decade. Yet, during this same period private sector real estate finance and development theory and practice have undergone enormous change.

This article focuses on five key business elements that affect an agency and private operator partnership: contract term, rate administration, compensatory interest in real property, return to the Government, and oversight and management. Provided in the next section is an overview of each agency's general business structure and details on each of these elements.

The following is a description of business structures provided by public sector partners, specifically, the Forest Service, National Park Service, and the U.S. Corps of Army Engineers.

Business structures provided by public sector partners—

Forest Service—The Forest Service issues and administers special use permits for recreation uses that serve the public, promote public health and safety, and protect the environment. There are six categories of uses involved that include: (1) group use, (2) individual use, (3) lodging, (4) facility-related activities, (5) facility-related services, and (6) winter recreation.

There are four categories of permit structures including (1) ski area permits, (2) other term permits (that include assets such

Timberline Lodge, Mt. Hood National Forest in Oregon. (Photograph courtesy of Margaret Bailey)

as lodging, resorts, and marinas), (3) outfitter and guide (non-asset term) permits, and (4) Granger-Thye permits. The permit system for each of these structures varies. The following paragraphs begin with a discussion of the business elements of term and return to the Government for each of the four permit types. Then the elements of compensable interest, rate and oversight, and management will be discussed as they relate to all permit types.

Ski area permits—Terms: Currently, ski areas are authorized under either the Organic Act of 1897/ Term Permit Act of 1915, or the National Forest Ski Area Permit Act of 1986 (Ski Area Permit Act). Terms for ski areas can be up to 40 years long.

Return to the Government: The Government return on ski area permits is based on the Graduated Rental System and varies based on level of adjusted gross revenue generated by the operation. For ski areas, the schedule varies based on the authorizing document. If the permit was issued under the Ski Permit Act, the beginning rental fee is 1.5 percent of total revenue and the top rate is 4.0 percent of total revenue. As of fiscal year 2009, the thresholds were as follows: 1.5 percent for revenue up to $4.3 million, 2.5 percent for between $4.3 and $21.6 million, 2.75 percent for resort revenues between 21.6 and $72 million; and 4 percent for mega resorts over $72 million. Fees collected are sent directly to the U.S. Department of the Treasury for re-appropriation to the Forest Service.

Term permits: Term permits are typically limited to 20 years; however, in special situations, regional foresters may approve a longer term not to exceed 30 years. These longer terms typically apply when the required private sector capital investment exceeds $1 million.

Return to the Government: Other term permits have their fees set according to the formula established within the Graduated Rate Fee System (GRFS). This system operates by applying a selected rate from an established schedule of rates applied to the concessioner's gross sales. The rate, or rates, to be used are determined by the proportioned relationship of the concessioner's sales to Gross Fixed Assets (GFA). As sales increase in relation to GFA, a higher rate from the schedule of graduated rates is applied to the higher increment of sales and the total fee increases. The calculation of the GRFS is based upon an analysis of the sales by business category, evaluation of break-even point by type of business, and then computation of a rate percentage based upon the amount of sales at various break even rates. The rate base for break-even sales ranges from 0.75 percent for grocery businesses to 4.5 for rental services. The balance of sales rates (for revenue above break-even) range from 1.13 percent for grocery to 6.75 percent for rental and services. These fees are sent directly to the U.S. Department of the Treasury for re-appropriation to the Forest Service.

Outfitter and guide permits—Terms: Priority versus temporary use permits are authorized for up to 10 years.

Return to the Government: The procedure for calculating return to the Government for outfitters and guides is based upon one of two options. Option A: The fee is based on an average client-day charge using a Forest Service schedule of rates. The minimum average client-day charge begins at $0.25 per client for client fees up to $8 and increases to $10 per client for fees up to $400 per day. The Forest Service receives 3 percent of the client fees if the fees are over $400 per day. Option B: The fee is 3 percent of the annual adjusted gross revenue, minus any applicable adjustment for use of National Forest System lands. These fees are retained at the forest level based upon the recent passage of the Federal Land Recreation Enhancement Act, which allows for outfitter and guide fees to be retained at the site where they are generated.

Granger-Thye permits—Terms: Terms for Granger-Thye permits are 5 years with the option of a 5-year extension at the discretion of the authorizing officer. If the permit is going to include reconstruction or other improvements costing more than $250,000, then 10-year initial terms are possible.

Return to the Government: The fee for a Granger-Thye permit should represent the full value of the use, consisting of a fee for the land use plus a fee for the use of Federal-owned improvements (buildings). The land use fee is determined based upon Forest Service policy, and the appropriate fee for the use of Government-owned improvements is set at 6 percent of the value of the improvements. With the exception of the maintenance fee offsets (agreed to within each permit), the remainder of the fee is sent directly to the U.S. Department of the Treasury for re-appropriation to the Forest Service.

Compensatory interest in real property: For all term permits (excluding Granger-Thye permits, which include the management and operation of government improvements), the permit holder typically creates the improvements. The permit creates an obligation against the United States by requiring the United States to pay for any improvements authorized by permits which the Forest Service revokes for reasons other than breach of contract prior to the end of the term. However, when a term permit expires, the United States is not obligated to pay for the holder's improvements or to issue a new contract. If a decision is made not to issue a new contract, the holder is responsible for removing improvements according to the provisions of the permit.

Rate approval: Term permits include language indicating "prices and services may be regulated by the [Forest Service] provided that the holder shall not be required to charge prices significantly different than those charged by comparable or competing enterprises." This is similar to language within the Granger-Thye Permit.

Oversight and management: The preponderance of day-to-day special use permit administration occurs at the district level of the Forest Service. The district ranger is responsible for all special use activities within the district. Except for those responsibilities specifically reserved by the forest supervisor, it is the responsibility of the district ranger to ensure quality on-the-ground administration of the special-uses program, including, but not limited to:

• Maintaining communication with local individuals and organizations with interest in the special-uses program
• Monitoring and evaluating special-use activities to determine the effects on other resources and ensure compliance with the forest land and resource management plans
• Evaluating special-uses applications under the district ranger's authority
• Completing appropriate environmental documentation prior to issuing these authorizations.

Information on the scope and scale of the Forest Service's Special Use program is managed through multiple databases in a decentralized manner. As such, global data on the number of authorizations by type and total revenue are not readily available. Data on the fees collected under the Federal Land Recreation Enhancement Act, as well as term permit authorities, is provided in the following table 4.10.

Over the last 5 years, the most immediate direct impact on the Forest Service has been the ability to retain at the forest level the special recreation permit fees. As seen in the

Table 4.10—U.S. Forest Service 5-year trend of special recreation permit fees from 2006 through 2010

Year	Special recreation permits[a]	Recreation special uses[b]
2006	$9,700,000	$48,740,000
2007	$10,000,000	$48,570,000
2008	$10,005,000	$51,700,000
2009	$9,359,200	na
2010	na	$53,319,000

na = Not available.
[a] Special use permits for recreation events, outfitting and guides, and miscellaneous recreation uses have terms of < 10 years.
[b] Special use permits fees for ski areas, resorts, marinas, and concession campground fees in excess of fee-offset. Fees sent directly to the U.S. Department of the Treasury.
Source: Bailey (2011a).

exhibit above this has resulted in approximately $10 million being generated and retained. If more outfitter and guiding businesses are authorized, the opportunities for additional fees to be generated and retained would increase. Recreation special use revenue is not directly retained at the site level, rather it is sent directly to the U.S. Department of the Treasury for re-appropriation. Special use fees have been increasing over the last 5 years.

National Park Service—Chapter 10 of the National Park Service management policies frames the key elements of the National Park Service Commercial Services Program. The two methods that commercial visitor services are authorized are concession contracts or commercial use authorizations. The guiding agreement outlining specific terms and conditions associated with the operation of concession services is a concession contract. A commercial use authorization (CUA) is a permit that authorizes certain commercial services within park areas to support visitor access but is limited in scope with specific conditions and is not considered a concession contract. CUAs may be issued only for commercial operations with annual gross receipts of not more than $25,000, resulting from services originating and provided solely within a unit of the National Park System, with a requirement that the commercial operation that provides the service must originate and terminate outside the boundaries of the park unit. The following paragraphs provide an overview of the five business structure elements of a National Park Service concession contract.

Term: National Park Service management policy states that the term of a concession contract will generally be 10 years or less. However, the director of the National Park Service may

El Tovar Hotel, Grand Canyon National Park in Arizona. (Photograph courtesy of Margaret Bailey)

award a contract for a term of up to 20 years if it is determined that the contract's terms and conditions, including the required construction of capital improvements, warrant a longer term.

Rate administration: The National Park Service must approve all rates charged by concessioners. The reasonableness of a concessioner's rates and charges to the public will, unless otherwise provided in the contract, be judged primarily on the basis of comparison with current rates and charges for facilities and services of comparable character under similar conditions.

Compensatory interest in real property: All buildings under concession contract are National Park Service-owned structures. The title remains with the Federal Government. Depending on the contract, the concessioner may have a contractual right of compensation in the form of a leasehold surrender interest or possessory interest in one, some, or all of the buildings. Possessory interest (PI) was the term used in concession contracts issued under the previous concession law, U.S. Public Law 89-249, to provide a contractual right of compensation to park concessioners for improvements to facilities they acquired or constructed for use by their businesses. U.S. Public Law 105-391 introduced the concept of leasehold surrender interest (LSI) to provide a contractual right of compensation for capital improvements made by concessioners under a concessions contract. The value of LSI in a capital improvement is the amount equal to the initial value of the construction cost of the capital improvement, adjusted by changes in the Consumer Price Index, minus depreciation of the capital improvement. U.S. Public Law 105-391 also provided that a concessioner that obtained a PI under the terms of a concessions contract is entitled to receive compensation for such PI improvements as provided in the concessions contract. This amount carries over into a new concession contract as the initial value of such LSI.

Return to the Government: Franchise fees provide the mechanism by which concession contracts return fair revenue to the Federal Government. U.S. Public Law 105-391 states that franchise fees shall be based on the "probable value of the contract." Probable value is defined as "a reasonable opportunity for net profit in relation to the capital invested and the obligations of the contract." National Park Service policy has outlined for contracts with gross receipts below $250,000 that the franchise fee will be 3 percent. For contracts between $250,000 and $500,000, the franchise fee can range between 3 and 5 percent. The National Park Service requires a franchise fee analysis be conducted for those contracts with gross revenue over $500,000. A franchise fee analysis considers the historical operations, evaluates the future financial performance, recognizes the potential investments that are being considered, and then estimates a reasonable return on invested capital and operations for the operator. The excess return above and beyond the operator's reasonable return is provided as the return to the Government and is paid out as a franchise fee and can also include a maintenance reserve. This analysis is conducted by either the National Park Service or an external business advisor if the gross revenues are above $3 million. Eighty percent of all franchise fees are retained at the park level and 20 percent are retained by the national office of the National Park Service's Commercial Services Program.

Oversight and management: The National Park Service's Commercial Services Program oversees approximately 560 concession contracts in over 123 national parks. The program's key functional responsibilities include contract development, contract management, facility asset management, and financial management. Currently this program area is managed by approximately 300 National Park Service employees, of whom approximately 50 percent are collateral duty. The scope and scale of the National Park Service concession program

Table 4.11—National Park Service 5-year trend of commercial services franchise fees from 2005 through 2009

Year	Gross revenue	Franchise fee	Franchise fee as a percent of gross revenue
2005	$885,236,076	$30,510,367	3.4
2006	$908,950,212	$35,859,989	3.9
2007	$963,922,228	$41,195,093	4.3
2008	$1,039,064,735	$55,698,954	5.4
2009	$1,007,631,889	$67,654,944	6.7

Source: Bailey (2011b).

Hide Away Cover Marina, Lake Sidney Lanier in Georgia. (Photograph courtesy of U.S. Army Corps of Engineers)

from 2005 to 2009, the most recent period for which data is available, is presented in table 4.11.

As this exhibit illustrates, franchise fees have increased over the period from 2001 to 2006. This is a combination of both increases in gross revenue as well as a revised approach to analyzing the probable value of each business opportunity.

The distribution of National Park Service concession revenue by category for the most recent year of available data is provided in figure 4.5. With nominal changes in business opportunities in the parks, these ratios have remained relatively stable over the last 5-year period for which data was available.

U.S. Army Corps of Engineers—The U.S. Army Corps of Engineers enters into leases with private sector operators for commercial concession purposes.

The U.S. Army Corps of Engineers has a standard lease for all commercial services. Key elements of these leases include:

Term: Lease terms can be up to 25 years. There is no direct preference for renewal but leases have been renewed based upon satisfactory performance. In those situations where leases are extended, the terms of extension are subject to review and discussions with each respective district real estate division.

Rate administration: The U.S. Army Corps of Engineers requests in their leases that the "rates and prices charged by the Lessee or its sub-lessees shall be reasonable and comparable to rates charged for similar goods and services by others in the area." Additionally, "the District Engineer shall have the right to review such rates and prices and require an increase or reduction when it is determined that this objective has been violated."

Compensatory interest in real property: Under U.S. Army Corps of Engineers leases, the development and maintenance of structures are the responsibility of the lessee. All structures and equipment furnished by the lessee shall be and remain the property of the lessee. Therefore, all title to structures remains with the lessee. At the end of the lease term, the lease states that the lessee "shall vacate the premises, remove the property there from, and restore the premises to a condition satisfactory to the District Engineer." Depending on the decision of the district engineer, the property could remain, but the lessee receives no compensatory interest from the U.S. Army Corps of Engineers. Leases can be sold but approval for transfer is subject to the district real estate division.

Return to the Government: Compensation to the Government is based upon a graduated revenue fee system,

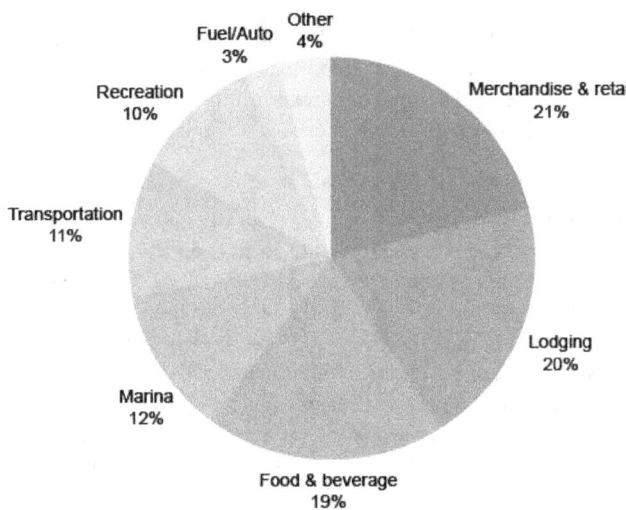

Figure 4.5—National Park System commercial services program distribution of revenue by business category. Source: Bailey (2011b).

which starts at 2 percent for operations that generate revenue below $50,000, increasing to 2.1 percent for revenue between $50,000 and $200,000 and then increases at 0.1 percent for each $200,000 dollar increase in revenue up to a cap of 4.6 percent for revenue above $5 million. Currently, only 25 percent of the concessionaire revenue is returned to the Treasury for reallocation back to the U.S. Army Corps of Engineers in the form of appropriated funding, while 75 percent is retained by the local counties in which the lake is located. This payment is meant to be in lieu of taxes. No fees are available at the unit level.

Oversight and management: On U.S. Army Corps of Engineers projects, the lake manager has day-to-day oversight responsibility for both concession and government facilities at the site level. The lake manager does not have responsibility for determining the structure or terms of leases for concessionaires on his lake. This responsibility lies at the district level under the real estate division. Should problems with the concessionaire occur, it is the district real estate personnel who have direct oversight responsibility. The real estate division at the district reports to the deputy chief of staff for real estate at the headquarters level.

The scope and scale of the U.S. Army Corps of Engineers program is presented in table 4.12. Over the last decade, the number of leases on U.S. Army Corps of Engineers land has remained relatively stable, but the distribution of leases has shifted more to private concessionaires from quasi-public agencies. Comparative Lease Revenue information was not available.

Observations—

The business structure of each Federal agency reviewed above varies. Following is a comparison of each key business structure element across these agencies. Overall, the review presented above of private partnerships with these three land management agencies provides an informative picture of private concession trends in the Federal sector.

Terms—The terms for business structures range from 5 to 40 years. In most cases, the terms match the elements of the business structures. Those involving capital investments and lack of guaranteed compensatory interest are longer in term, and those that require less capital investment and/or are more operational in nature (e.g., Forest Service Granger-Thye) provide for shorter terms. Both the Forest Service and the U.S. Army Corps of Engineers provide the potential for term extensions based upon satisfactory performance or plans for additional capital investment. The Forest Service has term limits on Granger-Thye and outfitter and guide permits, and the National Park Service also has a limit on their terms. All permits require the use of a competitive bid process. The private sector will always seek to gain a longer contract term for business security reasons and to provide a suitable period to amortize capital investments in real property assets. Public agencies must carefully evaluate capital investment requirements and investor return expectations as each contract term is considered. Capital investment requirement and investor return expectations relate closely to the potential success of a business opportunity.

Compensatory interest in real property—The only agency that provides compensatory interest in real property is the National Park Service. The Forest Service provides a level of compensation if the Forest Service terminates the permit for their interests. U.S. Army Corps of Engineers operator agreements do not provide for a compensable interest in real property improvements. Both the Forest Service and the U.S. Army Corps of Engineers require the private sector partner to remove real property at the end of the term if the business use is no longer desired by the Agency. While the National Park Service's compensatory interest would be a desirable term to a concessioner, there are other ways to satisfy private sector operators. If the term of the concession allows for an amortization of the desired/required investment, the opportunity for sale and transfer of the asset, and a clear understanding of compensation terms, the private sector can appropriately consider and evaluate the risk of the business opportunity.

Return to the Government—The process and methods for evaluating and establishing the appropriate return to the Government vary greatly between Federal agencies. Return to

Table 4.12—U.S. Army Corps of Engineers scope of lease program and trend data on leases (exhibit 1) in 1999 and 2008

	1999	2008
Leasing entity	Leases	Leases
	number	number
Concessionaires	172	364
State	593	571
Local	600	593
Quasi public	421	284
Federal	67	53
Total	1,853	1,865

Source: Bailey (2011c)

the Government is a topical area that comes under great scrutiny by Congress. Past Congressional and Office of Inspector General reports have focused on the issue of attaining a fair return to the Government for the opportunity it affords private partners to profit from the use of Federal lands. Recognizing the diversity of approaches and results between the agencies as well as the opportunities offered it is a reasonable area for review.

At one end of the spectrum is the U.S. Army Corps of Engineers, which has a standard lease rate that is applied to adjusted gross revenue thresholds regardless of the business type. No feasibility analysis is conducted to determine if there is excess return available to the Government. This is similar to the process used by the Forest Service for their ski permit fee estimates with the exception of the revenue threshold, to which the fee is applied, being adjusted upward by the Consumer Price Index (CPI). A CPI adjustment is not contemplated within U.S. Army Corps of Engineers leases. The Forest Service term permit fee process does evaluate a business's break-even point in their multi-step calculation. However, the analysis does not include an assessment of return on capital invested. The Forest Service Granger-Thye permit requires that a return to the Government is based on a process that recognizes the use of the Government's land and its associated improvements. The Forest Service outfitter and guide permits have estimated an invested capital return based upon the price the client is charged by the operator and the share of that price for which the Forest Service should benefit. The most comprehensive analysis for returns on capital invested is undertaken by the National Park Service. The National Park Service has established standard franchise fees for smaller contracts below $250,000 and a franchise fee range up to 5 percent for contracts that generate gross receipts between $250,000 and $500,000. Above this dollar threshold, in-depth financial analysis is conducted

to determine the franchise fee. Depending on the scale and scope of the operation, in-depth financial analysis would be the recommended approach for determining the return to the Government, and only the National Park Service is using this approach.

While the business structure terms can vary by agency, fundamental to each is the private sector's expectations for return. This can and should be evaluated for each deal structure prior to the setting of the return to the Government. A combination of authorities, tradition, policies, and lack of skilled personnel in real estate finance and contract structuring has in many agencies impacted the successful use of best real estate investment practices. This is an area of specific reform within the U.S. Army Corps of Engineers and the Forest Service.

Oversight and management—While the business structures for private sector partners are based on statute and regulation, the contract oversight and management of these complex hospitality and recreation assets cannot be overlooked. Of particular importance is the host agency's knowledge of resource stewardship as well as hospitality and recreation operations and finance. A background and base of knowledge in both of these areas increases the ability of the host agency to interact with private sector operators in a meaningful and collegial way, while also measuring business decisions against any potential impact to the resource. All parties need to have a vested interest in maintaining the value of the hospitality and recreation assets in alignment with the mission of each respective agency. In essence, each respective agency and their staff are "stewards" of our Nation's visitor service assets.

With the exception of the National Park Service, which has onsite concession specialists at its largest concessions supported by regional and Washington office staff, the other Federal agencies discussed in this article do not have dedicated staff for oversight and management of private sector hospitality and recreation visitor services. Many have adjunct or collateral duty staff to assist with day-to-day oversight and regional or district support from a real estate or special use division. While this model allows staff to confer with internal agency real estate advisors, it does not necessarily lead to a robust oversight of business operations. This can be to the detriment of both the agency and the private sector operator. Without concession specialists, the agency is not in a good position to monitor operations in order to understand how their potential returns are being affected, nor does it provide the operator the opportunity to share with the agency issues that may be affecting their operation. In the long run, this impacts visitor services, financial returns to all parties, and the condition of real property assets.

End Invited Paper

INVITED PAPER

Concession Operations on Bureau of Land Management Lands

Phil Walker[3]

In a memorandum from the Washington Office of the Bureau of Land Management, U.S. Department of the Interior, dated April 6, 2010, and addressing the subject of "Evaluating the Potential of Expanding the Bureau of Land Management's Recreation Concession Management Program," the following description of the Bureau of Land Management's Concessions program was given:

Recreation concession leases/agreements are authorized under the Federal Lands Policy and Management Act of 1976 and managed under policies as outlined in BLM Manual Section (M-2930). The BLM [Bureau of Land Management] currently manages 16 recreation concession agreements along the Lower Colorado River District in California and Arizona and one Commercial Lease in Idaho along the Snake River. Recreation concessioners currently provide the BLM with approximately $600,000 in lease/franchise fees each year of which 100 percent is reinvested onsite.

Recreation concession agreements may be offered … where compatible with resource management objectives and applicable planning documents. Concessions opportunities are also encouraged where they forward the purposes of any special area or unit designation. In expanding and invigorating the BLM Recreation Concession's program, maintenance costs can be reduced, revenues increased, opportunities for small businesses in local communities can be provided, and the improvement of associated visitor service and recreation opportunities will be enhanced.

As joint partners with the BLM, concessioners provide a safe, quality recreational experience for an ever-growing segment of the recreating public by providing developed recreational and retail facilities. Some potential concession opportunities and funding sources may be linked to American Recovery and Reinvestment Act (stimulus), youth initiatives, and renewable energy projects. Recreation concession facilities have grown in local communities along with visitor demands brought about by the designation of special management areas, and cooperatively, the concessions have contributed

to the local, State, and regional economic long-term development. The relationship of the BLM's recreation concession program to community growth, and the resultant needs of local tourism-related business, contributes toward the health of gateway communities and provides a fair market value return to the public.…

The majority of the Bureau of Land Management's concession program in the Colorado River corridor is administered by Yuma and Lake Havasu Field Offices. There are 16 concessioner operations consisting of camping, lodging and hospitality, restaurants, swimming pools, marinas, golf courses, boat ramps, miniature golf, and storage along the lower Colorado River. Another concessioner is located on the Snake River in Idaho with similar amenities. In total, the Bureau of Land Management has 17 current concessioner run operations covering three States: California, Arizona, and Idaho. Recently, the Bureau of Land Management sent a data call to the field requesting concession opportunities.

A handful of potential results were gathered from 160 field offices. Several opportunities will be selected to begin a pilot agreement, as well as revamping the current Bureau of Land Management concession policy. An internal working group began reviewing this process the week of December 6–10, 2010, in Phoenix. The following concession opportunities have been proposed as potentially viable:

- Recreational hospitality opportunities, including food and beverage, photo service, overnight accommodations, recreational/trailer parks, merchandising
- Recreational visitor service opportunities, including marina, river shuttle or boat launch facilities or services, campgrounds/day use, visitor center, winter sports, biking, off-highway vehicle (OHV)
- Other specialized recreational opportunities, including horse or bike rides or tours, OHV/recreational vehicle/boat equipment storage, shooting ranges, and long-distance trail or Yurt systems.

End Invited Paper

Concessions and State Park Systems

Data from the annual information exchange—
Private-sector concessions have played a significant role in the delivery of visitor services within the 50 State park systems in the United States for decades. Among other aspects, the Annual Information Exchange (AIX) monitors concession operations across all the States. AIX is a project of the National Association of State Park Directors (NASPD). A major section of the AIX is "Revenue," which covers a number of financial topics such as operating expenses, capital

[3] Manager, National Recreation Concessions Program, Bureau of Land Management, U.S. Department of the Interior, Washington, DC 20250.

expenditures, budgets, fees and charges, and State taxes dedicated to parks and recreation. One of those sections is "Sources of Revenue," which lists the various categories of State park system revenues. Over the year from July 1, 2008 to June 30, 2009, the 50 State park systems raised more than $950 million in revenue from 10 different sources (table 4.13). Camping fees accounted for nearly 30 percent of these revenues, followed by entrance fees, and the miscellaneous "other" category. Together, these three categories accounted for just slightly more than two-thirds of all revenues.

A limitation of the AIX is that State-owned and private concession-owned revenue sources are not differentiated in the data. This masks the revenue role of concessions in State park systems in dollar terms. But, with the exception of entrance fees, we know that private concessions contribute at some level to generating revenue in all other categories listed in table 4.13. Concession operations are especially significant in the provision of State park lodges and restaurants. (The "Concessions" group in table 4.13 does not refer to private concessions in general, but rather to operations providing food and related items such as snacks and drinks and other items sold in State park camp stores or refreshment stands. No description of what constitutes the "other" category is included in the AIX report.)

One issue that makes revenue comparisons across States difficult, and a likely contributing factor why private concessions are not distinguished, is lack of standard definitions for the revenue categories. This is a recognized need by the NASPD leadership and the university cooperators who conduct the AIX. Phil McKnelly, President of NASPD, commented in personal communication that the revenue sources in table 4.13 are most likely a mix of in-house (State-owned) and concession operations, though the majority of revenue is probably from the State-owned resources. The AIX also reports that 31 States charge a licensing fee for concession operations. McKnelly indicated that some States with concession operations generate revenue as a percentage of the private partner's income without charging a concession license fee as such.

National Association of State Park Directors survey on land leases—In a special survey conducted jointly in 2008 with the National Association of State Park Directors and that organization's executive director, Phil McKnelly, a questionnaire was sent to State park directors to gain insight into concession and leasing policies for State parks. Results from the survey are summarized below.

Of the responding 15 State park systems, all have some type of agreement with private sector operators. Some receive payments from private concession operators as a total annual dollar amount, while a number of others receive payments as a price per acre where a land lease is involved. All receive payments also in the form of a percentage of revenues received from the private partner. These percentages range from a low of 2–4 percent in North Dakota to 11–20 percent in Kansas. Where land leases are involved, the amount per acre leased is typically a few hundred dollars per year. In some cases, the services provided by private partners can provide substantial revenues back to the State park system. In Florida, for example, the State realized concession revenues of over $5.5 million in the July 2007–June 2008 fiscal year.

Private partners working with State park systems or other public land managers can cover a wide variety of services. For example, in Michigan, the State's park and recreation areas have leases, contracts, and rental agreements covering food concessions, outdoor centers, dry hydrants, boating access sites, ski hills, equestrian trails, model aircraft flying fields, and canoe or kayak liveries. For these types of services, fees are based on competitive bidding, fair market value of the land under lease, or on cost savings to the State. In North Dakota, the State leases facilities and the right to provide such provisions as docks, slips, concession items, and boat fuel. Private concession operations of public lands such as State parks are a highly important means for meeting a wide range of recreation visitor service demands.

Table 4.13—Dollars and percent of revenue generated by source in U.S. State park systems, 2008–2009

Revenue source	U.S. dollars	Percent
Entrance fees	204,555,729	21.4
Camping fees	282,585,302	29.6
Cabins/cottages	77,775,008	8.1
Lodges	56,428,274	5.9
Group facilities	4,083,720	0.4
Restaurants	49,347,869	5.2
Concessions	64,590,808	6.8
Beaches/pools	6,719,803	0.7
Golf courses	51,204,550	5.4
Other	158,902,072	16.6
Total operations	954,657,346	100.1

Note: Revenue sources do not sum to 100.0 percent exactly because of rounding. Source: Leung and others (2010).

Chapter 5
Public Outdoor Recreation Resources

This chapter addresses objective 5 of this assessment report on outdoor recreation and protected land resources: to describe the status and trends of local, State, and Federal public lands and associated properties as recreation resources. This chapter examines the recreation opportunities provided by government and public lands (local, State, Federal), and the access to these resources through facilities (e.g., trails) and services (e.g., maps and information) they usually provide.

Publicly-owned parks, forests, reserves, refuges, and other recreation resources help define the culture of the United States. Public resources (land, water, and facilities) have traditionally been available to outdoor users at either nominal or no direct cost. Though user fees have become more prevalent in recent decades, these fees still typically represent a small fraction of the cost to visit a natural area or developed recreation site. Very often, individuals have deeply-held personal attachments to public lands as particular, special places. Many of these sites are highly scenic and sometimes sacred.

Like the private sector, the public sector plays an essential role in providing outdoor recreation opportunities, especially nature-based opportunities. Local governments—which include counties, townships, municipalities (cities and towns), school districts, library districts, and other special districts or authorities—are among the more important providers. Their resources include parks, athletic courts and fields, river access, lakes, greenways, zoos, and other outdoor resources. Such local outdoor facilities are especially significant because they tend to be located within or very near to the urban and rural communities they serve.

State governments provide a little different resource in the form of State parks, recreation areas, historic sites, wildlife management areas, and various other public sites that are often located at a special geographic or cultural feature (e.g., an old covered bridge or a lake). These State areas are there to serve citizens statewide and often visitors from other States and countries. Many of the State facilities also emphasize conservation of natural or cultural resources, along with recreation, and tend to be less developed than local government areas.

The Federal Government holds the most extensive system of land and water in the United States, with a long history of land and water conservation. Most of the Federal lands are natural (forests, range, desert, mountains, and sea coasts) and the sites and facilities developed on these lands tend to feature their natural character. An important trend associated with all public lands is the enormous proliferation of homes,

resorts, and accommodations near, adjacent to, or within the boundaries of public lands.

The map below is from an earlier national assessment of outdoor recreation, one conducted through the late 1930s and published in 1941 (USDI National Park Service 1941). The map, produced by hand, illustrates the keen interest Americans and national leaders have held over the decades in the conservation and availability of outdoor recreation resources for the United States (see photo).

The recreation resource information in this chapter is presented for each level of government from local to State to Federal. National statistics are presented, as are statistics for the four regions defined for the 2010 RPA Assessment— North, South, Rocky Mountains (which includes the Great Plains), and Pacific Coast. For each level of government we also present, where possible, recent trends in the amount and distribution of those resources. Some of the trend information is not straightforward because of changes in resource definitions, measurement standards, and methods over time.

Local Government as a Recreation Provider

Every national assessment of outdoor recreation in the United States, dating back to the 1930s Department of the Interior study and the Outdoor Recreation Resources Review Commission (ORRRC) report in 1962, has stressed the need for local recreation opportunities where people live, i.e., "close-to-home" recreation. Local governments

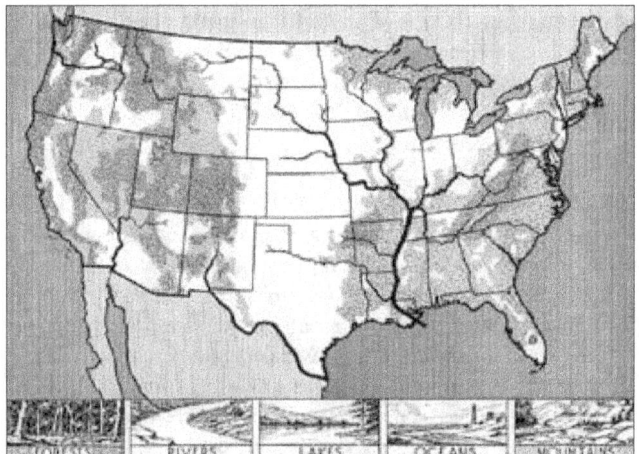

A Study of the Park and Recreation Problem of the United States. 1941. Chapter 2, Aspects of Recreation Planning, Figure 17. USDI National Park Service, U.S. Government Printing Office, Washington, DC. (http //www. cr.nps.gov/history/online_books/parks_america/images/photo17.jpg).

have traditionally been the major providers of community recreation opportunities. The Federal and State governments are also involved in providing close-to-home recreation through urban parks and recreation areas, but not nearly to the extent or reach of local government recreation and park systems. The private sector also plays a significant role in providing recreation in urbanized areas, but by virtue of being private can exclude some people through pricing or membership requirements.

A historic study by the National Park Service in 1935 reported the following:

> [A] national study of Municipal and County Parks in the United States, 1935, made by the National Park Service in cooperation with the National Recreation Association, gave the following figures on city park acreages: Of 1,425 cities reporting, 1,216 reported one or more parks, with a total acreage of 388,867. It may be fairly assumed that this comes very close to representing the total extent of city parks as of that date. Three hundred and forty-one cities reported no parks of less than an acre of park for each 2,000 of population, and in all probability most of the cities which failed to report belonged in this group.

> For the same study, 77 counties reported a total of 159,261.7 acres of park land. Most of the large county systems are found in metropolitan regions and of the 77 systems reported in the county classification, four are Ohio metropolitan park districts, one is the East Bay District in California, located in and serving principally two counties, and one is the Boston Metropolitan Park District, located in and serving several counties. (USDI National Park Service 1941).

The U.S. Census Bureau describes the structure of local government in the United States to "include, in addition to the Federal Government and the States, thousands of local governments—counties, municipalities, townships, school districts, and many 'special districts'." In 2007, 76,425 local governments were identified by the Census of Governments, not counting school districts.

> As defined by this Census, governmental units include all agencies or bodies having an organized existence, governmental character, and substantial autonomy. While most of these governments can impose taxes, many of the special districts—such as independent public housing authorities and local irrigation, power, conservation, and other types of districts—are financed from rentals, charges for services, benefit assessments, grants from other governments, and other nontax sources. The count of governments excludes semi-autonomous agencies through which States, cities, and counties sometimes provide for certain functions—for example, "dependent" school systems, State institutions of higher education, and certain other "authorities" and special agencies which are under the administrative or fiscal control of an established governmental unit. (U.S. Census Bureau 2007a).

A local government park and recreation agency can range from a part-time, one-person staff that administers sports or other programming in facilities shared with other agencies or schools to a major urban department such as those in New York City or Los Angeles that employ several thousand people, professionals, and specialists, full-time and part-time. One professional employee is the minimum standard we have adopted to delineate a local government provider as a department or agency. Included in this chapter is an invited paper by Peter Harnik and others that describes the largest city systems.

A wide variety of facilities, programs, and outdoor areas are offered by local government park and recreation departments in the United States. Some smaller departments emphasize programming more than park land acquisition and development. Much more indoor recreation is provided by local governments than by State or Federal-supplied resources. In any event, nearly all local government recreation agencies will include some public land for public use, even if it's shared with another government agency or school district. The best source of information about local government recreation and park agencies in the United States is the U.S. Census Bureau's Census of Governments.

Local Government Recreation and Park Agencies

The U.S. Census Bureau conducts the Census of Governments every 5 years (years ending in "2" or "7," the first occurring in 1957), which includes government organization, employment, and finances. In this section, we examine the organization of local government units and public employment with respect to parks and recreation. A listing of local governmental units organized by type (county, municipal and township, and special district governments) is provided. In addition, data on full-time, part-time, and full-time equivalent employment by type of government and function is given. Overseeing parks and recreation is one of more than two dozen different functions performed by local governments. This report examines trends in recreation and park employment since the 1997 Census of Governments as an indicator of trends in recreation resources provided by local governments.

The number of local governments increased a modest 3.3 percent between 2002 and 2007 (table 5.1), mainly due to the increase in the number of special district governments,

Table 5.1—Number of local government units in the United States and percent change, from 1997 to 2007, by type of government

Type of government unit	1997	2002	Percent change 1997–2002	2007	Percent change 2002–2007
County	3,043	3,034	-0.3	3,033	0.0
Municipal	19,372	19,429	0.3	19,492	0.3
Town or township	16,629	16,504	-0.8	16,519	0.1
Special district	34,683	35,052	1.1	37,381	6.6
U.S. total	73,727	74,019	0.4	76,425	3.3

Source: U.S. Census Bureau (2007c).

Table 5.2—Number and percent of local government units in the United States that provide parks and recreation services by type of government and region in 2007

Type of government unit	North Parks & Rec.	North All govts.	North % of reg.	South Parks & Rec.	South All govts.	South % of reg.	Rocky Mountains Parks & Rec.	Rocky Mountains All govts.	Rocky Mountains % of reg.	Pacific Coast Parks & Rec.	Pacific Coast All govts.	Pacific Coast % of reg.	U.S. total Parks & Rec.	U.S. total All govts.	U.S. total % of nat.
County	429	1,006	42.6	577	1,286	44.9	139	592	23.5	106	149	71.1	1,251	3,033	41.2
Municipal	2,280	9,250	24.6	1,902	6,119	31.1	805	2,973	27.1	678	1,150	59.0	5,665	19,492	29.1
Town or township	1,166	12,476	9.3	0	0	0.0	4	4,043	0.1	0	0	0.0	1,170	16,519	7.1
Special District	398	14,473	2.7	73	8,269	0.9	131	9,581	1.4	164	5,058	3.2	766	37,381	2.0
All local units	4,273	37,205	11.5	2,552	15,674	16.3	1,079	17,189	6.3	948	6,357	14.9	8,852	76,425	11.6

Note: "Parks & Rec." = Parks and Recreation, "All govts." = All governments, "% of reg." = Percent of region, "% of nat." = Percent of Nation.
Source: U.S. Census Bureau (2007c).

Table 5.3—Number of people employed in local government parks and recreation agencies and percent change, from 1997 to 2007, by region

North 1997	North 2007	North Percent change	South 1997	South 2007	South Percent change	Rocky Mountains 1997	Rocky Mountains 2007	Rocky Mountains Percent change	Pacific Coast 1997	Pacific Coast 2007	Pacific Coast Percent change	U.S. total 1997	U.S. total 2007	U.S. total Percent change
Full-time employees														
53,490	57,585	7.7	47,817	56,964	19.1	13,495	18,771	39.1	27,572	32,212	16.8	142,374	165,532	16.3
Part-time employees														
62,960	87,502	39.0	31,818	42,239	32.8	22,497	30,162	34.1	31,067	41,813	34.6	148,342	201,716	36.0
Full-time equivalent employees														
74,972	85,452	14.0	60,313	74,925	24.2	20,725	28,420	37.1	39,447	48,194	22.2	195,457	236,991	21.2

Source: U.S. Census Bureau (2007c).

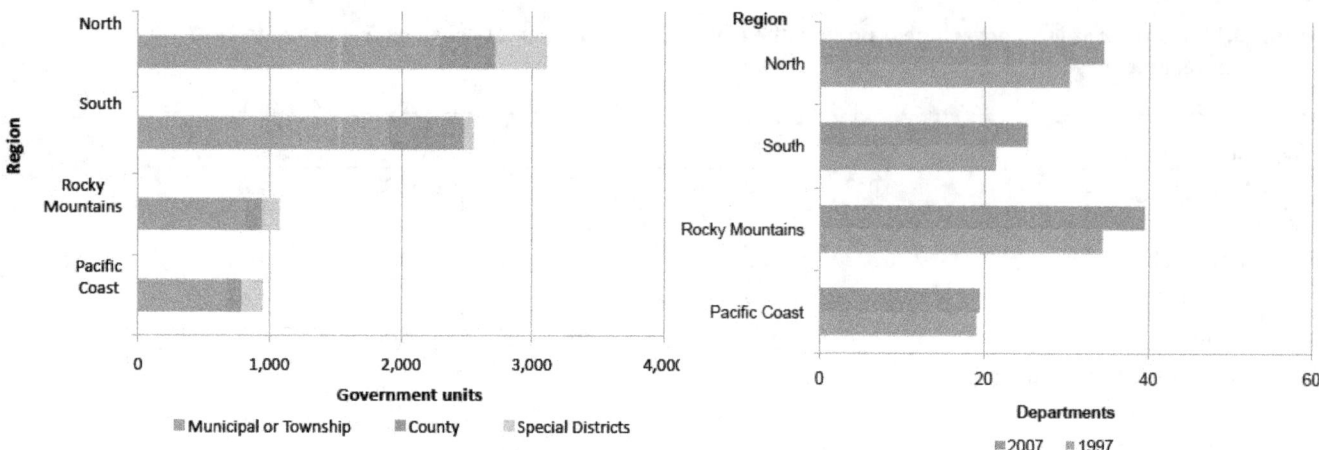

Figure 5 1—Number of local government units that provide parks and recreation services by type of government and region, 2007. Source: U.S. Census Bureau (2007c).

Figure 5.2—Number of local government parks and recreation departments per million people by region, 1997 and 2007. Source: U.S. Census Bureau (2007c).

which grew at a rate of 6.6 percent. Special districts are authorized by State legislatures to perform a single function or a limited number of functions, including but not limited to, water-sewer districts, irrigation districts, fire districts, school districts, community college districts, and hospital districts. Park and recreation services are included among these, sometimes as a sole purpose, and in other cases as one of many purposes, such as in conservancy or water-sewer districts. Necessary characteristics of special district governments are: existence as an organized entity, governmental character which includes the power to levy taxes, and substantial autonomy. A small proportion of U.S. special districts are engaged in providing park and recreation services; however, such districts are a primary local government provider in several States. About 12 percent— more than 8,800—of the Nation's local government units provide recreation and park services (table 5.2). These services are most prevalent in county governments (41 percent of counties), followed by municipal, township, and special districts. For all jurisdictions, the region with the highest proportion of local governments providing recreation and park services was the South (16 percent) and the lowest was the Rocky Mountains (6 percent).

The North region had 48 percent of the total number of local government units providing parks and recreation (fig. 5.1) with virtually all the township recreation departments and the largest number of municipal government recreation departments (nearly 2,300). County recreation and park departments were most numerous in the South, but the highest proportion of all counties that provide recreation was the Pacific Coast, with more than 71 percent of county governments (table 5.2). More than half of all special district recreation and park departments were in the North, but

the Pacific Coast and Rocky Mountains had the highest proportions of all recreation departments that were provided by special districts.

In terms of number of departments per capita, the Rocky Mountains led all regions with nearly 40 departments per 1 million residents, followed by the North (34), South (25), and Pacific Coast (20) (fig. 5.2 and Web site appendix table A5.1). All regions had increased in number of departments per capita since 1997, though the Pacific Coast grew only slightly.

These data on the number of local government parks and recreation departments are one indicator of recreation resources provided at the local level of government in the United States; however, as mentioned, they do not include any information on the amount or type of resources managed. Figure 5.3 shows the delivery of local government recreation and park services by county across the United States for the three types of local governments: county, municipal/township combined, and special district. The delivery of local government recreation services varies by State with respect to the three types of local governments. For example, township governments provide parks and recreation only in 20 Midwest and Northeastern States; special recreation districts are absent in many States but prevalent in others. (See Web site appendix tables A5.2 to A5.5 for detailed local government parks and recreation statistics by type and State.)

Another indicator of level of local outdoor recreation opportunities is the level of employment in parks and recreation departments. The definition chosen to indicate a local government recreation and parks department was simply the presence of one or more full-time equivalent (FTE) employees. There were nearly 237,000 FTE

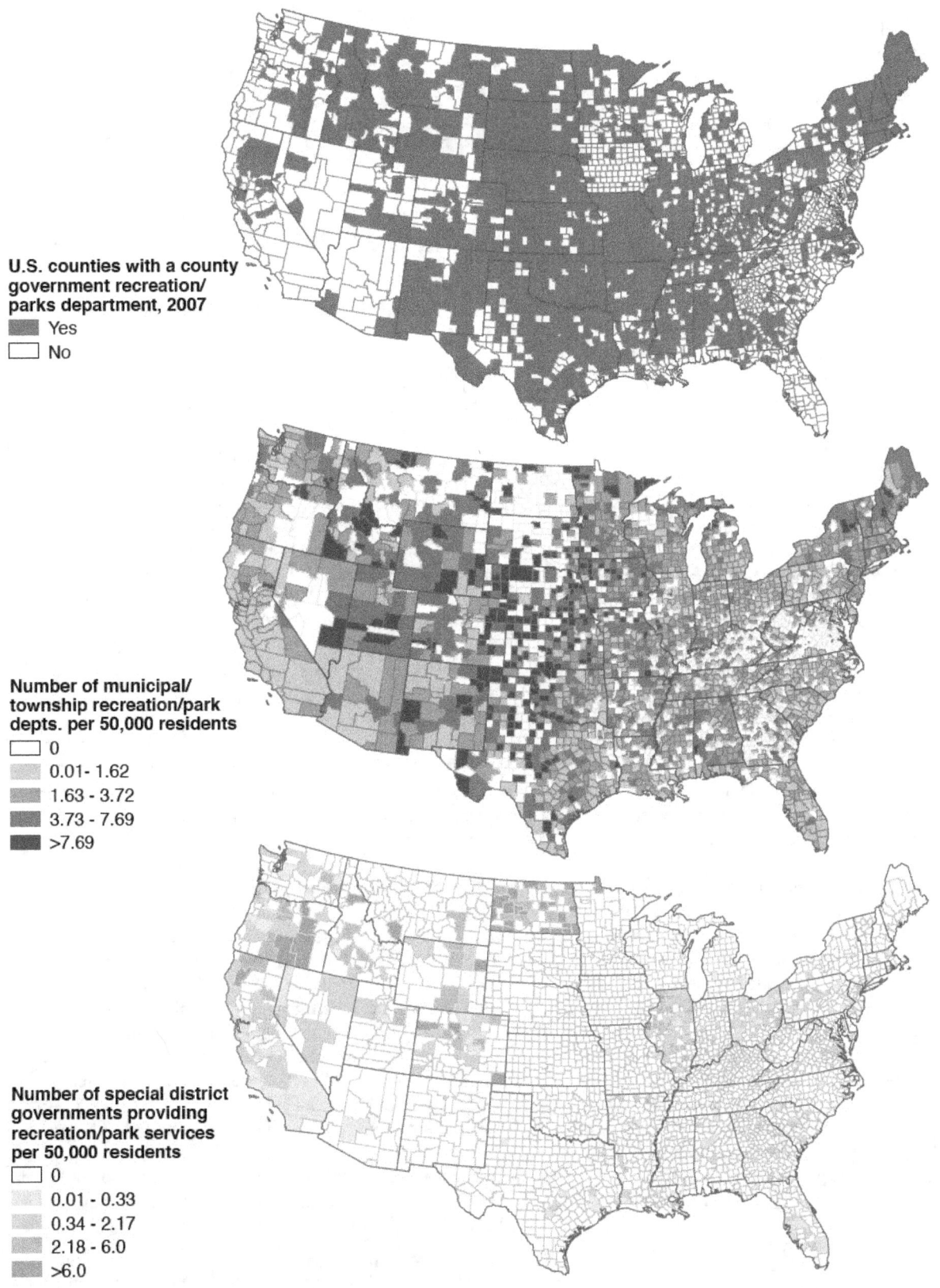

U.S. counties with a county government recreation/parks department, 2007

- Yes
- No

Number of municipal/township recreation/park depts. per 50,000 residents

- 0
- 0.01- 1.62
- 1.63 - 3.72
- 3.73 - 7.69
- >7.69

Number of special district governments providing recreation/park services per 50,000 residents

- 0
- 0.01 - 0.33
- 0.34 - 2.17
- 2.18 - 6.0
- >6.0

Figure 5.3—Distribution of three types of local government recreation and park agencies by county in the conterminous United States, 2007.
Source: U.S. Census Bureau (2007c).

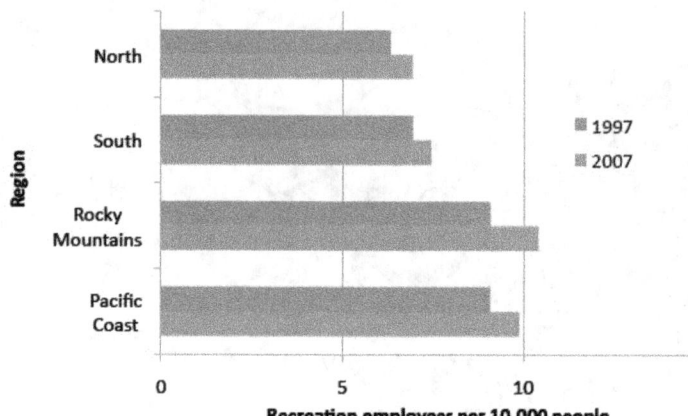

Figure 5.4—Number of local government parks and recreation full-time equivalent employees per 10,000 people by region, 1997 and 2007. Source: U.S. Census Bureau (2007c).

employees working in local government parks and recreation departments in the United States in 2007 (table 5.3). About 165,000 of these individuals were full-time workers.

Employment is shown by full-time and part-time status to indicate how much local government agencies rely on part-time employment. Part-time employees grew at a much higher rate (36 percent) between 1997 and 2007 than full-time employees. The Rocky Mountains region grew much faster in full-time employees than the other regions. On a per capita basis, the two western regions each had about 10 FTE employees per 10,000 population compared to about seven in the two eastern regions (fig. 5.4). Every region's parks and recreation employment kept pace with population growth since 1997, with the Rocky Mountains region registering the largest percentage increase (Web site appendix table A5.6).

While a single staff person does not necessarily make a "department," per se, it indicates a financial commitment to provide park and recreation services. A limitation of using employment as an indicator, though, is that it does not differentiate level of services provided between outdoor and indoor facilities and sites. For example, staffing of an indoor aquatic center could not be counted as an outdoor recreation resource, but staffing for a public outdoor swimming pool would. We make the assumption that public spending for any type of parks and recreation employee is positively related to the provision of outdoor recreation resources by the local government. Local government outdoor recreation resources require management by employees, even if a local agency manages only a single municipal park or playground.

INVITED PAPER

Parks for City People: Greenspace in the Metropolis

Peter Harnik, Ben Welle, and Coleen Gentles[1]

The total area covered by urban parkland in the United States exceeds 1 million acres, with parks ranging in size from the jewel-like 1.7-acre Post Office Square in Boston to the gargantuan 490,125-acre Chugach State Park in Anchorage. The total number is not known, although a study by The Trust for Public Land's Center for City Park Excellence identified 20,705 parks in the Nation's 77 most populous cities.

City parks provide playfields, teach ecology, offer exercise trails, mitigate flood waters, host concerts, provide beauty, protect wildlife, supply space for gardens, give a respite from commotion, and do much more. Some parks, such as Washington Square in New York City, are celebrated in books, songs, and films; others operate in obscurity, frequented and beloved only by those who live in the vicinity. They were our first parks, dating back to the 17th century in Boston, the 16th century in St. Augustine, FL, and to prehistory in the large Native American cities of the past. Their usage dwarfs that of the national parks—New York City's Central Park gets about 25 million visits annually, more than five times as many as the Grand Canyon.

With the general decline of cities and their parks in the second half of the 20th century, followed by the economic rebound beginning in the late 1990s, there came renewed interest in understanding more precisely the relationship between cities and the open space inside them.

Historical perspective—Beginning in 1859, when Frederick Law Olmsted, Calvert Vaux, and more than 3,000 laborers created Central Park, a wave of enthusiasm for urban "pleasure grounds" swept the Nation. Thousands of parks were constructed and millions of words were written about their features and attributes. Over the next eight decades, the purpose and design of parks metamorphosed, but parks remained so important to cities that, even during the depths of the Great Depression, many park systems received large influxes of money and attention through the Federal Government's relief and conservation programs.

During the height of the city park movement, from about 1870 to 1940, great efforts were made to plan for parkland, understand the relationship between parks and surrounding neighborhoods,

[1] Director, former Assistant Director, and Director of Marketing of the Center for City Park Excellence at The Trust for Public Land (www.TPL.org), Washington, DC 20250, respectively.

Fitness zones are easy-to-use, accessible outdoor gyms designed to promote general health within a park experience, creating a supportive social context for getting fit. (Photo courtesy of richreidphotography.com).

and measure the impact of parks. Leaders in Boston, Buffalo, Seattle, Portland, Denver, Baltimore, and elsewhere proudly and competitively labored to convert their cities from drab, polluted industrial cores into beautiful, culturally uplifting centers. These leaders believed a well designed and maintained park system was integral to their mission.

Inspired by boulevard systems in Minneapolis and Kansas City and by Olmsted's "Emerald Necklace" in Boston, many cities sketched out interconnected greenways linking neighborhoods, parks, and natural areas. The Emerald Necklace is a chain of parks about 1,100-acre in total that links parkways and waterways in Boston. Careful measurements were made of the location of parks and the travel distance (by foot, generally) for each neighborhood and resident. Through the National Conference on Outdoor Recreation, the Federal Government provided funding for collection, research, analysis, and dissemination of data on parks.

After World War II, the Nation's attention turned toward the development of suburbs, and the commitment to the urban public domain began to wane. There was even a naïve assumption that private, suburban backyards could replace most of the services provided by public city parks. Many of the ideas regarding the roles of parks in city plans and community socialization were lost. More important, ideas about measuring park success, assuring equity, and meeting the needs of changing users languished.

Over the next half century, the vast urban park system fell on hard times. Few cities provided adequate maintenance, staffing, and budgets, and most cities deferred critically needed capital investment. Many parks suffered from overuse—trampled plants and grass, deteriorated equipment, erosion, and loss of soil resiliency and health. Others declined from underuse—graffiti, vandalism, invasion of noxious weeds, theft of plant resources, and crime. The decline was camouflaged. In the older northern cities, general urban deterioration grabbed headlines and made parks seem of secondary importance. In the new cities of the South and West, low-density development made parks seem superfluous. Intellectual inquiry into city "green space" dwindled to almost nothing (with the single exception of the new ecological "urban natural area").

But every pendulum, it seems, eventually swings back. The effort to revive city park systems slowly gained momentum. When The Trust for Public Land was founded in 1972, it was the first national conservation organization with an explicit urban component to its work. At the same time, fledgling neighborhood groups began forming to save particular parks, either through private fundraising or public political action. There arose a new appreciation of the genius of Frederick Law Olmsted, and in 1980 the Central Park Conservancy was founded. In that same year, pioneering research by William H. Whyte resulted in the publication of "The Social Life of Small Urban Spaces" and the formation of the Project for Public Spaces. The rise of the urban community gardening

San Pedro Springs Park in San Antonio, TX, is the tenth oldest city park in the country, was created from naturally occurring springs, and dates from 1729, although the modern lake/pool was built in 2003. (Photo courtesy of San Antonio Parks & Recreation Department, San Antonio, TX)

movement and the spread of park activism to other cities led in 1994 to a $12 million commitment by the Lila Wallace-Reader's Digest Foundation and the creation of the Urban Parks Institute and the City Parks Alliance. Meanwhile, city park directors formed their own loose network within the National Recreation and Park Association.

Beginning in 1995, many older cities, such as Chicago, Boston, Washington, Atlanta, Denver, and New York, started bouncing back from years of population loss and fiscal decline. With new residents and a greater sense of optimism, they began seeking a competitive edge by combining their strong geographies and histories with their newfound economies. Elsewhere, in fast-growing, lower-density places such as Charlotte, NC, Dallas, Houston, and Phoenix, planners were belatedly trying to establish true urbanism through vibrant downtowns and pedestrian-friendly neighborhoods. In both old cities and new, there was rising interest in the use of parks to help shape vitality.

Acreage and facilities—According to "2009 City Park Facts," produced by the Center for City Park Excellence, the 77 largest cities have 184 different agencies providing parks, including city, county, metro, State or Federal entities, as well as port authorities, water districts, and conservancies. Together, they operate more than 1.3 million acres of parkland. These systems range from almost 40 percent of a city's land area down to 1.6 percent, with a median of 8.6

percent. Measured per capita, they provide from 1,794 acres per 1,000 residents down to only 1 acre per 1,000, with a median of 12.9 acres.

There are several ways to compare cities with regard to their parkland. As a percentage of total city area, New York City, San Francisco, Boston, San Diego, Raleigh,NC, and Austin,TX are among the leaders. But very crowded cities, of course, cannot provide as much parkland on a per-capita basis; under that alternative measure, Jacksonville, FL, Albuquerque, El Paso, Virginia Beach, and Kansas City, MO, do particularly well. (The city that offers the most parkland is sprawling Anchorage, thanks to having Chugach State Park inside its municipal borders.) Older, more densely-populated cities that still provide residents with relatively big swaths of green space include St. Paul, Minneapolis, Washington, DC, and Seattle (table 5.4).

City parks vary not only in size but also by type. Some are natural areas—usually pristine wetlands, forests, or deserts—left largely undisturbed and managed for their conservation and ecological values. In some cases, they are formerly used areas that have been left to return to nature. While they may have trails and occasional benches, they are not developed for recreation much beyond walking. Designed areas, on the other hand, are parklands that have been created, constructed, planted, and managed primarily for human use. They include playgrounds, neighborhood parks, mini-parks, picnic

Table 5.4—Park acres per 1,000 persons in selected U.S. cities, grouped by city population density levels, 2009

City	Population	Park acres	Acres per 1,000 persons
High density cities			
Washington, DC	588,292	7,617	12.9
Philadelphia	1,449,634	10,886	7.5
Los Angeles	3,834,340	23,761	6.2
New York	8,310,212	38,229	4.6
Miami	424,662	1,359	3.2
Intermediate-high density cities			
St. Paul, MN	277,251	4,976	17.9
Oakland	401,489	5,217	13.0
Seattle	594,210	6,170	10.4
Cleveland	438,042	3,127	7.1
Anaheim, CA	333,249	864	2.6
Intermediate-low density cities			
San Diego	1,266,731	45,492	35.9
Phoenix	1,552,259	41,980	27.0
San Antonio	1,328,984	19,620	14.8
Atlanta	519,145	3,846	7.4
Mesa, AZ	452,933	2,619	5.8
Low density cities			
Jacksonville	805,605	103,760	128.8
Albuquerque	518,271	34,630	66.8
Austin	743,074	26,271	35.4
Tulsa	384,037	7,336	19.1
Tucson	525,529	3,658	7.0

Source: The Trust for Public Land (2009).

meadows, sports fields, plazas, boulevards, and all areas served by roadways, parking lots, and service buildings and facilities. Most cities have also reserved land for future parks that are not yet open to the public. While the ratio of natural to developed parkland varies greatly city to city, in the aggregate the total among the Nation's 77 largest cities comes to an almost perfect 50-50 split.[2]

In 2009, big-city park departments offered their 56 million urban residents myriad recreational opportunities: 12,712 basketball hoops, 10,419 playgrounds, 9,078 tennis courts, 8,575 ball diamonds, 2,362 recreation centers, 1,290 swimming pools, 386 golf courses, 243 beaches, 183 nature/environment centers, 146 ice skating rinks, and 3,957 miles of bikeways. In addition to these more traditional opportunities, there are newer types of facilities and opportunities now being provided: 466 dog parks, 198 skateboard parks, and 12,988 community garden plots. (For hungry park-goers, there are also 268 restaurants and kiosks.)

In addition to land, park departments naturally need sufficient public revenue for land management and programs. This entails both an adequate operating budget and a regular infusion of capital funds for major construction, repairs, and land acquisition. A detailed survey of the 77 biggest cities showed that, in fiscal year 2007, the "adjusted park budget"—the amount spent by each city on parks operations and capital combined—came to $5.7 billion, or an average of $99 per resident.[3]

Naturally, the average masks considerable variation. The best funded major city park and recreation departments in 2007 were in San Francisco ($300 per resident), Chandler, AZ ($279), Washington, DC ($277), Seattle ($259), and Minneapolis ($214). On the other hand, several cities spent less than $50 per resident. On average, the per-resident spending broke out at $71 on operational costs and $28 on capital improvements and land acquisition in that fiscal year.

Another critical asset to public parks is an effective, complementary private fundraising effort—one that serves not only signature parks but also the whole system. Although private efforts must never be designed to let the local government off the hook, they can be valuable in undertaking monumental projects or in raising work to levels of beauty and extravagance that government on its own could not afford. Private campaigns are also effective in mobilizing the generosity of wealthy individuals, corporations, and foundations that would not contribute to government agencies.

---

[2] This data refers only to the principal park agencies in each city; subsidiary agencies, including Federal, State, county, and regional agencies with urban parkland were not tabulated as to natural and developed.

[3] In order to maintain a "level playing field" between cities, such non-standard big-ticket items as park department-owned stadiums, zoos, museums, aquariums, and cemeteries were not tabulated.

What makes city parks work?—Cities are economic entities made up of structures entwined with open space. In successful cities, private and public spaces complement each other with the sum greatly surpassing the parts. Thus, the value of a park system extends beyond the boundaries of the parks themselves. In fact, a well done city park system is a form of "natural infrastructure" that provides many services for the city as a whole including:

- cleaner air, as trees and vegetation filter out pollutants by day and produce oxygen by night
- cleaner water, as roots trap silt and contaminants before they flow into streams, rivers, and lakes
- reduced health costs from sedentary syndromes such as obesity and diabetes, thanks to walking and running trails, sports fields, recreation centers, bikeways, golf courses, and other opportunities for physical fitness
- improved learning opportunities from "outdoor classrooms" in forests, meadows, wetlands, and even recovering brownfields and greyfields (previously used tracts)
- increased urban tourism based on attractive, successful parks, with resulting increased commerce and sales tax revenue
- increased business vitality based on employer and employee attraction to quality parks
- natural beauty and respite from traffic and noise.

Taken collectively, well designed and managed parks have been shown not only to increase the property value of nearby residences, but to be so valuable that they routinely generate far more economic value than they cost to maintain.

Proximity—With 83 percent of Americans living in metropolitan areas, the actual location of parks may be more important than the amount of acreage or the number of facilities. The general philosophy behind city park systems is that they are to be accessible to everyone regardless of residence, physical abilities, or financial resources.

Large unspoiled natural areas, of course, cannot be equidistant from all city residents since they are predicated on topography, such as mountains, wetlands, canyons, and stream valleys, and on availability of space. But created parks—squares, plazas, playgrounds, neighborhood parks, ball fields, linear greenways—can usually be sited in such a way that every neighborhood and every resident is served. Preferably, people and parks are no farther than 10 minutes apart by foot in dense areas or 10 minutes apart by bicycle in spread-out sections. These standards take into account such significant physical barriers as uncrossable highways, streams, and railroad corridors, or heavily-trafficked roads. Numerous modern studies show that modern Americans are rarely willing to walk a mile or more on foot. Some are physically incapable of that distance; others are scared to cross

neighborhood boundaries; others simply do not have the time. When seniors, children and pets are taken into consideration, the time or capability equations become even more complex. Not every city has a resident distance goal, but some do. These range from one-tenth of a mile to a mini park in Chicago, to a quarter-mile to a neighborhood park in Detroit, Miami, St. Paul, and Seattle, and to 2 miles to a community park in Atlanta and Charlotte, NC.

Parks and transportation—Many people, of course, are so far from a park that they are forced to skip the trip or else must drive. But driving brings its own issues: knowing few if any of the people when you arrive, getting younger children and teens to the park and back again, finding places to park a vehicle, impacting the surrounding neighborhood with a flood of cars, and devoting more of the park's surface area to parking. In addition, without the walk the fitness and health values go down. According to a 2004 study on obesity, community design, and physical activity, every additional hour per day spent in a car is associated with a 6 percent increase in the likelihood of obesity. Conversely, each additional kilometer walked per day is associated with a 4.8 percent reduction in the likelihood of obesity (Frank and others 2004). The National Household Transportation Survey also shows a nearly identical level of growth between miles driven in cars and the percentage of Americans classified as overweight.

Parks surrounded by low-density housing with little or no mass transportation are only accessible to those with automobiles. Parks can serve a wider range of residents when

Children take over the road with bicycles and scooters in Piedmont Park. Atlanta's most visited park receives upwards of 3 million users per year. (Photo courtesy of Piedmont Park Conservancy, Atlanta, GA)

the parks are close to where many people live or work and when the parks are easily reachable by a range of good transit options. Most of the high-population-density cities rely on residents to walk, use mass transit, or ride bikes to visit parks. It is the mid-density and low-density cities that often have problems with too many cars.

Eight of the 11 most heavily used parks in American cities have subway or light-rail access within one-quarter of a mile of the park, and all of these parks have bus service that comes even closer than a quarter of a mile of the park. Outside of New York City (whose parks almost invariably have subway service), examples of parks best-served by rail are the Boston Common, Forest Park in St. Louis, Hermann Park in Houston, Millennium Park in Chicago, and the National Mall in Washington, DC.

Naturally, instituting transit service, especially rail, to major parks is expensive. But another way to increase access, bringing the parks to the people, is to use trails and greenways as fingers into outlying neighborhoods. Greenways along creeks and waterfronts, as well as trails along abandoned rail

Baltimore residents attend a festival near the famous Pagoda in Patterson Park. The city's oldest park, Patterson was created in 1827. (Photo courtesy of Friends of Patterson Park)

corridors, serve as slender parks on their own and also allow users to walk, run, bike, and rollerblade to major parks along the route. In Washington, DC, the Capital Crescent Trail (built on a former railroad) enables thousands of residents and suburbanites to access both Rock Creek Park and the National Mall, neither of which provide more than minimal space for auto storage. The more people living within walking distance of a park, the fewer who need to drive and deal with their cars when they get there.

Parks and revitalization—Parks can play a role in urban renewal. While new or expanding cities form parks mostly through conservation (saving virgin lands like forests, farms, and ranches), in built-out cities, it's just the opposite: parks themselves are a type of development—and they often serve as the anchor for the old and new buildings around them. From Boston to San Francisco, even cities that are considered "built out" have used redevelopment to increase parkland. Outmoded facilities like closed shipyards, underutilized rail depots, abandoned factories, decommissioned military bases and filled landfills have been converted to parks, and sunken highways and railroad tracks have been decked over with parkland. Denver de-paved its old Stapleton Airport, restoring the original land contours and transforming it into a 4,700-acre "walkable," mixed-use community with 1,100 acres of parks.

In New York City, the New York City Department of Parks and Recreation collaborated with the New York City Department of Transportation to convert 2,008 asphalt traffic triangles and paved medians into "greenstreets"—pocket parks and tree-lined malls that are maintained by community residents and businesspersons. In other cities, school systems and park departments have broken down historic bureaucratic barriers and signed joint use agreements to make schoolyard fields available for neighborhood use after school hours.

City parks do not exist in a vacuum. Every city is a complex and intricate interplay between the private space of homes and offices; the semi-public spaces of shops, stores, and restaurants; and the fully public space of parks, plazas, streets, preserves, and natural areas. When cities apply the principles of smart growth—affordable housing, increased density, green buildings, mixed-use areas, "walkability," better transit—with increased green infrastructure such as parks, a vision of park systems enriching cities will reciprocate with cities nourishing their parks. Carefully considered growth has the potential to convert cities from sprawl, vacant property or disinvestment into lively, beautiful neighborhoods with parks, plazas, and bike lanes supporting jobs, retail, housing, and other amenities. This is the vision and the reality of urban parks in 21st century America.

End Invited Paper

State Government as a Recreation Provider

Origins of the State park systems and of the role of States in providing outdoor recreation opportunities were expressed in an anthology to the 1930 National Conference on State Parks written by Herbert Evison (1930):

> It was not until automobiles became fairly numerous, and sufficient good or fair roads had been built to permit ready access to areas at a distance from centers of population, that the State-park movement may be said to have been fairly launched. Such State parks as had been established in the meantime had generally been created to preserve some outstandingly scenic area, such as the Niagara Reservation in New York or the Yosemite Valley in California, and resulted from a strong public opinion that was concerned as a rule only with a single project, and that had little or no vision of a day when most of our States would be building up systems of State parks.

Outdoor recreation resources provided by the 50 State governments occupy a sort-of middle ground between the heavily natural-land dependent Federal agencies and the much more facility and development-oriented local governments. The late well-known recreation economist Marion Clawson and others chose the term "intermediate" as the best descriptor of State government recreation resources. But that is really just a generic description of the resources that fall somewhere between city parks and recreation areas and the Federal wilderness system and other primitive backcountry resources.

State government recreation resources defy easy categorization because they cover the full spectrum from highly developed urban recreation areas to wild and remote land and water areas. Though not nearly to the extent of the Federal Government, State governments provide some backcountry opportunities, mainly for hiking and scenery appreciation. A key feature of most State resources is their proximity to populated areas and, thus, users. This is especially true in the Eastern United States, where State parks and other State resources play a much more significant role in providing outdoor recreation opportunities than in the West, where Federal land dominates.

Every State has a division or agency dedicated to providing outdoor recreation and educational opportunities: the State park system. A "system" is the correct terminology, given that these organizations are comprised of much more that just State parks alone. Most of the State park systems have received considerable investments in facilities and services from their State legislatures—though some States lag far behind others—and are managed specifically not only to provide outdoor recreation opportunities for State residents but also to attract tourists and their associated spending.

The two other State agencies that provide resources for outdoor recreation do so as a by-product of their primary missions: State forests and State wildlife and fish areas. These resources are not managed directly for recreation, but recreation is an allowable use on many, if not most, of the properties. In some States, these properties are not really promoted or advertised as public use areas, at least not nearly to the degree that State park systems are. Almost all of the State forest and wildlife and fish areas are lightly developed in terms of facilities, providing the kinds of backcountry and primitive recreational experiences that are not available in some State parks. Some States do not even have a recognized recreation program within their State forestry and wildlife divisions, but recreation occurs on those areas nonetheless.

A fourth State government recreation resource that warrants mentioning is the State trust land. Though limited to the States west of the Mississippi River, the State trust or school lands play an important role in providing undeveloped, natural land and water, mostly for the traditional pursuits of hunting and fishing. Perhaps just as important, they often provide access to other public lands through leases or use agreements with other State agencies. Recreation-related data about these other State agencies are limited, so the main focus of the State government section of this report is the State park systems, supplemented by brief sections on State forests, State wildlife and fish areas, and State trust lands.

State Park Systems

In 1938, the National Park Service prepared a report for the Land Planning Committee of the National Resources Board on Recreational Use of the Land in the United States. That report concluded that:

> [T]oday [in 1938], 46 of the 48 States possess State parks or areas differently named, but set aside wholly or primarily for recreational use—Colorado and Montana being the exceptions. Their holdings total approximately 3,755,985.49 acres. Accurate figures on attendance are not procurable, since few States take them, but in 1930 the National Conference on State Parks estimated, on the basis of reports received from nearly all of the States, that it was approximately 45,000,000 in that year. Figures submitted to the National Resources Board in August of this year indicate a 1933 attendance of approximately 61,297,683 persons. In addition, it is estimated that State forests and game and fish properties in 23 States have approximately 5,000,000 visitors each year.

State parks have expanded over the years and have become a major source of outdoor recreation opportunity.

Keyhole State Park near Moorcroft, WY. (Photograph courtesy of Wyoming State Parks)

We use two principal sources of State park systems data in this section. First is the National Association of State Park Directors (NASPD), an organization founded in 1962, which lists first among its five goals "to provide a common forum for the exchange of information about State park programs." This goal is a major focus of NASPD and is accomplished through the organization's Annual Information Exchange (AIX) which is managed in partnership with the Department of Parks, Recreation, and Tourism Management at North Carolina State University. AIX data covering the period July 1, 2008, through June 30, 2009, are presented in this chapter. Each year the AIX compiles basic statistical information about the systems in each State covering inventory (land and water), facilities, visitation and use, capital expenses, financing, personnel, and park support groups. We present here only the inventory and facilities portions of the AIX, except for a short analysis of concessions data in chapter 4.

Despite relatively good control over the data collection process by the NASPD and its academic partners, there are still nuances and caveats about making data trend comparisons. This is true for three basic reasons. First, the AIX relies on each individual State to complete and return the standardized questionnaire; however, some States simply do not respond or submit an incomplete form. The second issue is that consistency of record-keeping within a State is sometimes not maintained due to staff turnovers, changes in department operating procedures, database systems, and the like. A third problem is that management responsibilities within State natural resource departments occasionally change too, such as a State parks system site being reclassified, transferred out of the department, or shut down. All of these are reasons that hamper consistent data collection and comparability. Despite these concerns about consistency, they are not serious enough to preclude a discussion of trends for some of the basic statistics of State park system inventory and facilities.

A second source of data is an individual park area inventory across the 50 States conducted during 2009 by the Forest Service, U.S. Department of Agriculture (specifically, the Southern Research Station research work unit in Athens, GA) and the University of Georgia. Basic data about the size (acreage), location (latitude/longitude), and site type or classification were collected on every State park system unit based on available information from State government Web sites, printed materials, and email queries. This is the only source of data available at the individual State park resolution level.

Recreation resources in the State Park Systems—
States manage more than 6,500 individual parks and other categories of areas covering nearly 14 million acres (table 5.5), representing a 16 percent increase in areas and a 6 percent increase in total acreage since 2002. An area is any managed entity that is summarized in one of five system categories: State parks, recreation areas, historic sites, natural areas, and other areas. State parks, the flagship category, are always identified and named as such and typically provide a level of visitor facilities and services that indicates a significant investment from the State. Across all States, parks are most consistently and easily categorized for reporting purposes. Most of the growth in both State park system areas and acreage occurred in the historic site, natural areas, and other areas categories. While some real growth in the number of areas undoubtedly occurred, much of the 16 percent increase can be explained by either re-classifications within State properties or by more complete reporting by the State agencies. This is undoubtedly the case in the North region. "Other areas" is a miscellaneous category that may include State forests, fish and wildlife areas, and such. Some of the "new" properties may have simply been transferred from another State entity such as a State forestry agency.

State parks represent one-third of all State park system units in the United States and nearly two-thirds of the total acreage (fig. 5.5). State recreation areas appear most frequently in the Pacific Coast region with more than half of the total U.S. acreage in this classification (table 5.5). Excluding Alaska, however, this percentage drops to about 37 percent. Nearly half of State historic sites are located in the North, but the South and Pacific Coast each trail the North closely in historic site acreage indicating larger sites on average in those regions. Nationwide, historic sites comprise 9 percent of all State park system units, but they make up < 1 percent of the total acreage. In many States, however, historic sites are administered through travel and tourism divisions, departments of cultural resources, or other agencies rather than through the State park system.

About 57 percent of all State park system units in the Nation are located in the North, which has twice as many areas as any other region. This number is skewed somewhat by New York, which reported more than 1,000 State forests and fish and wildlife areas that are managed by the State's Department of Environmental Conservation. The North and Pacific Coast regions lead with a near-identical 5.2 million acres, each having about 37 percent of the total U.S. system (fig. 5.6). Almost 70 percent of all U.S. State park system areas and slightly more than half of all acreage are in the two eastern regions. Alaska has the most acreage of any State, more than twice that of the State with the next largest, California. With Alaska and its huge parks excluded, the eastern proportion of acreage rises to nearly 70 percent, with almost 49 percent of the 10.6 million non-Alaskan acreage in the North region.

Though the total amount of State park system acreage is just a fraction, about 2 percent, of the amount of Federal land in the United States, the key to its effectiveness is location and accessibility. First and foremost, unlike Federal land, State park land is not heavily concentrated in the Western States. State park system units exist in all 50 States and are generally evenly distributed geographically within each State (fig. 5.7). Moreover, a great number of State park units are located in close proximity to counties with high population density, especially the highest population concentrations of more than 500 people per square mile. A few examples from figure 5.7 are the numerous parks around the greater New York City area, in New England, and surrounding the metropolitan areas of southern California and northern California's Bay Area. The large number of urban-proximate parks is complemented by an equally large number of State park units in more rural and remote areas, where their contributions to local and regional economic developments are significant.

Another indicator of the extent of State park systems in the United States is acreage by county (fig. 5.8). Noteworthy is not only the large number (a majority) of U.S. counties that have State park acreage, but also the extensive acreages of 7,000 acres or more in some counties. New England States, Florida, Minnesota, and California are examples. Further, State parks are distributed throughout the 14 ecosystem divisions as identified by Forest Service geographer Robert G. Bailey (Bailey 1995) (fig. 5.9). About one-half of 1 percent of the U.S. land area is protected in State park systems (table 5.6). Six of the 14 divisions have more than 1.0 percent of their area thus protected, six have < 0.5 percent, and two divisions equal the national percentage of 0.5 percent. The Savanna, Marine, Tundra, and Mediterranean divisions are the leading divisions in terms of proportion protected in State parks, however, Savanna and Marine are two of the three smallest divisions in total area. Temperate Steppe and Tropical/Subtropical Steppe have the smallest percentage protected with 0.1 percent. Temperate Steppe has by far the largest land area of any division with nearly one-fourth of the total U.S. land area.

One difficulty with the AIX data is with those units which are not classified as State parks, recreation areas, or historic sites. (The Southern Research Station database was limited to these classes with very few miscellaneous sites included.) These three categories are mostly straightforward across all States. The other two classifications, "natural areas" and "other areas," are considerably less standardized from State to State. The natural areas class may include environmental education and scientific units, in addition to State natural areas and preserves. Natural areas are by far most prevalent in the South, with more than half of the Nation's 1.1 million acres of State natural areas. The generic "other areas" category may include forests, fish and wildlife areas, and various other miscellaneous State park system sites that vary by State. These unclassified sites are particularly numerous in the North region. They comprise more than one-fourth of all State park system units nationwide and about 18 percent of the acreage.

Though State parks are not exactly an "equalizer" for the relative lack of Federal land in the East region, their greater presence in the East gives them a more prominent role in public sector recreation opportunities than in the West Region. Still, given the lower population in most of the West, there are more State park system acres per capita in the West than in the Eastern States (table 5.7). Nationally, there are 46 State park system acres for every 1,000 residents, which represent an increase of < 1 percent since 2002. This limited growth was due primarily to reclassification of other areas to State park status in the North while the other three regions showed declines in State park system acres between 2002 and 2009. Further, nationwide per capita increases in historic sites, natural areas, and other areas masked the decline in State parks and recreation areas, the two classes used most frequently for outdoor recreation. State park acres per capita decreased in every region and recreation area acres per capita dropped in all but the North. (See Web site appendix table A5.7 and A5.8, respectively, for State park system acreage and per capita statistics by State.)

State recreation areas, which are frequently characterized by smaller acreage and more concentrated uses, are most prevalent in the Pacific Coast region, with about 54 percent of the Nation's total acres (table 5.5). Acreage in State recreation areas has contracted slightly since 2002, either through reclassifications or closures. Although frequently the urban units of many State systems are designated as "recreation areas" (as opposed to State parks), many if not most of the State recreation areas on the West Coast are State beaches and Pacific Ocean access sites. Almost three-fourths of historic sites are located in the eastern regions, but the proportion of acreage is lower due to the presence of some large historic site properties in the West, particularly in California. Massachusetts ranks second in historic site acreage. Land

Table 5.5—Number and acres of State park system units by type of unit and region in 2009

Type of State park system area	Units	North	Percent	South	Percent	Rocky Mountains	Percent	Pacific Coast	Percent	United States	Percent change, 2002–2009
State parks	No.	1,128	52.3	462	21.4	279	12.9	287	13.3	2,156	7.9
	Acres	2,203,943	24.8	1,487,408	16.7	903,049	10.2	4,299,731	48.3	8,894,131	1.9
Recreation areas	No.	227	28.9	94	12.0	138	17.6	327	41.6	786	-2.8
	Acres	282,216	23.3	81,155	6.7	191,155	15.8	658,760	54.3	1,213,286	2.7
Historic sites	No.	302	49.6	143	23.5	60	9.9	104	17.1	609	18.9
	Acres	36,104	31.1	32,387	27.9	16,885	14.6	30,642	26.4	116,018	33.2
Natural areas	No.	428	60.2	76	10.7	149	21.0	58	8.2	711	16.7
	Acres	189,366	16.9	556,948	49.8	230,547	20.6	141,713	12.7	1,118,574	16.1
Other areas	No.	1,669	73.0	29	1.3	423	18.5	165	7.2	2,286	33.0
	Acres	2,472,222	93.6	59,555	2.3	54,177	2.1	56,110	2.1	2,642,064	19.9
All areas	No.	3,754	57.3	804	12.3	1,049	16.0	941	14.4	6,548	15.8
	Acres	5,183,851	37.1	2,217,453	15.9	1,395,813	10.0	5,176,228	37.0	13,973,344	6.2

Change is measured from Annual Information Exchange data collected during the period July 1, 2001 to June 30, 2002.
Note: Region percentages sum across to 100; may not equal 100 exactly due to rounding. Natural areas include environmental education sites and areas classified as scientific sites. Other areas include forests, fish and wildlife areas, and other miscellaneous State park system sites.
Source: Leung and others (2010).

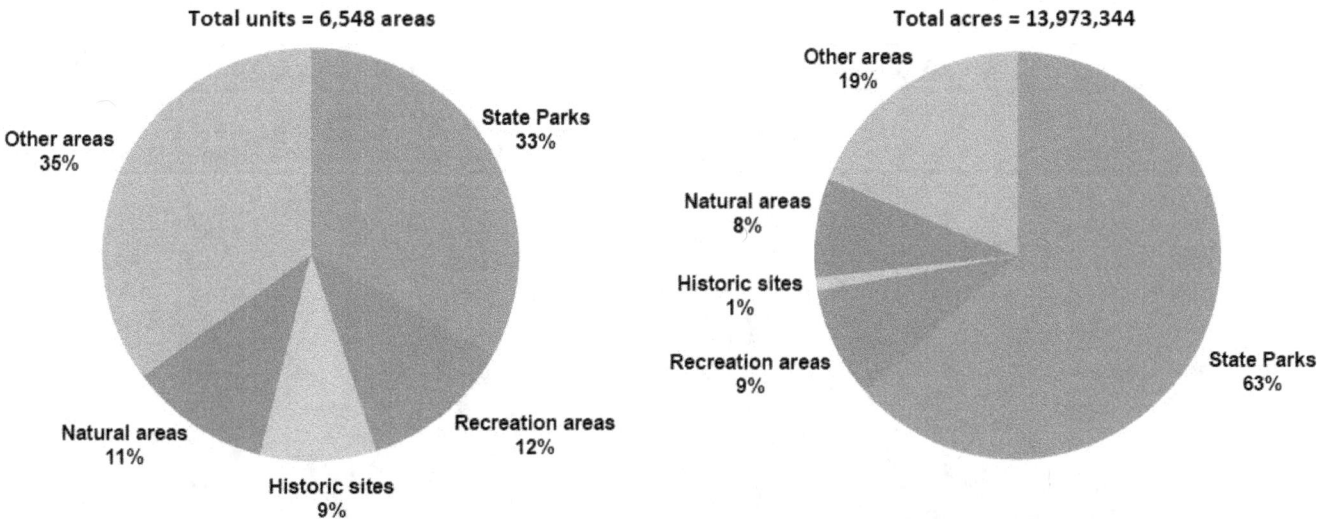

Figure 5.5—Percent of State park system units and acres in the United States by type of system area, 2009. Note: Natural areas include environmental education sites and areas classified as scientific sites. Other areas include forests, fish and wildlife areas, and other miscellaneous State park system sites. Source: Leung and others (2010).

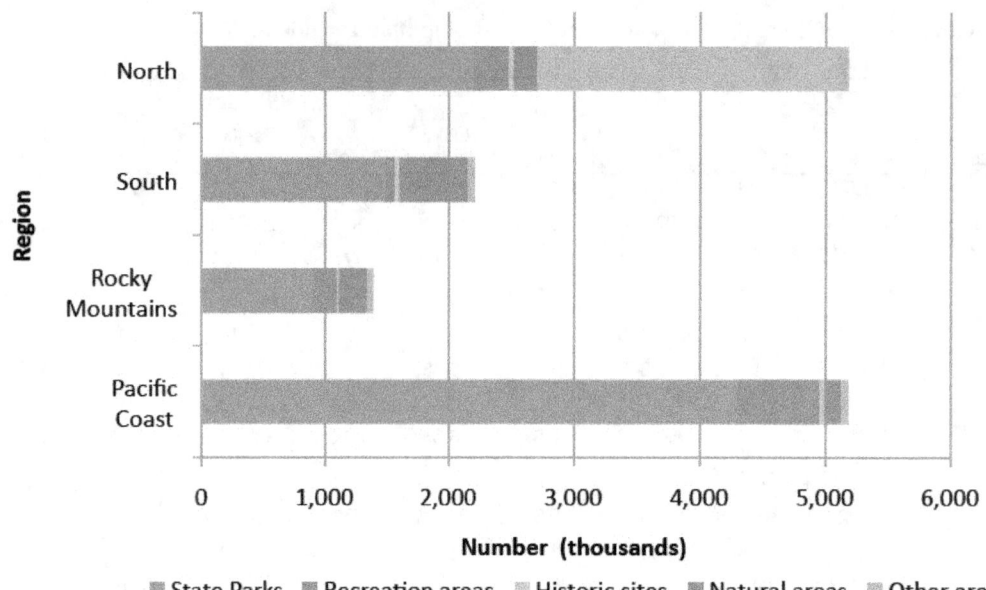

Figure 5.6—Acres in State park systems by type of area and region, 2009. Source: Leung and others (2010).

Table 5.6—State park system acres by Bailey's ecosystem division and percent of division protected in State park systems in 2009

		Ecosystem division			State park systems		
Code	Name	Acres (thousands)	Percent of total U.S. area		Acres	Percent of total State park area	Percent protected in State park systems
120	Tundra	90,816.0	4.2		1,500.0	12.7	1.7
130	Subarctic	92,864.0	4.3		438.0	3.7	0.5
210	Warm Continental	122,176.0	5.6		1,493.0	12.7	1.2
220	Hot Continental	239,680.0	11.0		2,430.0	20.6	1.0
230	Subtropical	268,736.0	12.4		1,043.0	8.9	0.4
240	Marine	43,712.0	2.0		1,064.0	9.0	2.4
250	Prairie	190,912.0	8.8		527.0	4.5	0.3
260	Mediterranean	87,808.0	4.0		1,468.0	12.5	1.7
310	Tropical/Subtropical Steppe	162,432.0	7.5		158.0	1.3	0.1
320	Tropical/Subtropical Desert	142,784.0	6.6		541.0	4.6	0.4
330	Temperate Steppe	520,512.0	24.0		588.0	5.0	0.1
340	Temperate Desert	198,272.0	9.1		325.0	2.8	0.2
410	Savanna	4,992.0	0.2		173.0	1.5	3.5
420	Rainforest	4,160.0	0.2		22.0	0.2	0.5
	All divisions	2,169,856.0	99.9		11,770.0	100.0	0.5

Note: Total State park system acres in this database does not match total acres in Leung and others (2010) because their database includes 'other areas' that consist of some State forests, fish and wildlife areas, and other miscellaneous State park system sites.
Sources: U.S. Geological Service (2004), USDA Forest Service (2009a).

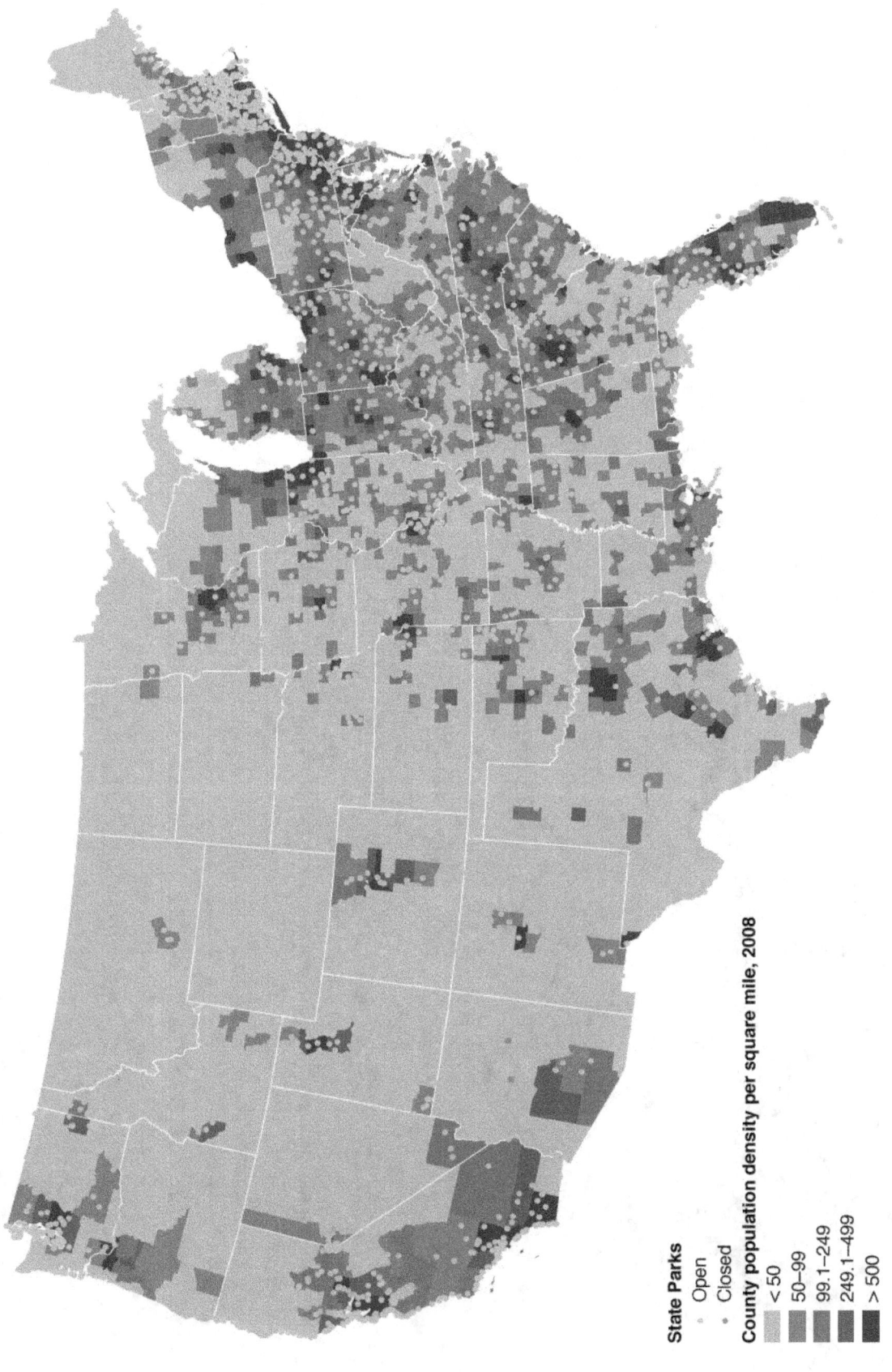

State Parks
- Open
- Closed

County population density per square mile, 2008
- < 50
- 50–99
- 99.1–249
- 249.1–499
- > 500

Figure 5.7—State park system units in the contiguous United States (2009) and county population density (persons per square mile), 2008. Source: USDA Forest Service (2009a).

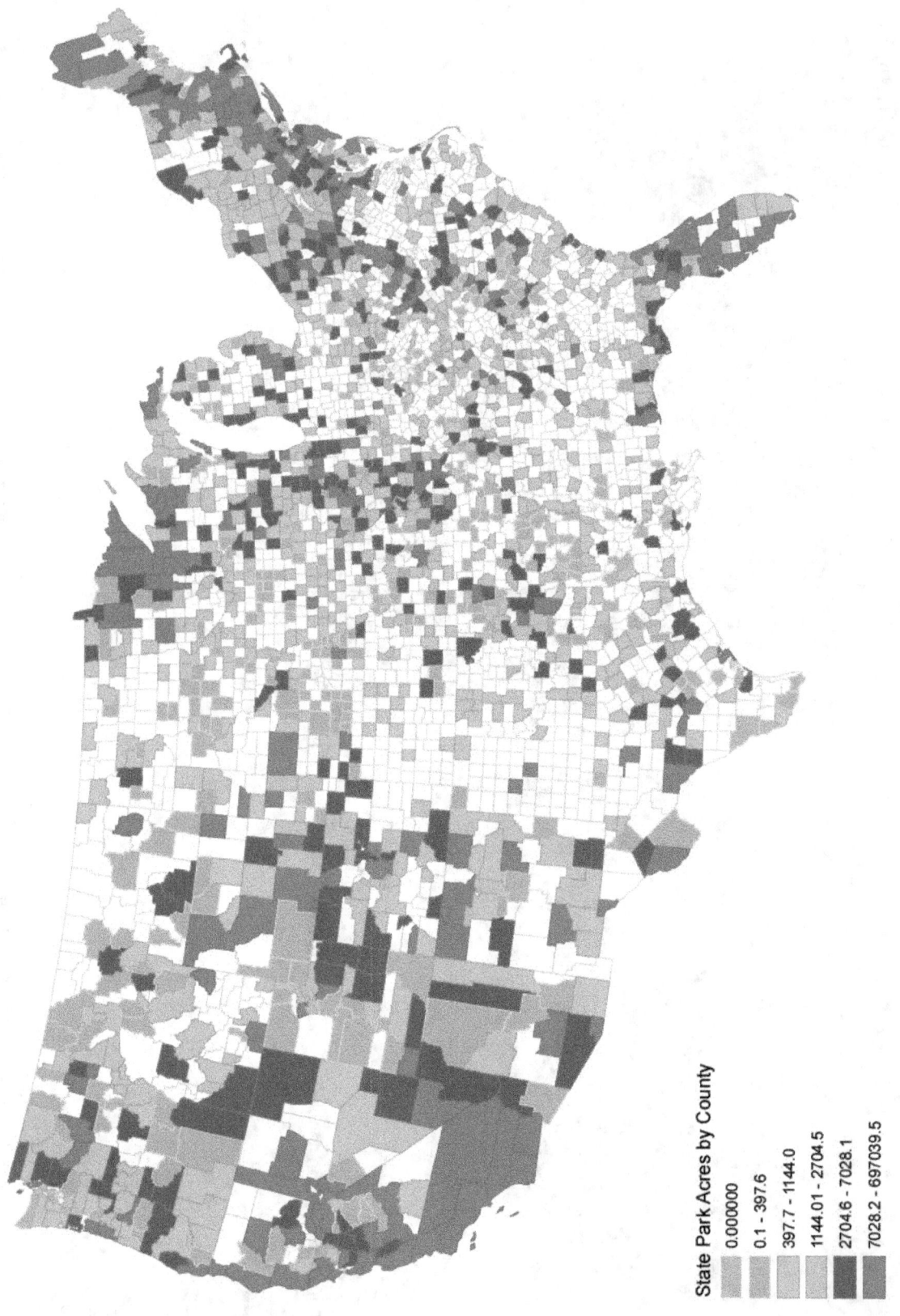

State Park Acres by County

	0.000000
	0.1 - 397.6
	397.7 - 1144.0
	1144.01 - 2704.5
	2704.6 - 7028.1
	7028.2 - 697039.5

Figure 5.8—State park system acres by county in the contiguous United States, 2009. Source: USDA Forest Service (2009a).

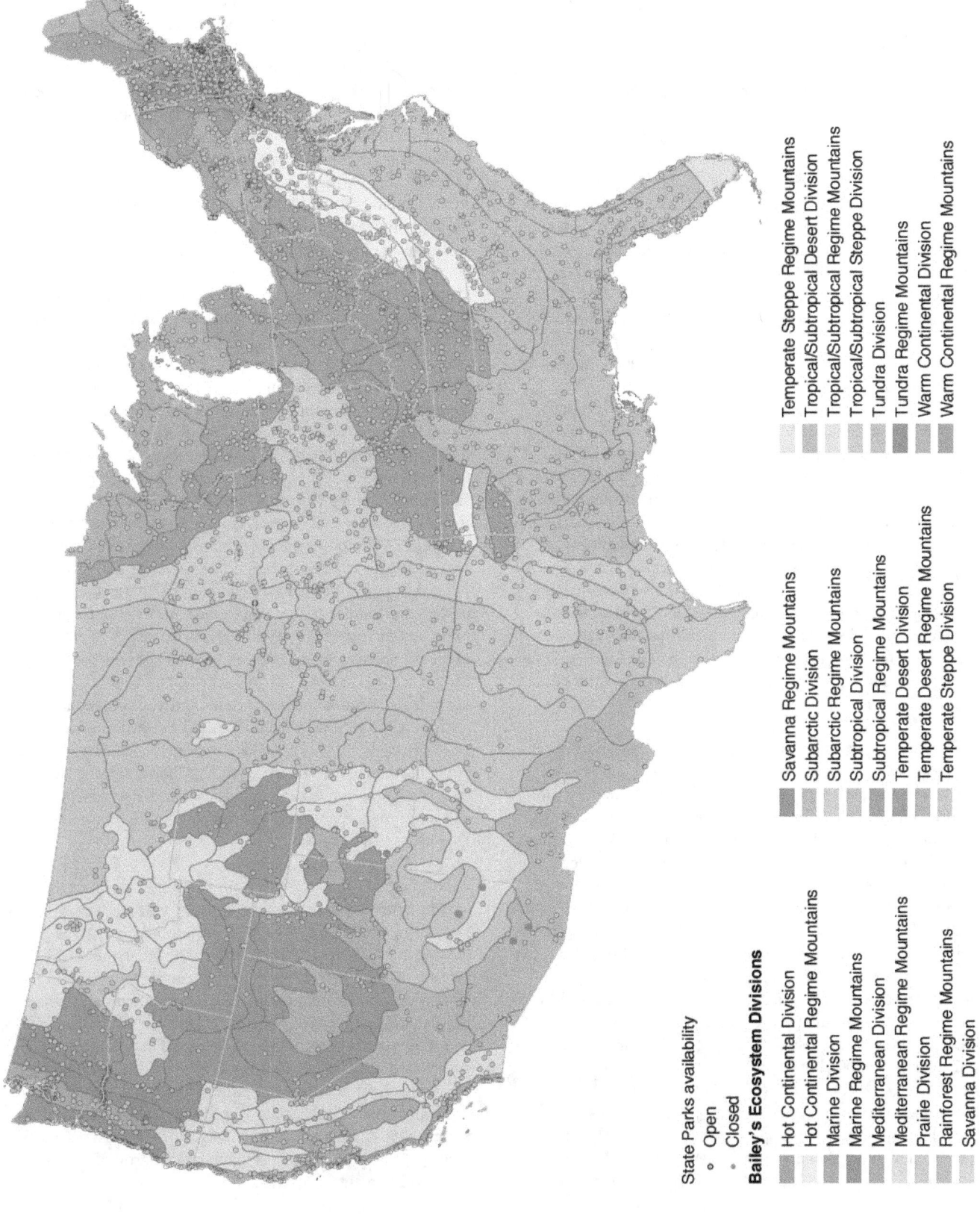

State Parks availability
  ○ Open
  • Closed

Bailey's Ecosystem Divisions

▨	Hot Continental Division
▨	Hot Continental Regime Mountains
▨	Marine Division
▨	Marine Regime Mountains
▨	Mediterranean Division
▨	Mediterranean Regime Mountains
▨	Prairie Division
▨	Rainforest Regime Mountains
▨	Savanna Division

▨	Savanna Regime Mountains
▨	Subarctic Division
▨	Subarctic Regime Mountains
▨	Subtropical Division
▨	Subtropical Regime Mountains
▨	Temperate Desert Division
▨	Temperate Desert Regime Mountains
▨	Temperate Steppe Division

▨	Temperate Steppe Regime Mountains
▨	Tropical/Subtropical Desert Division
▨	Tropical/Subtropical Regime Mountains
▨	Tropical/Subtropical Steppe Division
▨	Tundra Division
▨	Tundra Regime Mountains
▨	Warm Continental Division
▨	Warm Continental Regime Mountains

Figure 5 9—State park system units overlaid on Bailey ecosystem divisions. Sources: USGS (2004) and USDA Forest Service (2009a).

area in historic sites grew significantly nationwide since 2002, more than 33 percent. However, this growth partly reflects the small base number of historic site acres which are by far the least of any category.

Natural areas, which include environmental education and other areas classified as "scientific" sites, are far more common in the East with 71 percent of sites and 67 percent of acreage. Areas classified as "natural areas" increased 16 percent since 2002. Florida and Colorado lead in natural area acreage by a wide margin. All totaled, the distribution of land and water in the State park systems is much more aligned to the U.S. population distribution than are the Federal resources, but their much smaller total area implies much greater use pressures too.

Facilities—Most State park system units, State parks, and State recreation areas in particular, have outdoor facilities designed to serve a variety of recreation activities. In addition, most parks and recreation areas are large enough to have significant undeveloped areas, some largely undeveloped, such as Baxter State Park in Maine. In parks that do not allow backcountry camping and backpacking, there are usually opportunities to experience nature on hiking, canoe, or other trails. At the other end of the spectrum there are a number of State units which specifically cater to the tourist market, which means full services and amenities. Frequently these State parks have the word "resort" in their name. A few States specialize in tourism with the objective of contributing to regional economic development. Table 5.8 lists the 2009 AIX count of selected recreational facilities across the State park systems by region (see Web site appendix table A5.9 for the same information by State). Figure 5.10 shows the same information broken out by region.

Campsites and trails are staples among State park recreation facilities. Most State parks offer camping facilities as a primary attraction and even more have trails, ranging from very short, highly interpreted nature trails to extensive backcountry trail systems. The 2009 AIX reports a total of nearly 5,900 separate trails in State park systems totaling almost 43,000 miles (table 5.8). The numbers represent increases of 22 percent in miles and almost 43 percent in the number of trails since 2002. The number of trails increased particularly fast in the Pacific Coast region. These numbers undoubtedly reflect many newly classified or re-classified trails, in addition to some newly developed ones. Trail reporting across States is difficult because of lack of standardized data collection and record-keeping procedures. (Three States reported no trails or trail mileage in the 2009 AIX.)

Total trail mileage managed by State park systems is just less than one-third of the approximately 133,000 trail miles provided by the National Forest System, yet the total State park system acreage is just 7 percent that of the U.S. Forest Service's total land area. Similarly, State parks provide almost three times the 14,900 miles of National Park Service trails in about one-sixth the land area. These statistics indicate the importance of State park systems in providing hiking and other trail opportunities. About 42 percent of trails and just under half of the trail mileage are in the two eastern regions. The Rocky Mountains region has the most trail mileage (although the North nearly equals it) but fewest trails, indicating the presence of long backcountry trails in mountain areas. Trails and trail mileage were among the largest facility increases per capita in the United States since 2002 (table 5.9) (fig. 5.11). Some of those gains are undoubtedly due to reclassifications or simply additions of existing trails to the State reports.

Campsites are classified as one of two types: (1) "improved" sites that typically have electric hook-ups, tent pads, picnic tables, and other improvements, and (2) "primitive" sites which have either very minimal or no developed facilities beyond being marked as a designated campsite. There are 151 more improved camping areas than primitive areas in State park systems, but the individual improved campsites outnumber primitive campsites more than threefold (table 5.8). The number of State park areas offering primitive camping increased more than 30 percent since 2002, although the total number of primitive campsites increased < 3 percent. Further, there is a rather large regional difference in the provision of improved and primitive camping areas and individual campsites. The eastern regions have nearly twice the number of improved camping areas than the western regions and more than three times the number of individual improved campsites. The West has approximately 60 percent of the primitive camping areas and campsites, with the Rocky Mountains region alone having almost 44 percent of primitive campsites, reflecting the presence of numerous backcountry settings in the mountain States. While areas that provide primitive camping on a per capita basis grew significantly since 2002, the number of campsites per 1 million residents declined by 3 percent. Improved campsites decreased 4 percent per capita nationally in that same period, with particularly sharp drops in the Pacific Coast region.

All of the other State park system recreation facilities that appear in table 5.8, i.e., cabins/cottages, golf courses, marinas, swimming pools, and stables, are also more likely to be located in the eastern regions than in the West. About 73 percent of State park areas with cabins or cottages, more than 80 percent of the total number of cabins/cottages and stables, more than 90 percent of State park golf courses (and holes), and more than 94 percent of the areas with swimming pools are located in the North and South regions. The total number of cabins or cottages in State parks grew about 10 percent, swimming pools grew about 12 percent, stables and marinas increased just slightly, and the number of golf courses and holes in State park units posted the largest growth, about 14 and 22 percent, respectively.

Table 5.7—Per capita acres of State park system units by type of area and region, and percent change from 2002 to 2009

Type of State park system area	North Acres/ 1,000 people 2009	North Percent change '02–'09	South Acres/ 1,000 people 2009	South Percent change '02–'09	Rocky Mountains Acre/ 1,000 people 2009	Rocky Mountains Percent change '02–'09	Pacific Coast Acres/ 1,000 people 2009	Pacific Coast Percent change '02–'09	United States Acres/ 1,000 people 2009	United States Percent change '02–'09
State Parks	17.7	-6.3	14.5	-2.9	32.5	-3.6	87.6	-2.7	29.3	-3.6
Recreation areas	2.3	5.6	0.8	-13.2	6.9	-11.6	13.4	-2.8	4.0	-2.9
Historic sites	0.3	141.7	0.3	-11.1	0.6	-19.7	0.6	44.2	0.4	26.7
Natural areas	1.5	7.8	5.4	2.3	8.3	8.5	2.9	32.0	3.7	9.9
Other areas	19.9	28.8	0.6	16.0	2.0	20.4	1.1	-77.5	8.7	13.4
All areas	41.7	9.6	21.6	-1.8	50.2	-2.5	105.5	-5.4	46.0	0.5

Note: Natural areas include environmental education sites and areas classified as scientific sites. Other areas include forests, fish and wildlife areas, and other miscellaneous State park system sites. U.S. population estimates are 287.73 million (2002) and 304.06 million (2008).
Source: Leung and others (2010).

Table 5.8—Number of State park system areas with selected recreation facilities and total number of facilities by region in 2009

Facility	North Number	North Percent	South Number	South Percent	Rocky Mountains Number	Rocky Mountains Percent	Pacific Coast Number	Pacific Coast Percent	United States Number	United States Percent change '02–'09
Trails: number	1,173	20.0	1,312	22.3	931	15.8	2,460	41.9	5,876	42.8
Trails: number of miles	15,447	35.9	5,941	13.8	15,858	36.9	5,735	13.3	42,980	22.0
Improved campsites: number of areas	713	40.6	439	25.0	409	23.3	194	11.1	1,755	5.2
Improved campsites: total number	87,034	53.3	36,327	22.2	24,971	15.3	15,109	9.2	163,441	1.3
Primitive campsites: number of areas	302	18.8	315	19.6	760	47.4	227	14.2	1,604	30.9
Primitive campsites: total number	12,411	24.9	8,178	16.4	21,795	43.8	7,387	14.8	49,771	2.6
Cabins: number of areas	331	44.5	208	28.0	116	15.6	88	11.8	743	27.0
Cabins: total number	3,327	45.7	2,708	37.2	724	9.9	524	7.2	7,283	9.8
Golf courses: total number	62	45.6	63	46.3	7	5.1	4	2.9	136	14.3
Golf holes: total number	1,035	46.0	1,026	45.6	144	6.4	45	2.0	2,250	21.8
Marinas: total number	135	47.2	75	26.2	61	21.3	15	5.2	286	-0.3
Swimming pools: total number	154	52.4	123	41.8	11	3.7	6	2.0	294	11.8
Stables: total number	33	33.3	54	54.5	11	11.1	1	1.0	99	2.1

Note: Also includes Annual Information Exchange data for the period July 1, 2001 to June 30, 2002. Region percentages sum across to 100; may not equal 100 exactly due to rounding.
Source: Leung and others (2010).

Table 5.9—State park system facilities per capita by region and percent change from 2002 to 2009

	North		South		Rocky Mountains		Pacific Coast		United States	
Facility	Number per 1 million people, 2009	Percent change '02–'09	Number per 1 million people, 2009	Percent change '02–'09	Number per 1 million people, 2009	Percent change '02–'09	Number per 1 million people, 2009	Percent change '02–'09	Number per 1 million people, 2009	Percent change '02–'09
Number of trails	9.4	23.6	12.8	2.9	33.5	91.5	50.1	47.5	19.3	35.2
Trails: number of miles	124.2	22.1	57.8	-0.7	570.1	-3.1	116.9	101.7	141.4	15.5
Improved campsites: number of areas	5.7	2.9	4.3	-6.6	14.7	8.2	4.0	-16.0	5.8	-0.5
Improved campsites: total number	699.8	0.1	353.4	0.7	897.7	8.7	307.9	-36.2	537.5	-4.2
Primitive campsites: number of areas	2.4	-15.9	3.1	-6.7	27.3	103.0	4.6	-5.9	5.3	23.9
Primitive campsites: total number	99.8	2.2	79.6	1.8	783.6	-8.2	150.5	-12.5	163.7	-2.9
Cabins: number of areas	2.7	30.4	2.0	12.2	4.2	6.9	1.8	20.1	2.4	20.2
Cabins: total number	26.8	9.6	26.3	-3.1	26.0	17.5	10.7	-7.5	24.0	3.9
Golf courses: total number	0.5	47.1	0.6	-9.0	0.3	-10.7	0.1	-52.9	0.5	9.8
Golf holes: total number	8.3	34.2	10.0	0.4	5.2	58.9	0.9	-40.6	7.4	15.3
Marinas: total number	1.1	-1.8	0.7	-7.6	2.2	-12.0	0.3	3.3	0.9	-6.0
Swimming pools: total number	1.2	26.5	1.2	-13.7	0.4	11.1	0.1	33.3	1.0	6.6
Stables: total number	0.3	-20.6	0.5	35.9	0.4	-33.3	0.0	-66.7	0.3	-2.9

Note: Also includes Annual Information Exchange data for the period July 1, 2001 to June 30, 2002. U.S. population estimates are 287.73 million (2002) and 304.06 million (2008). Source: Leung and others (2010).

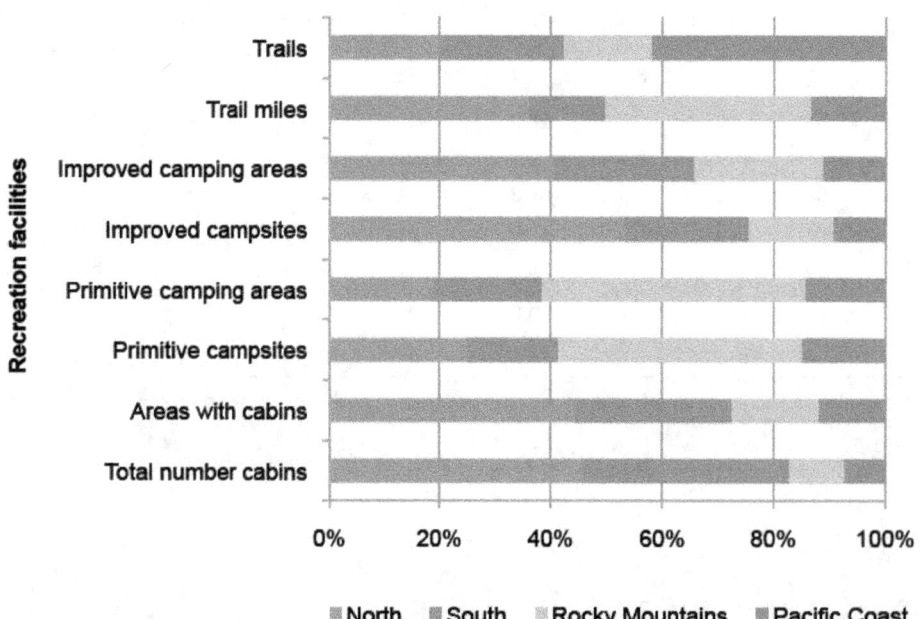

Figure 5.10—Percent of State park system areas with selected recreation facilities and total number of facilities by region, 2008. Source: Leung and others (2010).

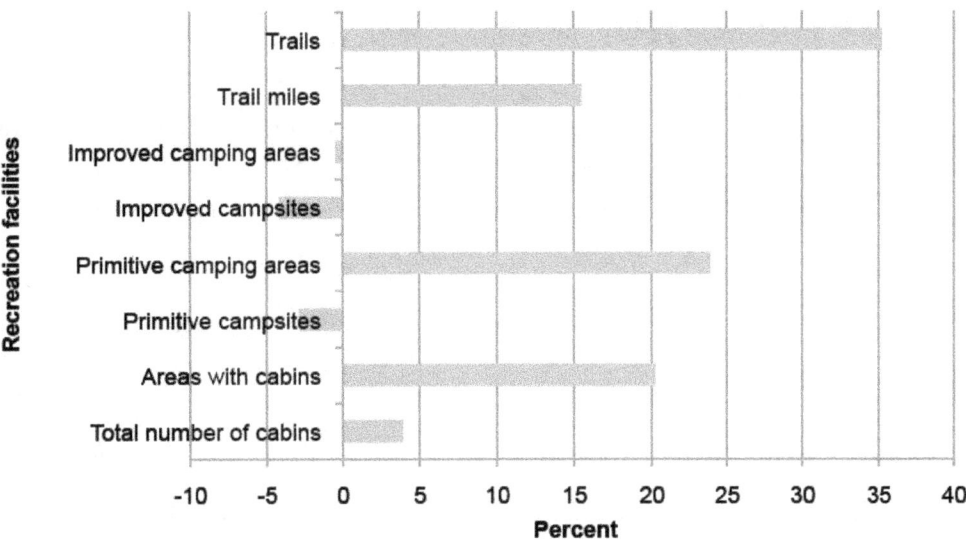

Figure 5.11—Percent change in number of State park system recreation facilities per 1 million people, 2002–2009. Source: Leung and others (2010).

State Forests

State forests provide a complement to the recreation opportunities found in State park systems in nearly every State, both through formal recreation programs and informal public access to the State-owned forests. Interestingly, many State parks began as parts of State forests in the first half of the last century. State forests tend to be less well known as recreation opportunities in that recreation is not a primary part of their modern mission. In most States, the State forestry agencies exist primarily to provide forest management assistance to private landowners, forest fire prevention and suppression, and related forest health, protection, planning, conservation, and education outreach. Urban forestry assistance is also an emphasis of many State forestry departments.

Many States manage a system of State forests and some demonstration forests that frequently are available for public recreational use. Principles of multiple-use management are often an emphasis in the State-owned forests, where recreation needs are balanced with other resource demands such as timber, water, wildlife habitat, and forage. Because recreational facility development is often minimal, State forests are especially suitable for more dispersed forms of recreation, such as wildlife observation, fishing, nature study, and horseback riding. States that have a formal recreation program within their State forest system are most likely to have developed facilities for intensive recreation use.

The National Association of State Foresters (NASF) is a nonprofit organization that represents the interests of the State forest agency directors on forestry policy issues

and legislation. One of the NASF's services is to collect information about the State forestry agencies every other year and publish the online report "State Forestry Statistics" (available through NASF or the NASF Web site: www. stateforesters.org). The latest report available is for 2006. Of interest to this assessment report are two sections entitled, "Resource Base" and "Programs/Personnel." Statistics from the 2006 NASF report are shown in table 5.10 for regions.

Nationally, there are 66.35 million acres of State-owned forest land with only about 25.3 million acres managed by State forestry agencies. The amount of State-owned forest has increased almost 8 percent since 2002. State forestry agency land area was not collected for the 2002 report, but State-owned forest data were taken from reports by the Forest Inventory and Analysis Program of the Forest Service, and include any State-owned forested land. The majority of these forest lands are managed through State departments of natural resources. Nationally, about 9 percent of all public or private forest land is State-owned. This proportion is highest in the Pacific Coast and North regions (about 13 percent) and lowest in the South. Land administered specifically by State forestry agencies makes up 3.4 percent of the Nation's forest resources. The proportion of forest land that is managed by State forest agencies is greatest among regions in the North (9.5 percent) and smallest in the South (< 1 percent).

The total national recreation spending by State forestry agencies was $23.1 million, 83 percent of which was by the North region who also had by far the largest proportion of the total budget spent on recreation at 5.2 percent. The increase in total recreation spending nationwide was $1.2 million

Table 5.10—Characteristics of State forestry agencies by region, in 2006

State forestry characteristic	Units	North Number	North Percent	South Number	South Percent	Rocky Mountains Number	Rocky Mountains Percent	Pacific Coast Number	Pacific Coast Percent	United States Number	United States Percent change '02–'09
All forest land	1,000 acres	170,587	23.0	208,317	28.1	148,200	20.0	213,980	28.9	741,084.0	0.2
State-owned forest land	1,000 acres	22,582	34.0	6,337	9.6	8,300	12.5	29,136	43.9	66,355.0	7.8
Forest land managed by State forestry agency	1,000 acres	16,235	64.3	1,498	5.9	2,503	9.9	5,033	19.9	25,268.7	na
Forest recreation budget	$1,000 (2006 $)	19,309	83.4	939	4.1	119	0.5	2,779	12.0	23,145.6	5.4
State forestry total expenditures	$1,000 (2006 $)	369,757	18.2	528,214	26.1	185,102	9.1	944,380	46.6	2,027,452.0	8.0

na = Not available
Note: Region percentages for acreages and budgets/expenditures sum across to 100; may not equal 100.0 exactly due to rounding. Illinois and Louisiana did not respond to the National Association of State Foresters (NASF) survey that provided these statistics. Forest land area for Alaska, Louisiana, and Illinois are from the 2004 NASF report. Eleven States did not provide program expenditure information; five States did not respond to the question about a forest recreation program in the State forestry agency. Forest land managed by the State forestry agency was not asked in 2002. Change in the final column for the two percentage characteristics is absolute change in percent from 2002 to 2006.
Source: National Association of State Foresters (2006).

(not adjusted for inflation), a 5 percent increase from the $21.9 million in 2002. Forest recreation accounts for just over 1 percent of the total State forest agency spending. Similar to State parks, the lack of reporting by some States hampers trend comparisons. Figure 5.12 shows how the proportions of State-owned forest land, forest area managed by State forestry agencies, total expenditures by State forestry agencies, and State forestry agency budgets for recreation are distributed across the four RPA regions. The North dominates in the amount of forest managed by State forestry agencies and in forest recreation budgets, while the Pacific Coast States are most prominent in total State-owned forest area and State forestry expenditures. The relative amounts of these indicators, except for forestry expenditures, are shown in figure 5.13 which emphasizes the significantly larger role of State forests as a provider of outdoor recreation in the North region.

State forestry statistics by State are listed in the Web appendix table A5.10 and appear in descending order of the proportion of their total State forest land that is in State forests. Minnesota, New Jersey, and Michigan manage more than 20 percent of their total State forest area as State forests. Pennsylvania, Washington, Wisconsin, Florida, Idaho, and Alaska have more than 1 million acres of land in State forests. Twenty States reported having a formal forest recreation program located within their State forestry agency, up from 19 States in 2002. The proportion of a State's total budget spent on recreation ranged from highs of 19 percent in Michigan, 15 percent in Indiana, and 13 percent in Missouri to several States with < 1 percent.

State Wildlife and Fish Areas

State wildlife and fish agencies are the third major type of State government provider of outdoor recreation opportunities. In many States they are sister agencies to the State park and State forestry agencies, all located within departments of natural resources or conservation. However, in an equal number of States, State wildlife and fish agencies are independent agencies that report directly to the governor or to a commission appointed by the governor. These agencies represent a diversity of opportunities for outdoor recreation with somewhat different policies, regulations, and resources, but the differences are not large.

One noticeable difference between State wildlife and fish systems and State park and forestry systems is the large amount of leased and cooperatively managed land and water with which they carry out their missions. State park and forest systems tend to own almost all of their properties. But much of the land and water managed by State wildlife and fish agencies is not "owned" by the State per se, and frequently the recreation management responsibilities belong to the partner or lessee. In any event, the regulation of wildlife and fish resources for recreation such as seasons, bag limits, and other rules is the administrative responsibility of the State wildlife and fish agencies.

The Wildlife Management Institute, a Washington, DC-based educational and scientific nonprofit organization, has

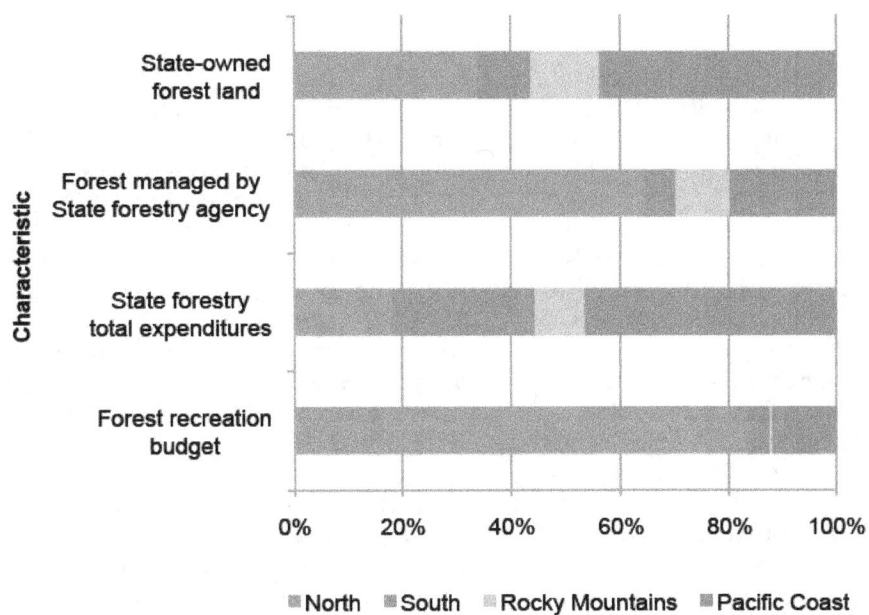

Figure 5.12—Percent of selected State forestry agency characteristics by region, 2006. Source: National Association of State Foresters (2006).

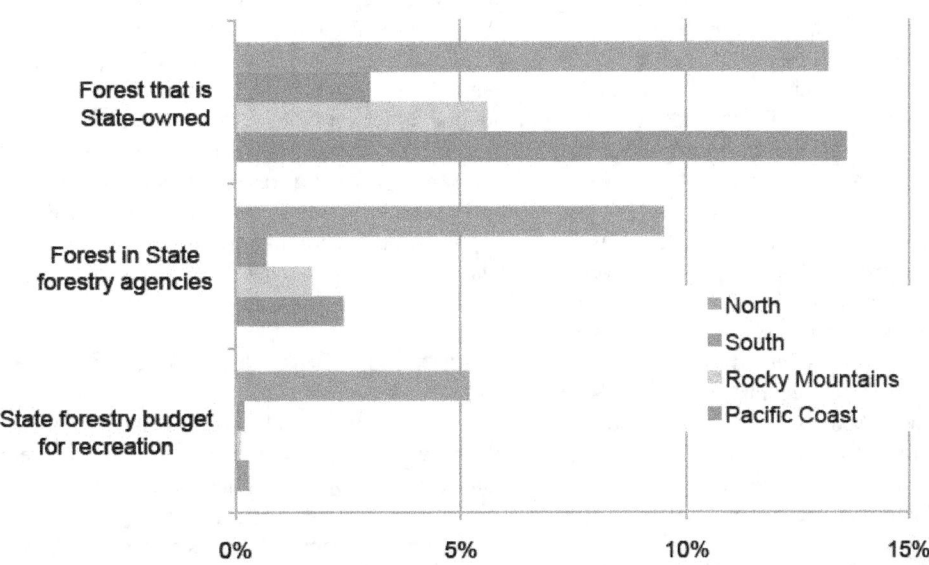

Figure 5.13—Percent of forest that is State-owned and in State forestry agencies, and percent of State forestry budgets for recreation by region, 2006.Source: National Association of State Foresters (2006).

in the past compiled information about the 50 State wildlife and fish agencies. The most recent of their reports (Wildlife Management Institute 1997) described the total land area either owned or managed by State fish and wildlife agencies in the United States. Reported was the sum of owned properties ("purchased" and "donated") and managed properties ("leased" and "easements"). Of the 30.3 million total land acres, about 11.5 million acres (38 percent) were managed rather than owned by the States. Nearly all of the managed properties, with the exception of a small fraction of land in easement, were leased from other owners. Another 57 million acres nationwide— nearly twice the amount owned or managed by States—was under cooperative agreements with other State or Federal Government agencies, industry, or with individual private landowners. Similar to State forests, the North region led other regions with just under half (49 percent) of all State wildlife and fish land and water that they either directly owned or managed. Unfortunately, no more recent summarized data for State wildlife and fish agencies exists since 1997.

Federal Land as a Recreation Resource

As described in chapter 3, there are almost 640 million acres of Federal land in the United States, about 28 percent of the total U.S. land area (table 5.11), not including U.S. Department of Defense properties, Indian tribal lands, and other miscellaneous Federal real estate. These lands are managed by seven different Federal land-managing agencies and provide valuable resources for outdoor recreation.

With the exception of some national wildlife refuges, areas reserved for science and research, and other administrative and operational sites, such as dams, nearly all Federal land is open and available to the public for recreation. In some cases, access to Federal lands is inhibited by inholdings (private land within proclamation boundaries), closed adjacent private land, and ownership fragmentation. About 97 percent of Federal land is under the jurisdiction of four agencies—Bureau of Land Management, Forest Service, U.S. Fish and Wildlife Service, and the National Park Service (fig. 5.14).

Nearly 70 percent of all Federal land is either Bureau of Land Management or Forest Service property; however, not counting Alaska, this proportion rises to 84 percent. More than 92 percent of Federal land is located in the Western United States, where essentially all Bureau of Land Management land is located. Even excluding Alaska—which has about 228.5 million Federal acres or 36 percent of the national total—Federal land is still predominantly western at 88 percent. Considering just the four largest land-managing agencies, the two western regions comprise 94 percent of the national acreage. However, considering the three water resource agencies (U.S. Army Corps of Engineers, Bureau

of Reclamation, and Tennessee Valley Authority), Federal acreage is almost evenly split between the West and East. Excluding water acres, about 37 percent of this land area is in the South and 12 percent in the North (fig. 5.15).Total Federal acreage changes very little over time, < 0.2 percent since 2002 (table 5.11) which amounts to a net decrease of about 1.4 million acres sold or transferred to other public and private entities. All of these transferred properties came from the Bureau of Land Management, most of it occurring in Alaska. Except for Alaska, there was actually a 1.5 percent increase in Federal land since 2002. \The large increase in U.S. Army Corps of Engineers acreage since 2002 is most likely the result of the change in that agency's data reporting systems whose Natural Resources Management System ceased operation in 1999.

Per capita acres of Federal land have decreased significantly, both nationally and by region. This is for the most part the result of national and regional population increases. In 2008, there were 2,105 acres per 1,000 U.S. residents (or about 2.1 acres per person). This represented a 5.6 percent decrease from the per capita amount in 2002 (fig. 5.16; and see Web appendix table A5.11 for per capita statistics by agency and region). This decline was largest in the Rocky Mountains and Pacific Coast regions, reflecting greater population growth in the West, but more modest in the eastern regions due to slower population increases. The decline in per capita Federal acres since 1995 was even more pronounced, mirroring the 14 percent population increase since then. These figures hint that there may be increasing congestion and sometimes competition for Federal recreation opportunities as population grows and the finite Federal land base remains about constant.

Recreation Management of Federal Lands

Management of Federal lands has always been and likely always will be a challenging proposition. As presented in chapter 4, development of nearby private land, increasing extractive use pressures from a variety of sources, and shrinking management budgets add to the challenge. Summaries of two papers invited for this chapter are added to address some of significant aspects of the challenge of managing recreation on Federal lands. The first of these papers, by Winter and others, describes opinions from managers concerning sustainable recreation management. The second paper, by Winter and Czetkovich, discusses trust between the public and a land management agency. Both sustainability and trust are keys to long-term management effectiveness. Only brief summaries of these papers are included here; the full texts are included in the Appendix located with the electronic version of this document at http://

Table 5.11—Acres of Federal land by agency and region in 2008

	United States					
Federal agency	North	South	Rocky Mountains	Pacific Coast	Total	Percent Change
	- - - - - - acres (thousands) - - - - - -					
U.S. Forest Service	12,240	13,320	99,419	67,734	192,713	0.1
National Park Service	1,349	5,195	11,080	61,201	78,825	0.1
U.S. Fish and Wildlife Service	1,711	4,357	9,893	78,544	94,504	4.5
Bureau of Reclamation	0	197	5,470	854	6,522	0.0
Bureau of Land Management	4	44	142,962	110,356	253,367	-3.1
Tennessee Valley Authority	0	248	0	0	248	0.0
U.S. Army Corps of Engineers	2,557	7,104	3,540	545	13,746	18.5
All Federal agencies	17,862	30,466	272,364	319,234	639,926	-0.2

Note: Beginning year in the percent change column is 2003 for the USDA Forest Service and USDI Fish and Wildlife Service, 2002 for the USDI National Park Service and USDI Bureau of Land Management, and 1999 for the U.S. Army Corps of Engineers. Earlier data were not available for the USDI Bureau of Reclamation and Tennessee Valley Authority. Sources: USDA Forest Service (2008), USDI National Park Service (2008), USDI U.S. Fish and Wildlife Service (2009), USDI Bureau of Reclamation (2008), USDI Bureau of Land Management (2008a), Tennessee Valley Authority (N.d.), U.S. Army Corps of Engineers (2006).

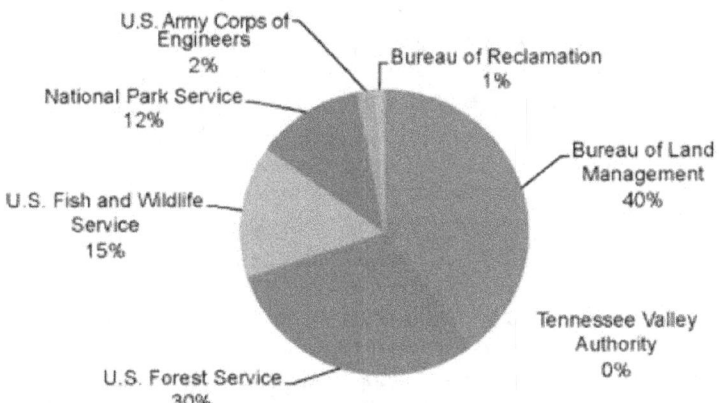

Figure 5 14—Percent of Federal land by agency, including Alaska, 2008. Sources: USDA Forest Service (2008), USDI National Park Service (2008), USDI Fish and Wildlife Service (2009), USDI Bureau of Reclamation (2008), USDI Bureau of Land Management (2008a), Tennessee Valley Authority (N.d.), U.S. Army Corps of Engineers (2006).

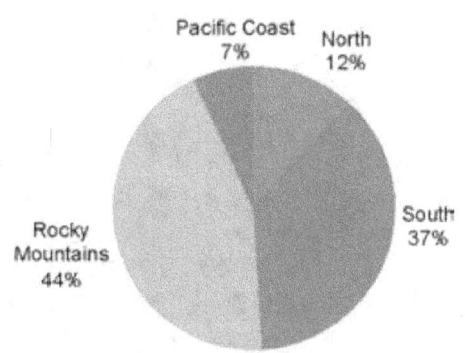

Figure 5.15—Percent of Federal land in the three water-resource agencies (U.S. Army Corps of Engineers, Bureau of Reclamation, Tennessee Valley Authority), by region, 2008. Sources: USDA Forest Service (2008), USDI National Park Service (2008), USDI Fish and Wildlife Service (2009), USDI Bureau of Reclamation (2008), USDI Bureau of Land Management (2008a), Tennessee Valley Authority (N.d.), U.S. Army Corps of Engineers (2006).

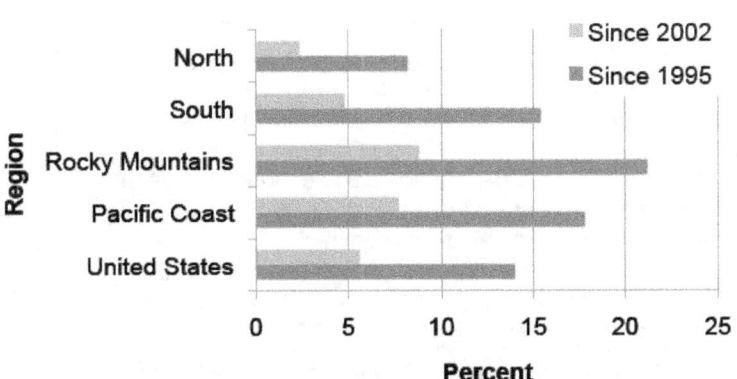

Figure 5 16—Percent decrease in per capita acres of Federal land, including Alaska, 1995 and 2002–2008. Sources: USDA Forest Service (2008), USDI National Park Service (2008), USDI Fish and Wildlife Service (2009), USDI Bureau of Reclamation (2008), USDI Bureau of Land Management (2008a), Tennessee Valley Authority (N.d.), U.S. Army Corps of Engineers (2006).

Sustainability in Outdoor Recreation and Tourism

There are many threats to nature-based recreation and tourism. Addressing threats such as land development or loss of access can in part be facilitated through application of a sustainability framework. Sustainability with regard to any natural land use must consider three dimensions: (1) economic, (2) social, and (3) environmental. These dimensions are interdependent and balance between them is essential to sustainability (United Nations Environment Programme and World Tourism Organization 2005). To help better understand this interdependence as it applies to management of recreation on Federal lands, a study was conducted of Forest Service personnel to gain insight into current perceptions, barriers, facilitators, and other concerns related to sustainable recreation on national forest lands.

Methods—This study was conducted in 2009 as a Web-based survey of Forest Service personnel with recreation management duties. Survey items were derived from a sustainable operations survey completed by the first author (Winter 2008), from concepts explored by Cottrell and others (see Cottrell and Vaske 2006; Cottrell and others 2007), and from items of particular interest, such as perceived impacts and responses to global climate change. We gathered names from directories, email lists, and direct contact through phone and email to verify appropriate personnel to include in our study.[1] Some examples of responses to sustainability questions are provided here. The full paper is published in this General Technical Report as an appendix (go to http://www.srs.fs.usda.gov/pubs/ and search for this publication. The full paper is available there.).

Educating the future. (Photo by Nate and Kelly Bricker).

Summary of primary findings—The majority of Forest Service respondents strongly agreed that they have a professional responsibility to practice sustainable business practices while also reducing environmental footprints (72.4 percent), that sustainability is important to the area they manage (71.1 percent), and that it warrants additional investment (62.5 percent). Respondents were in less agreement that sustainability is a Forest Service priority (47.5 percent agreed). Ratings of items important to sustainability reflect an understanding of the broader components of sustainability. For example, the majority rated environmental impacts (97.4 percent), increased environmental appreciation (95.0 percent), economic impacts (91.4 percent), increased appreciation of surrounding communities (80.1 percent), and improved health for the recreating public (77.1 percent) as important in sustainability. Issues that were of greatest concern included a lack of resources (especially funding and personnel), unmanaged use, increased use, and Agency relationship with the public. Inclusion of global climate change as a sustainability concern was given mixed responses.

Discussion—Sustainability was viewed as a shared concern and responsibility by respondents. Global climate change received a mixed response, with only a slight majority expecting impacts on recreation and tourism. Most Agency respondents did not think sustainability is an Agency priority as reflected in opinions that personnel and funding are inadequate. Many responding managers felt it important to have the Forest Service become a role model for sustainable management, including enhanced educational efforts. As part of being a role model, Forest Service respondents indicated that a broader perspective of benefits might be considered to include direct ecosystem or cultural enhancement benefits. Cultural enhancement could include partnering with community groups, volunteers, organizations, and local businesses.

---

[1]We aimed for a census of managers with primary recreation management duties at the regional, forest, and district level. Temporary and seasonal personnel were excluded, as were most classified as recreation technicians. Each employee was sent up to three emails requesting their participation in an online survey. We contacted 872 employees by email and received 433 usable surveys, giving us a 50.5 percent response rate. (Some of the employees were dropped from the response rate calculation because of an incorrect address, they were no longer in a recreation management position, or email inboxes that were not accepting messages through the duration of the study). Response rate, though varied by forest and district, was similar across the United States when examining Forest Service regions involved.

Trust and Recreation Management

(The full text of this paper is included in the Web appendix to this chapter.

Trust has been presented as an essential component of land management because it greatly influences how public citizens and agency managers interact. Drawing from a series of studies they conducted over the last few years, Winter and Cvetkovich summarize in their invited paper findings about the role of trust in outdoor recreation resource management. Each study they summarize approached trust through the "salient values similarity model," which suggests that perception of similarity of values between self and another helps predict existence of trust.

Across studies Winter and Cvetkovich have summarized, a common set of findings emerged. One such finding was that people tend to weigh agency actions in light of their own values regarding resource management (Cvetkovich and Winter 2003). Another finding was that perception of value similarity may exist if the public believes that agency staff personally share their values, even though in their agency role the staff may not be able to do what the public prefers. Perceived similarity of values is important because it is significantly associated with trust which is often associated with approval of management decisions. For example, the authors found that trust and similarity of values was significant in the predicting approval of management to protect threatened and endangered species such that recreation had to be banned in sensitive areas.

Archival photograph in 1957 of entrance sign to the Tonto National Forest (from the TNF website). The sign is on the "Apache Trail" highway, near Mesa, AZ. The Superstition Mountains are in the background. (Photo by D.O. Todd)

Some recent explorations of variations by gender within communities of color revealed a pattern of distrust among groups with typically greater social advantage (White and Asian males). This is an important finding because it challenges the predominate view that disadvantaged populations are more likely to distrust managing agencies. Across a number of studies the authors found a tendency towards trust rather than distrust in the Forest Service related to a number of management issues.

The authors' research has lent some important insights to help better understand trust or distrust between the public and agencies. It has pointed to the importance of similar values in trust, and thus the importance for agencies to clearly understand public values and to communicate their own core values underlying decisions. Once values are clearly outlined and similarities identified, an agency can benefit by considering and perhaps aligning with public values where possible. If an agency must take action deemed inconsistent with core values, it is beneficial to all concerned to communicate the reasons for that inconsistency. The authors' research points to the importance of paying attention to value-action consistency and to seeking legitimacy for inconsistency through clear communication of reasons for such decisions.

www.srs fs.usda.gov/pubs/ for the paper by Winter and others and for the paper by Winter and Czetkovich .

Congressionally Designated Federal Areas

Designated Wilderness—Federal land protected in the National Wilderness Preservation System has increased 3.3 percent since 2003 to a total of more than 109 million acres. This includes additions from the Omnibus Public Land Management Act of 2009 which was signed into law on March 30, 2009. Fifty-two new wilderness areas were established, and acreage was added to 26 existing areas, for a total addition of over 2 million acres, mostly Bureau of Land Management land. Given that the Bureau of Land Management started with a smaller amount of wilderness prior to 2004, its additions represent an increase of almost one-third to its current total of 8.7 million acres. Forest Service and National Park Service acreage in the National Wilderness Preservation System increased about 2.5 and 1.1 percent, respectively, since 2003. Combined, these two agencies manage about 73 percent of the National Wilderness Preservation System.

As with Federal land in general, the National Wilderness Preservation System is dominated by the western regions, in particular Alaska. More than 52 percent of the National Wilderness Preservation System is in Alaska, the large majority managed by the National Park Service and U.S. Fish and Wildlife Service (fig. 5.17). Including Alaska, about 96 percent of the NWPS is located in the West. Without Alaska, the proportion drops only slightly, to about 92 percent (Web site appendix table A5.12). Although the physical size of the National Wilderness Preservation System has increased recently, it has decreased 1.4 percent overall in per capita acres since 2003 as a result of declines in the South and Pacific Coast (table 5.12). Additions to the National Wilderness Preservation System and slower population growth in the North resulted in the largest per capita increase.

National Recreation Areas—In addition to special designation of selected Federal lands as wilderness areas, there are three other special Federal recreation systems. These are typically referred to collectively as Congressionally designated areas and include the National Recreation Areas, National Wild and Scenic Rivers, and National Recreation Trails. Each system traces its origins to the influence and recommendations of the 1958–1962 Outdoor Recreation Resources Review Commission.

The criteria for establishing national recreation areas were issued by the President's Recreation Advisory Committee in 1963, stipulating that all designations would be made by Congress. While other uses are allowed, outdoor recreation is the dominant purpose and accessibility to population centers is an important criteria. There are 41 national recreation areas,

which together cover more than 7.4 million acres (table 5.13). National recreation areas are managed primarily by the National Park Service and the Forest Service. There is a single Bureau of Land Management national recreation area in Alaska. More than 40 percent of the national recreation areas are located in the two eastern regions, but they account for just 10 percent of total acreage.

National Wild and Scenic River System—The National Wild and Scenic River System was established by Congress through the Wild and Scenic Rivers Act of 1968. Qualifying rivers or river sections were to be identified and designated as having one or more outstanding values classified as scenic, wild, or recreational. Rather than mandatory conservation measures, the Act is known more for helping to preserve the character of the designated rivers. There were more than 12,500 miles of designated wild and scenic rivers in the United States as of June, 2009 (table 5.14). Designated mileage in the Nation increased 11 percent since 2000, led by the Rocky Mountains and South regions, which grew by 50 and 31 percent, respectively. The Rocky Mountains led all regions in adding river mileage in each of the three value categories, particularly in the wild rivers class, which increased 87 percent. Nationally, additions to the wild and scenic categories far outpaced those rivers classified as recreational.

National Trails System—A National Trails System was created by the National Trails System Act of 1968, to include national scenic trails, national historic trails, and national recreation trails. Though scenic and historic trails have much recreational and tourism value, especially for long-distance hiking and trekking, only national recreation trails are covered in this report. National recreation trails may be managed by any government agency at the Federal, State, or local level, or may be privately owned as long as they are available for public use. The National Park Service oversees administration of the National Trails System, and the nongovernmental organization American Trails maintains a database of all the national recreation trails in the system. A goal of the Trails Act is to create a "national network of trails" with a stated objective for national recreation trails of being "reasonably accessible" to urban populations. National recreation trails may be designated and approved administratively every year and do not require Congressional designation.

After many years of limited activity, the national recreation trails program was revitalized in 2000. The number and miles of trails have continued to grow, reaching more than 1,000 national recreation trails and over 20,000 miles nationally in 2009 (table 5.15). These figures represent an increase of 20 percent in the number of trails and 52 percent in trail mileage in the previous 5 years. The increase in both number and miles of national recreation trails has been

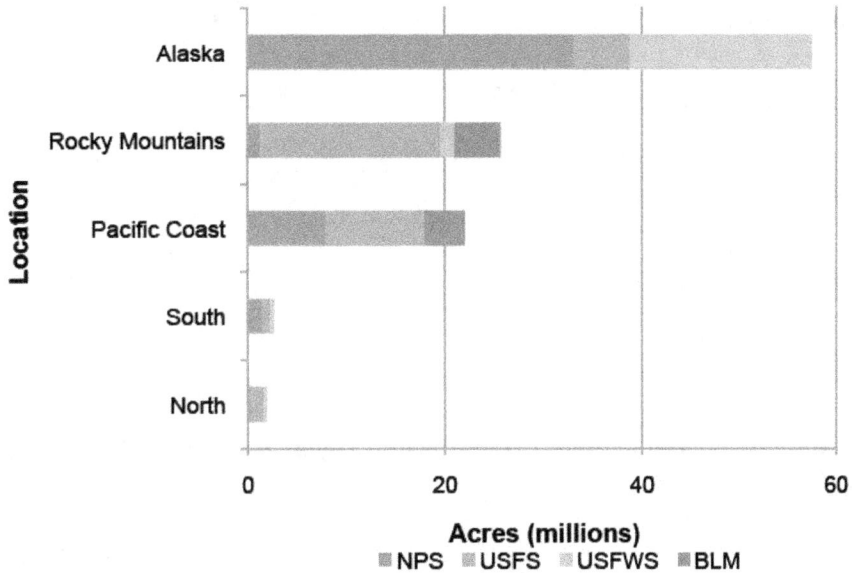

Figure 5 17—Acres of land in the National Wilderness Preservation System, by region (Alaska separate) and agency, 2009.
Source: Wilderness Institute (2009).

Table 5.12—Per capita acres (per 1,000 people) of National Wilderness Preservation System by agency and region, and percent change from 2003 to 2009

Federal agency	North		South		Rocky Mountains		Pacific Coast		United States	
	Acres per 1,000 people 2009	Percent change '02–'09	Acres per 1,000 people 2009	Percent change '02–'09	Acres per 1,000 people 2009	Percent change '02–'09	Acres per 1,000 people 2009	Percent change '02–'09	Acres per 1,000 people 2009	Percent change '02–'09
Bureau of Land Management	0.0	0.0	0.0	0.0	165.6	54.8	84.0	2.1	28.7	27.0
U.S. Fish and Wildlife Service	0.5	0.0	4.6	-6.1	52.7	-9.1	381.1	-4.5	68.1	-4.5
U.S. Forest Service	11.5	4.5	7.3	-3.9	654.6	-8.0	321.4	-1.1	118.9	-2.1
National Park Service	1.4	27.3	14.5	-6.5	48.3	25.8	833.1	-4.4	144.3	-3.6
U.S. total	13.4	5.5	26.4	-6.0	921.1	0.7	1,619.6	-3.5	360.1	-1.4

Note: U.S. population estimates are 290.21 million (2003) and 304.06 million (2008).
Source: Wilderness Institute (2009).

Table 5.13—Number and acres of National Recreation Areas by agency and RPA region in 2008

RPA region	National Park Service		U.S. Forest Service		Bureau of Land Management		Total	
	Number	Acres	Number	Acres	Number	Acres	Number	Acres
North	4	81,373	5	146,769	0	0	9	228,142
South	4	117,076	4	377,875	0	0	8	494,951
Rocky Mountains	4	2,820,555	7	1,513,219	0	0	11	4,333,774
Pacific Coast	6	394,396	6	952,689	1	998,702	13	2,345,787
United States	18	3,413,400	22	2,990,552	1	998,702	41	7,402,654

RPA = Resources Planning Act.
Source: USDA Forest Service (2008), USDI National Park Service (2008), USDI Bureau of Land Management (2008a).

Table 5.14—Miles of National Wild and Scenic Rivers by river classification and RPA region in 2000 and 2009

RPA region	Wild 2000	Wild 2009	Wild Percent Change	Scenic 2000	Scenic 2009	Scenic Percent Change	Recreational 2000	Recreational 2009	Recreational Percent Change	Total 2000	Total 2009	Total Percent Change
North	172	174	1.5	935	1,014	8.5	964	1,007	4.4	2,070	2,195	6.0
South	187	284	51.8	318	414	30.2	112	112	0.0	617	810	31.3
Rocky Mountains	710	1,328	87.1	288	380	31.9	532	587	10.5	1,530	2,295	50.0
Pacific Coast	4,280	4,370	2.1	911	936	2.7	1,886	1,946	3.2	7,077	7,252	2.5
United States	5,349	6,156	15.1	2,452	2,743	11.9	3,493	3,652	4.6	11,294	12,552	11.1

RPA = Resources Planning Act.
Source: Interagency Wild and Scenic Rivers Council (2009).

Table 5.15—Number and miles of National Recreation Trails by RPA region, 2004 and 2009

RPA region	Number 2004	Number 2009	Number Percent change	Miles 2004	Miles 2009	Miles Percent change
North	226	312	38.1	4,119	7,319	77.7
South	220	264	20.0	3,578	6,577	83.8
Rocky Mountains	254	292	15.0	2,969	3,380	13.8
Pacific Coast	198	209	5.6	2,622	2,944	12.3
United States	898	1,077	19.9	13,288	20,220	52.2

RPA = Resources Planning Act.
Source: American Trails (2009).

significantly higher in the two eastern regions since 2004, with mileage increasing more than 75 percent in both the North and South.

National Scenic Byways Program—Driving for pleasure and sightseeing are two of the most popular outdoor recreation activities in the United States. They reflect dependence and affection by Americans for the automobile. Most scenic roads are two-lane rather than four-lane highways. In 1992 the Federal Highway Administration in the U.S. Department of Transportation established the National Scenic Byways Program in response to demand for scenic driving roads and regional economic development through tourism.

The National Scenic Byways Program does not fund new construction of highways, but instead works with local and regional grass-roots organizations and State governments to recognize, preserve, and enhance selected roads with one or more of the following intrinsic qualities: scenic, historic, cultural, archeological, recreational, and natural. The program does include grant monies for which managing organizations may apply, in eligible categories such as corridor management plans, safety improvements, byway facilities, and access to recreation. Since 1992, 2,832 projects have been funded for State and nationally designated byway routes in all 50 States, and the District of Columbia.

Scenic byways are designated by the U.S. Secretary of Transportation as either All-American Roads or National Scenic Byways based on one or more of the six intrinsic qualities. The first designations occurred in 1996. To receive National Scenic Byway designation a road or highway must have at least one of the qualities while All-American Roads must possess at least two of the six qualities. These roads are generally considered the most scenic highways in the Nation with features that do not exist elsewhere. The latest additions to the National Scenic Byways system occurred in 2009 with the addition of five All-American Roads and 37 National Scenic Byways in 26 States. Overall, 46 States are represented in the system. As of November 2010, there are a grand total of 150 byways in the system, 31 of which are All-American Roads (fig. 5.18). The All-American Roads along with their State(s) and year of designation are listed in table 5.16.

In addition to the Federal Highway Administration's National Scenic Byways Program, two other Federal agencies have their own scenic byways programs. The Forest Service's "National Forest Scenic Byways" and the Bureau of Land Management "Back Country Byways" include many roads that are also designated by the National Scenic Byways Program. Further, most individual States have their own scenic byway programs apart from the National Scenic Byways Program. These programs are usually administered through the State Department of Transportation or Division of Tourism offices or some combination of State agencies. The State programs

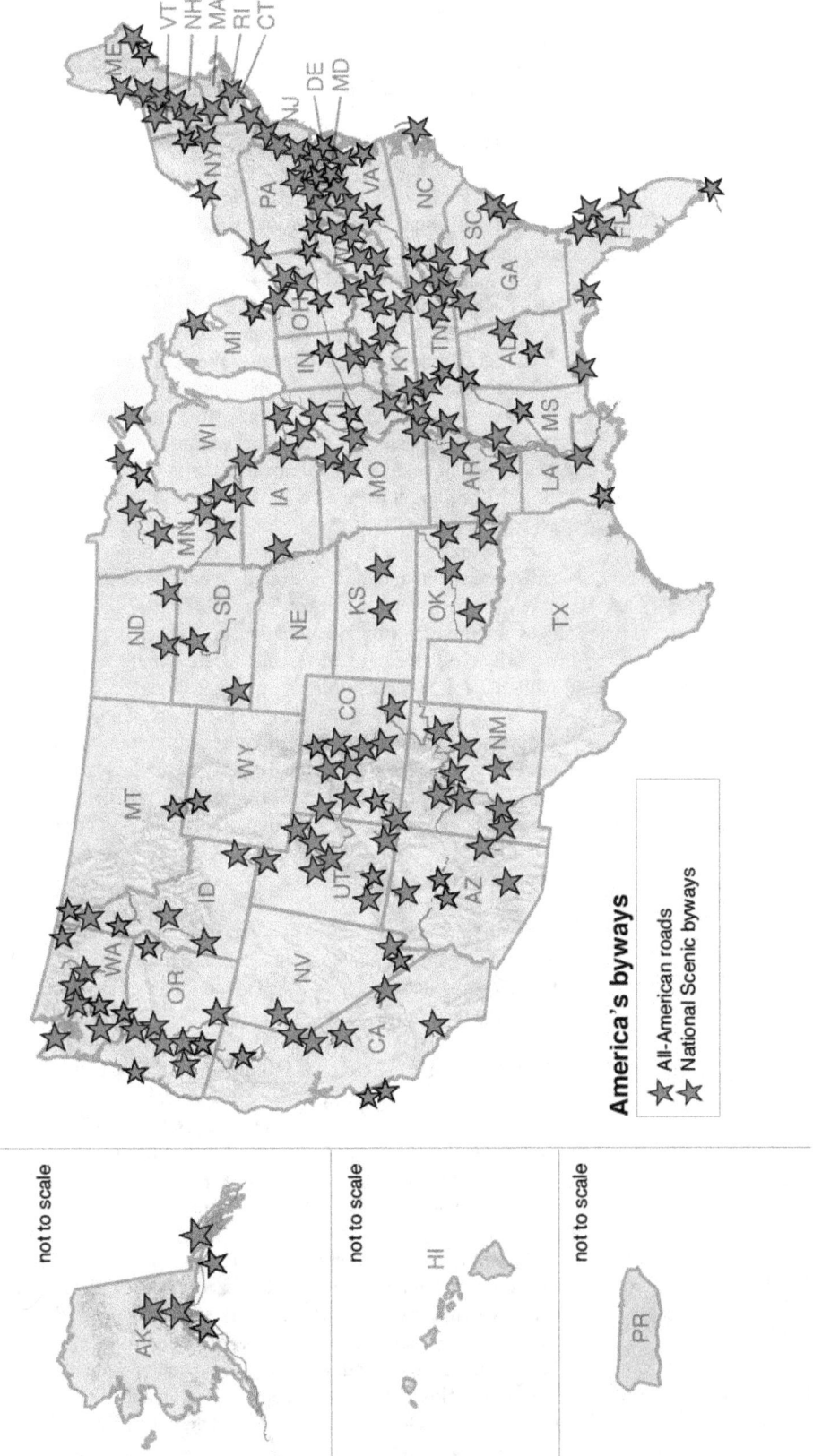

Figure 5 18—Highways in the National Scenic Byways Program by designation, 2010. Note: Byways receive a symbol on the map for each State where they are located. Source: National Scenic Byways Program (2010).

America's byways

★ All-American roads
★ National Scenic byways

not to scale

not to scale

not to scale

Table 5.16—All-American Roads in the National Scenic Byways Program with State(s) and year of designation, 2010

Acadia All-American Road (ME - 2009)

Alaska's Marine Highway (AK - 2005)

Beartooth Highway (MT - 2002, WY - 2000)

Blue Ridge Parkway (VA - 2005, NC - 1996)

Chinook Scenic Byway (WA - 1998)

Colonial Parkway (VA - 2005)

Creole Nature Trail (LA - 2002)

Florida Keys Scenic Highway (FL - 2009)

George Washington Memorial Parkway (VA - 2005)

Harriet Tubman Underground Railroad Byway (MD - 2009)

Hells Canyon Scenic Byway (OR - 2000)

Historic Columbia River Highway (OR - 1998)

Historic National Road
(MD - 2002, WV - 2002, IN - 2002, PA - 2002, IL - 2002, OH - 2002)

Historic Route 66 (AZ - 2009)

International Selkirk Loop (ID - 2005, WA - 2005)

Lakes to Locks Passage (NY - 2002)

Las Vegas Strip (NV - 2000)

Natchez Trace Parkway (AL - 1996, MS - 1996, TN - 1996)

North Shore Scenic Drive (MN - 2002)

Northwest Passage Scenic Byway (ID - 2005)

Pacific Coast Scenic Byway - Oregon (OR - 2002)

Red Rock Scenic Byway (AZ - 2005)

Route 1 - Big Sur Coast Highway (CA - 1996)

Route 1 - San Luis Obispo North Coast Byway (CA - 2002)

San Juan Skyway (CO - 1996)

Scenic Byway 12 (UT - 2002)

Selma to Montgomery March Byway (AL - 1996)

Seward Highway (AK - 2000)

Trail Ridge Road/Beaver Meadow Road (CO - 1996)

Volcanic Legacy Scenic Byway (OR - 1998, CA - 2002)

Woodward Avenue (M-1)–Automotive Heritage Trail (MI - 2009)

Note: Some All-American Roads received designations in more than one State in different years.
Source: National Scenic Byways Program (2010).

recognize the National Scenic Byways roads as part of their systems but also have additional State-designated highways and roads which have not applied for or received the National Scenic Byway or All-American Roads designations.

Federal recreation facilities—The Recreation One-Stop Initiative is a Federal program coordinated by the U.S. Department of the Interior that provides a customer-friendly Internet information portal (www.recreation.gov) about recreation opportunities on Federal lands, across all agencies. The Initiative provides information about Federal recreation areas using standardized definitions across agencies presented in a consistent format. The Recreation Information Data Base (RIDB), created for the rec.gov Web site, has more than 9,000 records in its facilities database. A "facility" is defined as a specific recreation site as opposed to a larger recreation "area," such as a national forest, that encompasses a number of facilities. The database is a binary (yes/no) format with data across 22 different recreation activities and/or facilities. Nearly 96 percent of the 9,000-plus Federal recreation facilities provide campgrounds (table 5.17). Hiking and fishing opportunities are a distant second and third at around 34 percent of the national sites. Figure 5.19 shows the top 10 facilities/activities at Federal sites and their distribution by region. As expected, the large majority (73 percent) of all sites are located in the Western United States, although this proportion is much smaller than the 92 percent of Federal land in the two western regions. This reflects a higher concentration of Federal recreation facilities per land area in the East where the majority of the Nation's population resides. Interpretive programs and visitor centers are particularly highly represented in the North region and boating facilities stand out in the South, although there are not as many boating facilities as in the western regions.

Federal recreation facilities on a per capita basis (per 1 million people) are shown in table 5.18. The more than 9,000 Federal facilities translate to just under 30 such facilities per 1 million people in the United States, or about 1 per 33,500 people. These ratios are much higher in the West, as expected. The Rocky Mountains region has more than 10 times the number of available Federal facilities per capita than both the North and South and nearly twice as many as the Pacific Coast. This disparity in per capita provision of facilities demonstrates not only the abundance of western facilities but also the much larger population in the East that is being served.

Trend data are not available for the RIDB since it is a fairly new database that originated in the early 2000s. Moreover, it is an evolving source of information which is populated by the Federal agencies with varying levels of completeness and comprehensiveness. It does appear to be comprehensive for the most highly developed Federal recreation sites such as campgrounds. However, some of the data appear incomplete, e.g., the North and South regions have just 10 sites each that

Table 5.17—Number of Federal recreation facilities by activity availability (or type of facility) and region, 2009

Activity or facility	North Number	North Percent	South Number	South Percent	Rocky Mountains Number	Rocky Mountains Percent	Pacific Coast Number	Pacific Coast Percent	United States Number	United States Percent of total
Camping	1,030	11.9	1,147	13.2	3,374	38.9	3,131	36.1	8,682	95.7
Hiking	181	5.7	184	5.8	1,826	57.7	975	30.8	3,166	34.9
Fishing	166	5.4	248	8.0	1,779	57.5	900	29.1	3,093	34.1
Boating	232	12.9	437	24.2	632	35.1	502	27.8	1,803	19.9
Picnicking	10	0.6	10	0.6	1,214	71.8	456	27.0	1,690	18.6
Recreational vehicles	0	0.0	0	0.0	1,056	64.7	575	35.3	1,631	18.0
Biking	50	3.9	37	2.9	901	70.9	282	22.2	1,270	14.0
Horseback riding	17	1.6	44	4.2	764	72.5	229	21.7	1,054	11.6
Hunting	49	4.8	78	7.6	689	67.3	208	20.3	1,024	11.3
Wildlife viewing	16	1.7	12	1.3	559	58.6	367	38.5	954	10.5
Auto touring	1	0.2	5	1.0	374	74.9	119	23.8	499	5.5
Water sports	0	0.0	1	0.3	179	48.1	192	51.6	372	4.1
Interpretive programs	102	27.9	68	18.6	130	35.5	66	18.0	366	4.0
Visitor center	118	32.6	78	21.5	110	30.4	56	15.5	362	4.0
Off highway vehicle	0	0.0	0	0.0	258	81.1	60	18.9	318	3.5
Wilderness	0	0.0	0	0.0	167	59.2	115	40.8	282	3.1
Winter sports	3	1.4	0	0.0	175	81.4	37	17.2	215	2.4
Swimming site	0	0.0	1	0.5	60	30.6	135	68.9	196	2.2
Historic and cultural site	21	13.3	4	2.5	110	69.6	23	14.6	158	1.7
Fish hatchery	17	25.8	16	24.2	20	30.3	13	19.7	66	0.7
Day use area	0	0.0	0	0.0	39	65.0	21	35.0	60	0.7
Climbing	0	0.0	0	0.0	42	82.4	9	17.6	51	0.6
All facilities	1,183	13.0	1,240	13.7	3,454	38.1	3,198	35.2	9,075	100.0

Note: The number of facilities do not sum down to the total ("All facilities") because more than one facility/activity may occur at a given recreation site. Region percentages sum across to 100. Source: U.S. Department of the Interior (2009).

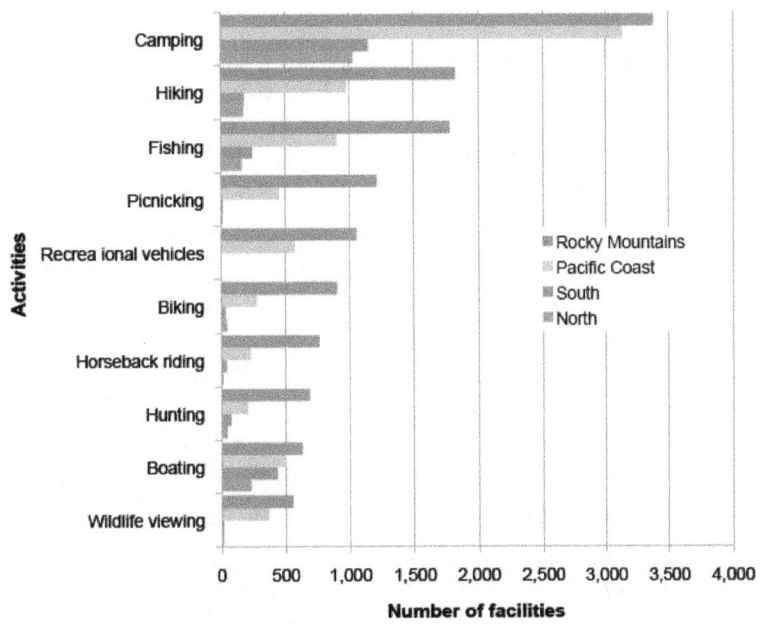

Figure 5.19—Number of Federal recreation facilities by activity availability (or type of facility) and region, 2009.
Source: U.S. Department of the Interior (2009).

Table 5.18—Federal recreation facilities per capita by activity availability (or type of facility) and region, 2009

Activity or facility	North	South	Rocky Mountains	Pacific Coast	United States
Camping	8.3	11.2	121.3	63.8	28.6
Hiking	1.5	1.8	65.6	19.9	10.4
Fishing	1.3	2.4	64.0	18.3	10.2
Boating	1.9	4.3	22.7	10.2	5.9
Picnicking	0.1	0.1	43.6	9.3	5.6
Recreational vehicles	0.0	0.0	38.0	11.7	5.4
Biking	0.4	0.4	32.4	5.7	4.2
Horseback riding	0.1	0.4	27.5	4.7	3.5
Hunting	0.4	0.8	24.8	4.2	3.4
Wildlife viewing	0.1	0.1	20.1	7.5	3.1
Auto touring	0.0	0.0	13.4	2.4	1.6
Water sports	0.0	0.0	6.4	3.9	1.2
Interpretive programs	0.8	0.7	4.7	1.3	1.2
Visitor center	0.9	0.8	4.0	1.1	1.2
Off highway vehicle	0.0	0.0	9.3	1.2	1.0
Wilderness	0.0	0.0	6.0	2.3	0.9
Winter sports	0.0	0.0	6.3	0.8	0.7
Swimming site	0.0	0.0	2.2	2.8	0.6
Historic and cultural site	0.2	0.0	4.0	0.5	0.5
Fish hatchery	0.1	0.2	0.7	0.3	0.2
Day use area	0.0	0.0	1.4	0.4	0.2
Climbing	0.0	0.0	1.5	0.2	0.2
All facilities	9.5	12.1	124.2	65.2	29.8

Note: Based on 2008 U.S. population estimate of 304.06 million.
Source: U.S. Department of the Interior (2009).

offer picnicking and no sites offering recreation vehicle sites. More likely, almost every one of the camping sites also offers picnicking and some surely provide recreational vehicle camping. Despite these shortcomings, the RIDB is the best single source of Federal recreation facilities data.

CHAPTER 6
Geospatial Patterns of Recreation Resources

This chapter addresses objective 6 of this assessment report on outdoor recreation and protected land resources: to map and describe the geospatial distribution of selected recreation and protected land resources as percent of total land area and per capita for counties in the United States. The primary focus in this chapter is on the geographic distribution of recreation and land resources by region and sub-region of the country and comparatively across counties. We take a broad perspective to include land, water, facilities, and services, just as was done in previous chapters. People tend to select recreation activities in part because of the availability of appropriate or highly desirable land, water, facilities, and services.

Availability is an important attribute of resources that fundamentally defines whether a resource is or is not a recreation resource. As referenced in this assessment, availability is largely a function of location relative to potential recreation users, that is, where the population resides. Generally, the closer a site or facility is to a populated area, the lower the transportation costs and the greater the probability of use. Thus, the spatial aspect of recreation resources is very important in determining the patterns of people's recreation participation across different activities. For this chapter, we spatially consider nine basic resources that form the foundation for nature-based outdoor recreation:

- Federal and State park land
- Water
- Non-Federal forest
- Non-Federal open range and pasture
- Ocean and Great Lakes coast
- Mountains
- Snow cover
- Specially designated Federal lands
- Private recreation businesses

Data and Methods

Resource data were compiled for every county in the United States. Eight of the nine resources are summarized in tables showing the following statistics for the Nation, for each of four major RPA regions, and for each of eight sub-regions: acres occupied by the resource, per capita quantity, percent of the total surface area represented by the resource, and average county percentage. The ninth resource, private recreation businesses, lists the total number of businesses and the number per 10,000 people. In addition, spatial patterns of relative abundance (or scarcity)

of these resources across individual counties of the lower 48 States are mapped.

Population and total surface acres for each sub-region, region, and the Nation are shown in table 6.1. The two eastern regions—North and South—had just under three-fourths of the Nation's 304 million people as of 2008, and about 43 percent of its land area. Conversely, the two western regions—Rocky Mountains (including Great Plains) and Pacific Coast (including Alaska and Hawaii)—had just over one-fourth of the Nation's population, but about 58 percent of the land area. Alaska alone accounts for almost 18 percent of the U.S. land area. Discounting Alaska, the East and West are very close in size, with the East slightly larger.

Relative proximity is an important attribute to choosing places for outdoor recreation by a county's residents. Thus, an additional element of the spatial mapping analysis describes resources as they occur within three distance zones for each county. These zones roughly represent local trip, day trip, and overnight trip and are defined as:

- Home county—Quantity of the resource within the boundaries of each U.S. county. Resource statistics for each home county are simply (a) the percent of the county's land surface area occupied by that resource and (b) the per-capita area.
- 75 mile zone—Resources within the home county and in nearby counties whose centroids (geographic center) are within 75 miles of the home county centroid. Resource statistics are expressed as (a) the percent of total land area of the counties included within the 75-mile zone occupied by that resource and (b) the per-capita area for the population within the combined counties. Recreation opportunities represented by resources within 75 miles can be roughly considered to be within a 2-hour drive, which would capture the large majority of the outdoor recreation day trips.
- 75-125 mile zone—Quantity of resource added across counties whose centroids are between 75 and 125 miles from each home county centroid. This zone forms an outer ring or "donut" and can be considered as resources within a 2- to 4-hour drive. This distance would capture most overnight trips which are taken for the purpose of outdoor recreation and not include longer, extended vacations. Quantities are expressed as the percent of total land area occupied by the resource across counties in the donut and per-capita total quantity for the population within the donut counties combined.

Maps were developed to show the pattern of the nine resources across counties of the contiguous United States. Three maps in sequence were developed, one for each of the three distance zones, to show how apparent access to resources compares based on distances from home county center.

Results

The following tables summarize the nine categories of resources important for outdoor recreation for each region and sub-region of the United States, as well as for the Nation as a whole. The maps that follow the tables focus on two different metrics related to spatial availability of recreation resources. The first metric is percent of total land area of each home county, of the counties in the 75-mile zone, and of the counties in the 75-125 mile zone that is composed of a particular recreation resource. The second is the quantity of that particular recreation resource per capita.

Federal and State Park Land

Federal and State park land represents what people often believe is the "Great Outdoors," i.e., larger tracts of mostly undeveloped and wild or backcountry land and water. Federal

land includes all property in the six major land-managing agencies: National Park Service, U.S. Forest Service, U.S. Fish and Wildlife Service, Bureau of Land Management, Tennessee Valley Authority, and U.S. Army Corps of Engineers. (The Bureau of Reclamation is not included because most of its areas are cooperatively managed by other agencies.) Federal land especially is composed of many vast, wild, and primitive landscapes, including designated wilderness. These resources stand in contrast to the more highly developed local parks. However, many Federal recreation areas and almost all State parks do have significant investments in developed facilities and services for visitors. Federal and State park land combined account for more than 627 million acres, about one-fourth of the Nation's land and water base (table 6.2). State park land includes all areas managed by State park agencies regardless of whether they are classified formally as a park. In addition to State parks, most State park systems include State recreation areas, sometimes State forests, and many also manage State historic sites, natural areas, and other scientific and environmental education sites.

State park areas comprise only about 2 percent of the combined Federal and State park system land, with more State park land in the East than in the West. So the dominant influence of the western Federal lands is apparent with nearly 50 percent of Pacific Coast land area and 35 percent of the Rocky Mountains

Table 6.1—Total population and total surface acres by RPA sub-region and region, 2008

Sub-region and region	Total population		Total surface area	
	Number	Percent	Number	Percent
	thousand		*acres (thousand)*	
Northeast	63,245.9	20.8	141,088.1	5.8
North Central	61,122.0	20.1	329,186.6	13.6
North total	124,368.0	40.9	470,274.6	19.4
Southeast	49,485.4	16.3	162,425.1	6.7
South Central	53,320.2	17.5	401,215.2	16.5
South total	102,805.6	33.8	563,640.3	23.2
Great Plains	6,031.2	2.0	196,766.0	8.1
Intermountain	21,729.6	7.1	552,682.9	22.8
Rocky Mountains total	27,760.9	9.1	749,448.9	30.9
Alaska	683.2	0.2	424,491.0	17.5
Pacific Northwest	10,339.3	3.4	108,595.4	4.5
Pacific Southwest	38,044.9	12.5	111,761.0	4.6
Pacific Coast total	49,067.4	16.1	644,847.4	26.6
U.S. total	304,001.8	100.0	2,428,211.3	100.0

RPA = Resources Planning Act.
Source: U.S. Census Bureau (2000, 2008).

region in Federal and State park land (table 6.2). Those proportions are just 5 and 4 percent, respectively, for the North and South regions. Further, while the average county nationally is about 9 percent Federal and State park system land, those numbers are much higher in the Pacific Coast (31 percent) and Rocky Mountains (20 percent). The real disparity in East and West is seen in per capita area of Federal and State park land. The combination of larger population and much smaller resource areas in the East results in fewer than 0.3 acres per capita for both eastern regions. In the West, the per capita amounts are 9.4 acres per person in the Rocky Mountains and 6.5 in the Pacific Coast. The Intermountain Sub-region, with its large Federal land base and relatively smaller population, has more than twice the per capita area of Federal and State park system land than any other sub-region, excluding Alaska.

The widespread availability of the Federal and State park lands in the West is evident in the county pattern maps for both percent of area and acres per capita. In percent of area, most of the West is covered in the darkest shades, not only for the home county, but with very little change over the other two distance zones (fig. 6.1). Many counties in the lower Great Plains and scattered counties in the Southeast and Midwest have no Federal and State park land as is evident from the home county zone. Every U.S. county has at least some Federal and State park land within the two distance zones

(75 mile and 75-125 mile zones), although a large band of Great Plains counties has < 1 percent in both. The same is true for sections of the lower Great Lakes States and upstate New York. The two distance zone maps highlight the extent of Federal and State park lands surrounding the Appalachian and Ozark/Ouachita Mountains, as well as the upper Great Lakes States, New England, and Florida.

The county distribution of Federal and State park land per capita looks quite similar to the pattern for percent of area for the home county (fig. 6.2). In the two distance zones, there are fewer western counties in the darkest shade (> 19.4 acres per capita), which reflects the presence of the western metropolitan areas. In both distance zones in the East, a band of the lightest shade (< 0.08 acres per capita) runs from roughly the Chicago metropolitan area eastward to the coast. Another large group of these counties is in Texas. Most of the eastern counties occupy the middle category of between 0.08 to 1.39 acres per capita.

Water Area

Water is a highly valued recreation resource. Frequently referred to as a "magnet" for outdoor recreation, water resources include streams, rivers, ponds, lakes, oceans, and

Table 6.2—Total and per capita acres of Federal and State park land, percent of total surface area, and mean county percent by RPA sub-region and region, 2008

Sub-region and region	Federal and State park land			
	Acres	Per capita acres	Percent of total area	Mean county percent
	thousand			
Northeast	5,519.6	0.09	3.9	4.0
North Central	14,395.8	0.24	4.4	3.1
North total	19,915.4	0.16	4.2	3.3
Southeast	12,043.0	0.24	7.4	5.9
South Central	16,231.2	0.30	4.0	4.4
South total	28,274.2	0.28	5.0	4.9
Great Plains	6,666.5	1.11	3.4	2.4
Intermountain	252,976.2	11.64	45.8	39.9
Rocky Mountains total	259,642.7	9.35	34.6	20.0
Alaska	231,739.8	339.18	54.6	43.8
Pacific Northwest	41,449.4	4.01	38.2	27.0
Pacific Southwest	46,297.7	1.22	41.4	29.6
Pacific Coast Total	319,486.9	6.51	49.5	30.7
U.S. total	627,319.2	2.06	25.8	8.6

RPA = Resources Planning Act.
Note: Federal and State park land is the sum of Federal land-managing agency area and State park system areas. See table 6.1 for population and total surface area acreage.
Sources: USDA Forest Service (2008, 2009b); USDI National Park Service (2008); USDI Fish and Wildlife Service (2009); USDI Bureau of Land Management (2008b); Tennessee Valley Authority (N.d.). U.S. Army Corps of Engineers (2006).

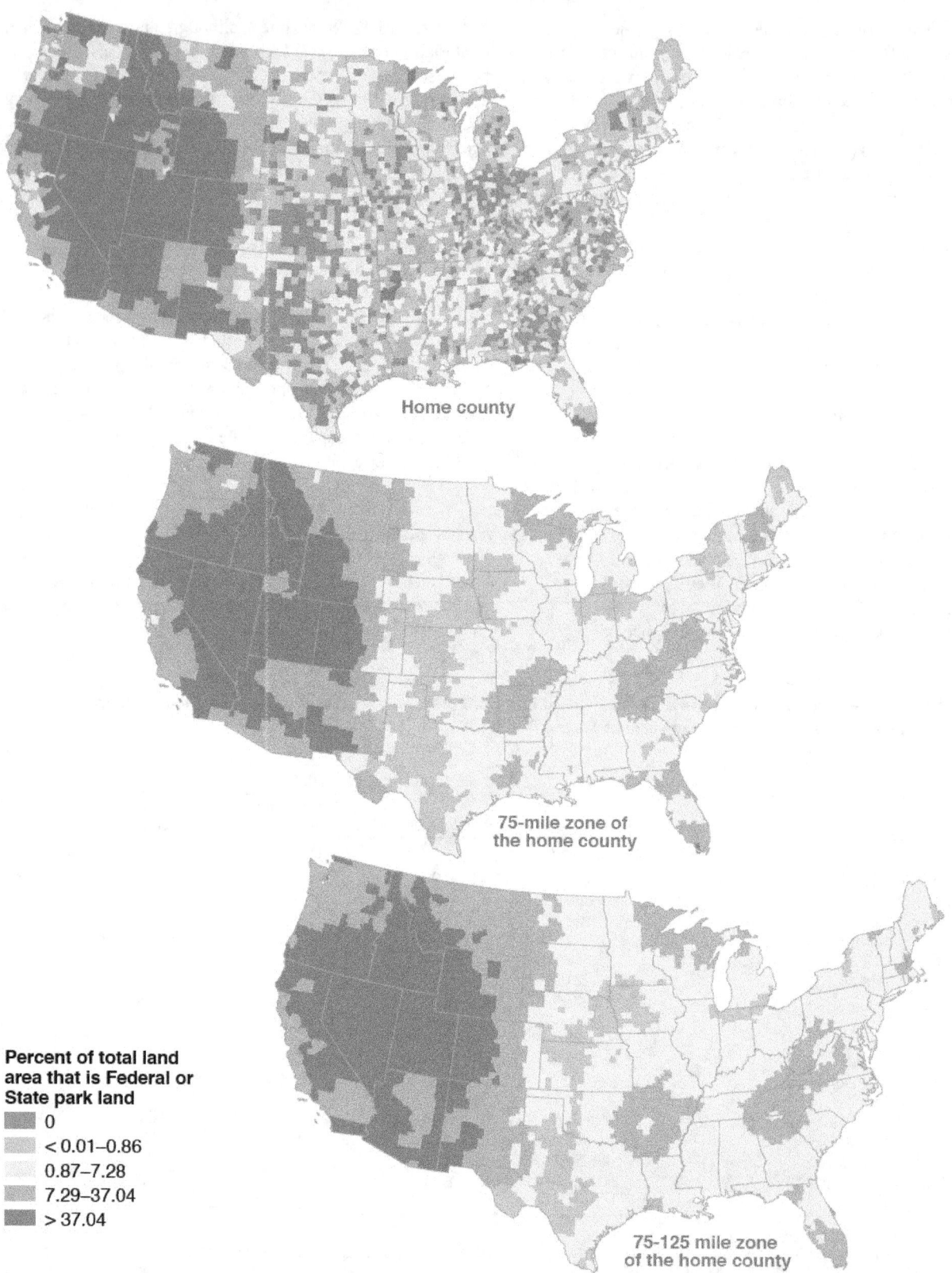

**Percent of total land
area that is Federal or
State park land**
- 0
- < 0.01–0.86
- 0.87–7.28
- 7.29–37.04
- > 37.04

Home county

75-mile zone of
the home county

75-125 mile zone
of the home county

Figure 6.1— Percent of total land area that is Federal and State park land, 2008, within home county, within the 75-mile distance zone, and within the
75-125 mile distance zone. Sources: USDA Forest Service (2008, 2009b), USDI National Park Service (2008), USDI Fish and Wildlife Service (2009),
USDI Bureau of Land Management (2008b), Tennessee Valley Authority (N.d.), U.S. Army Corps of Engineers (2006).

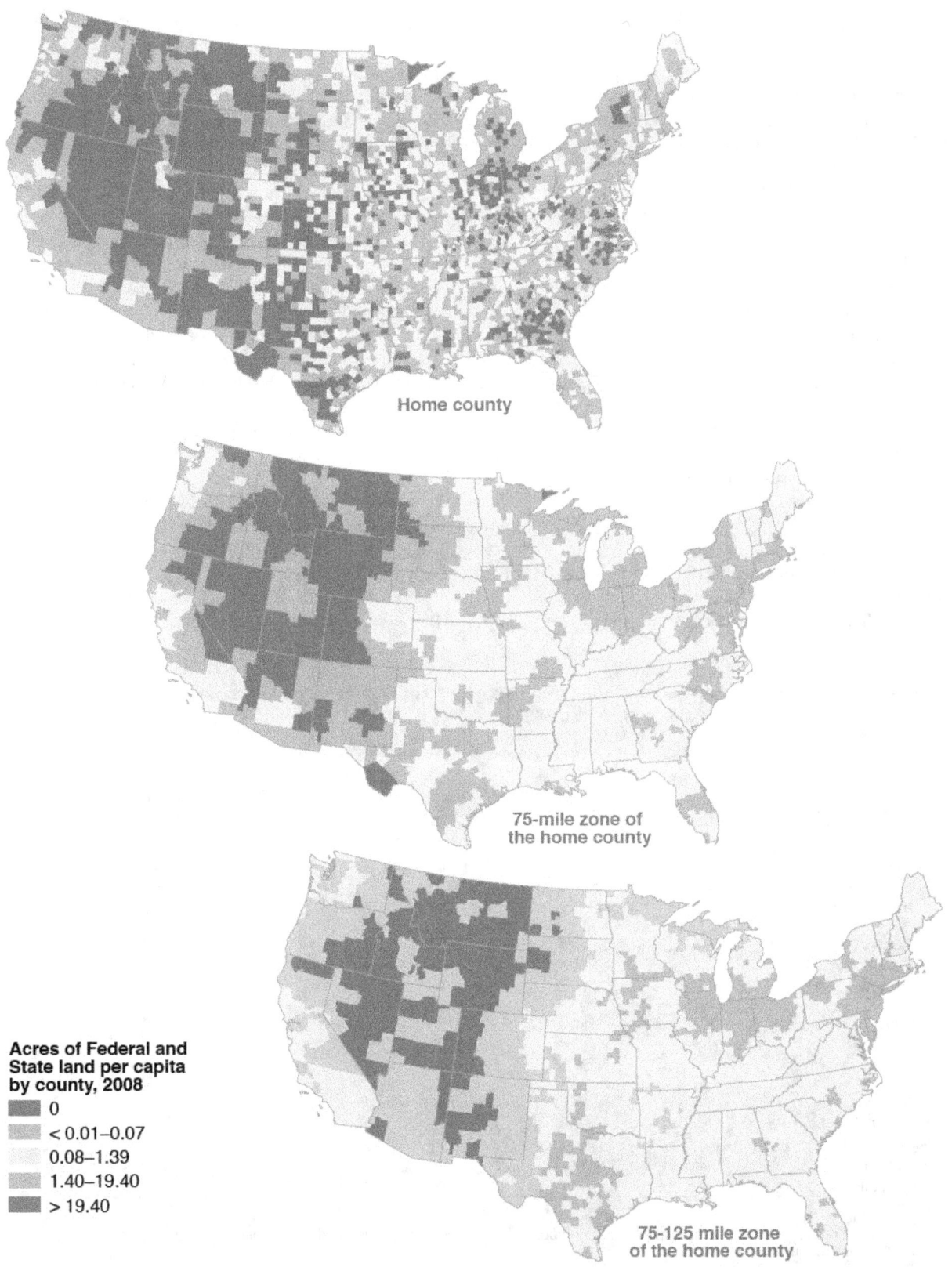

Figure 6.2—Acres of Federal and State park land per capita, 2008, within the home county, within the 75-mile distance zone, and within the
75-125 mile distance zone. Sources: USDA Forest Service (2008, 2009b), USDI National Park Service (2008), USDI Fish and Wildlife Service (2009),
USDI Bureau of Land Management (2008b), Tennessee Valley Authority (N.d.), U.S. Army Corps of Engineers (2006).

bays, i.e., any running or body of water that is suitable for water-based recreational activities. An ideal database for a recreation assessment analysis would include not only the surface area of available water, but also the management and site attributes that are conducive to recreational use. Management inputs would include facilities such as boat ramps, rafting and kayaking launching spots, marinas and boat slips, and other similar boating facilities. For swimming, the primary management inputs would be managed beach areas and associated bathhouse facilities. Two primary physical site attributes for water-based recreation are water quality and attractiveness of the water resource, which is closely associated with quality. Scenic attributes, for example, mountain settings are also highly desirable. Finally, managed facilities such as campgrounds and picnic grounds are not water-based facilities per se, but can be greatly enhanced and more attractive to users in the presence of water. Such a comprehensive database of all these management inputs and water resource attributes is not available, however, so this assessment uses a straightforward measure of water surface area.

The Census Bureau's Topologically Integrated Geographic Encoding and Referencing system (TIGER) database is the source of basic water area coverage, summed to county totals for this assessment. The Census Bureau classifies water as one of four types—inland, coastal, territorial, and Great Lakes—however, only the sum total of these are included in this report. Nationwide there are more than 164 million surface acres of water, about 7 percent of the total area (table 6.3). The West accounts for about 78 million acres (48 percent of the national total), however, 58 million acres of this (75 percent) are in Alaska. Excluding Alaska, water resources are much more disproportionately located in the Eastern United States, which has more than 81 percent of the non-Alaska water area. Three of the four eastern sub-regions exceed 9 percent of their total area in water resources, whereas in the West only the Pacific Southwest (excluding Alaska) has at least 7 percent total water area and this is heavily influenced by the waters surrounding Hawaii. On a per capita basis, the North region at 0.46 is close to the national average of 0.54 surface acres of water per person. All western sub-regions except Alaska are below the national per capita amount. In the Pacific Coast, the water acres per capita would drop to about 0.25 if Alaska were not considered.

The influence of the coastal and Great Lakes waters is evident in the county pattern maps that show percent of total surface area that is water for the three distance zones, particularly for the home county (fig. 6.3). Nearly every U.S. home coastal county is in the darkest shade category (> 11.24 percent) with the only additional counties in that

Table 6.3—Total and per capita acres of total water area, percent of total surface area, and mean county percent by RPA sub-region and region, 2008

Sub-region and region	Water area			
	Acres	Per capita acres	Percent of total area	Mean county percent
	thousand			
Northeast	14,328.5	0.23	10.2	9.3
North Central	42,505.3	0.70	12.9	6.0
North total	56,833.8	0.46	12.1	6.9
Southeast	15,068.8	0.30	9.3	6.1
South Central	14,213.4	0.27	3.5	3.1
South total	29,282.1	0.28	5.2	4.2
Great Plains	2,495.3	0.41	1.3	1.1
Intermountain	4,793.4	0.22	0.9	1.1
Rocky Mountains total	7,288.8	0.26	1.0	1.1
Alaska	58,442.2	85.54	13.8	22.3
Pacific Northwest	4,569.2	0.44	4.2	6.5
Pacific Southwest	7,836.5	0.21	7.0	11.3
Pacific Coast total	70,848.0	1.44	11.0	10.9
U.S. total	164,252.7	0.54	6.8	4.9

RPA = Resources Planning Act.
Note: Census Bureau water is classified as one of four types: inland, coastal, territorial, and Great Lakes. See table 6.1 for population and total surface area acreage.
Source: U.S. Census Bureau (2000).

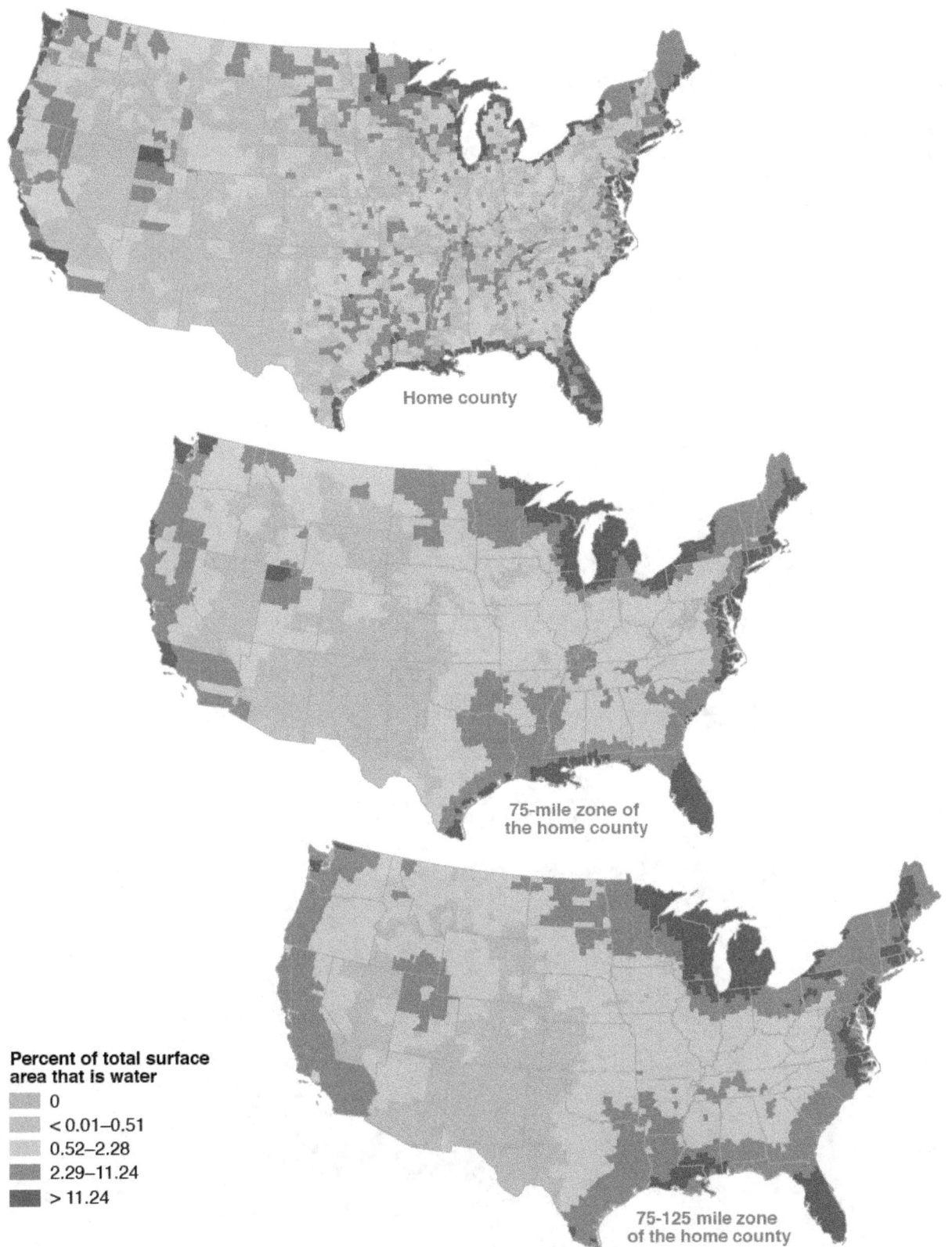

Percent of total surface area that is water

- 0
- < 0.01–0.51
- 0.52–2.28
- 2.29–11.24
- > 11.24

Home county

75-mile zone of the home county

75-125 mile zone of the home county

Figure 6.3—Percent of total surface area that is water, 2008, within the home county, within the 75-mile distance zone, and within the 75-125 mile distance zone. Source: U.S. Census Bureau (2000).

Home county

75-mile zone of
the home county

**Acres of total water area
per capita by county, 2008**

- 0
- < 0.01–0.06
- 0.07–0.40
- 0.41–2.24
- > 2.24

75-125 mile zone
of the home county

Figure 6.4—Acres of total water area per capita, 2008, within the home county, within the 75-mile distance zone, and within the 75-125 mile distance zone. Source: U.S. Census Bureau (2000).

class limited to a few in Minnesota and the Great Salt Lake region. For the two distance zones the Great Lakes, Gulf of Mexico, Florida below the panhandle, and the upper Atlantic counties have the most relative amount of total water area. The least-water category (< 0.51 percent) for home counties is quite evenly distributed throughout the country but the arid and semi-arid regions of the Great Plains and West dominate this category in the two distance zones. The medium-dark shade category is dominant in the distance zones near the lakes in Minnesota and the Dakotas, the Mississippi, Ohio, and Tennessee Rivers, and much of east Texas, Arkansas, Oklahoma, and Louisiana.

Counties with the largest relative amount of water per capita are not clustered along the coasts, but rather are much more scattered, especially in the low population counties of the West and northern Great Plains (fig. 6.4). Some coastal counties, especially along the Gulf of Mexico, also appear in the highest category for home counties (> 2.24 acres per capita), but as the analysis shifts to the two distance zones, the counties with most availability are almost exclusively in the west and upper Midwest, with the only exception being northern Maine. A large swath of counties in the two distance zones with the lowest availability (lightest shade, < 0.07 acres per capita) exists from Pennsylvania south to the Carolinas and Georgia (broken up only by the Tennessee Valley counties) and as far west as eastern Illinois.

Non-Federal Forest

Forests are a major land cover in the United States, providing the setting for numerous "nature-based" outdoor recreation activities, ranging from camping, backpacking, and picnicking to hiking, hunting, mountain biking, and nature study. Forests are also frequently a setting of choice for people participating in water-based activities, whether on reservoirs, alpine lakes, rivers, or streams. Forests cover approximately 29 percent of the surface area of the United States with the North, South, and Pacific Coast regions being between 26 and 28 percent forest and the more arid Rocky Mountains region 19 percent forest.

The focus of this section is on non-Federal forest land, which consist primarily of privately owned and State and local government forests, accounting for 386 million acres (19 percent of the total land area in the lower 48 States) (table 6.4). (Non-Federal forest data were not available for Alaska and Hawaii.) Estimates of non-Federal forest are included in the USDA Natural Resources Conservation Service (NRCS) National Resources Inventory which was used by Forest Service research scientist David Wear (2011) to develop estimates of non-Federal forest land in 2010. More than 30 percent of the land area in both eastern regions is non-Federal forest while that in the Rocky Mountains is only 4 percent and the Pacific Coast is 17 percent. Although the East has nearly 83 percent of the contiguous States' non-Federal forest

Table 6.4—Total and per capita acres of non-Federal forest land, percent of total surface area, and mean county percent by RPA sub-region and region, 2010

| Sub-region and region | Non-Federal forest land | | | |
	Acres	Per capita acres	Percent of total area	Mean county percent
	thousand			
Northeast	74,844.6	1.18	53.0	47.4
North Central	72,917.0	1.20	22.2	19.9
North total	147,761.6	1.19	31.4	27.8
Southeast	69,499.7	1.40	42.8	46.6
South Central	102,310.2	1.90	25.5	31.3
South total	171,809.9	1.66	30.5	36.8
Great Plains	3,280.3	0.54	1.7	2.1
Intermountain	25,205.6	1.16	4.6	5.8
Rocky Mountains total	28,485.9	1.02	3.8	3.8
Pacific Northwest	24,300.1	2.31	22.4	27.4
Pacific Southwest	13,435.5	0.36	12.0	17.0
Pacific Coast total	37,735.6	0.79	17.1	22.9
U.S. total	385,793.0	1.27	19.3	26.8

RPA = Resources Planning Act.
Note: Non-Federal forest land projections were not done for Alaska and Hawaii.
See table 6.1 for population and total surface area acreage.
Source: Wear (2011).

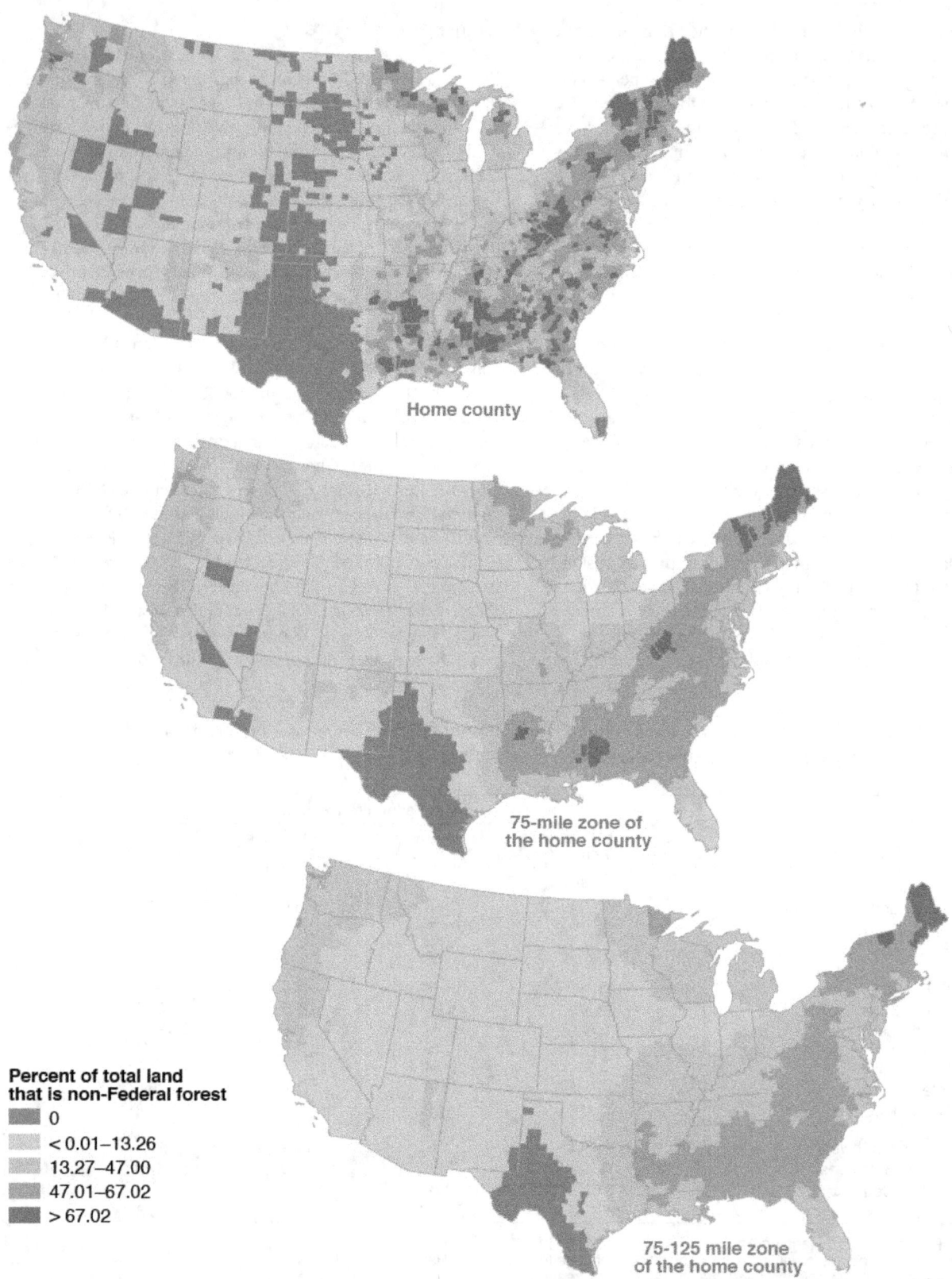

Home county

75-mile zone of
the home county

**Percent of total land
that is non-Federal forest**
- 0
- < 0.01–13.26
- 13.27–47.00
- 47.01–67.02
- > 67.02

75-125 mile zone
of the home county

Figure 6.5—Percent of total land area that is non-Federal forest, 2010, within the home county, within the 75-mile distance zone, and within the 75-125 mile distance zone. Source: Wear (2011).

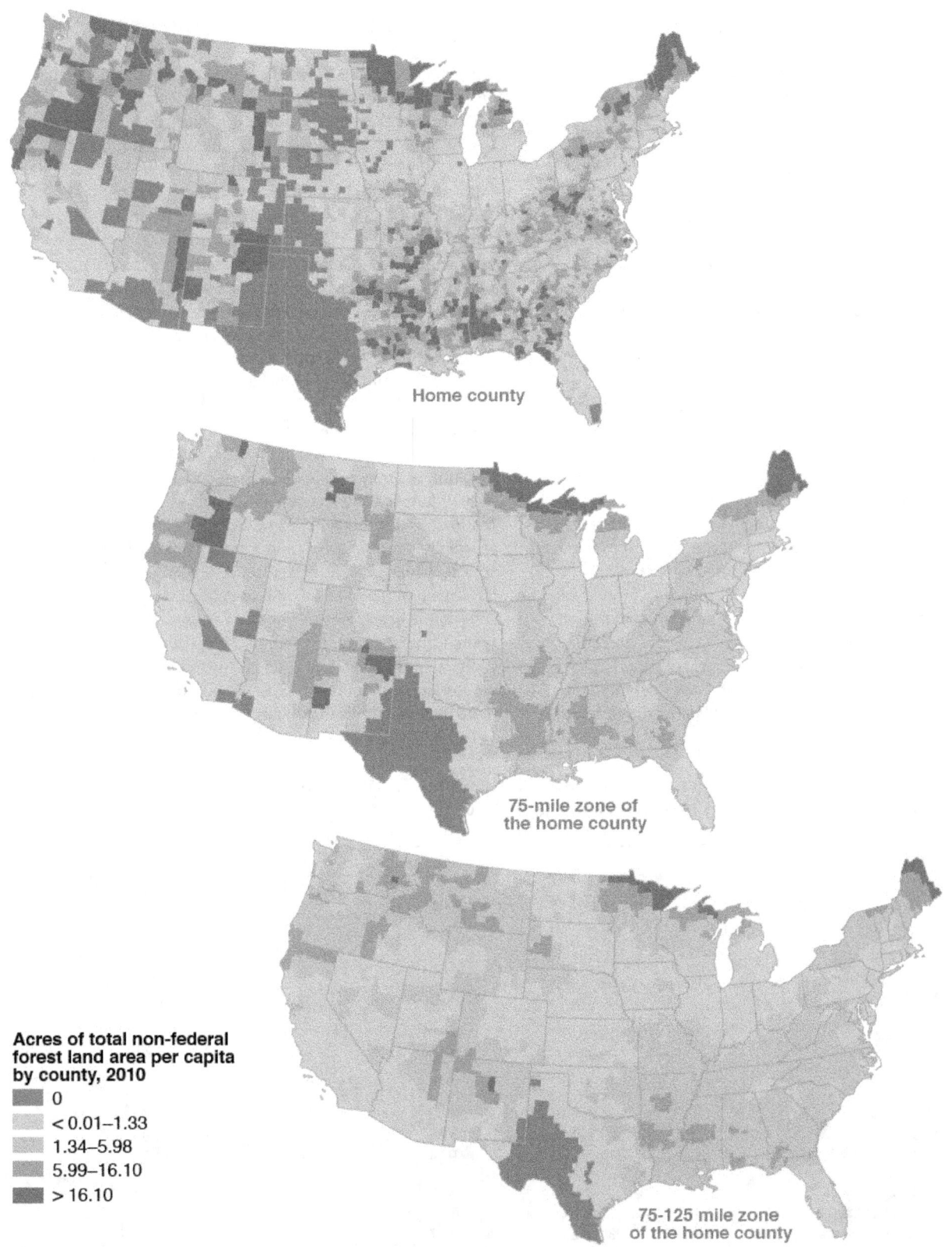

Home county

75-mile zone of
the home county

**Acres of total non-federal
forest land area per capita
by county, 2010**

- 0
- < 0.01–1.33
- 1.34–5.98
- 5.99–16.10
- > 16.10

75-125 mile zone
of the home county

Figure 6.6—Acres of total non-Federal forest land area per capita, 2010, within the home county, within the 75-mile distance zone, and within the
75-125 mile distance zone. Source: Wear (2011).

land, the per capita amounts of non-Federal forest are not considerably larger than in the West. The South leads all regions with almost 1.7 acres of non-Federal forest per capita while the Pacific Coast trails the other regions with less than 0.8 acres per person.

The eastern dominance of non-Federal forest is apparent in the county pattern maps (fig. 6.5). The East contains every county with the darkest shade (> 67 percent), except for one Oregon county. A majority of counties in the Great Plains and many in the Intermountain West have no non-Federal forest land in the home county zone while much of Texas has no forest even within the two distance zones. The 75 mile zone and 75-125 mile zone each have large regions of non-Federal forest in the lightest shade (< 13.26 percent, not counting 0) that extends west from eastern Texas and Oklahoma, Missouri, and most of Minnesota all the way to Northern California and the Pacific Northwest along with much of Illinois, Indiana, and northwest Ohio.

There is not a regional disparity in non-Federal forest acres per capita (fig. 6.6). The highest category (darkest shade, > 16.1 acres per capita) is distributed throughout all regions with the exception of the Great Plains and lower Great Lakes States. In the two distance zones there is a more even distribution of non-Federal forest, with larger concentrations of counties in the middle shade and above (> 1.34 acres per capita) in the Southeast, the upper Great Lakes States, along the Appalachian Mountains up through New England, and in much of the Rocky Mountains west and Pacific Coast regions.

Non-Federal Open Range and Pasture

Open non-forested lands are very extensive in the contiguous United States, covering 514 million acres, slightly more than one-fourth of the total area of the 48 States (table 6.5). These non-Federal open lands consist of range and pasture as measured by the USDA-NRCS National Resources Inventory (NRI), and estimated for 2010 by Forest Service research scientist David Wear (2011). The NRI defines range as primarily native grasses, grass-like plants, and forbs or shrubs suitable for grazing and browsing. These would include grasslands, savannas, many wetlands, some deserts, and tundra. Pasture, according to the NRI, is land that is usually but not necessarily managed for livestock grazing. It has a vegetative cover of grasses, legumes, and/or forbs, regardless of whether or not it is being grazed by livestock. Pasture does not include cultivated agricultural lands.

While much of range is publicly owned, most pasture is privately owned. Recreation occurs on almost all these acres in one form or another, though most likely not to the extent that it does in forested environments. Nevertheless, open range and pasture provide many opportunities for nature-based recreation, especially nature viewing and learning activities, off-highway vehicle driving, and other activities. The West has just under 60 percent of the 514 million non-Federal range and pasture acres while nearly all of the eastern range and pasture is in the South Central sub-region (mainly Texas and Oklahoma). Per capita acres of open range and pasture are by far the largest in the Rocky Mountains, which at almost 10 acres per person is more than five times that of any other region.

Table 6.5—Total and per capita acres of open range and pasture, percent of total surface area, and mean county percent by RPA sub-region and region, 2010

Sub-region and region	Open range and pasture			
	Acres	Per capita acres	Percent of total area	Mean county percent
	thousand			
Northeast	7,185.9	0.11	5.1	5.7
North Central	28,438.5	0.47	8.6	9.9
North total	35,624.4	0.29	7.6	8.7
Southeast	15,632.7	0.32	9.6	9.1
South Central	155,780.2	2.90	38.8	31.8
South total	171,412.9	1.66	30.4	23.7
Great Plains	77,639.2	12.82	39.5	34.7
Intermountain	192,921.0	8.88	34.9	34.8
Rocky Mountains total	270,560.2	9.74	36.1	34.7
Pacific Northwest	17,918.7	1.70	16.5	15.1
Pacific Southwest	18,493.3	0.50	16.5	18.9
Pacific Coast total	36,412.0	0.77	16.5	16.7
U.S. total	514,009.5	1.70	25.7	20.5

RPA = Resources Planning Act.
Note: Open range and pasture projections were not done for Alaska and Hawaii. Does not include cultivated agricultural lands. See table 6.1 for population and total surface area acreage. Source: Wear (2011).

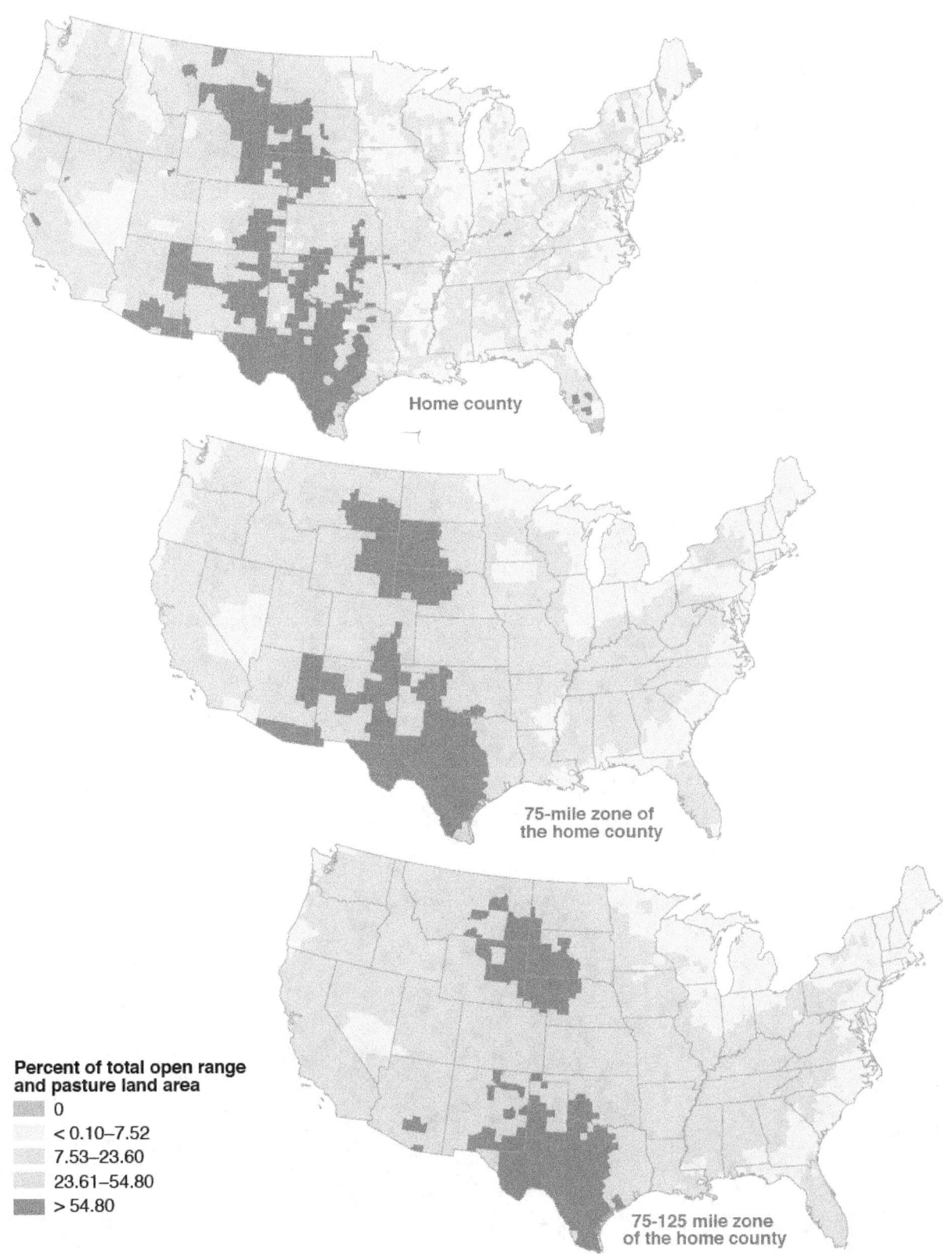

Percent of total open range and pasture land area

- 0
- < 0.10–7.52
- 7.53–23.60
- 23.61–54.80
- > 54.80

Home county

75-mile zone of the home county

75-125 mile zone of the home county

Figure 6.7—Percent of total land area that is open range and pasture, 2010, within the home county, within the 75-mile distance zone, and within the 75-125 mile distance zone. Source: Wear (2011).

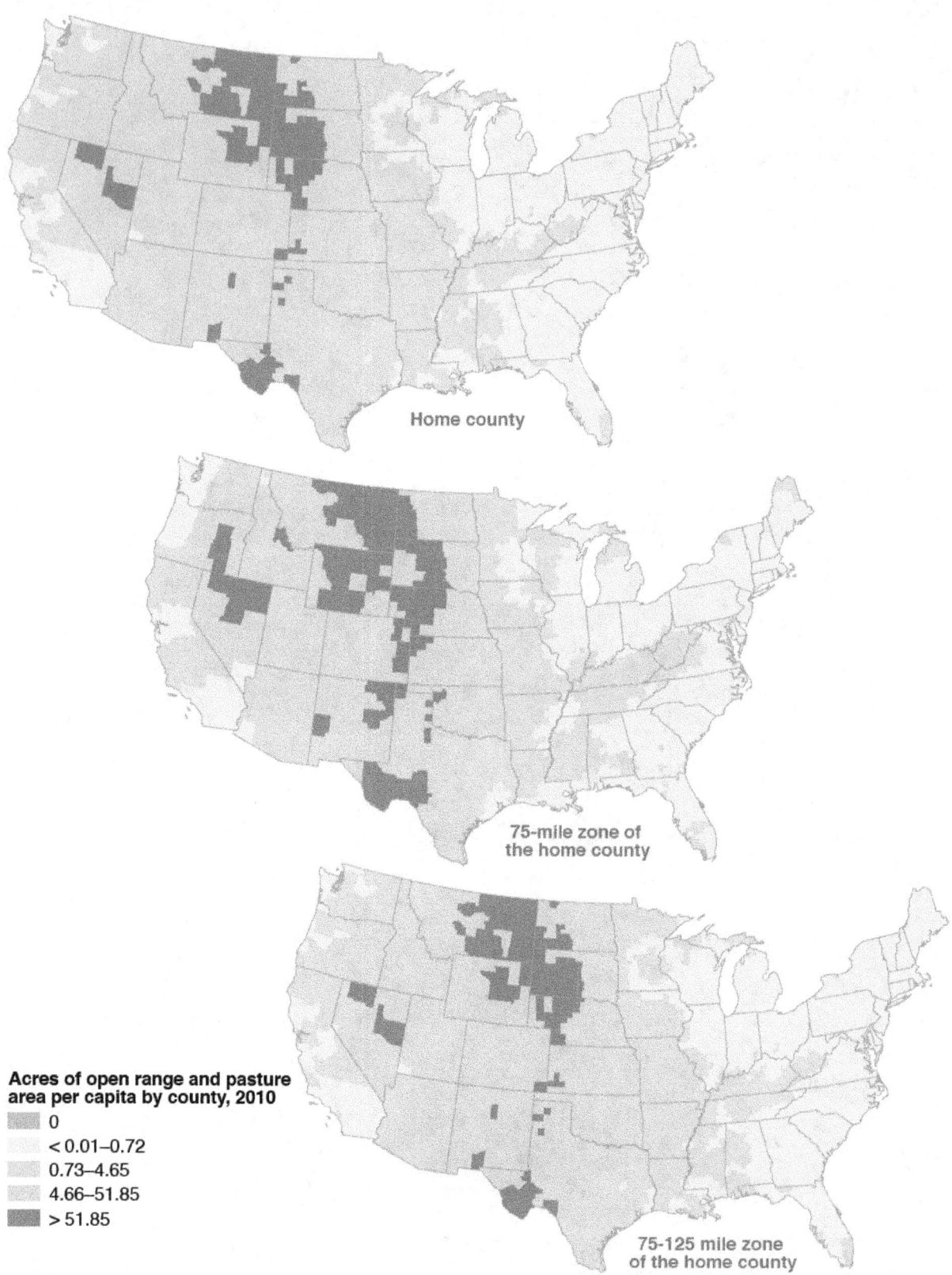

Home county

75-mile zone of
the home county

**Acres of open range and pasture
area per capita by county, 2010**

- 0
- < 0.01–0.72
- 0.73–4.65
- 4.66–51.85
- > 51.85

75-125 mile zone
of the home county

Figure 6.8—Acres of total open range and pasture area per capita, 2010, within the home county, within the 75-mile distance zone, and within the
75-125 mile distance zone. Source: Wear (2011).

Except for a few counties in Florida and Arkansas, the county pattern maps of the percent of open range and pasture land show that all other eastern counties with the darkest shade (> 54.8 percent) are located in either Texas or Oklahoma (fig. 6.7). All other high percentage range and pasture land are in the West. Expanding out to the two distance zones, a number of high percentage counties remain throughout Texas, New Mexico, and the high plains areas of Nebraska, Wyoming, South Dakota, and Montana. Areas with the lowest percentages (lightest shade, < 7.53 percent) for the two distance zones follow a band from the Great Lakes to the eastern seaboard to northern Florida. The three county maps showing acres per capita look very similar to the area percentage maps with the relatively high shadings (nearly 52 acres per person) primarily in the West and low shadings (< 0.73 acres per capita) in the East (fig. 6.8).

Table 6.6—Total and per capita acres of coastal county area, percent of total surface area, and mean county percent by RPA sub-region and region, 2008

Sub-region and region	Coastal county area			
	Acres	Per capita acres	Percent of total area	Mean county percent
	thousand			
Northeast	70,765.2	1.12	50.2	46.8
North Central	97,211.8	1.59	29.5	18.5
North total	167,976.9	1.35	35.7	26.7
Southeast	85,955.6	1.74	52.9	41.3
South Central	61,039.7	1.14	15.2	11.9
South total	146,995.3	1.43	26.1	23.0
Great Plains	0.0	0.00	0.0	0.0
Intermountain	0.0	0.00	0.0	0.0
Rocky Mountains total	0.0	0.00	0.0	0.0
Alaska	300,892.8	440.40	70.9	85.2
Pacific Northwest	32,901.9	3.18	30.3	41.3
Pacific Southwest	60,740.5	1.60	54.3	54.0
Pacific Coast total	394,535.1	8.04	61.2	53.3
U.S. total	709,507.4	2.33	29.2	21.4

RPA = Resources Planning Act.
Note: Coastal counties meet one of the following criteria: 1) at least 15 percent of a county's total land area is located within the Nation's coastal watershed; or 2) a portion of or an entire county accounts for at least 15 percent of a coastal cataloging unit, i.e., although a county does not have at least 15 percent of its total area within the coastal watershed, it still has a large land area within a coastal watershed. See table 6.1 for population and total surface area acreage.
Source: USDC National Oceanic and Atmospheric Administration (2004).

Ocean and Great Lakes Coast

The coastal counties of the United States make up 17 percent of the U.S. contiguous land area and contain more than half of the country's population. With Alaska and Hawaii included, the percentage jumps to 29 percent, or about 710 million acres (table 6.6). There are 673 U.S. coastal counties which are made up of a wide variety of landscapes from mountainous to flat tidewater areas. This considers both ocean coastal and Great Lakes coastal counties. The National Oceanic and Atmospheric Administration (NOAA) defines a coastal county as not only those which are physically about the coast but also those counties which have at least 15 percent of their total land area located within the coastal watershed. NOAA also classifies as "coastal" some counties which do not meet the 15 percent watershed criterion but have a large land area located within the coastal watershed. Excluding Alaska's 300 million acres, coastal area in the East outpaces that in the West by a factor of more than three to one. The Rocky Mountains region obviously has no coastal acres. Excluding Alaska, coastal acres per capita are higher in the West (particularly Pacific Northwest sub-region) than in the East.

The tremendously high beach visitation throughout the United States only begins to describe the popularity of coastal environments as a recreation resource. Besides the attractiveness of beaches for family outings and vacations (swimming, diving, and surfing activities), coastal settings also attract saltwater fishers, a variety of boaters, and nature lovers who appreciate the scenery, birds, and wildlife found in marine and other coastal settings. In addition, may people visit the National Wildlife Refuges, the majority of which were established in flyways in the Nation's coastal and estuarine areas.

The home county map in figure 6.9 shows coastal counties in the lower 48 States as defined by NOAA. An interesting aspect of the two distance zone maps is the large number of U.S. counties that are located within both 75 miles and 75-125 miles from the coast. All of Michigan and most Northeastern States lie within these two distance zones. The proportion of the Nation's population living in all of those counties is considerably over one-half because more than one-half live in the coastal counties alone. Coastal acres per capita in the home county are highest (black shade, > 44.3 acres per person) in northern California, the Pacific Northwest, scattered counties throughout the Gulf of Mexico, portions of New York and Maine, and the upper Great Lakes States (fig. 6.10). No home counties along the eastern seaboard are among the coastal counties with the most acreage per capita. The two distance zone maps show that the same areas, especially the upper Great Lakes, Maine, and the Pacific Coast north of California's Bay Area, still have the highest relative amount of coastal acres per capita.

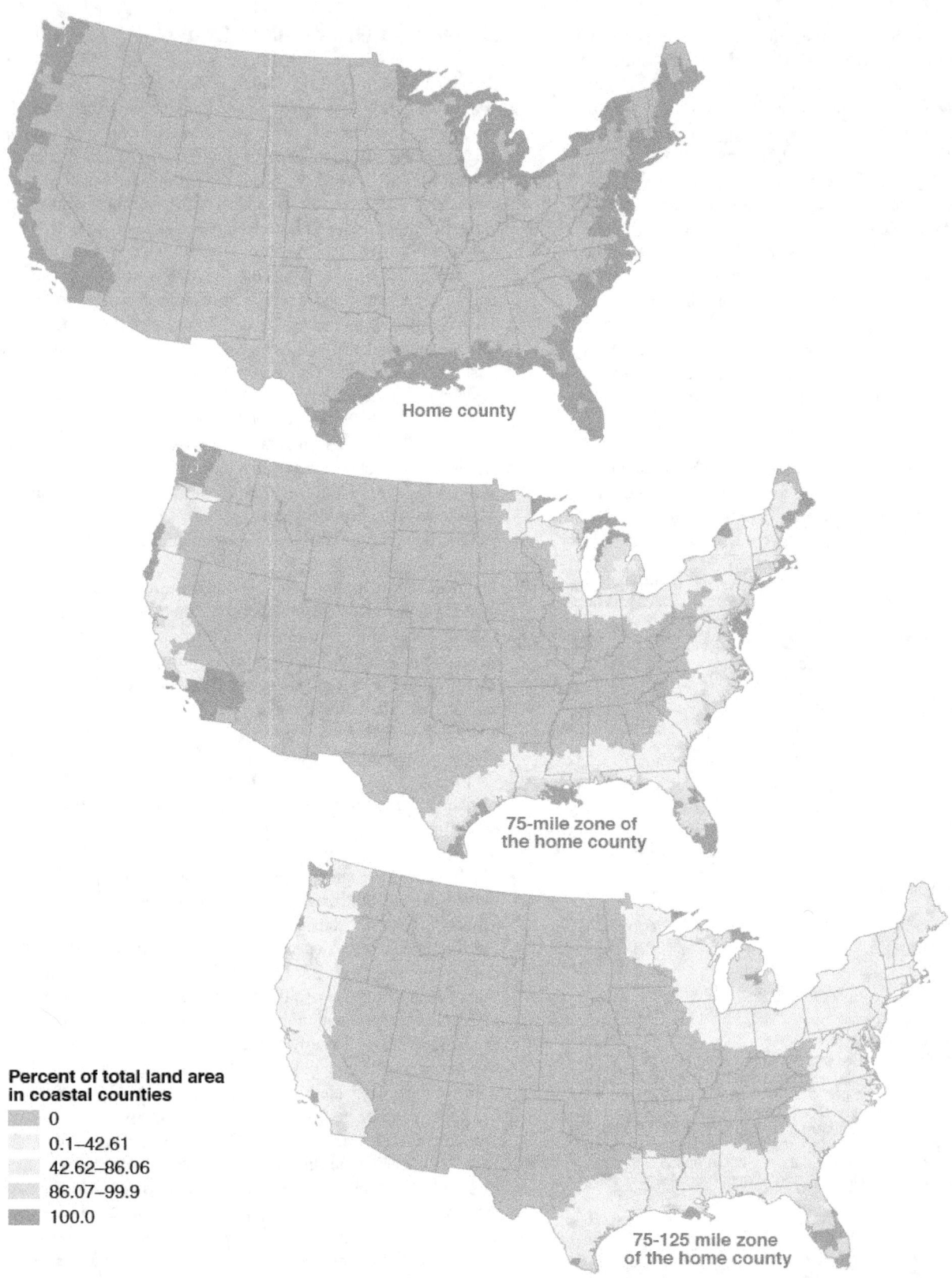

Percent of total land area in coastal counties

- 0
- 0.1–42.61
- 42.62–86.06
- 86.07–99.9
- 100.0

Home county

75-mile zone of the home county

75-125 mile zone of the home county

Figure 6.9—Percent of total land area that is in coastal counties, 2010, within the home county, within the 75-mile distance zone, and within 75-125 mile distance zone. Source: USDC National Oceanic and Atmospheric Administration (2004).

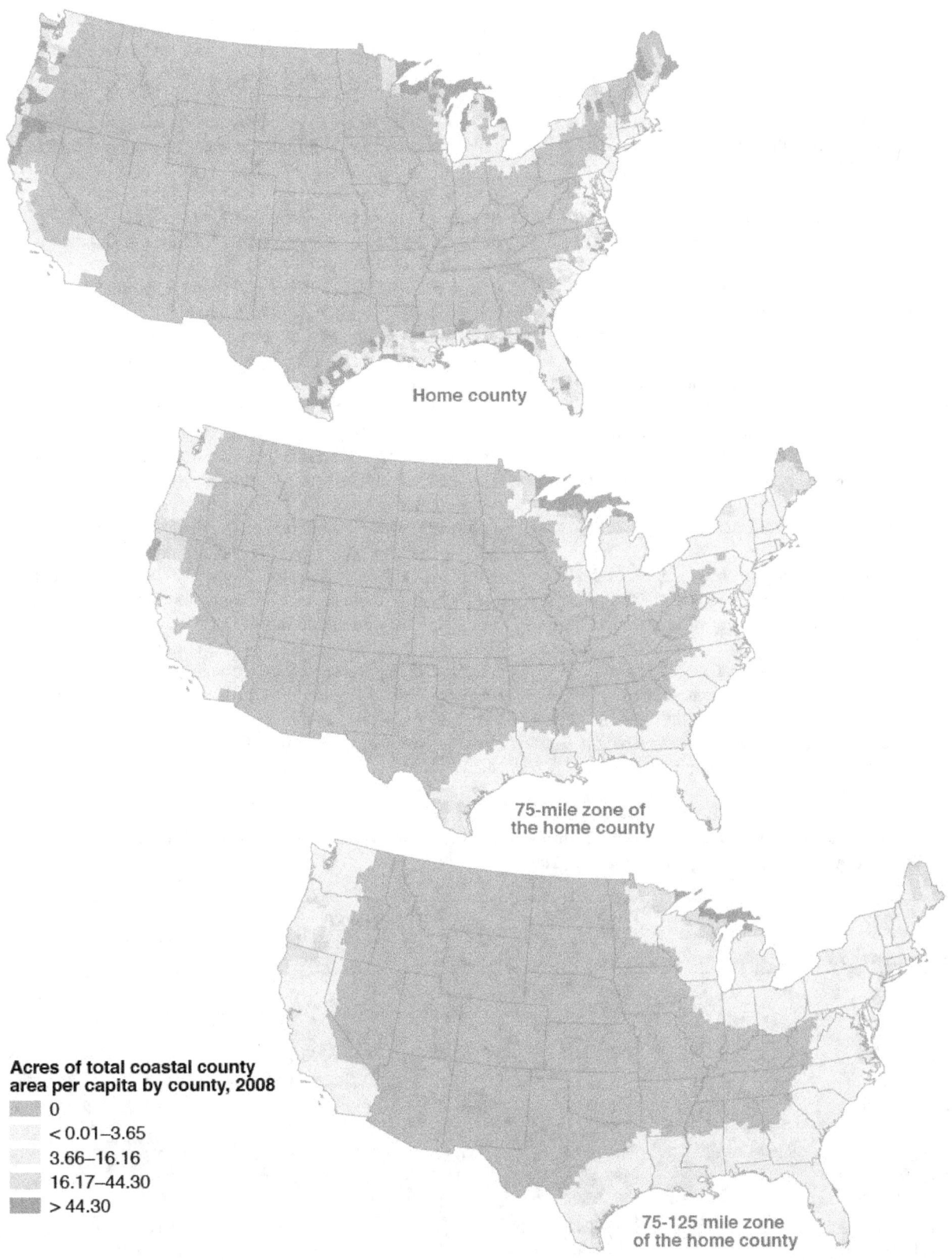

Home county

75-mile zone of
the home county

**Acres of total coastal county
area per capita by county, 2008**
- 0
- < 0.01–3.65
- 3.66–16.16
- 16.17–44.30
- > 44.30

75-125 mile zone
of the home county

Figure 6 10—Acres of total coastal county area per capita, 2008, within the home county, within the 75-mile distance zone, and within the
75-125 mile distance zone. Source: USDC National Oceanic and Atmospheric Administration (2004).

Mountains

Mountains are a highly significant natural amenity that draws tourists and sometimes new residents. With improvements in computing and communications, especially the Internet, over the past few decades, telecommuting has increasingly been an option for people who choose to live and work in mostly rural, mountain environments. Much of the Nation's public land is concentrated in mountain environments, as are most of the backcountry resources that support more primitive forms of outdoor recreation. The wide variety of nature-based recreation that occurs in mountainous areas include camping, hiking, backpacking, mountain biking, mountain and rock climbing, nature study, sightseeing, driving for pleasure, and many other land-based activities. Many water-based activities are also highly dependent on mountains, among them kayaking, rafting, and fly fishing. In addition, activities which require snow or ice such as alpine and nordic skiing, snowboarding, snowmobiling, and ice climbing, occur predominantly in mountain environments. Areas classified by Forest Service geographer Robert Bailey as belonging to mountain ecosystems are shown in table 6.7 for the contiguous United States.

In the 48 States, nearly 1 in 5 acres are mountainous, with the two western regions accounting for 78 percent (298 million acres) of this area. The Pacific Northwest sub-region has the largest proportion of mountains with over 50 percent, followed by the Pacific Southwest with 47 percent, and the Northeast and Intermountain sub-regions, both with more than 33 percent. The North Central sub-region is the only one with no mountain environments. The Rocky Mountains region easily leads all others with about 6.8 mountainous acres per

capita. Pacific Coast is second with 2.3 acres per capita, well ahead of the eastern regions, which both have fewer than 0.5 acres of mountains per person.

County pattern maps showing the percent of total land area that is mountainous highlight the major mountain chains in the contiguous United States (fig. 6.11). In the home county map, all but a handful of counties west of the Great Plains have some mountain environments, which indicates the extent of the Rocky Mountains, Sierra Nevada, and the Cascade Range. In the East, the Appalachian Mountains stretch from Georgia to Maine, with the only other mountains being the Ozark and Ouachita Mountains of Arkansas and Oklahoma. (Technically, the one county in west Texas with mountains is in the South region.) The two distance zone maps are pretty similar to the home county map for the western mountains, but in the East these zones demonstrate the large regions beyond the home counties that surround the Appalachian and Ozark/Ouachita Mountains. (For example, with the exception of two counties in western New York, every county in all of the States north of Virginia is located within 125 miles of mountains.) The distance zone maps indicate that the majority of the Nation's counties are located within a 2- to 4-hour drive and slightly fewer counties within even 1 hour of mountains. The county pattern maps for per capita acres of mountains shows that with the exception of upper New York and Maine, home counties in the West dominate the highest category with more than 116.63 acres per person (fig. 6.12). In the 75-mile zone, no counties in the East have more than 25 mountainous acres per person and in the 75-125 mile zone, only a few New York, Vermont, and Maine counties have more than 4.13 acres per capita.

Table 6.7—Total and per capita acres of mountainous area, percent of total surface area, and mean county percent by RPA sub-region and region, 2008

Sub-region and region	Mountainous area			
	Acres	Per capita acres	Percent of total area	Mean county percent
	thousand			
Northeast	49,174.8	0.78	34.9	30.9
North Central	0.0	0.00	0.0	0.0
North total	49,174.8	0.40	10.5	8.9
Southeast	20,185.2	0.41	12.4	17.5
South Central	12,363.4	0.23	3.1	3.3
South total	32,548.6	0.32	5.8	8.6
Great Plains	2,077.2	0.34	1.1	0.6
Intermountain	185,477.6	8.54	33.6	39.6
Rocky Mountains total	187,554.7	6.76	25.0	18.9
Pacific Northwest	58,024.8	5.61	53.4	54.8
Pacific Southwest	52,514.4	1.38	47.0	54.0
Pacific Coast total	110,539.2	2.28	50.2	54.5
U.S. total	379,817.3	1.25	19.0	12.7

RPA = Resources Planning Act.
Note: Mountainous area data were not available for Alaska and Hawaii. See table 6.1 for population and total surface area acreage. Source: Bailey (1995).

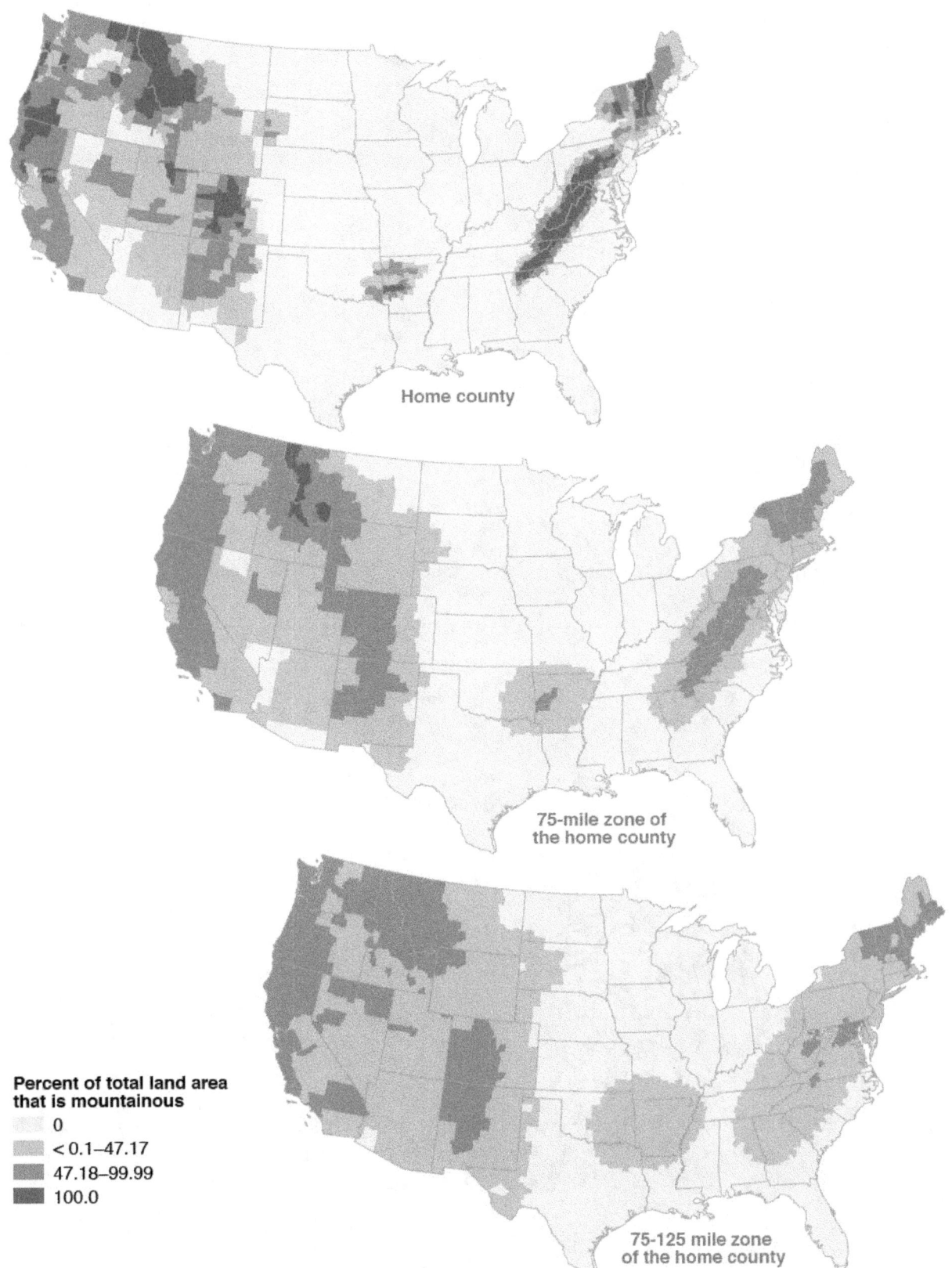

Home county

75-mile zone of
the home county

**Percent of total land area
that is mountainous**

0

< 0.1–47.17

47.18–99.99

100.0

75-125 mile zone
of the home county

Figure 6.11—Percent of total land area that is mountainous, 2008, within the home county, within the 75-mile distance zone, and within the
75-125 mile distance zone. Source: Bailey (1995).

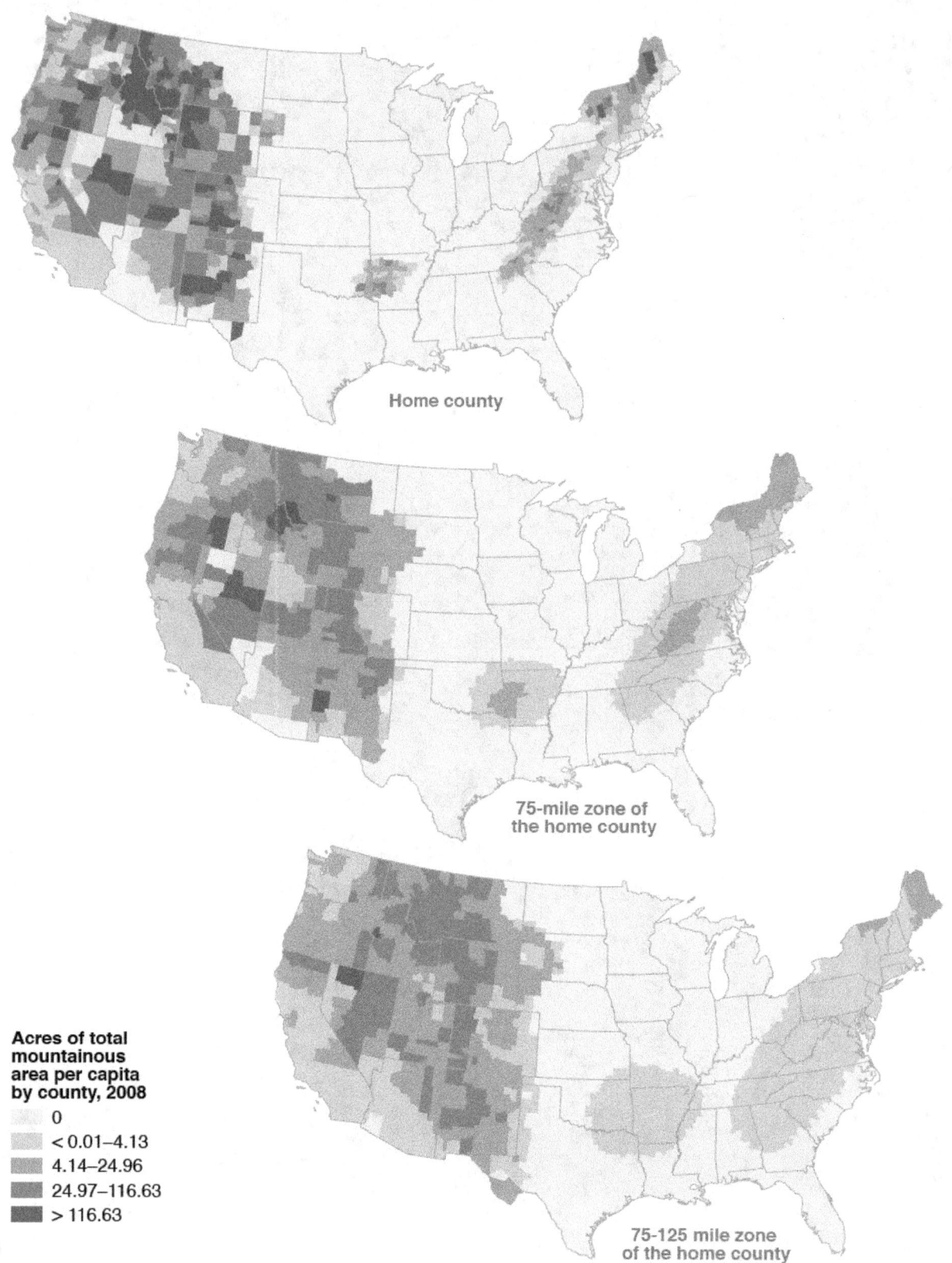

Home county

75-mile zone of
the home county

**Acres of total
mountainous
area per capita
by county, 2008**

0
< 0.01–4.13
4.14–24.96
24.97–116.63
> 116.63

75-125 mile zone
of the home county

Figure 6.12—Acres of total mountainous area per capita, 2008, within the home county, within the 75-mile distance zone, and within the
75-125 mile distance zone. Source: Bailey (1995).

Snow Cover

Counties with adequate winter snowfall are conducive to promoting a variety of snow sport activities for both residents and visitors, and in some places, may attract new residents. Alpine or downhill skiing areas require large investments in facilities and infrastructure and, in addition to artificial snow-making, are very dependent on adequate snowfalls. Similarly, snowboarding, which has recently increased tremendously in popularity, also makes use of such downhill skiing facilities. Cross-country skiing and snowshoeing, though less dependent on developed facilities than alpine skiing, still require snowfall. The amounts and periodicity of snowfall vary greatly across the country, ranging from places that get none to others that receive many feet of snow in an average winter. Based on data from NOAA's National Climatic Data Center, we define a "snow county" as one that has an average of 28.5+ days/year with 1 or more inches of measured snow depth (table 6.8). (The "average" refers to the mean value from a number of snow reporting stations that NOAA has installed in every U.S. county.) This represents a fairly stringent definition of snow resources for recreation since even some counties with ski areas, for example in North Carolina and southern California, do not qualify. Those areas likely depend mostly on manmade snow equipment.

About 581 million acres (29 percent) of the total area in the lower 48 States is classified as a "snow county," which is interpreted as being capable of supporting snow-based recreation in a sustainable manner. These snow areas are dominated by the Rocky Mountains and North regions which contain about 91 of the total snow county area. The remainder is in the Pacific Coast and one county in Virginia that qualifies. Although the North has less snow county acreage than the Rocky Mountains, more than half of its land is classified as a snow county. For the Rocky Mountains it is 39 percent, followed by 24 percent in the Pacific Coast. However, the Rocky Mountains' 10.4 snow acres per capita is more than five times that of any other region.

The county pattern maps show the percent of area in snow counties in the United States for the home county and two distance zones (fig. 6.13). By definition, a home county that is a "snow county" has 100 percent of its area so classified. In the two distance zones, only counties in the high-mountain West and northernmost counties in the East have 100 percent snow area located within a 1-hour or 2- to 4-hour drive. Also in the distance zones, the lightest shade (< 28.46 percent of area in the zone within snow counties) extends a bit farther south but not a great deal. This demonstrates that snow recreation resources as defined here within a 2- to 4-hour drive are limited primarily to the western and northern regions of the 48 States. Snow acres per capita in the home counties are greatest in the Rocky Mountains, Oregon, Nevada, and upper Minnesota and Wisconsin (fig. 6.14). Aside from upper New England and New York, all snow counties in the two distance zones east of Michigan are in the lightest class or shade (< 11.86 snow acres per capita).

Table 6.8—Total and per capita acres of snow county area, percent of total surface area, and mean county percent by RPA sub-region and region, 2008

Sub-region and region	Snow county area			
	Acres	Per capita acres	Percent of total area	Mean county percent
	thousand			
Northeast	94,673.1	1.50	67.1	50.8
North Central	143,440.8	2.35	43.6	28.7
North total	238,113.8	1.91	50.6	35.1
Southeast	271.0	0.01	0.2	0.4
South Central	0.0	0.00	0.0	0.0
South total	271.0	0.00	0.0	0.1
Great Plains	21,110.6	3.50	10.7	7.6
Intermountain	267,830.2	12.33	48.5	58.9
Rocky Mountains total	288,940.8	10.41	38.6	31.7
Pacific Northwest	49,785.9	4.82	45.8	30.7
Pacific Southwest	3,781.5	0.10	3.4	5.2
Pacific Coast total	53,567.4	1.11	24.3	19.5
U.S. total	580,893.0	1.92	29.0	18.7

RPA = Resources Planning Act.
Note: A "snow county" is one that has 28.5 days or more per year with 1 or more inches of measured snow depth. Data not available for Alaska and Hawaii. See table 6.1 for population and total surface area acreage.
Source: USDC National Oceanic and Atmospheric Administration (2005).

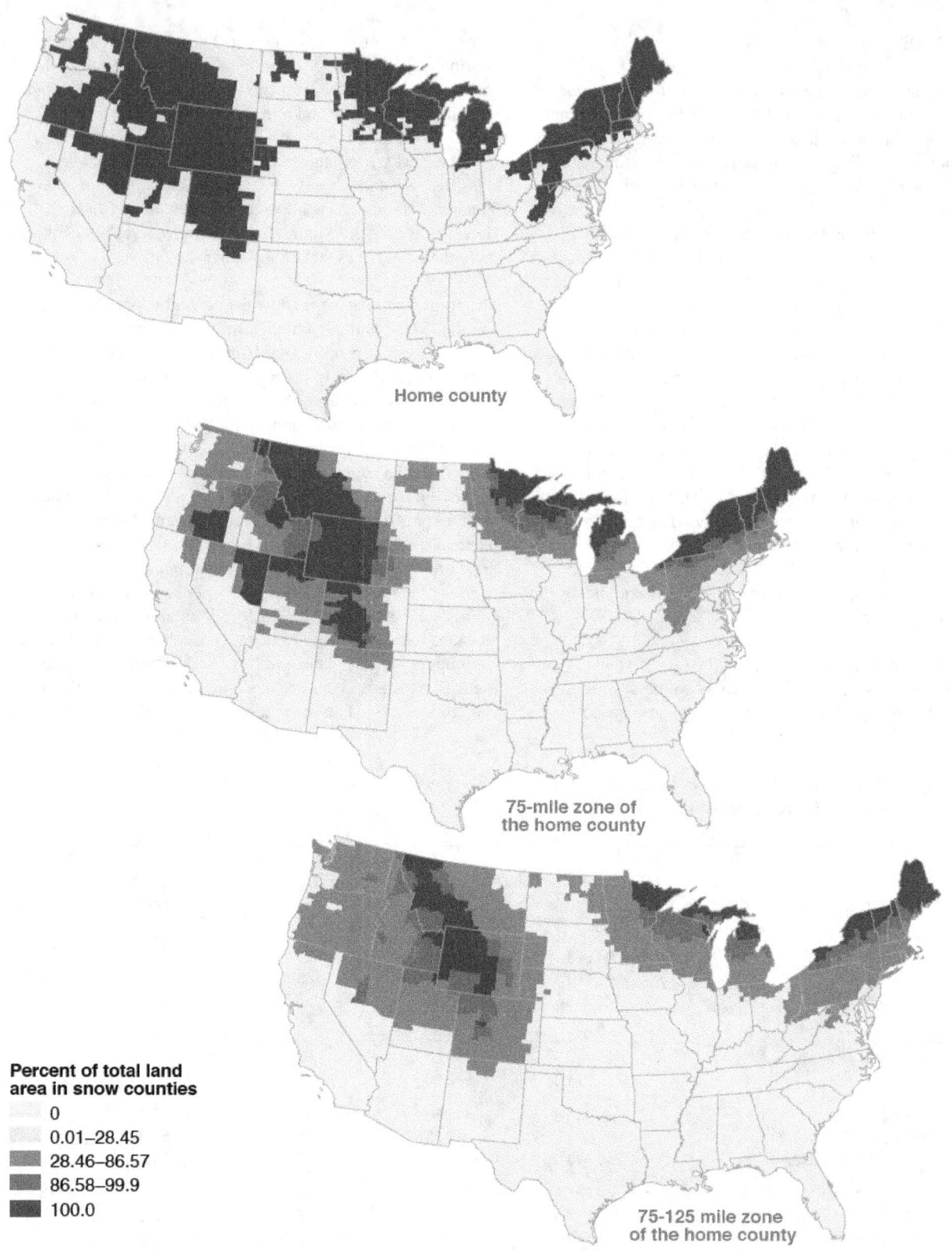

Home county

75-mile zone of
the home county

**Percent of total land
area in snow counties**

- 0
- 0.01–28.45
- 28.46–86.57
- 86.58–99.9
- 100.0

75-125 mile zone
of the home county

Figure 6.13—Percent of total land area that is in snow counties (>28.5 mean days with 1+ inches of snow depth), 2008, within the home (snow) county, within the 75-mile distance zone, and within the 75-125 mile distance zone. Source: USDC National Oceanic and Atmospheric Administration (2005).

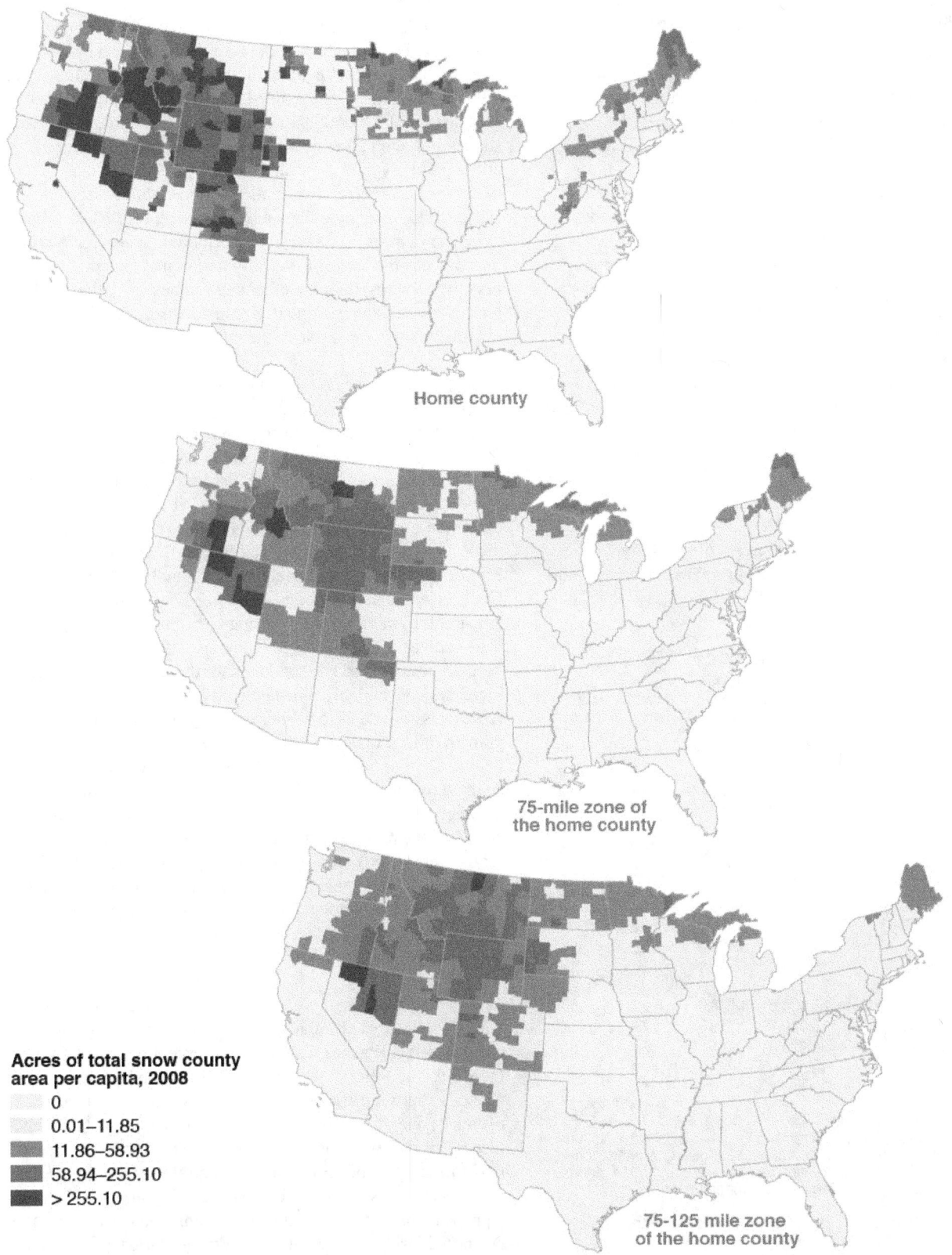

Home county

75-mile zone of
the home county

**Acres of total snow county
area per capita, 2008**

- 0
- 0.01–11.85
- 11.86–58.93
- 58.94–255.10
- > 255.10

75-125 mile zone
of the home county

Figure 6.14—Acres of total snow county area per capita, 2008, within the home county, within the 75-mile distance zone, and within the
75-125 miles distance zone. Source: USDC National Oceanic and Atmospheric Administration (2005).

Specially-Designated Federal Lands

Some Federal lands have special designation status. Best known are Federal lands in the National Wilderness Preservation System, National Park System, and National Recreation Area System. Sources of data covering these Systems are the National Park Service, Forest Service land offices, the Wilderness Institute at the University of Montana, and the Bureau of Land Management. These specially designated Federal lands are for the most part protected, large in size, offer backcountry recreation opportunities, and often offer dramatic scenery. Some units of the National Park System offer many developed facilities and some are located in urban areas, as are some of the national recreation areas. Wilderness areas by definition must be wild, such that they are "untrammeled" by people, in the words of the Wilderness Act. The Act also States that Wilderness is suitable for "primitive and unconfined recreation." In any event, the intent of this category is to examine the availability of the special places that make up the three resource systems.

Table 6.9—Total and per capita acres of specially designated Federal land, percent of total surface area, and mean county percent by RPA sub-region and region, 2008

| Sub-region and region | Specially designated Federal land | | | |
	Acres	Per capita acres	Percent of total area	Mean county percent
	thousand			
Northeast	794.2	0.01	0.6	0.6
North Central	2,214.4	0.04	0.7	0.2
North total	3,008.6	0.02	0.6	0.3
Southeast	4,495.3	0.09	2.8	1.4
South Central	2,466.3	0.05	0.6	0.5
South total	6,961.6	0.07	1.2	0.9
Great Plains	383.4	0.06	0.2	0.1
Intermountain	34,228.4	1.58	6.2	5.1
Rocky Mountains total	34,611.8	1.25	4.6	2.5
Alaska	88,036.5	128.85	20.7	18.7
Pacific Northwest	8,340.0	0.81	7.7	7.0
Pacific Southwest	16,928.9	0.44	15.1	9.1
Pacific Coast total	113,305.5	2.31	17.6	9.7
U.S. total	157,887.5	0.52	6.5	1.5

RPA = Resources Planning Act.
Note: Specially designated Federal land includes units in the National Wilderness Preservation System, National Park Service units (non-wilderness), and U.S. Forest Service and Bureau of Land Management National Recreation Areas. See table 6.1 for population and total surface area acreage.
Sources: USDA Forest Service (2008), USDI National Park Service (2008), Wilderness Institute (2009).

Nationwide, there are nearly 158 million acres of specially designated Federal lands, with more than 56 percent in Alaska (table 6.9). Almost 94 percent of all such lands are in the West, 85 percent if Alaska is excluded. These are about the same proportions of Federal lands in general. The Pacific Southwest sub-region, with numerous national parks, recreation areas, and wilderness in California especially, has more than twice the percentage of specially- designated Federal lands (15 percent) than any other sub-region except for Alaska. On a per capita basis, however, the Intermountain sub-region has nearly twice the acres of specially designated Federal land per person (1.6 acres) than the other sub-regions, with the Pacific Northwest a distant second (0.8 acres per capita). Alaska is obviously not comparable to the other sub-regions.

Although large acreages are in the West, the distribution of specially designated Federal lands by county is much more evenly distributed across the country with nearly every State having at least one home county with a percentage greater than zero (fig. 6.15). The highest percentage areas are indeed in the West (darkest shade, > 16.61 percent), with the exception of the Boundary Waters Canoe Area of Minnesota, the Everglades and Big Bend National Park regions of Florida and Texas respectively, the Okefenokee Wilderness in Georgia, and a handful of counties in and around the southern Appalachian mountains, including Great Smoky Mountains National Park. The number of counties with at least some specially designated Federal lands for the two distance zones increases considerably. The latter distance zone, which represents about a 2- to 4-hour drive, includes at least 90 percent of U.S. counties, the only exceptions being scattered counties throughout the Great Plains and upper Midwest, and a single remote county in northwestern Nevada. In the two distance zone maps, it is easy to see the influence (darkest shade) of the regions surrounding the Greater Yellowstone and Grand Teton areas of Wyoming, the Sawtooth Mountains in Idaho, Glacier National Park in Montana, Mount Ranier and North Cascades National Parks in Washington, the special mountain and desert lands in southern California, Nevada, and Arizona, and the Everglades region in Florida.

On a per capita basis, the West dominates the highest category (darkest shade, > 13.82 acres per person) for the home county and two distance zones with just a few exceptions (fig. 6.16). Only a few counties in the East are in the second highest category (between 1.36 and 13.82 acres per capita) in the two distance zones. Eastern counties in the third highest class of the distance zones, which is a relatively small land area of between 0.07 to 1.35 acres per capita, are concentrated in the upper Great Lakes States, upstate New York and New England, the southern Appalachians and Ozark/Ouachita regions, southern Georgia/northern Florida, the Everglades region of Florida, and portions of western Texas and Oklahoma.

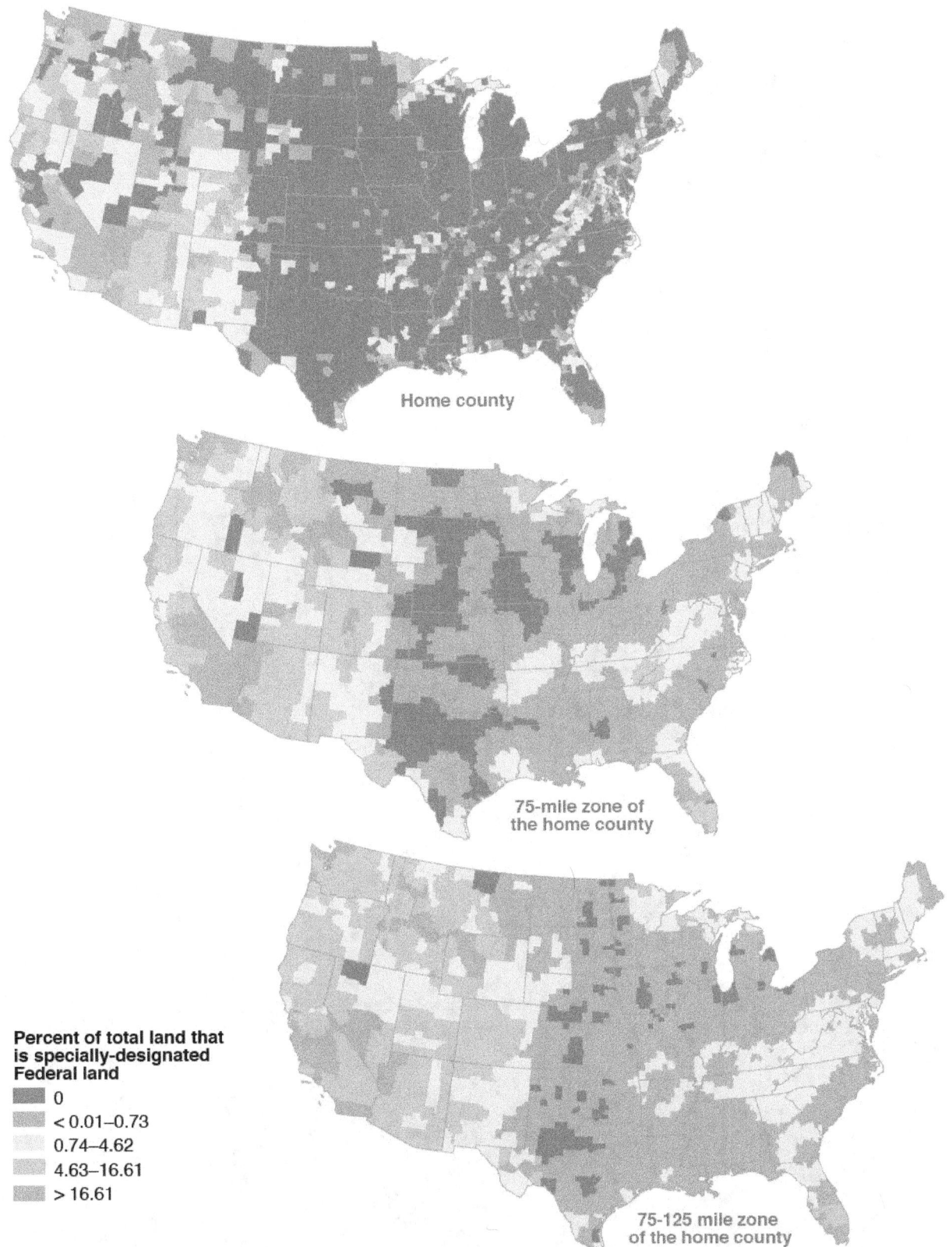

Home county

75-mile zone of
the home county

**Percent of total land that
is specially-designated
Federal land**

- 0
- < 0.01–0.73
- 0.74–4.62
- 4.63–16.61
- > 16.61

75-125 mile zone
of the home county

Figure 6 15—Percent of total land area that is specially designated Federal land, 2008, within the home county, within the 75-mile distance zone,
and within the 75-125 mile distance zone. Sources: USDA Forest Service (2008), USDI National Park Service (2008), and Wilderness Institute (2009).

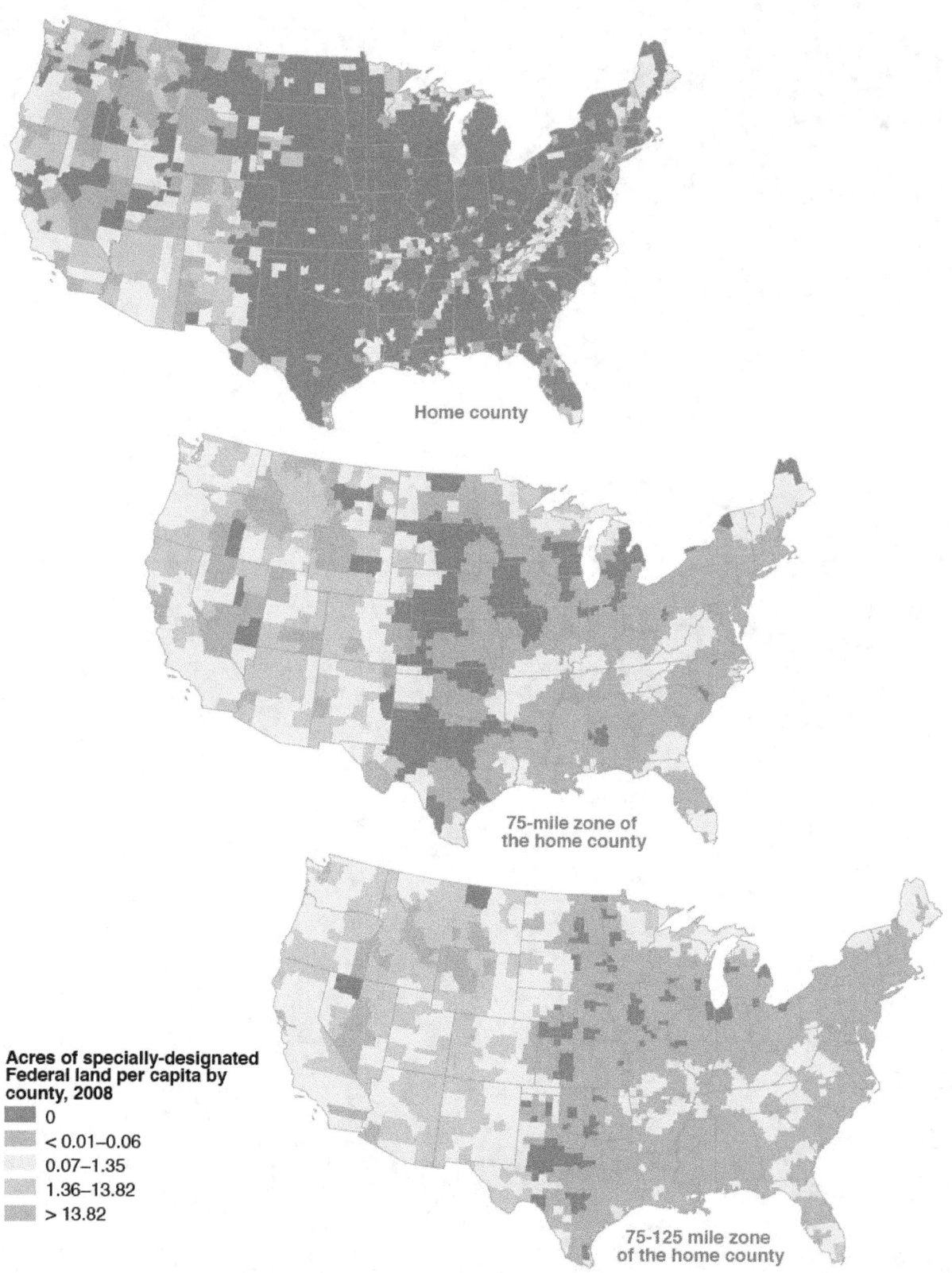

Home county

75-mile zone of
the home county

**Acres of specially-designated
Federal land per capita by
county, 2008**

- 0
- < 0.01–0.06
- 0.07–1.35
- 1.36–13.82
- > 13.82

75-125 mile zone
of the home county

Figure 6.16—Acres of specially designated Federal land per capita, 2008, within the home county, within the 75-mile distance zone, and within the 75-125 mile distance zone. Sources: USDA Forest Service (2008), USDI National Park Service (2008), and Wilderness Institute (2009).

Private Recreation Businesses

The U.S. Census Bureau maintains its Business Register, a file of all known single and multi-establishment companies, and conducts the Economic Census for the United States every 5 years. These are the Bureau's sources of data covering private business employment and finance as well as the number of establishments, organized by North American Industry Classification System (NAICS) codes. Data are analyzed and reported in the *County Business Patterns*, which was last published in 2007. Private businesses are important resources for outdoor recreation because they provide not only access to privately owned land and water resources and other facilities for recreation, but also may provide outfitter and guide services, without which many people would be precluded from participating. An example is a whitewater rafting outfitter which not only has the rafts and other necessary equipment that a person may not own, but also the leadership expertise to guide clients on a trip they may not be qualified to handle by themselves.

Presented in this section is an index of the level of private-sector recreation-related business establishments for each U.S. county, summarized by region and sub-region (table 6.10). The index consists of the simple summation of nine separate business types:

1. marinas
2. skiing facilities
3. private-sector historical sites
4. private-sector zoos and botanical gardens
5. recreational vehicle parks and campgrounds
6. private-sector nature parks
7. private golf courses and country clubs
8. amusement and theme parks
9. recreational and vacation camps (except campgrounds)

These businesses represent the extent of recreation-related industrial sectors in the *County Business Patterns* data that may confidently be called "outdoor recreation businesses." The index is not intended to be representative of all outdoor recreation-oriented businesses. One limitation of these Census data is that many recreation businesses are included in the miscellaneous category "All Other Amusement and Recreation Industries," which are not included in the index because this category includes as many if not more indoor recreation-oriented businesses than outdoor. Data are limited to number of recreation businesses and the number per capita. (An area measurement is not applicable.)

The two East regions account for more than 20,000 (76 percent) of the nearly 27,000 total businesses nationwide. This is nearly identical to the 75 percent of population in the East (see table 6.10). The per capita number of recreation businesses nationally is slightly less than 0.9 per 10,000 people (or 9 per 100,000) with the four regions much more closely centered around this mean, than say for example, some of the public land resources which have much higher per capita values in the West. The Rocky Mountains barely leads the North, both with slightly over 1 business per 10,000 people, while the South and Pacific Coast trail not far behind with 0.75 and 0.69 per capita, respectively. The only real notable patterns in the county maps for the three distance zones are the lack of any businesses in many Great Plains home counties and scattered counties elsewhere, and relatively low numbers of businesses per capita for the two distance zones in the South, Midwest, and southern California (fig. 6.17). Similar to many other resources, recreation businesses per capita are relatively highest (darkest shade > 4.19 per 10,000) in the high amenity areas of the Rocky Mountains, upper Great Lakes States, and New England.

Table 6.10—Total number of recreation businesses, and number per 10,000 people by RPA sub-region and region, 2007

Sub-region and region	Recreation businesses, 2007	
	Number of businesses	Per 10,000 people
Northeast	6,530.0	1.03
North Central	6,200.0	1.01
North total	12,730.0	1.02
Southeast	4,188.0	0.85
South Central	3,548.0	0.67
South total	7,736.0	0.75
Great Plains	785.0	1.30
Intermountain	2,153.0	0.99
Rocky Mountains total	2,938.0	1.06
Alaska	209.0	3.06
Pacific Northwest	1,124.0	1.09
Pacific Southwest	2,055.0	0.54
Pacific Coast total	3,388.0	0.69
U.S. total	26,792.0	0.88

RPA = Resources Planning Act.
Note: "Recreation businesses" as presented in this table is an index of the level of private-sector recreation-related business establishments that exist in each U.S. county. It is the sum of nine distinct business types: marinas, skiing facilities, private-sector historical sites, private-sector zoos and botanical gardens, recreational vehicle parks and campgrounds, private-sector nature parks, (private) golf courses and country clubs, amusement and theme parks, and recreational and vacation camps (except campgrounds). See table 6.1 for population and total surface area acreage.
Source: U.S. Census Bureau (2007b).

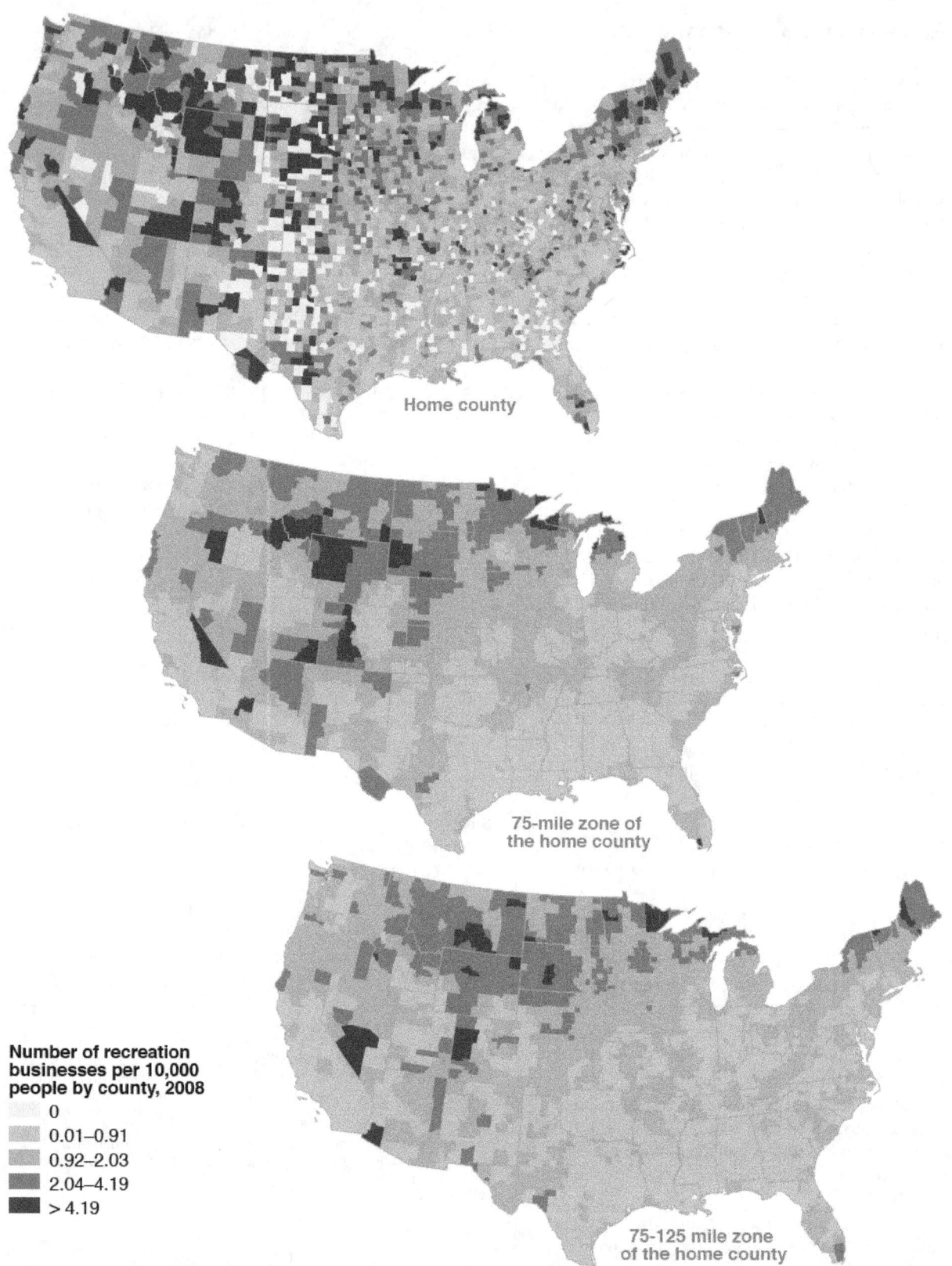

Number of recreation businesses per 10,000 people by county, 2008

- 0
- 0.01–0.91
- 0.92–2.03
- 2.04–4.19
- > 4.19

Home county

75-mile zone of the home county

75-125 mile zone of the home county

Figure 6.17—Number of recreation businesses per 10,000 people, 2008, within the home county, within the 75-mile distance zone, and within the 75-125 mile distance zone. Source: U.S. Census Bureau (2007b).

CHAPTER 7
Projections of Future Recreation Resources

This chapter addresses objective 7 of this national assessment on outdoor recreation and protected land resources: to tabulate and map projections of future per capita recreation resources for the 75-mile distance zone. The primary focus is on projections of the geospatial distribution of these resources by region and sub-region of the country. County-level maps of the contiguous United States are presented which show expected relative availability in the year 2060 for the same 9 recreation resources described in chapter 6. The projected recreation resources, driven by forecast population changes between the present and 2060, can be interpreted as becoming less "available" as more people are competing to use them. The focus is on the 75-mile recreation distance zone, which is generally interpreted as the distance encompassing recreation opportunities within a 1- to 2-hour drive of people's homes. To review, the nine basic outdoor recreation resources include:

- Federal and State park land
- Water
- Non-Federal forest
- Non-Federal open range and pasture
- Ocean and Great Lakes coast
- Mountains
- Snow cover
- Specially-designated Federal lands
- Private recreation businesses

Data and Methods

Recreation resource data compiled for all U.S. counties allowed basic projections of how the availability of those resources would change given projected changes in population. Non-Federal forest, range and pasture projections to 2060 were used in this assessment forecasting (Wear 2011). Current resource levels were maintained for the remaining resources. County population projections at 10-year intervals from 2010 to 2060 for the moderate or A1B scenario were used, which closely followed Census Bureau national population projections that were then further disaggregated to the county-level for the forecasting sections of the RPA Assessment (Zarnoch and others 2010).

These population projections were used to produce county-level maps for the nine recreation resources showing their current and projected relative per capita abundance (or scarcity), followed by maps showing the proportion of per capita availability in 2060 relative to that in 2008, or what we call a "change proportion." (Forest and open range/pasture show the change proportion from the base year 2010.) Maps in chapter 6 to show amount of

resource per capita located within the 75-mile distance zone of each county, defined as the quantity of resource within both the home county and all other counties whose center or centroid are within 75 miles of each home county centroid. Recreation opportunities represented by resources within 75 miles can be considered to be within a 2-hour drive.

Results

Preceding each resource map is a table showing the current and projected resource per capita for RPA regions and sub-regions, as well as the change proportion of per capita availability in 2060 relative to that in 2008 (2010 for non-Federal forest and open range/pasture). A proportion less than 1.0 indicates a decline in resources per capita. At the more aggregated scale represented by the table cells (9 resource columns by 14 nation/region/sub-region rows), projected 2060 population increases result in change proportions for all resources of less than 1.0. At the resolute scale represented by the county-level maps, however, some change proportions are greater than 1.0, which indicates that population is expected to decrease resulting in more resources per capita in 2060 than in 2008. Projected 2060 population and current total surface area acres for each sub-region, region, and the Nation are shown in table 7.1.

Federal and State Park Land

Federal land agencies include the National Park Service, the U.S. Forest Service, the U.S. Fish and Wildlife Service, the Bureau of Land Management, the Tennessee Valley Authority, and the U.S. Army Corps of Engineers. State park land includes all areas managed by State park agencies regardless of their classification. Nationally, there will be a projected 1.4 acres of Federal and State park land per capita in 2060, which is about two-thirds of the 2.1 acres per capita in 2008 (table 7.2). The two western regions will still far outpace the eastern regions by 2060 in acres per capita, especially the Intermountain and Pacific Northwest sub-regions (not considering Alaska). However, because of expected population growth, the Rocky Mountains region, especially the Intermountain sub-region, will experience the largest decline in per capita acres, as indicated by the 2060/2008 proportion. The impact should be minimal region-wide, since the Intermountain sub-region will still have more than twice the acreage of any other sub-region. However, recreationists in selected hotspots throughout the Rocky Mountains that are projected to have large population increases will likely experience declines in availability and/or increasing congestion.

Counties with the most acres per person in the 75-mile distance zone in both 2008 and 2060 (darkest shade, > 19.40) are entirely in the West (fig. 7.1). Regions of the United States with the lowest relative availability will be the urbanized Northeast, upper Midwest, and the large mid-section of Texas and Oklahoma to a lesser extent. Counties with a proportion greater than 1.0 in figure 7.2 will lose population in 2060, thus resulting in more acres per capita. Most of these counties

are in the Great Plains sub-region and along the Mississippi Valley, with just a few scattered counties throughout Northeast. The smallest change proportions are throughout the West, especially the Intermountain sub-region, the Southeast, east Texas, the Ozark/Ouachita region, and portions of Minnesota and Wisconsin. High population growth in these areas will have the most relative effect on per capita levels of existing Federal and State park land resources.

Table 7.1—Projected 2060 total population and current total surface area acres by RPA sub-region and region

Sub-region and region	Projected 2060 population		Total surface area (thousand acres)	
	Number	Percent	Number	Percent
	thousand		*thousand*	
Northeast	80,049.2	17.9	141,088.1	5.8
North Central	77,548.7	17.3	329,186.6	13.6
North region	157,597.9	35.2	470,274.6	19.4
Southeast	83,107.9	18.6	162,425.1	6.7
South Central	80,565.9	18.0	401,215.2	16.5
South region	163,673.8	36.6	563,640.3	23.2
Great Plains	7,915.8	1.8	196,766.0	8.1
Intermountain	41,779.9	9.3	552,682.9	22.8
Rocky Mountains region	49,695.6	11.1	749,448.9	30.9
Alaska	1,158.9	0.3	424,491.0	17.5
Pacific Northwest	16,838.7	3.8	108,595.4	4.5
Pacific Southwest	58,343.1	13.0	111,761.0	4.6
Pacific Coast region	76,340.6	17.1	644,847.4	26.6
U.S. total	447,308.0	100.0	2,428,211.3	100.0

RPA = Resources Planning Act.
Source: Zarnoch and others (2010), U.S. Census Bureau (2000).

Table 7.2—Current (2008) and projected (2060) per capita acres of Federal and State park land and proportion of current acres projected for 2060 by RPA sub-region and region

Sub-region and region	Federal and State park land			
	Total acres 2008	Per capita acres, 2008	Projected per capita acres, 2060	Proportion of 2008 acres projected for 2060
	thousand			
Northeast	5,519.6	0.09	0.07	0.79
North Central	14,395.8	0.24	0.19	0.79
North region	19,915.4	0.16	0.13	0.79
Southeast	12,043.0	0.24	0.14	0.60
South Central	16,231.2	0.30	0.20	0.66
South region	28,274.2	0.28	0.17	0.63
Great Plains	6,666.5	1.11	0.84	0.76
Intermountain	252,976.2	11.64	6.05	0.52
Rocky Mountains region	259,642.7	9.35	5.22	0.56
Alaska	231,739.8	339.18	199.97	0.59
Pacific Northwest	41,449.4	4.01	2.46	0.61
Pacific Southwest	46,297.7	1.22	0.79	0.65
Pacific Coast region	319,486.9	6.51	4.19	0.64
U.S. total	627,319.2	2.06	1.40	0.68

RPA = Resources Planning Act.
Note: Federal and State park land is the sum of Federal land-managing agency area and State park system areas. Acreage is held constant at the 2008 level. See table 7.1 for projected population and total surface area acreage.
Sources: USDA Forest Service (2008, 2009b), USDI National Park Service (2008), USDI Fish and Wildlife Service (2009), USDI Bureau of Land Management (2008b), Tennessee Valley Authority (N.d.); U.S. Army Corps of Engineers (2006), and Zarnoch and others (2010).

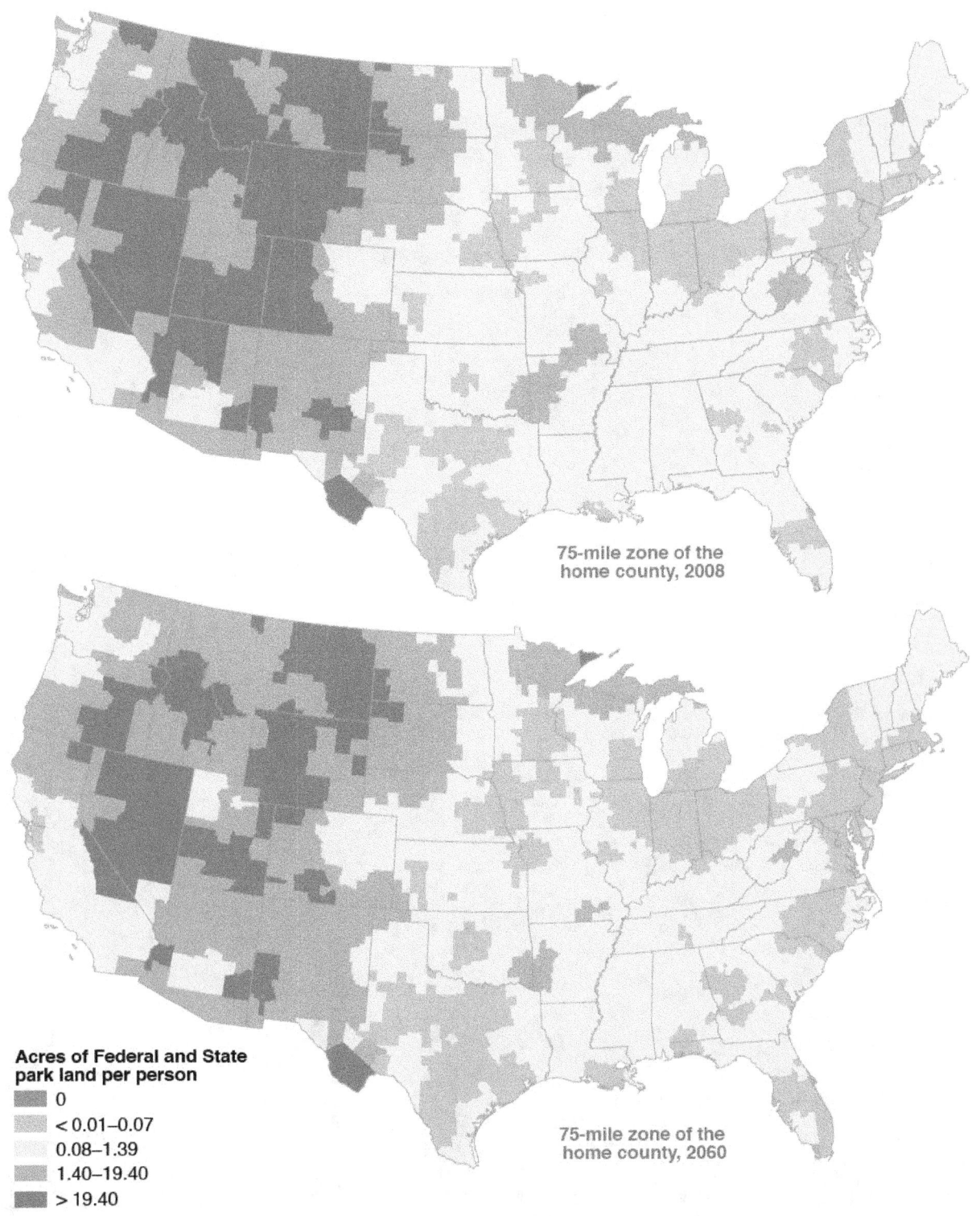

Figure 71— Acres of Federal and State park land per person, 2008 and 2060, within the 75-mile distance zone. Sources: USDA Forest Service (2008, 2009b), USDI National Park Service (2008), USDI Fish and Wildlife Service (2009), USDI Bureau of Land Management (2008b), Tennessee Valley Authority (N.d.), U.S. Army Corps of Engineers (2006), and Zarnoch and others (2010).

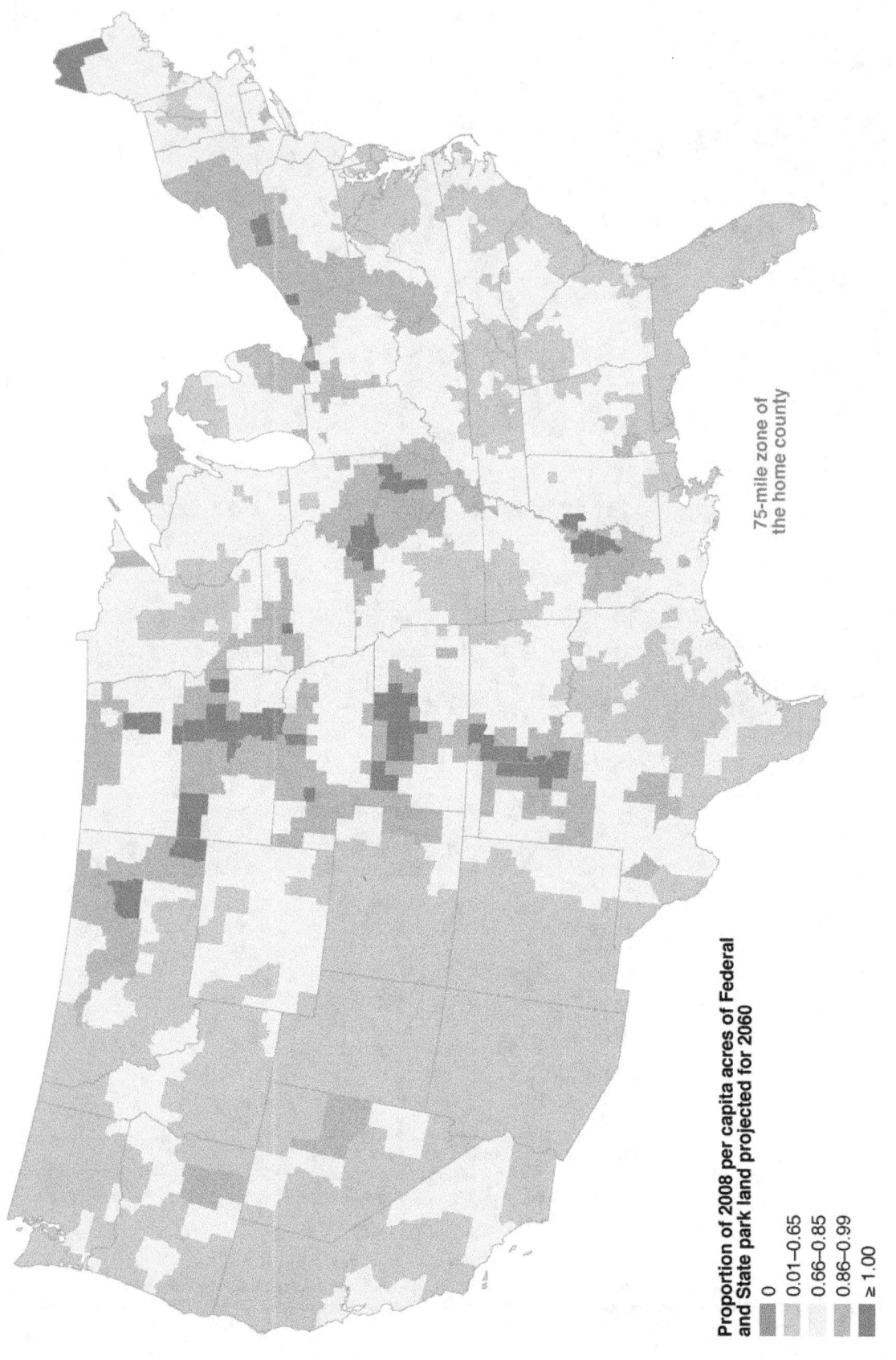

Proportion of 2008 per capita acres of Federal and State park land projected for 2060

- 0
- 0.01–0.65
- 0.66–0.85
- 0.86–0.99
- ≥ 1.00

75-mile zone of the home county

Figure 7.2—Proportion of 2008 per capita acres of Federal and State park land projected for 2060, within the 75-mile distance zone. Sources: USDA Forest Service (2008, 2009b), USDI National Park Service (2008, 2009b), USDI Fish and Wildlife Service (2009), USDI Bureau of Land Management (2008b), Tennessee Valley Authority (N.d.), U.S. Army Corps of Engineers (2006), and Zarnoch and others (2010).

Water Area

Water resources, including streams, rivers, ponds, lakes, and ocean will continue to be a major factor that attracts both local residents and visitors for outdoor recreation. Given the expected population increase, water acres per capita in the United States are projected to fall from slightly more than 0.5 acres per person in 2008 to less than 0.4 acres per person in 2060 (table 7.3). The largest decline will be in the Rocky Mountains region, which has the least amount of water area (about 7.3 million surface acres), that is, only about one-fourth the water area of the next closest region, the South. Water recreation opportunities in the West could feel these effects, especially around metropolitan areas such as Denver, Phoenix, and Salt Lake City.

County pattern maps for the 75-mile distance zones show the largest acres per capita in 2008 and 2060 (darkest shade, > 2.24 acres per person) in the West, upper Great Plains, and Great Lakes States, with the West tailing off some in 2060 (fig. 7.3). The change proportion map shows a definite shift to lower per capita water resources in the West and Southeast, a result of the high projected population growth in those areas, especially the Pacific Coast and Rocky Mountains regions (fig. 7.4). The highest relative change proportions are located in northern Maine, along the Great Lakes, in the Mississippi Valley, and scattered throughout the Great Plains.

Table 7.3—Current (2008) and projected (2060) per capita acres of total water area and proportion of current acres projected for 2060 by RPA sub-region and region

Sub-region and region	Water area			
	Total acres 2008	Per capita acres, 2008	Projected per capita acres, 2060	Proportion of 2008 acres projected for 2060
	thousand			
Northeast	14,328.5	0.23	0.18	0.79
North Central	42,505.3	0.70	0.55	0.79
North region	56,833.8	0.46	0.36	0.79
Southeast	15,068.8	0.30	0.18	0.60
South Central	14,213.4	0.27	0.18	0.66
South region	29,282.1	0.28	0.18	0.63
Great Plains	2,495.3	0.41	0.32	0.76
Intermountain	4,793.4	0.22	0.11	0.52
Rocky Mountains region	7,288.8	0.26	0.15	0.56
Alaska	58,442.2	85.54	50.43	0.59
Pacific Northwest	4,569.2	0.44	0.27	0.61
Pacific Southwest	7,836.5	0.21	0.13	0.65
Pacific Coast region	70,848.0	1.44	0.93	0.64
U.S. total	164,252.7	0.54	0.37	0.68

RPA = Resources Planning Act.
Note: Census Bureau water is classified as one of four types: inland, coastal, territorial, and Great Lakes. Acreage is held constant at the 2008 level. See table 7.1 for projected population and total surface area acreage.
Sources: U.S. Census Bureau (2000), Zarnoch and others (2010).

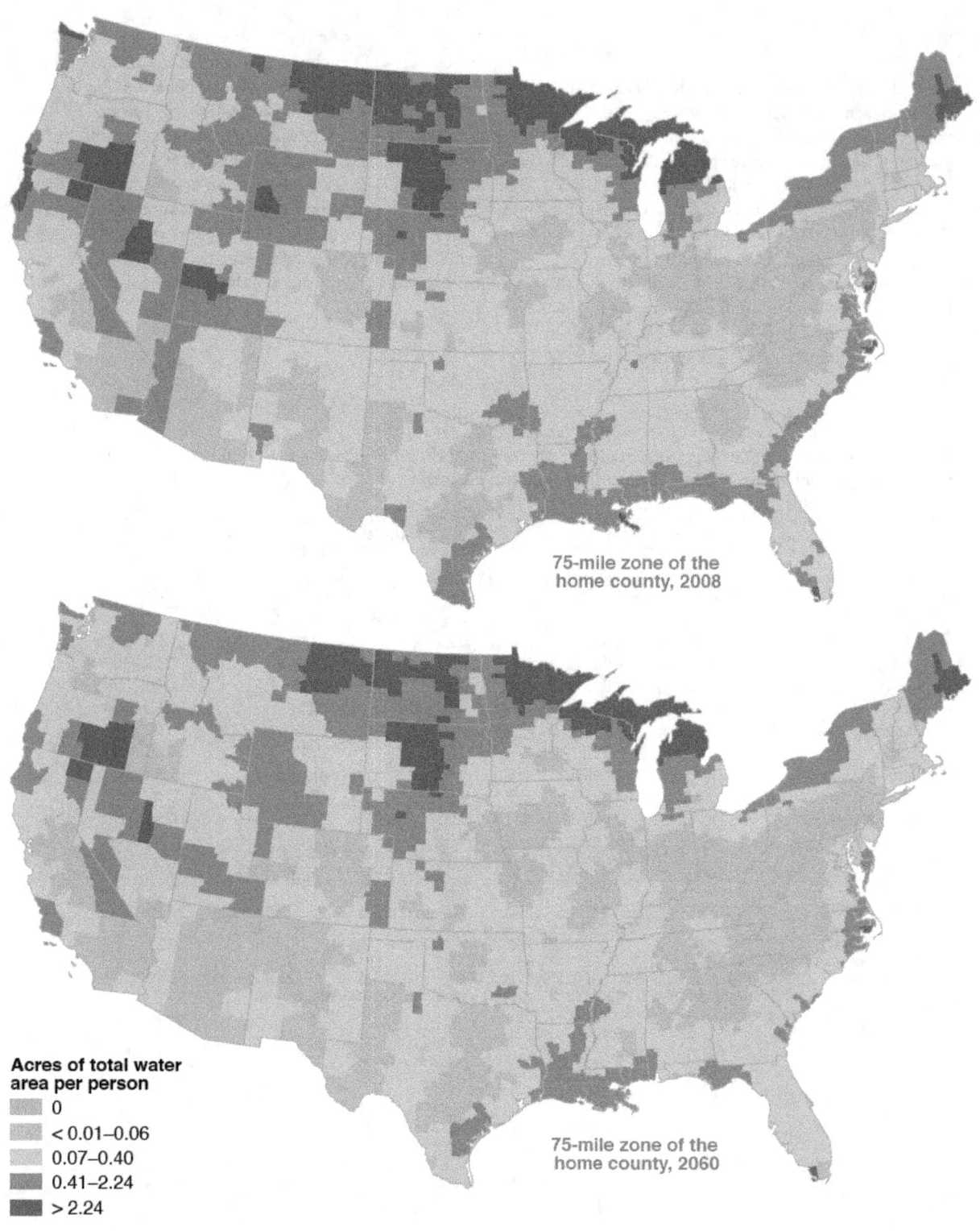

75-mile zone of the home county, 2008

Acres of total water area per person

- 0
- < 0.01–0.06
- 0.07–0.40
- 0.41–2.24
- > 2.24

75-mile zone of the home county, 2060

Figure 7.3—Acres of total water area per person, 2008 and 2060, within the 75-mile distance zone.
Sources: U.S. Census Bureau (2000), and Zarnoch and others (2010).

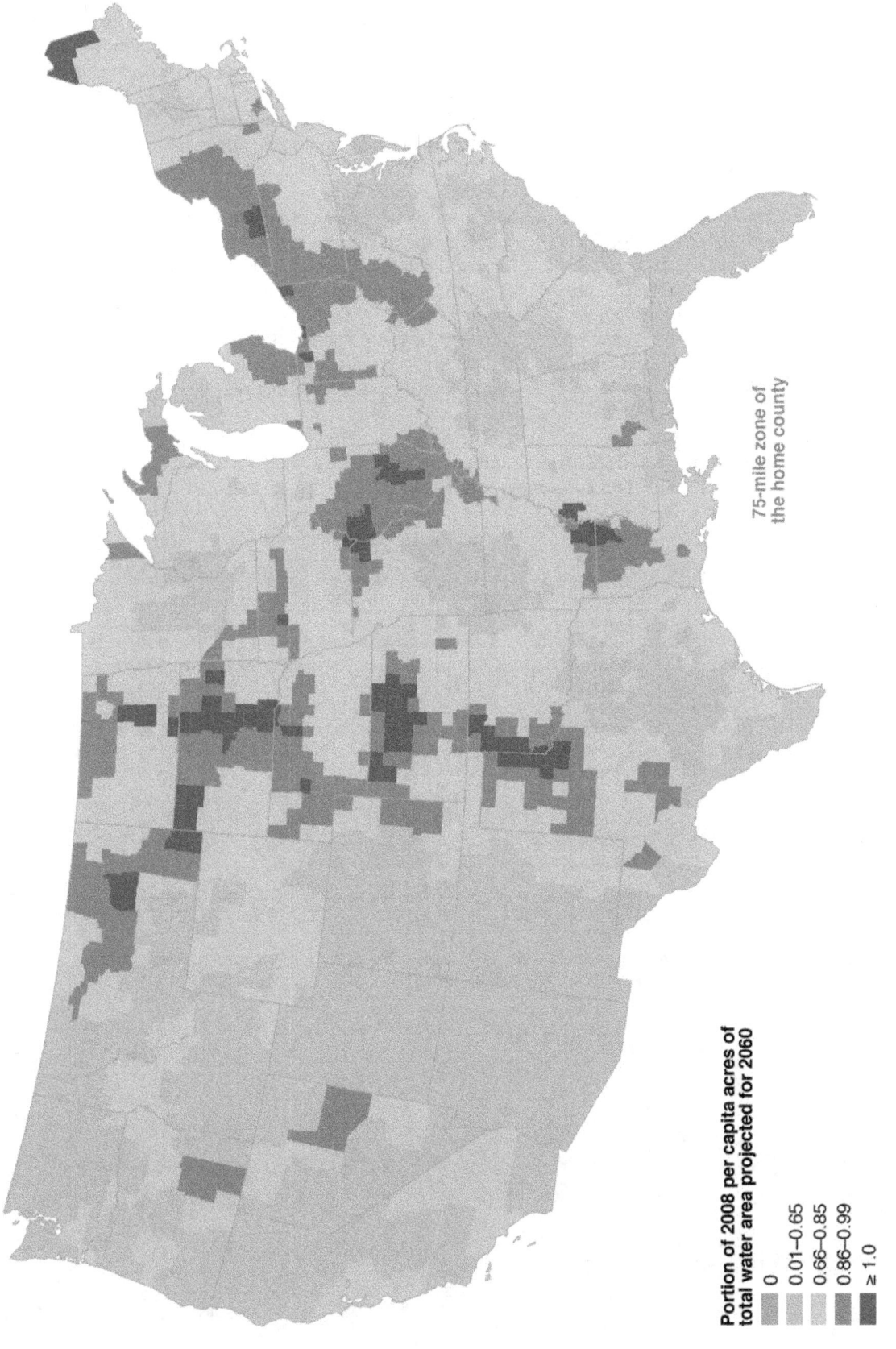

Portion of 2008 per capita acres of total water area projected for 2060

- 0
- 0.01–0.65
- 0.66–0.85
- 0.86–0.99
- ≥ 1.0

75-mile zone of
the home county

Figure 7.4—Proportion of 2008 per capita acres of total water area projected for 2060, within the 75-mile distance zone. Sources: U.S. Census Bureau (2000), and Zarnoch and others (2010).

Non-Federal Forest

Forests are a major land cover and use in the United States. Currently, the total area of public and private forest resources covers approximately 29 percent of the surface area of the country. Similar to chapter 6, the focus of this section is on non-Federal forest land. Based on RPA land use projections (Wear 2011), non-Federal forest area in the 48 States is expected to decline 7.8 percent between 2010 and 2060 for the A1B scenario, from about 386 million acres to 356 million (table 7.4). The projected decline in forest acres per person is also significant, from 1.27 in 2010 to 0.8 in 2060. In two high-population growth sub-regions, Intermountain and Southeast, the 2060 per capita forest land is projected to be just 0.50 and 0.52, respectively, which is about half the level in 2010.

Acres of non-Federal forest area per capita by county in the 75-mile distance zones in 2010 and 2060 are shown in figure 7.5. The highest per capita counties (darkest shade, > 16.10 acres per person) in 2008 are mostly in the Northeast, upper Great Lakes regions, and scattered throughout the West, with a few counties falling out of the highest class in 2060. Almost all of west Texas and a handful of other western counties have no non-Federal forest located within 75 miles. Similar to the other natural resources, most counties in the West and Southeast have the largest declines (lightest shades) in per capita non-Federal forest area in 2060 (fig. 7.6). Also included in this class are concentrations of counties in the Ozark/Ouachita highlands, Minnesota, and upper Wisconsin. The positive expected changes in the Great Plains States are somewhat misleading because of relative lack of forest resources in that region.

Table 7.4—Current (2010) and projected (2060) per capita acres of non-Federal forest and proportion of current acres projected for 2060 by RPA sub-region and region

Sub-region and region	Non- Federal forest land land			
	Total acres 2060	Per capita acres, 2010	Projected per capita acres, 2060	Proportion of 2010 acres projected for 2060
	thousand			
Northeast	69,168.0	1.18	0.86	0.73
North Central	68,839.6	1.20	0.89	0.74
North region	138,007.6	1.19	0.88	0.74
Southeast	60,119.0	1.40	0.72	0.52
South Central	94,555.9	1.90	1.17	0.62
South region	154,674.9	1.66	0.95	0.57
Great Plains	3,183.5	0.54	0.40	0.74
Intermountain	24,373.2	1.16	0.58	0.50
Rocky Mountains region	27,556.7	1.02	0.55	0.54
Pacific Northwest	22,759.1	2.31	1.35	0.59
Pacific Southwest	12,509.2	0.36	0.21	0.59
Pacific Coast region	35,268.3	0.79	0.47	0.59
U.S. total	355,507.5	1.27	0.80	0.63

RPA = Resources Planning Act.
Note: Non-Federal forest land projections were not done for Alaska and Hawaii. See table 7.1 for projected population and total surface area acreage. Sources: Wear (2011), and Zarnoch and others (2010).

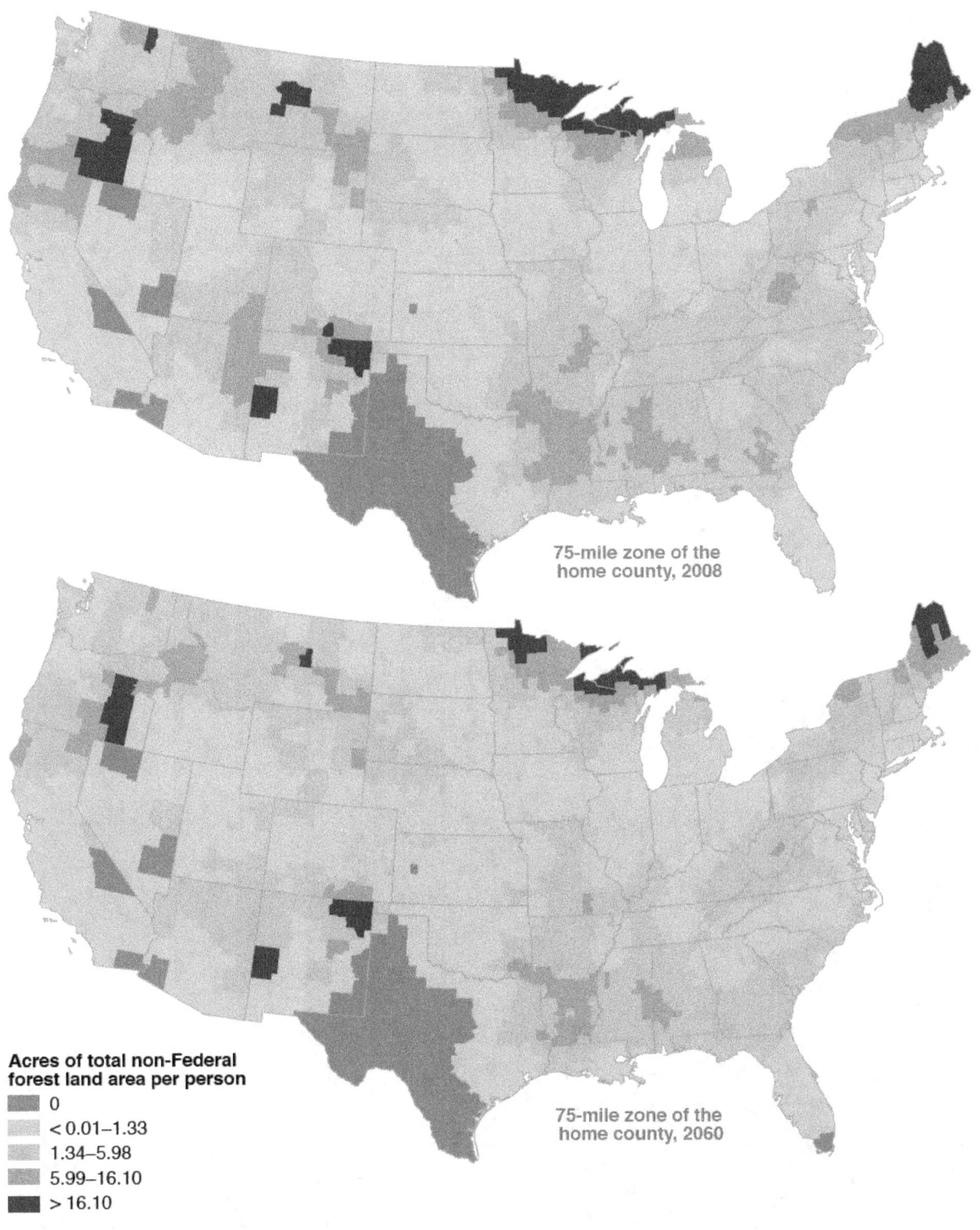

Acres of total non-Federal
forest land area per person

- 0
- < 0.01–1.33
- 1.34–5.98
- 5.99–16.10
- > 16.10

75-mile zone of the
home county, 2008

75-mile zone of the
home county, 2060

Figure 7.5—Acres of total non-Federal forest land area per person, 2008 and 2060, within the 75-mile distance zone.
Sources: Wear (2011), and Zarnoch and others (2010).

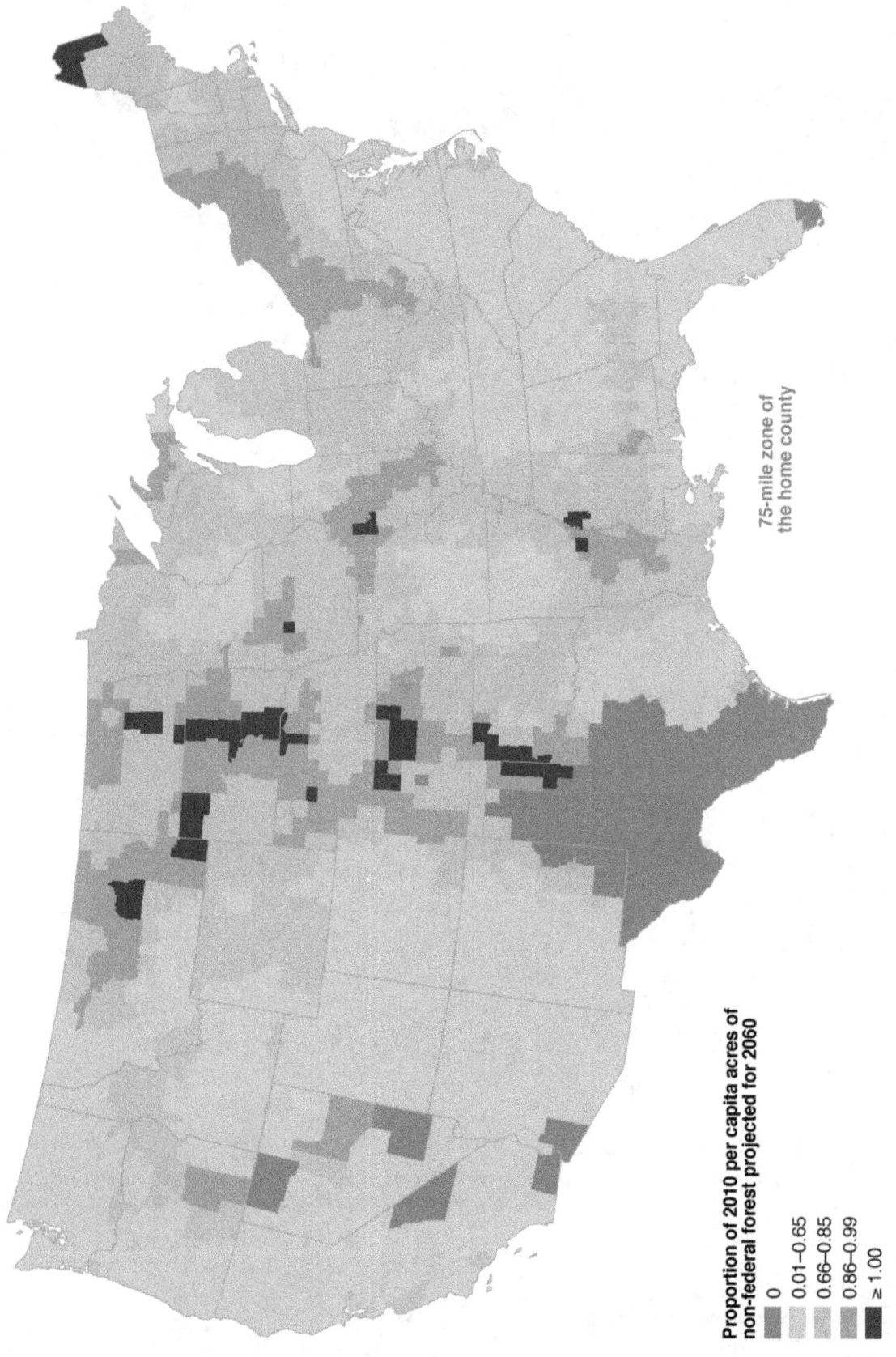

**Proportion of 2010 per capita acres of
non-federal forest projected for 2060**

- 0
- 0.01–0.65
- 0.66–0.85
- 0.86–0.99
- ≥ 1.00

75-mile zone of
the home county

Figure 7.6—Proportion of 2010 per capita acres of non-Federal forest projected for 2060, within the 75-mile distance zone. Sources: Wear (2011), and Zarnoch and others (2010).

Non-Federal Open Range and Pasture

Open non-forested lands are very extensive in the United States. Besides non-Federal forest, open range and pasture is the only category of recreation resources considered in this report for which projected changes in area to the year 2060 exist (Wear 2011). In 2060, non-Federal open range and pasture are projected to be about 497 million acres in the 48 States, down about 3 percent from the 514 million acres in 2010 (table 7.5). While much of range is publicly owned (especially by the Bureau of Land Management, but Federal lands are not included in this analysis), most pasture is privately owned. Recreation occurs on almost all these acres in one form or another. Per capita open range and pasture land is expected to be about 1.1 acres per person nationally in 2060, about two-thirds what it was in 2010. The largest changes are expected in the Intermountain and Southeast sub-regions, due largely

to population growth, though the Southeast has just a fraction of the acreage of open range and pasture land compared to the Intermountain. The Great Plains will still dwarf all other sub-regions in acres per person by 2060, despite the 9.7 projected acres per person which is a decline from 12.8 acres in 2010.

Current and projected acres of open range and pasture per capita within the 75-mile distant zone are dominated by the western regions, as shown in the county pattern maps for 2008 and 2060 (fig. 7.7). The projected change proportion in per capita acres from 2010 to 2060 will show the least declines and some gains (i.e., ≥ 1.0) in the Great Plains, where range and pasture is plentiful and population is slow growing or declining, and also in the lower Mississippi Valley and coastal plain of the Southeastern United States (fig. 7.8). The Midwest and Northeast States will remain fairly constant because of their relatively small amount of range and pasture resources.

Table 7.5—Current (2010) and projected (2060) per capita acres of non-Federal open range and pasture and proportion of current acres projected for 2060 by RPA sub-region and region

| Sub-region and region | Non-Federal open range and pasture | | | |
	Total acres 2060	Per capita acres, 2010	Projected per capita acres, 2060	Proportion of 2010 acres projected for 2060
	thousand			
Northeast	6,514.4	0.11	0.08	0.72
North Central	26,635.1	0.47	0.34	0.73
North region	33,149.5	0.29	0.21	0.73
Southeast	13,917.9	0.32	0.17	0.53
South Central	150,183.3	2.90	1.86	0.64
South region	164,101.2	1.66	1.00	0.60
Great Plains	76,744.1	12.82	9.70	0.76
Intermountain	188,934.7	8.88	4.52	0.51
Rocky Mountains region	265,678.8	9.74	5.35	0.55
Pacific Northwest	17,299.2	1.70	1.03	0.60
Pacific Southwest	16,862.2	0.50	0.29	0.58
Pacific Coast region	34,161.4	0.77	0.45	0.59
U.S. total	497,090.9	1.70	1.11	0.66

RPA = Resources Planning Act.
Note: Open range and pasture projections were not done for Alaska and Hawaii. Does not include cultivated agricultural lands. See table 7.1 for projected population and total surface area acreage.
Sources: Wear (2011), and Zarnoch and others (2010).

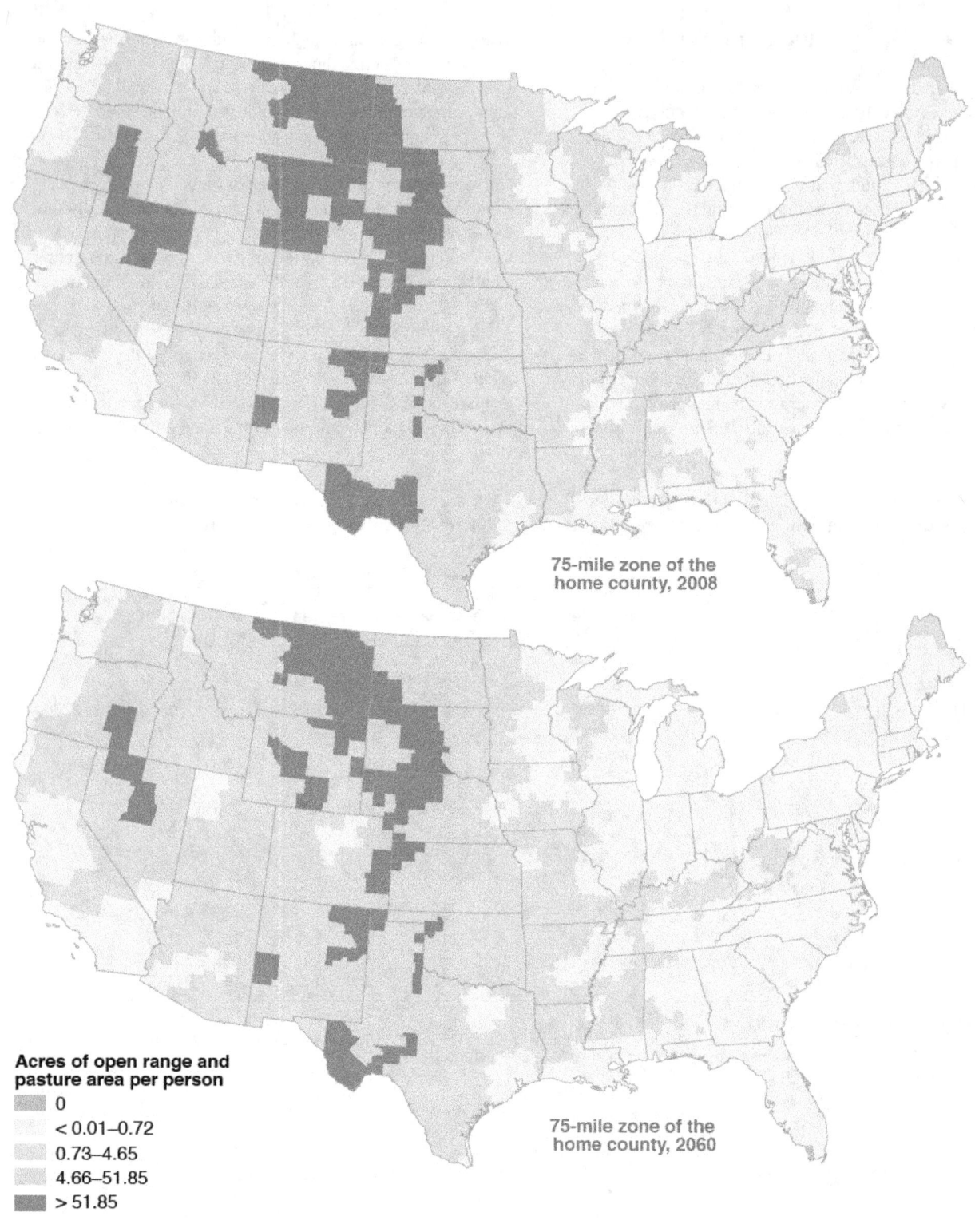

75-mile zone of the
home county, 2008

**Acres of open range and
pasture area per person**

- 0
- < 0.01–0.72
- 0.73–4.65
- 4.66–51.85
- > 51.85

75-mile zone of the
home county, 2060

Figure 7.7—Acres of open range and pasture area per person, 2008 and 2060, within the 75-mile distance zone. Sources: Wear (2011), and Zarnoch and others (2010).

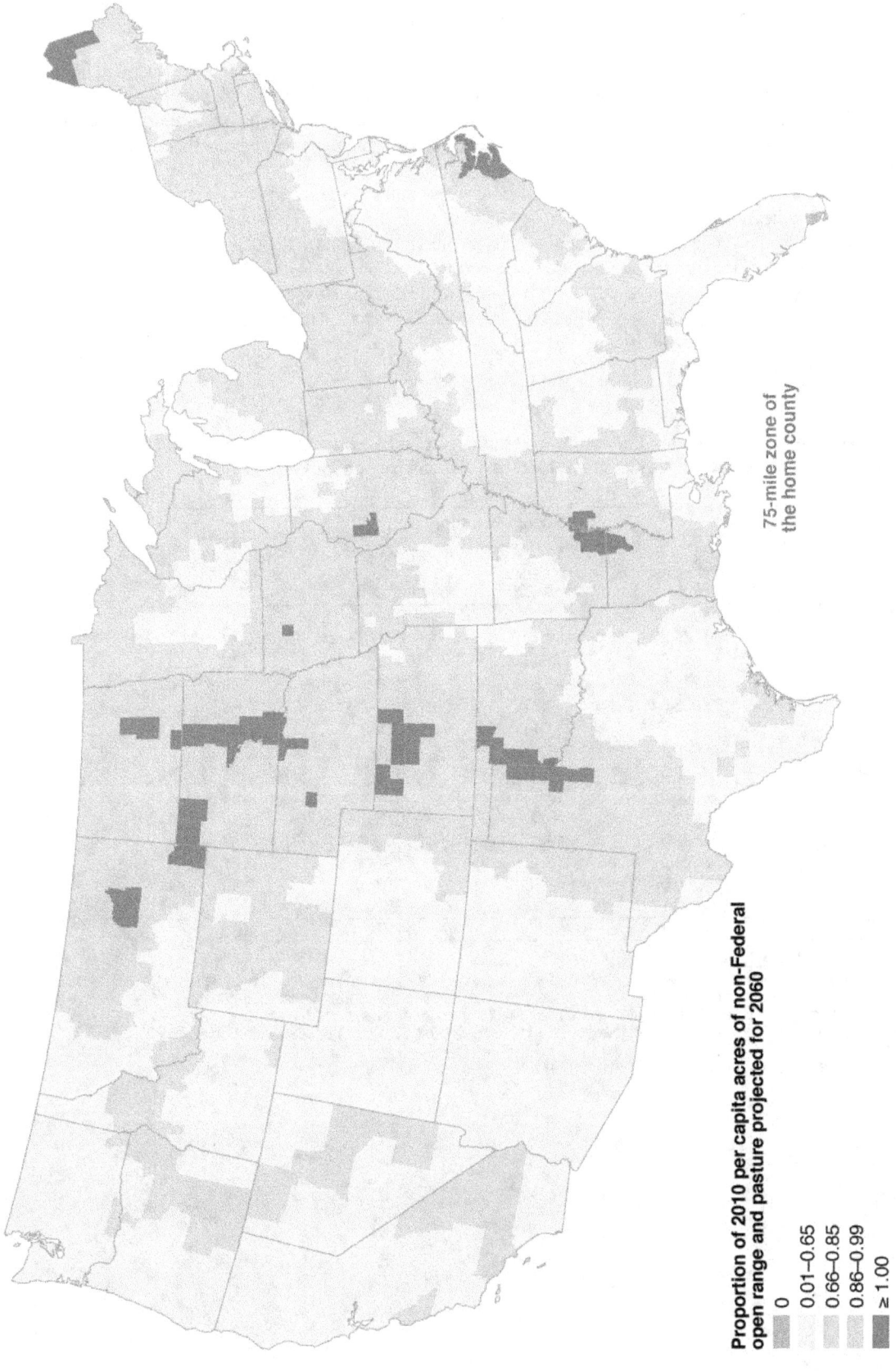

Proportion of 2010 per capita acres of non-Federal open range and pasture projected for 2060

0

0.01–0.65

0.66–0.85

0.86–0.99

≥ 1.00

75-mile zone of the home county

Figure 7.8—Proportion of 2010 per capita acres of non-Federal open range and pasture projected for 2060, within the 75-mile distance zone. Sources: Wear (2011), and Zarnoch and others (2010).

Ocean and Great Lakes Coast

Coastal counties contain 17 percent of the U.S. contiguous land area, have more than half of the country's population, and cover a variety of landscapes from oceans, to the Gulf of Mexico, and Great Lakes. Given the projected population growth in the United States, per capita acres of coastal county area are expected to decline from 2.3 acres per person in 2008 to 1.6 in 2060 (table 7.6). The Southeast and Pacific Northwest sub-regions should experience the largest decline in per capita change proportions relative to the other regions, though the differences are slight among all sub-regions.

The county pattern maps for 2008 and 2060 highlight the counties in the Great Lake States, Maine, and a few in

northern California and Oregon as having the most coastal land per capita within the 75-mile distance zone (fig. 7.9). Conversely, they also show that the Southeast will have noticeably fewer counties with high per capita coastal acreage in 2060. The change proportions indicate that the counties that will decline the most relative to other coastal counties are in California, Pacific Northwest, and along the southeastern coast (especially Florida) and stretching into the Gulf States to Texas (fig. 7.10). Many Great Lakes counties are expected to stay nearly constant (in the 0.86 to 0.99 proportion class) in coastal acres per capita due to lower projected population gains, while all others except in Northern Michigan will be in the 0.66 to 0.85 change proportion category.

Table 7.6—Current (2008) and projected (2060) per capita acres of ocean and Great Lakes coastal county area and proportion of current acres projected for 2060 by RPA sub-region and region

| Sub-region and region | Coastal county area | | | |
	Total acres 2008	Per capita acres, 2008	Projected per capita acres, 2060	Proportion of 2008 acres projected for 2060
	thousand			
Northeast	70,765.2	1.12	0.88	0.79
North Central	97,211.8	1.59	1.25	0.79
North region	167,976.9	1.35	1.07	0.79
Southeast	85,955.6	1.74	1.03	0.60
South Central	61,039.7	1.14	0.76	0.66
South region	146,995.3	1.43	0.90	0.63
Great Plains	0.0	0.00	0.00	na
Intermountain	0.0	0.00	0.00	na
Rocky Mountains region	0.0	0.00	0.00	na
Alaska	300,892.8	440.40	259.64	0.59
Pacific Northwest	32,901.9	3.18	1.95	0.61
Pacific Southwest	60,740.5	1.60	1.04	0.65
Pacific Coast region	394,535.1	8.04	5.17	0.64
U.S. total	709,507.4	2.33	1.59	0.68

RPA = Resources Planning Act; na= Not applicable.
Note: Coastal counties meet one of the following criteria: 1) at least 15 percent of a county's total land area is located within the Nation's coastal watershed; or 2) a portion of or an entire county accounts for at least 15 percent of a coastal cataloging unit, i.e., although a county does not have at least 15 percent of its total area within the coastal watershed, it still has a large land area within a coastal watershed. Acreage is held constant at the 2008 level. See table 7.1 for projected population and total surface area acreage.
Source: USDC National Oceanic and Atmospheric Administration (2004).

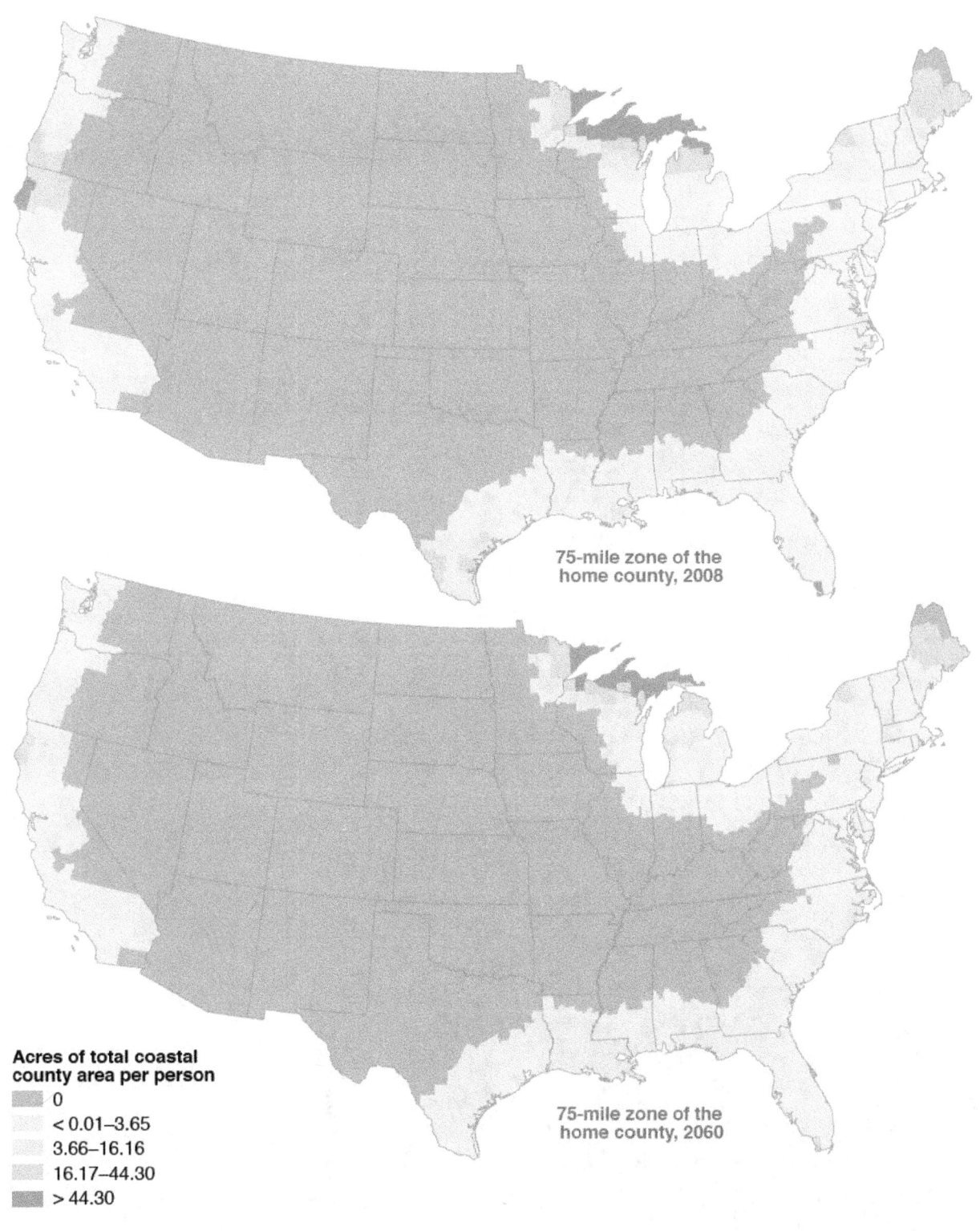

75-mile zone of the
home county, 2008

**Acres of total coastal
county area per person**

- 0
- < 0.01–3.65
- 3.66–16.16
- 16.17–44.30
- > 44.30

75-mile zone of the
home county, 2060

Figure 7.9—Acres of coastal county area per person, 2008 and 2060, within the 75-mile distance zone.
Source: USDC National Oceanic and Atmospheric Administration (2004).

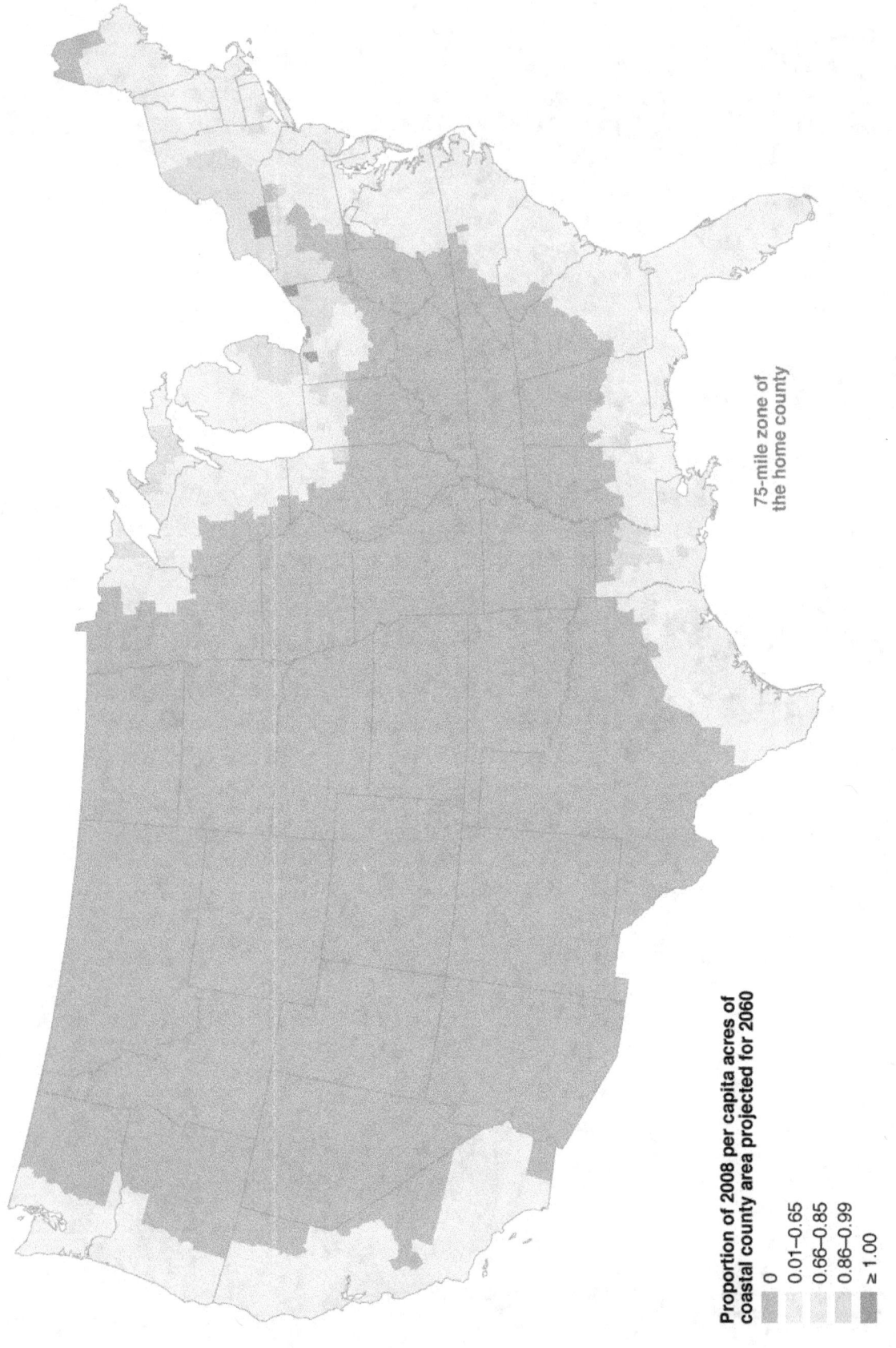

Proportion of 2008 per capita acres of coastal county area projected for 2060

- 0
- 0.01–0.65
- 0.66–0.85
- 0.86–0.99
- ≥ 1.00

75-mile zone of the home county

Figure 7.10—Proportion of 2008 per capita coastal county acres projected for 2060, within the 75-mile distance zone. Source: USDC National Oceanic and Atmospheric Administration (2004).

Mountains

Mountains are a highly significant natural amenity that supports a myriad of outdoor recreation opportunities that attract residents and tourists. Much of the Nation's public land is concentrated in mountain environments, especially in the West, but also along the Appalachians and Ozark/Ouachita ranges. Mountains are a resource that will obviously change very little, if at all, over a 50-year planning horizon. However, mountain acres per capita will decline as population rises, as shown by the projected 0.85 acres per capita in 2060 which is a decrease from 1.25 acres per person in 2008 (table 7.7). Based on projected population, the Intermountain sub-region will experience the sharpest decline; however, its 4.4 mountain acres per person will still lead all other sub-regions by a significant margin. The only other sub-region with more than 1 acre per person will be the Pacific Northwest with 3.5. The Northeast sub-region will continue to have the most mountain acres per capita in the Eastern United States.

County pattern maps for mountain acres in the 75-mile distance zones for 2008 and 2060 show that every county in the highest category is now and will continue to be located in the West (fig. 7.11). Counties in the contiguous United States in this category having more than 116.63 mountainous acres per person represent the top 10 percent of counties, many of which are sparsely populated. The only eastern county that is not in the lower two classes in 2060 is the northernmost county in Maine. Many western counties will remain in the two middle categories, between 4.14 and 116.63 acres per capita. Based on the change proportions, many western counties, especially in the Intermountain sub-region, will have fewer mountain acres per person in 2060 than in 2008, however, some western counties will remain in the darker shades, with a few even increasing in per capita acres (fig. 7.12). Conversely in the East, very few counties are expected in the lowest change proportion class, which reflects slower population growth than in the West.

Table 7.7—Current (2008) and projected (2060) per capita acres of mountains and proportion of current acres projected for 2060 by RPA sub-region and region

Sub-region and region	Mountains			
	Total acres 2008	Per capita acres, 2008	Projected per capita acres, 2060	Proportion of 2008 acres projected for 2060
	thousand			
Northeast	49,174.8	0.78	0.61	0.79
North Central	0.0	0.00	0.00	na
North region	49,174.8	0.40	0.31	0.79
Southeast	20,185.2	0.41	0.24	0.60
South Central	12,363.4	0.23	0.15	0.66
South region	32,548.6	0.32	0.20	0.63
Great Plains	2,077.2	0.34	0.26	0.76
Intermountain	185,477.6	8.54	4.44	0.52
Rocky Mountains region	187,554.7	6.76	3.77	0.56
Pacific Northwest	58,024.8	5.61	3.45	0.61
Pacific Southwest	52,514.4	1.38	0.90	0.65
Pacific Coast region	110,539.2	2.28	1.47	0.64
U.S. total	379,817.3	1.25	0.85	0.68

na = Not applicable; RPA = Resources Planning Act.
Note: Mountain area data were not available for Alaska and Hawaii. Acreage is held constant at the 2008 level.
See table 7.1 for projected population and total surface area acreage.
Source: Bailey (1995).

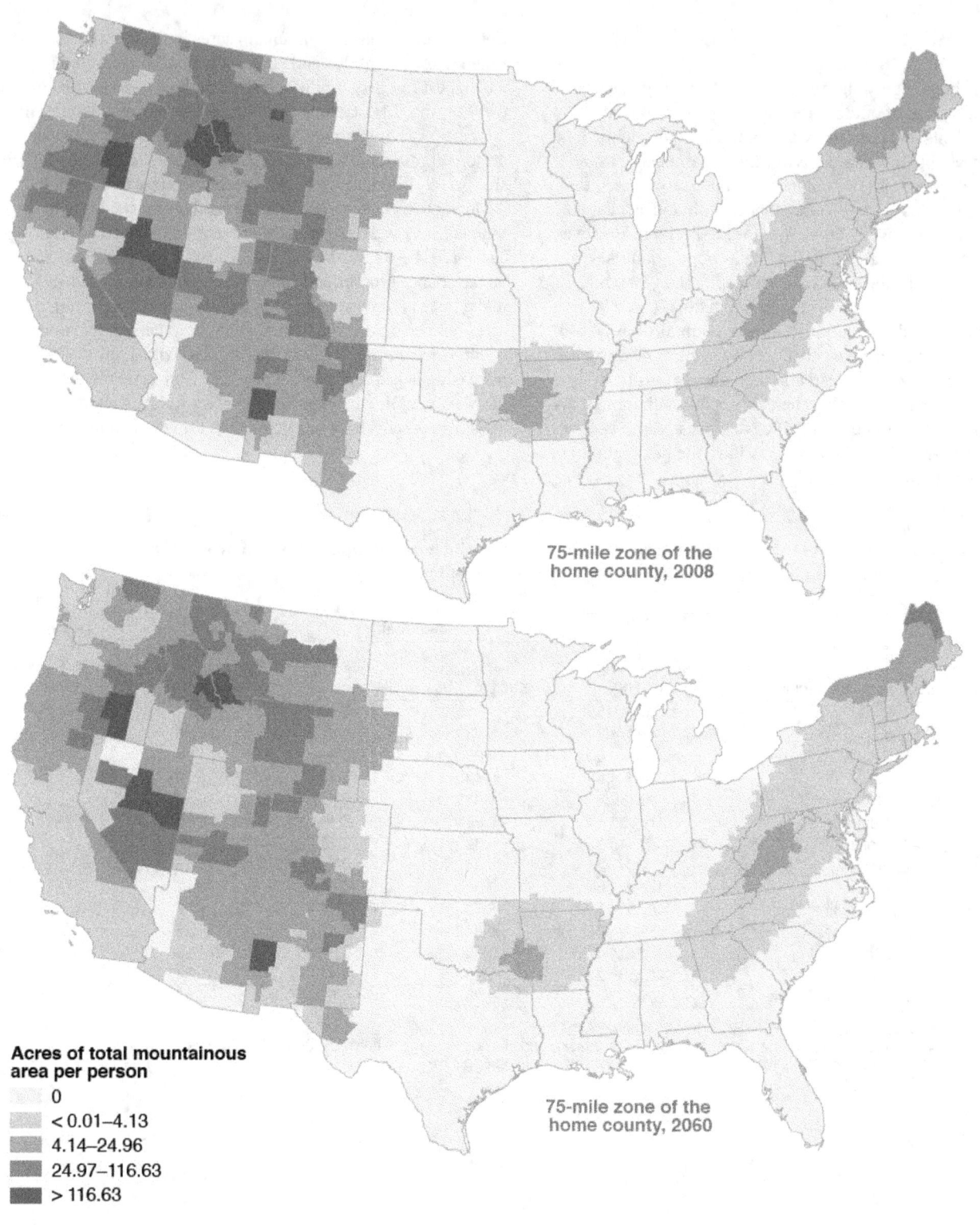

Acres of total mountainous area per person

0
< 0.01–4.13
4.14–24.96
24.97–116.63
> 116.63

75-mile zone of the home county, 2008

75-mile zone of the home county, 2060

Figure 7.11—Acres of mountains per person, 2008 and 2060, within the 75-mile distance zone. Source: Bailey (1995).

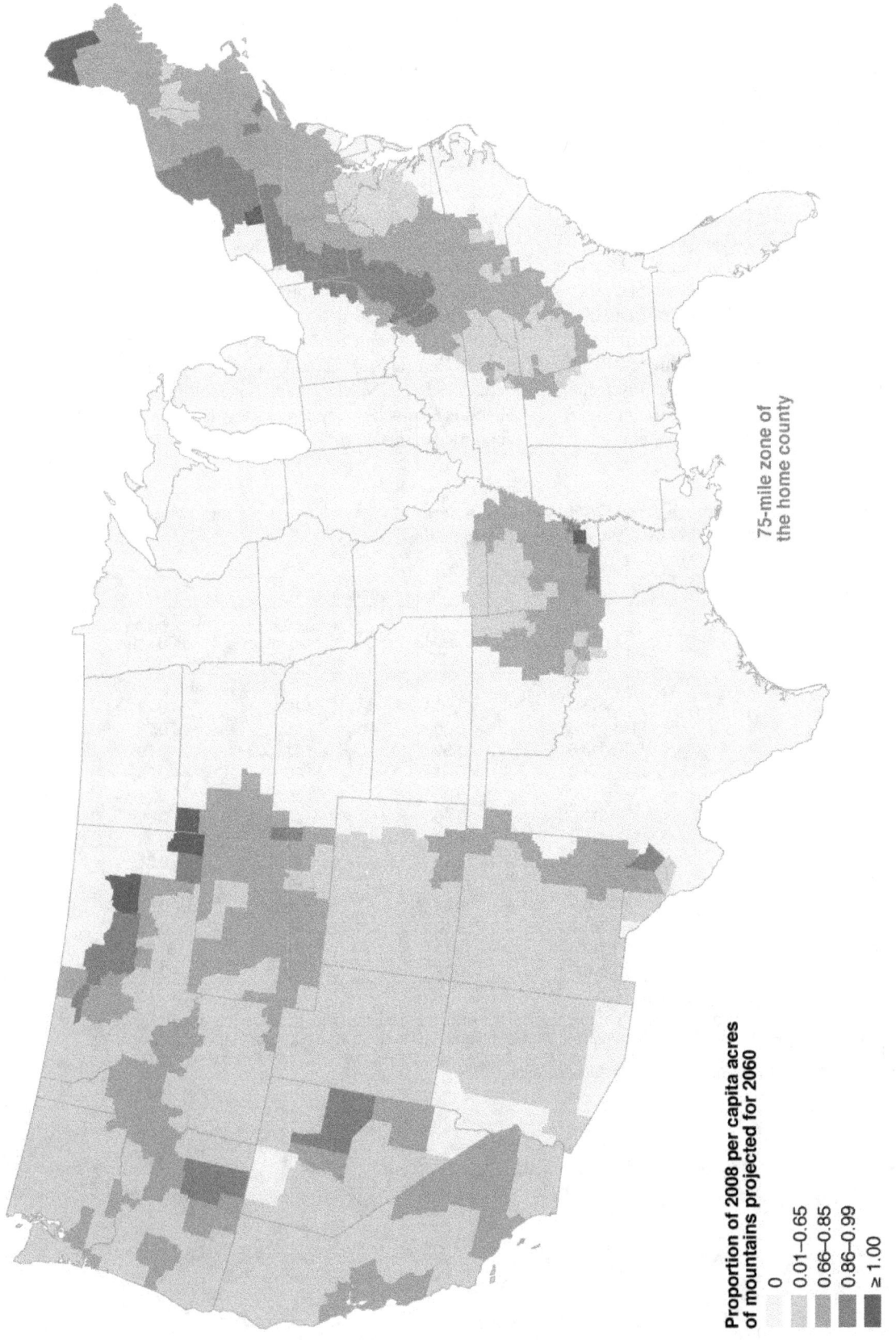

Proportion of 2008 per capita acres
of mountains projected for 2060

0
0.01–0.65
0.66–0.85
0.86–0.99
≥ 1.00

75-mile zone of
the home county

Figure 7.12—Proportion of 2008 per capita acres of mountains projected for 2060, within the 75-mile distance zone. Source: Bailey (1995).

Snow Cover

Regions of the United States with sufficient winter snowfall support a number of snow and ice-based recreational activities that are not available in the other regions. Snowfall amounts and periodicity vary greatly across the country, generally increasing as latitudes move farther north. Based on data from the National Oceanic and Atmospheric Administration's National Climatic Data Center, we define a "snow county" as one that has an average of 28.5 days or more per year with 1 or more inches of measured snow depth. Projections of snowfall data are not available, but projected population increases resulted in an estimate of 1.30 snow county acres per person in 2060 for the contiguous United States, down from 1.92 acres in 2008 (table 7.8). The Rocky Mountains region will drop significantly from 10.41 acres per person to 5.81 acres. The Intermountain sub-region, in particular, will be affected by population

growth and will have just a little more than half of the per capita acres in 2060 (6.41) than it had in 2008 (12.33). This is significant because the Intermountain sub-region accounts for about 46 percent of the total snow county area in the contiguous United States.

A handful of counties in the West and North Central States will remain in the highest category of per capita snow acres in the 75-mile distance zone (darkest shade, > 255.10 acres per person), with many changing to a lower category by 2060 due to projected population growth (fig. 7.13). The darkest shade in figure 7.14 shows counties with a change proportion of 1.0 or greater, indicating an increase in per capita snow acres between 2008 and 2060. Just a few counties in the West and North Central States are expected to be in this class. Most counties in the Northeast and much of the Midwest will not decline as much in per capita snow acres as the majority of counties in the West.

Table 7.8—Current (2008) and projected (2060) per capita acres of snow county area and proportion of current acres projected for 2060 by RPA sub-region and region

Sub-region and region	Snow county area			
	Total acres 2008	Per capita acres, 2008	Projected per capita acres, 2060	Proportion of 2008 acres projected for 2060
	thousand			
Northeast	94,673.1	1.50	1.18	0.79
North Central	143,440.8	2.35	1.85	0.79
North region	238,113.8	1.91	1.51	0.79
Southeast	271.0	0.01	0.00	0.60
South Central	0.0	0.00	0.00	–
South region	271.0	0.00	0.00	0.63
Great Plains	21,110.6	3.50	2.67	0.76
Intermountain	267,830.2	12.33	6.41	0.52
Rocky Mountains region	288,940.8	10.41	5.81	0.56
Pacific Northwest	49,785.9	4.82	2.96	0.61
Pacific Southwest	3,781.5	0.10	0.06	0.65
Pacific Coast region	53,567.4	1.11	0.71	0.64
U.S. total	580,893.0	1.92	1.30	0.68

na = Not applicable; RPA = Resources Planning Act.
Note: A "snow county" is one that has 28.5 days or more per year with 1 or more inches of measured snow depth. Acreage is held constant at the 2008 level. See table 7.1 for projected population and total surface area acreage. Data not available for Alaska and Hawaii.
Source: USDC National Oceanic and Atmospheric Administration (2005).

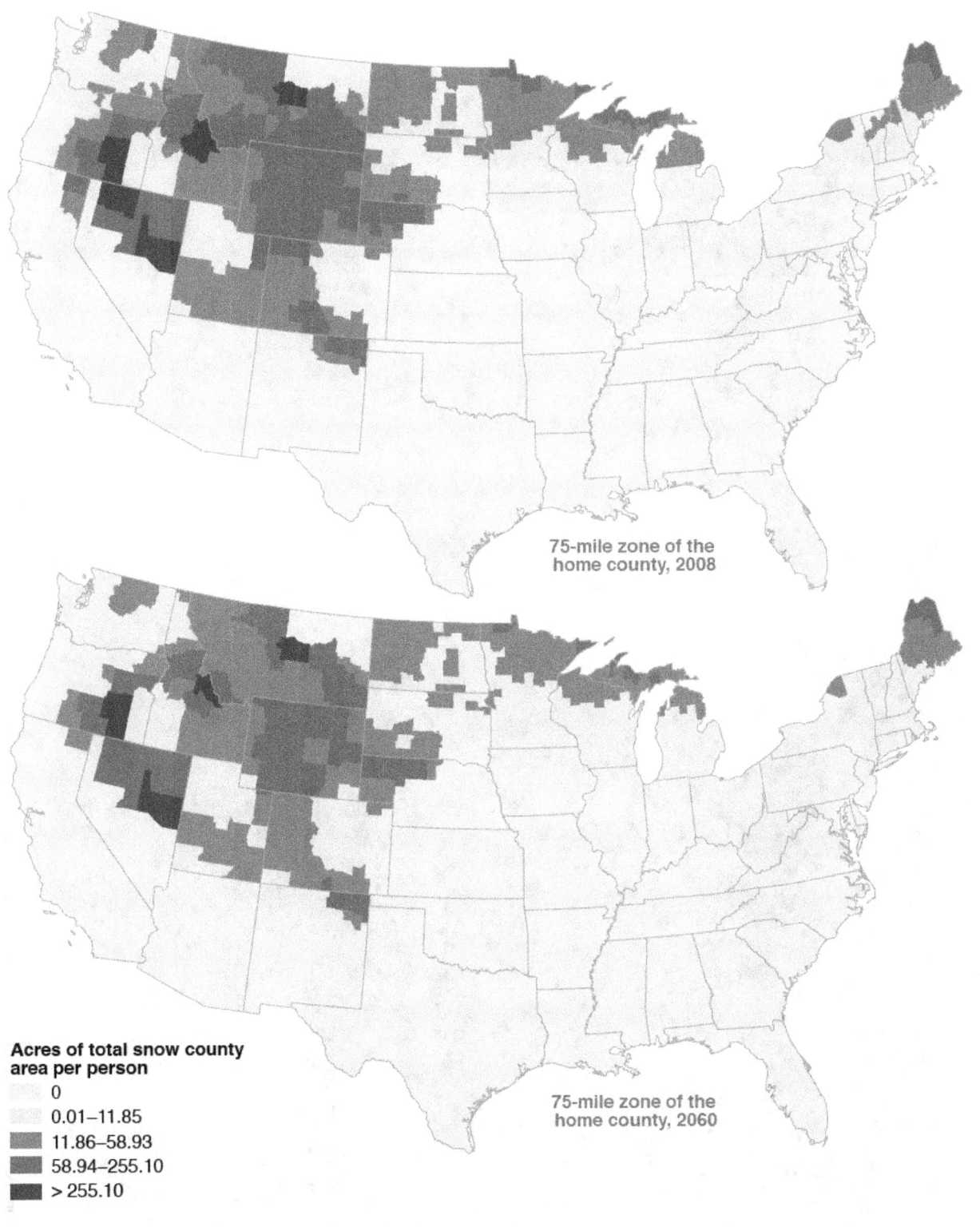

75-mile zone of the
home county, 2008

**Acres of total snow county
area per person**

0
0.01–11.85
11.86–58.93
58.94–255.10
> 255.10

75-mile zone of the
home county, 2060

Figure 7.13—Acres of snow county area per person, 2008 and 2060, within the 75-mile distance zone.
Source: USDC National Oceanic and Atmospheric Administration (2005).

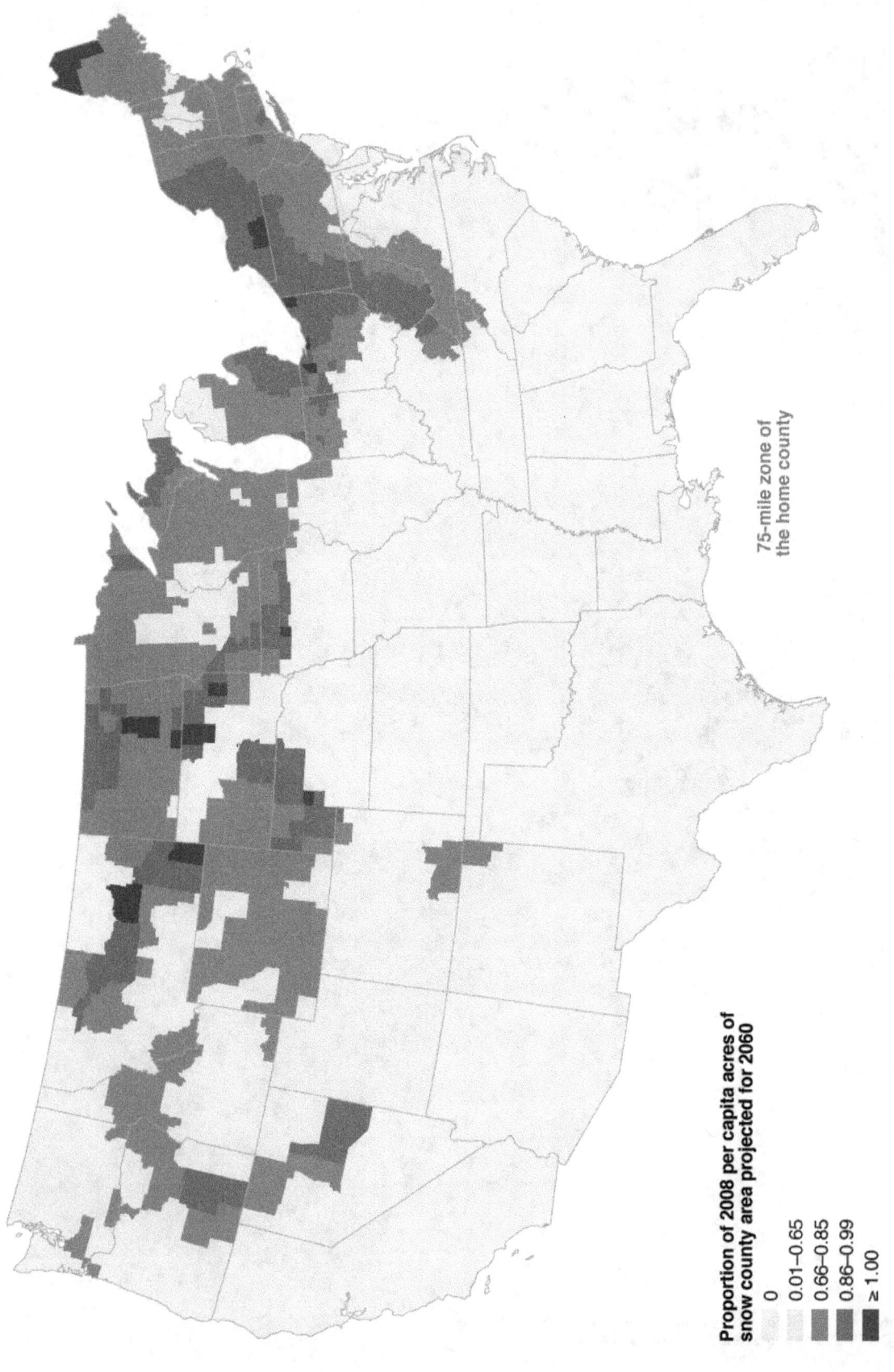

**Proportion of 2008 per capita acres of
snow county area projected for 2060**

0
0.01–0.65
0.66–0.85
0.86–0.99
≥ 1.00

75-mile zone of
the home county

Figure 7.14—Proportion of 2008 per capita snow county acres projected for 2060, within the 75-mile distance zone. Source: USDC National Oceanic and Atmospheric Administration (2005).

Specially-Designated Federal Lands

Federal lands classified as "specially designated" in this chapter include many of the Nation's most wild and primitive environments. These areas have special protection status and thus can provide unique recreation opportunities not found elsewhere. These special Federal lands include land and water in three designated systems: (1) the National Wilderness Preservation System, (2) National Park System, and (3) National Recreation Areas. Some national parks and national recreation areas have designated wilderness but it is not double-counted in this analysis. The specially designated Federal land areas are typically large in size, offer backcountry recreation opportunities, and often offer dramatic scenery.

Projections of land areas in these special systems are not available, but per capita amounts of these resources are expected to decline because of population growth. Projected acres per capita of special Federal land in the 50 States are expected to be 0.35, down from 0.52 in 2008 (table 7.9). Excluding Alaska, the Intermountain sub-region has more than twice the acreage of any other sub-region, but it will also be most affected by population growth. Per capita acres of specially designated land in that sub-region will be cut almost in half, from just under 1.6 acres per person in 2008 to slightly more than 0.8 acres in 2060.

Many counties in the West will still be in the highest category of acres per capita within the 75-mile distance zone in 2060 (darkest shade, > 13.82 acres per person) but the number of those counties will decrease somewhat (fig. 7.15). Relatively high areas in the East are clustered around the eastern mountain ranges and the Boundary Waters area of northern Minnesota. A few dozen counties will have an increase (i.e., change proportion of > 1.0) in special Federal acres per capita from 2008 to 2060, due to their location in remote counties projected to lose population (fig. 7.16). However, many more counties that are expected to have fewer acres per capita in 2060 are in the West. This change proportion is due to the western regions having many fast-growing metropolitan areas such as Denver, Phoenix, Tucson, and Albuquerque. These specially designated Federal lands are a national resource because most draw visitors from well outside the 2-hour distance zone used in this analysis. With the exception of much of the Great Plains, parts of the upper Midwest, and a few other scattered counties, all other U.S. counties are located within 75 miles of specially designated Federal lands.

Table 7.9—Current (2008) and projected (2060) per capita acres of specially designated Federal land and proportion of current acres projected for 2060 by RPA sub-region and region

Sub-region and region	Specially designated Federal land			
	Total acres 2008	Per capita acres, 2008	Projected per capita acres, 2060	Proportion of 2008 acres projected for 2060
	thousand			
Northeast	794.2	0.01	0.01	0.79
North Central	2,214.4	0.04	0.03	0.79
North region	3,008.6	0.02	0.02	0.79
Southeast	4,495.3	0.09	0.05	0.60
South Central	2,466.3	0.05	0.03	0.66
South region	6,961.6	0.07	0.04	0.63
Great Plains	383.4	0.06	0.05	0.76
Intermountain	34,228.4	1.58	0.82	0.52
Rocky Mountains region	34,611.8	1.25	0.70	0.56
Alaska	88,036.5	128.85	75.97	0.59
Pacific Northwest	8,340.0	0.81	0.50	0.61
Pacific Southwest	16,928.9	0.44	0.29	0.65
Pacific Coast region	113,305.5	2.31	1.48	0.64
U.S. total	157,887.5	0.52	0.35	0.68

RPA = Resources Planning Act.
Note: Specially designated Federal land includes units in the National Wilderness Preservation System, National Park Service units (non-wilderness), and U.S. Forest Service and Bureau of Land Management National Recreation Areas. Acreage is held constant at the 2008 level. See table 7.1 for projected population and total surface area acreage.
Sources: USDA Forest Service (2008), USDI National Park Service (2008), and Wilderness Institute (2009).

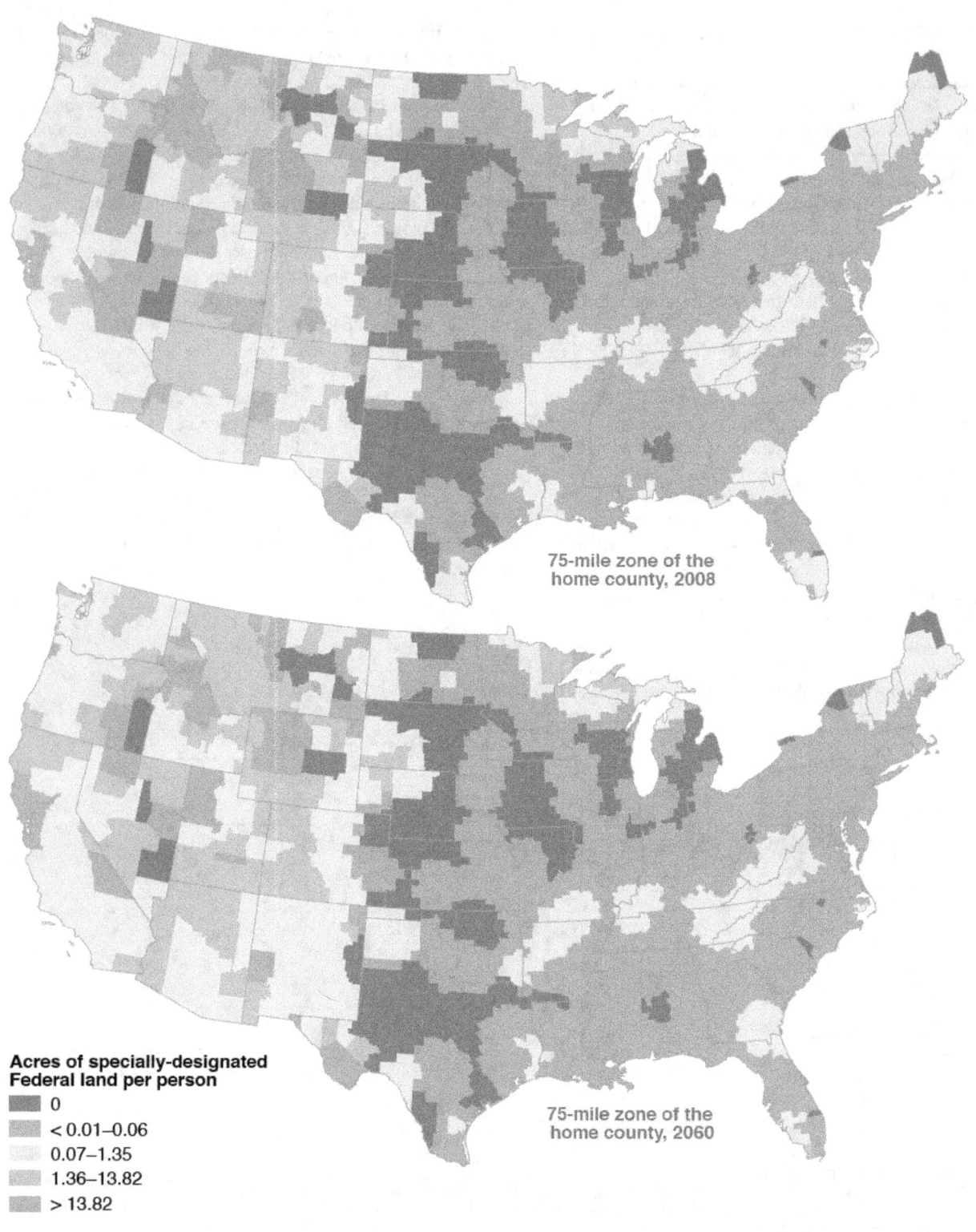

75-mile zone of the
home county, 2008

**Acres of specially-designated
Federal land per person**
- 0
- < 0.01–0.06
- 0.07–1.35
- 1.36–13.82
- > 13.82

75-mile zone of the
home county, 2060

Figure 7.15—Acres of specially designated Federal land per person, 2008 and 2060, within the 75-mile distance zone.
Sources: USDA Forest Service (2008), USDI National Park Service (2008), and Wilderness Institute (2009).

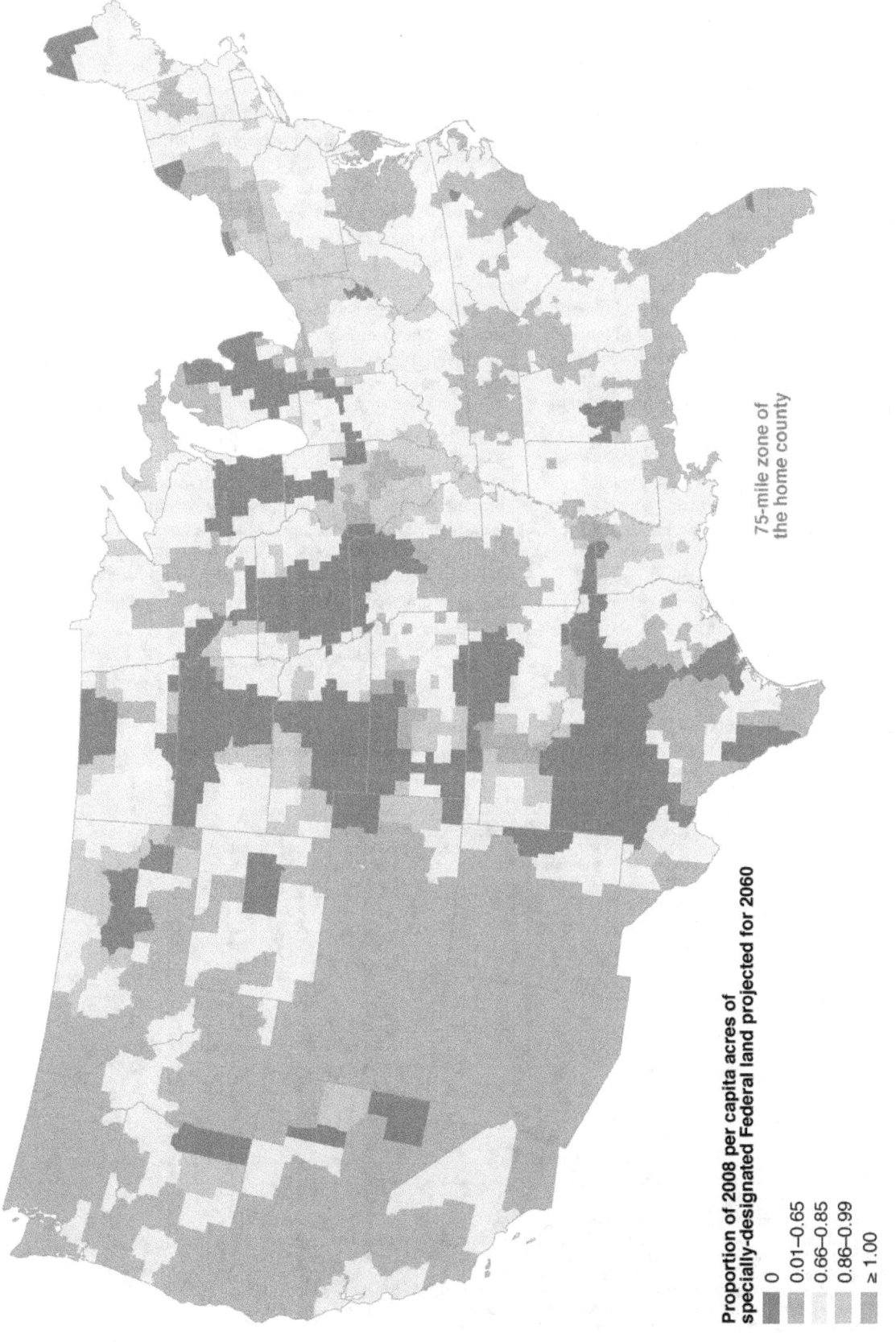

Proportion of 2008 per capita acres of specially-designated Federal land projected for 2060

- 0
- 0.01–0.65
- 0.66–0.85
- 0.86–0.99
- ≥ 1.00

75-mile zone of the home county

Figure 7.16—Proportion of 2008 per capita acres of specially designated Federal land projected for 2060, within the 75-mile distance zone. Sources: USDA Forest Service (2008), USDI National Park Service (2008), and Wilderness Institute (2009).

Private Recreation Businesses

The U.S. Census Bureau maintains its Business Register and conducts the Economic Census for the United States. The Register is the Census Bureau's source of data covering private employer establishments. Data are analyzed and reported in the *County Business Patterns*, most recently published in 2007. (Businesses per capita are reported as 2008 because that is the population estimate year used.) Private businesses are important resources for outdoor recreation, especially in the rental and sale of equipment and provision of outfitter and guide services and also in supplying privately owned land and water for recreation. We created an index by summing the number of establishments in nine private-sector recreation-related business types for each U.S. county. The nine types of enterprises are the only discernible outdoor recreation-related businesses that are tracked in the *County Business Patterns* data. They include marinas, skiing facilities, private-sector historical sites, private-sector zoos and botanical gardens, recreational vehicle parks and campgrounds, private-sector nature parks, private golf courses and country clubs, amusement and theme parks, and recreational and vacation camps (except campgrounds).

No forecast of the future numbers of these establishments is available, but change is certainly expected by 2060 due to the usual volatility of small businesses in general. As demand for a given recreation business increases (decreases),

an increase (decrease) in the supply of establishments would be expected in response to the shifting demand. Given the projected population increases by 2060, the per capita number of recreation businesses in the Nation is expected to drop to about 0.60 businesses per 10,000 people (6 per 100,000) which is down from 0.88 in 2008 (table 7.10). Similar to the other resource analyses that were based on population gains, the Rocky Mountains will likely feel the effects more than the other regions. In 2008, the Rocky Mountains led all regions with 1.06 businesses per 10,000 people but drops to second place behind the North region, with 0.59 businesses per capita in 2060.

The county pattern maps for the 75-mile distance zones shows that per capita number of recreation businesses are projected to decline in many areas from 2008 to 2060, under the assumption that the number of businesses establishments as reported in the 2007 *County Business Patterns* report will remain constant (fig. 7.17). The exception is most of the Southeast and South Central States, which had relatively fewer businesses per capita in 2007 anyway. In figure 7.18, which depicts the change proportion in recreation businesses per capita from 2008 to 2060, a shift to fewer businesses in the West is evident. The same situation is true throughout much of the South Central and Southeast sub-regions, especially in Florida. This lowest category means that many of the counties will have roughly two-thirds or less the number of recreation businesses per capita in 2060 than they had in 2008.

Table 7.10—Current (2008) and projected (2060) per capita (per 10,000 population) number of recreation businesses and proportion of current number of businesses projected for 2060 by RPA sub-region and region

Sub-region and region	Recreation businesses			
	Number of businesses, 2007	Businesses per capita, 2008	Projected businesses per capita, 2060	Proportion of 2008 businesses projected for 2060
Northeast	6,530	1.03	0.82	0.79
North Central	6,200	1.01	0.80	0.79
North region	12,730	1.02	0.81	0.79
Southeast	4,188	0.85	0.50	0.60
South Central	3,548	0.67	0.44	0.66
South region	7,736	0.75	0.47	0.63
Great Plains	785	1.30	0.99	0.76
Intermountain	2,153	0.99	0.52	0.52
Rocky Mountains region	2,938	1.06	0.59	0.56
Alaska	209	3.06	1.80	0.59
Pacific Northwest	1,124	1.09	0.67	0.61
Pacific Southwest	2,055	0.54	0.35	0.65
Pacific Coast region	3,388	0.69	0.44	0.64
U.S. total	26,792	0.88	0.60	0.68

RPA = Resources Planning Act.
Note: "Recreation businesses" as presented in this table represent an index of the level of private-sector recreation-related business establishments that exist in each U.S. county. It is the sum of nine separate business types: marinas, skiing facilities, private-sector historical sites, private-sector zoos and botanical gardens, recreational vehicle parks and campgrounds, private-sector nature parks, (private) golf courses and country clubs, amusement and theme parks, and recreational and vacation camps (except campgrounds). The number of businesses is held constant at the 2007 level. See table 7.1 for projected population and total surface area acreage. Businesses per capita are listed as 2008 because the 2008 Census population estimate is used. Source: U.S. Census Bureau (2007b).

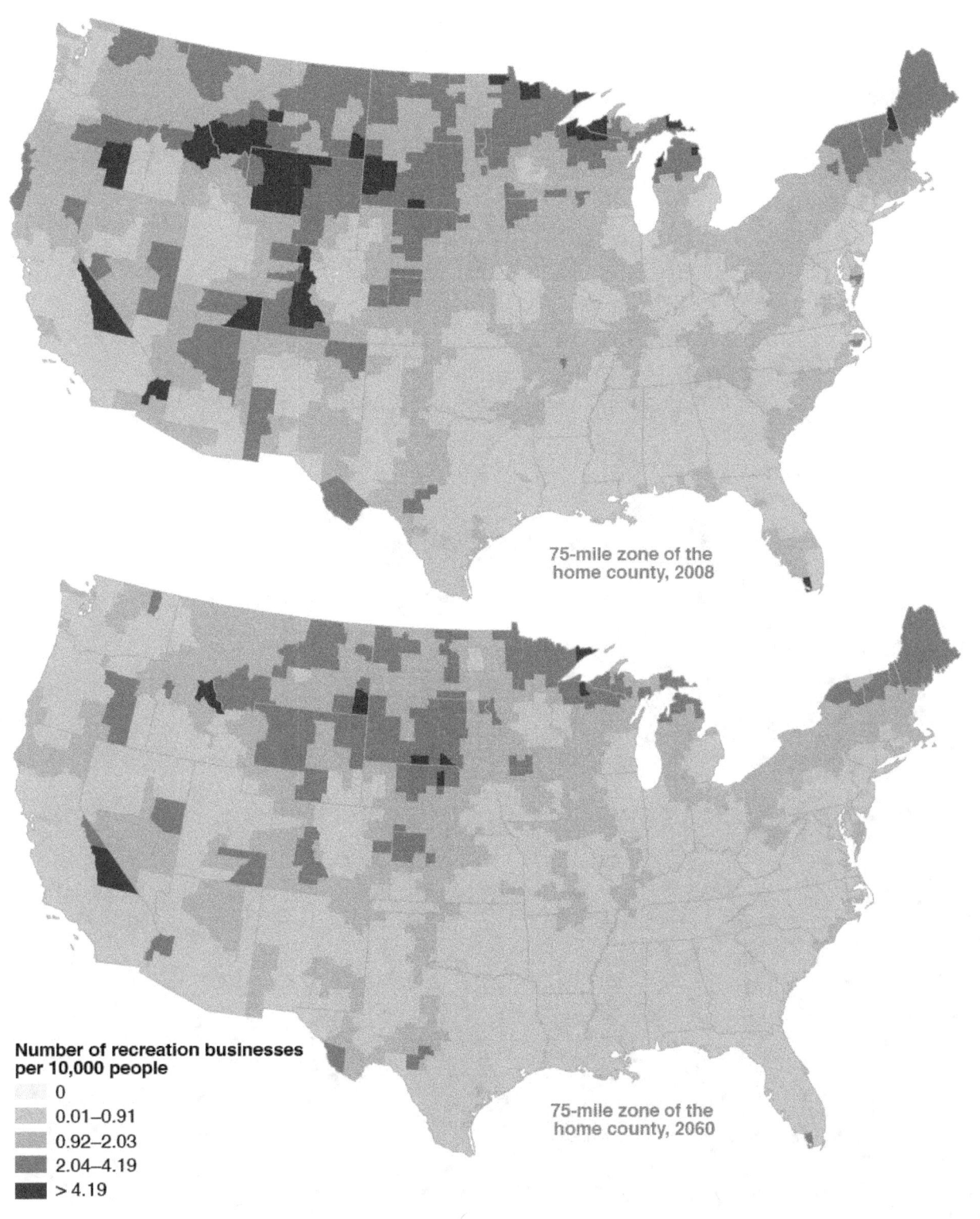

75-mile zone of the
home county, 2008

**Number of recreation businesses
per 10,000 people**
- 0
- 0.01–0.91
- 0.92–2.03
- 2.04–4.19
- > 4.19

75-mile zone of the
home county, 2060

Figure 7 17—Number of recreation businesses per 10,000 people, 2008 and 2060, within the 75-mile distance zone. Source: U.S. Census Bureau (2007b).

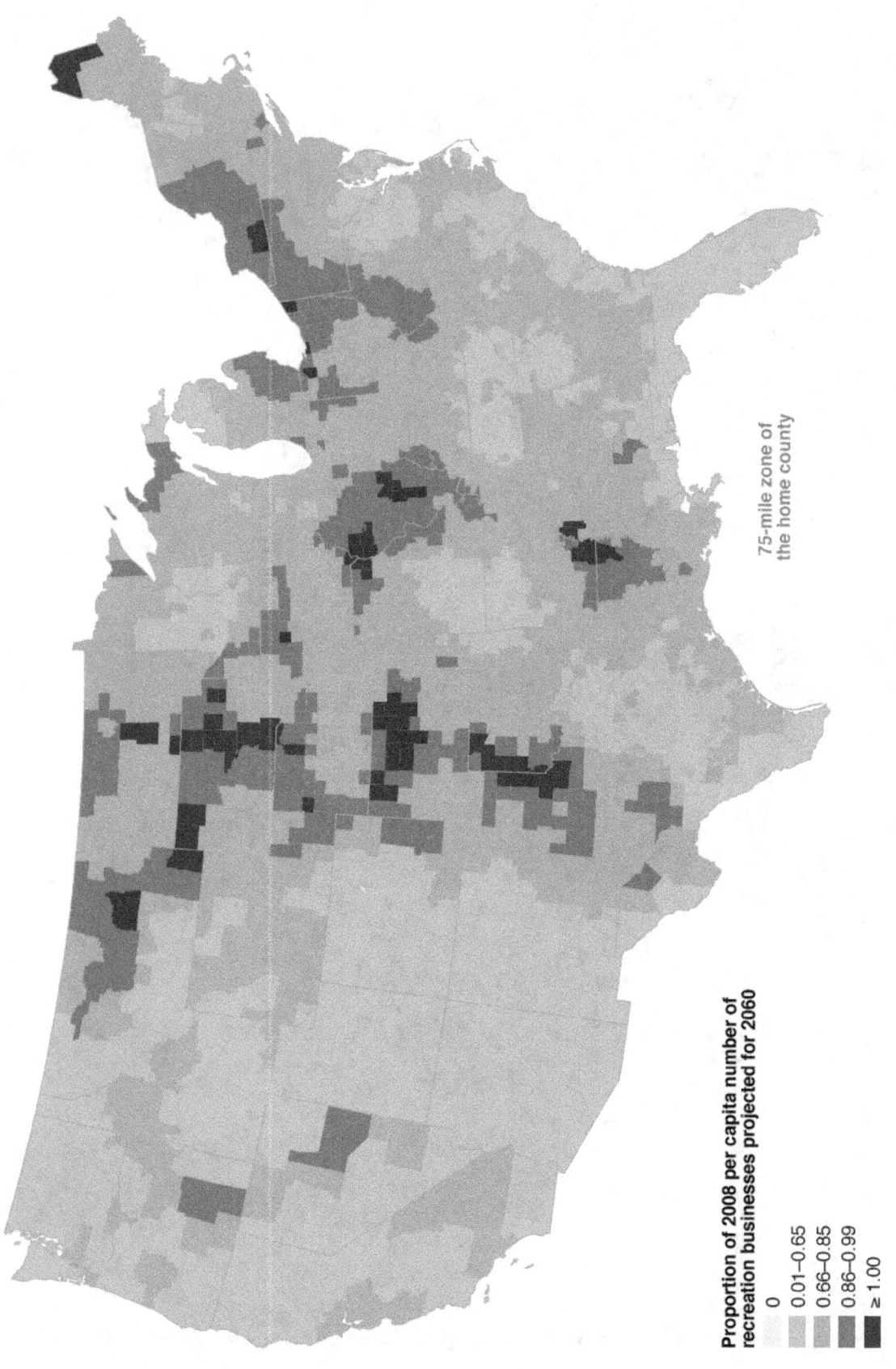

Proportion of 2008 per capita number of recreation businesses projected for 2060

- 0
- 0.01–0.65
- 0.66–0.85
- 0.86–0.99
- ≥ 1.00

75-mile zone of
the home county

Figure 7.18—Proportion of 2008 number of recreation businesses per 10,000 people projected for 2060, within the 75-mile distance zone. Source: U.S. Census Bureau (2007b).

CHAPTER 8
Summary

This General Technical Report presents the results of an analysis of public and private outdoor recreation and protected land resources in the United States. This analysis includes examination of the present status and future trends of land and other natural resources (to 2060) for the Nation and its regions and sub-regions. To help in visualizing land status and future trends, geospatial maps showing patterns of change across U.S. counties have been provided. This is one of several reports the Forest Service, U.S. Department of Agriculture, has developed for the national 2010 Resource Planning Act (RPA) Assessment (described in chapter 1). As context for summarizing the status and futures for outdoor recreation resources, a brief overview of demand trends follows below.

Outdoor Recreation Demand Trends— A Brief Overview

Outdoor recreation plays a large role in American lifestyles and in land management by both the public and private sectors. For context in thinking about the importance of recreation resources, a summary of major recreation trends, as reported in a companion RPA report (Cordell, 2012), follows:

(1) Outdoor recreation choices by people today are noticeably different from those made by and available to previous generations of Americans.

(2) There is an overall increase in outdoor recreation participation even though some traditional activities have been in decline.

(3) There is growth in one group of nature-based activities in particular, that of "viewing and photographing nature."

(4) Different segments of society choose different mixes of outdoor activities.

(5) There is evidence that America's youth spend time outdoors, and, among some young people, this time is substantial.

(6) Public lands remain highly important for the recreation opportunities they offer.

(7) Trends in visitation vary by Federal land management agency and between Federal and State jurisdictions.

(8) A national study of motivations showed there are various reasons why people seek different forms of outdoor recreation.

(9) Future trends in terms of per capita participation and total number of participants appear to increase for some activities and decline for others.

Land and Water Resources

The total area of the United States is about 2.43 billion acres. Of this, 2.26 billion acres is land (60 percent of which is privately owned), and 169 million is water. Land with natural cover includes forest (612 million acres), shrublands (583 million acres), grasslands (319 million acres), and wetlands (124 million acres). Together, these natural land covers make up about 62 percent of the total land and water area of the United States. Of these natural lands, publicly owned lands are critical resources for nature-based outdoor recreation. While the amount of public land managed by local governments is modest, it provides highly important outdoor recreation opportunities near or within communities. State lands, too, are important because they not only are located near where people live but they also typically offer larger, more natural areas. Federally managed land includes about 640 million acres, of which the majority is managed either for raw resource production (e.g., wood) or to remain in its wild natural condition. Private lands constitute the majority of total land area across the United States, with Kansas having the greatest proportion at 99 percent and Nevada having the smallest at 13 percent. Although the overall ownership pattern is quite constant over time, the use and ownership of private lands change frequently, resulting in a shifting spectrum of opportunities for outdoor recreation.

There has been growing interest in protection of public and private land and water resources. The need for protection is evident when one realizes the many risk factors that can limit a sustained flow of benefits, services, and raw materials from the these lands. The United States loses about 2 million acres of forest, farm, and other open space each year through conversion to developed uses. In reaction to these losses, land trusts, State and local governments, and Federal Government agencies have dedicated funding and coordinated efforts to conserve rural land. Most significant of the protected lands of the United States are the Federal lands held in public trust. These 640 million acres of Federal land include National parks, national forests, national wildlife refuges, and other Federal ownerships. Private and public lands with some level of protection status make up the majority of opportunities for nature-based outdoor recreation for the American public.

The Roles of Private and Public Sectors as Outdoor Recreation Providers

The private sector has made vital contributions in providing outdoor recreation opportunities. This includes businesses operating on public lands, e.g., canoe outfitters, outdoor equipment manufacturers, information and touring services, resorts, and a vast array of businesses that offer other goods and services. The top business establishments in the United States dedicated to outdoor recreation include golf courses and country clubs, recreational vehicle parks and campgrounds, marinas, recreation and vacation camps, and historical sites. Vacation homes are an important and growing self-supplied private recreation resource.

In the public sector, local governments have been a major provider of community recreation opportunities for over two centuries. Currently, about 12 percent (over 8,800) of the Nation's local government units provide recreation and park services. State outdoor recreation opportunities are primarily provided by the State park systems. In 2009, State park agencies managed more than 6,500 individual units covering nearly 14 million acres.

The Federal Government provides a diverse array of outdoor recreation resources. Of the 640 million acres of Federal land, nearly all is available for recreation. There are three special Federal recreation resource systems that are Congressionally designated. They include national recreation areas, national wild and scenic rivers, and national recreation trails. These systems are made up of 41 national recreation areas totaling 7.4 million acres, 12,500 miles of national wild and scenic rivers, and more than 1,000 national recreation trails (totaling in excess of 20,000 trail miles).

Thumbnails on Availability of Recreation Resources

Recreation resource availability is largely a function of location relative to potential recreation users. To examine availability, nine resources were considered, including park land, water, forest, open range and pasture, ocean and Great

Top Privately operated canoe and boat outfitter and gift shop complex at "put in" to the Okefenokee Swamp National Wildlife Refuge. (Photographer Ken Cordell, 2009) Bottom The Minneapolis Sculpture Garden is one of Minnesota's crown jewels and its centerpiece, the Spoonbridge and Cherry, has become a Minnesota icon. The Sculpture Garden is essentially a free museum in a park. (Source Explore Minnesota Tourism)

Lakes, mountains, snow cover, designated Federal lands, and private recreation businesses. In addition to examining the current spatial pattern of these resources across the counties of the country, future per capita availabilities were projected to reflect the effects of continuing population growth.

Nationally, 1.4 acres of Federal and State park land per capita are projected for 2060. This is two-thirds of the acres per capita that existed in 2008. Although the western regions will far exceed per capita availability of these public lands in the eastern regions by 2060, significant projected population growth in the Rocky Mountains region will result in that region experiencing the largest proportion decline in the future (meaning acres per capita in 2060 relative to per capita acres in 2008).

A decline in water acres per capita is also projected, from over one-half acre per person in 2008 to less than 0.4 acres in 2060. As with public lands, the largest decline is projected for the Rocky Mountains region. The total acres of non-Federal forest is expected to decline by nearly 8 percent by 2060. This projection combined with population growth translates to a national per capita decline from 1.3 acres in 2010 to 0.8 acres by 2060. The greatest projected decrease is for the Intermountain and Southeast sub-regions. In 2060, non-Federal open range and pasture are projected to total 497 million acres in the lower 48 States, a 3 percent decline from 2010. With the further influence of population growth, per capita open range and pasture land is projected at 1.1 acres per capita in 2060, about two-thirds what it was in 2010. The largest decline is expected in the Intermountain and Southeast sub-regions.

Because of high population growth, per capita acres of coastal county area are expected to drop from 2.3 acres per person in 2008 to 1.6 in 2060. Mountain acres per capita are projected to decrease from 1.3 acres in 2008 to 0.9 acres in 2060. Further, it is estimated that there will be 1.3 snow county acres per person in 2060, down from 1.9 acres in 2008. Large projected population growth in the Rocky Mountains, especially the Intermountain sub-region, will result in a substantial drop in snow county acres per capita in that region. Federal lands classified as "specially designated" are expected to decline in the 50 States from 0.5 per capita in 2008 to 0.4 in 2060. Excluding Alaska, the Intermountain sub-region has over twice the acreage of any other sub-region, but its per capita acres of specially designated land are expected to decline to almost half by 2060.

Given the projected population increases, the per capita number of recreation businesses nationally is expected to drop from 0.9 per 10,000 people in 2008 to 0.6 in 2060. Similar to the other resource analyses that were based on population gains, the Rocky Mountains will likely feel the effects more than the other regions, declining from just over one business per 10,000 people to less than 0.6 in 2060.

Top Tributary creek flowing from the White River National Forest in Colorado, 2007. Bottom South beach, Jekyll Island State Park, east Atlantic Coast, near Brunswick, GA. (Photographs by Ken Cordell)

Concluding Observation

The future of outdoor recreation in the United States may not, and likely will not, unfold as simply as depicted in this report. There are many complicating factors in addition to population growth that will determine the future of recreation and protected land resources. But certainly population growth and all that comes with that growth will play a central, if not the determining role.

Mountains in northwest South Carolina overlook Jocassee Lake, 2007. (Photograph by Ken Cordell)

With population increases come pressures to use land for development or agriculture. As well, more population brings more people seeking places for the recreation activities of their choice. Fewer places, or places with less extensive undeveloped area, will be a major challenge for recreation providers of the future. These decisionmaking providers will have to weigh their choices carefully, because the results of many of those decisions will be irreversible. Once natural land is developed, or substantially altered from its natural state, there is little likelihood it would ever be allowed to revert back to a natural state.

Natural land is highly valued for its ecosystem services and for its aesthetic qualities. These services and qualities are at the core of most people's choice of place and time for outdoor recreation. For sure, lodging, food, travel, information, and a host of other services are extremely important to people's choices. But these recreation support services, such as lodging and travel, must be provided in or near the natural settings that make them desirable to the recreation seeker. Undoubtedly, if there are to be nature-based outdoor recreation opportunities in the future, measures will need to be taken to protect the natural character that makes these lands and water attractive. Land protection through land trusts or government action plays and will play an increasingly critical role in assuring future generations will have natural places for their recreation activities.

Acknowledgments

We thank the following for their reviews: Taylor Stein, Associate Professor, Ecotourism Research, University of Florida; Scott Shafer, Associate Professor, Department of Recreation, Park and Tourism Sciences, Texas A&M University; and Linda Langner, Renewable Resources Planning Act Assessment Program Lead, U.S. Department of Agriculture, Forest Service, Washington Office. We thank the authors for their contribution of topic papers to this publication, and we thank Shela Mou, Publications Specialist with the Athens Research Group, for her assistance with the preparation of this report.

Literature Citations

American Trails. 2009. National recreation trails database. http://tutsan.forest.net/trails/. [Date accessed: March 31, 2010].

Avery, T.E. 1975. Natural resources measurements. New York: McGraw-Hill Book Company. 339 p.

Bailey, Margaret. 2011a. USDA Forest Service special use program data. Available from Margaret Bailey, CHM Government Services, 548 Cabot Street, Beverly, MA 01915.

Bailey, Margaret. 2011b. USDI National Park Service commercial services program data. Available from Margaret Bailey, CHM Government Services, 548 Cabot Street, Beverly, MA 01915.

Bailey, Margaret. 2011c. U.S. Army Corps of Engineers real estate division data. Available from Margaret Bailey, CHM Government Services, 548 Cabot Street, Beverly, MA 01915.

Bailey, R.G. 1995. Description of the ecoregions of the United States. 2nd ed. Misc. Pub. No. 1391. http://www.fs.fed.us/land/ecosysmgmt/index.html. [Date accessed: September 2, 2011].

Barnes, C.A. 2010. 2001 national land cover data spreadsheet by state. Available from C.A. Barnes of Stinger Ghaffarian Technologies, a contractor to the U.S. Geological Survey, Earth Resources Observation and Science (EROS), 47914 252nd Street, Sioux Falls, SD 57198-0001.

Barry, J.J.; Hellerstein, D. 2004. Farm recreation. In: Cordell, H.K. Outdoor recreation for 21st century America. State College, PA: Venture Publishing, Inc.: 149-167.

Bastian, C.T.; McLeod, D.M.; Germino, M.J. [and others]. 2002. Environmental amenities and agricultural land values. Ecological Economics. 40(3): 337-349.

Brown, D.M.; Reeder, R.J. 2007. Farm-based recreation: a statistical profile, ERR-53. http://www.ers.usda.gov/publications/err53/err53.pdf. [Date accessed: August 23, 2011].

Brown, G.; Alessa, L. 2005. A GIS-based inductive study of wilderness values. International Journal of Wilderness. 11(1): 14-18.

Brown, T.C. 1999. Past and future freshwater use in the United States: a technical document supporting the 2000 USDA Forest Service RPA Assessment. Gen. Tech. Rep. RMRS-39. Fort Collins, CO: U.S. Department of Agriculture Forest Service, Rocky Mountains Research Station. 47 p.

Brown, T.C.; Hobbins, M.T.; Ramirez, J.A. 2005. The source of water supply in the United States. RMRS-RWU-4851. Discussion Paper. 57 p. Unpublished report. On file with: U.S. Department of Agriculture Forest Service, Rocky Mountains Research Station, 240 West Prospect, Fort Collins, CO 80526.

Butler, B.J. 2008. Family forest owners of the United States, 2006. Gen. Tech. Rep. NRS-27. Newtown Square, PA: U.S. Department of Agriculture Forest Service, Northern Research Station. 72 p.

Campaign for America's Wilderness. 2003. A mandate to protect America's Wilderness. Washington, DC: Campaign for America's Wilderness. 44 p.

Carr, M., ed. 2005. Earth…water…fire: the role and management of fire in aquatic ecosystems. In: Wildland Waters. FS-828. http://www.fs.fed.us/wildlandwaters/newsletters/wildlandwaters_summer05.pdf. [Date accessed: August 16, 2011].

Clawson, M.; Harrington, W. 1991. The growing role of outdoor recreation In: Frederick, K.D.; Sedjo, R.A., eds. America's renewable resources: historical trends and current challenges. Washington, DC: Resources For the Future: 249-279.

Clayton, S. 2003. Environmental identity: a conceptual and an operational definition. In: Clayton, S ; Opotow, S., eds. Identity and the natural environment: the psychological significance of nature. Cambridge, MA: Massachusetts Institute of Technology. 45-65.

Clayton, S.; Myers, G. 2009. Conservation psychology: understanding and promoting human care for nature. West Sussex, UK: Wiley-Blackwell. 264 p.

Clutter, M.; Mendell, B.; Newman, D. [and others]. 2005. Strategic factors driving timberland ownership changes in the U.S. South. Asheville, NC: U.S. Department of Agriculture Forest Service, Southern Research Station. 15 p.

Cole, D.N. 2004. Wilderness experiences: what should we be managing for? International Journal of Wilderness. 10(3): 25-27.

Cole, D.N.; Hall, T.E. 2008. Wilderness visitors, experiences, and management preferences: how they vary with use level and length of stay. Res. Pap. RMRS-RP-71. Fort Collins, CO: U.S. Department of Agriculture Forest Service, Rocky Mountains Research Station. 61 p.

Cordell, H.K. 1999. Outdoor recreation in American life: a national assessment of demand and supply trends. Champaign, IL: Sagamore Publishing. 449 p.

Cordell, H.K. 2012. Outdoor recreation trends and futures: a technical document supporting the Forest Service 2010 RPA Assessment. Gen. Tech. Rep. SRS-150. Asheville, NC: U.S. Department of Agriculture Forest Service, Southern Research Station. 167 p.

Cordell, H.K.; Heboyan, V.; Santos, F.; Bergstrom, J.C. 2012. Natural amenities and rural population migration: a technical document supporting the Forest Service 2010 RPA Assessment. Gen. Tech. Rep. SRS-146. Asheville, NC: U.S. Department of Agriculture Forest Service, Southern Research Station. 32 p.

Cordell, H.K. 2008. The latest on trends in nature-based outdoor recreation. Forest History Today. Spring: 4-10.

Cordell, H.K.; Bergstrom, J.C.; Bowker, J.M. 2005. The multiple values of wilderness. State College, PA: Venture Publishing. 298 p.

Cordell, H.K.; Overdevest, C. 2001. Footprints on the land: an assessment of demographic trends and the future of natural resources in the United States. Champaign, IL: Sagamore Publishing. 307 p.

Cottrell, S.P.; Vaske, J.J. 2006. A framework for monitoring and modeling sustainable tourism. e-Review of Tourism Research. 4(4): 74-84.

Cottrell, S.P.; Vaske, J.J.; Shen, F.; Ritter, P. 2007. Resident perceptions of sustainable tourism in Chongdugou, China. Society and Natural Resources. 20(6): 511-525.

Cvetkovich G.T.; Winter P.L. 2003. Trust and social representations of the management of threatened and endangered species. Environment and Behavior. 35(2): 286-307.

Dawson, C.P.; Hendee, J.C. 2009. Wilderness management: stewardship and protection of resources and values, fourth ed. Golden, CO: Fulcrum Publishing. 656 p.

Donovan, G.H.; Brown, T.C. 2007. Be careful what you wish for: the legacy of Smokey Bear. Frontiers in Ecology. 5(2): 73-79.

Duarte, L. 2010. GAP and the protected areas database of the United States (PAD-US) partnership. Gap Analysis Bulletin. http://www.gap.uidaho.edu/bulletins/17/Duarte.pdf. [Date accessed: May 6, 2011].

Evison, H. 1930. A state park anthology. Washington, DC: National Conference on State Parks. http://www.nps.gov/history/history/online_books/recreation_use/chap3-2.htm. [Date accessed: September 6, 2011].

Frank, L.D.; Andresen, M.A ; Schmid, T.L. 2004. Obesity relationships with community design, physical activity, and time spent in cars. American Journal of Preventive Medicine. 27(2): 87-96.

Hellerstein, D. 2010. Challenges facing USDA's conservation reserve program. http://www.ers.usda.gov/AmberWaves/June10/Features/ChallengesFacingCRP.htm. [Date accessed: October 24, 2011].

Hendee, J.C.; Dawson, C.P. 2004. Wilderness progress after forty years under the U.S. Wilderness Act. International Journal of Wilderness. 10(1): 4-7.

Hill, B.J. 1994. Wilderness valuation – preservation. http://www.findarticles.com [Date accessed: December 10, 2007].

Houlahan, J.E.; Findlay, C.S. 2004. Estimating the "critical" distance at which adjacent land-use degrades wetland water and sediment quality. Landscape Ecology. 19: 677–690.

Hurteau, M.D.; Hungate, B.A.; Koch, G.W. 2009. Accounting for risk in valuing forest carbon offsets. http://www.cbmjournal.com/content/4/1/1. [Date accessed: August 16, 2011].

Im, S.; Brannan, K.M ; Mostaghimi, S. 2003. Simulating hydrologic and water quality impacts in an urbanizing watershed. Journal of the American Water Resources Association. 39(6): 1465–1479.

Interagency Wild and Scenic Rivers Council. 2009. River mileage classifications for components of the June 2009 National Wild and Scenic Rivers System. http://rivers.gov/publications/rivers-table.pdf. [Date accessed: February 23, 2010].

Intergovernmental Panel on Climate Change (IPCC). 2007. Climate change 2007: synthesis report. http://www.ipcc.ch/publications_and_data/publications_ipcc_fourth_assessment_report_synthesis_report.htm. [Date accessed: September 30, 2011].

Jubenville, A. 1978. Outdoor recreation planning. Philadelphia, PA: W.B. Saunders Company. 290 p.

Kalabokidis, K.D. 2000. Effects of wildfire suppression chemicals on people and the environment: a review. Global Nest. 2(2): 129-137.

Krist, F.J.; Sapio, F.; Tkacz, B. 2007. Mapping risk from forest insects and diseases. FHTET-2007 06. Fort Collins, CO: U.S. Department of Agriculture Forest Service, Forest Health Technology Enterprise Team. 115 p.

Land Trust Alliance. 2006. 2005 National land trust census report. http://www.landtrustalliance.org/land-trusts/land-trust-census/2005-report.pdf. [Date accessed: January 14, 2011].

Leung, Y.-F.; Siderelis, C.; Serenari, C. 2010. Annual information exchange—statistical report of state park operations: 2008-2009. Raleigh, NC: North Carolina State University, Department of Parks, Recreation, and Tourism Management. 58 p.

Lubowski, R.N.; Vesterby, M.; Bucholtz, S. [and others]. 2006. Major uses of land in the United States, 2002. http://www.ers.usda.gov/publications/EIB14/eib14.pdf. [Date accessed: October 24, 2011].

Maczko, K.; Hidinger, L., eds. 2008. Sustainable rangelands: ecosystem goods and services. http://www.fs fed.us/rm/pubs_other/rmrs_2008_maczko_k001.pdf. [Date accessed: October 24, 2011].

Menakis, J.P. 2008. Mapping wildland fire potential for the conterminous United States. http://svinetfc4.fs.fed.us/RS2008/j_menakis/index.htm. [Date accessed: August 16, 2011].

Multi-Resolution Land Characteristics Consortium. 2001. National Land Cover Database 2001. http://www.mrlc.gov/nlcd2001.php. [Date accessed: June 24, 2011].

Munn, I.A.; Barlow, S.A.; Evans, D.L.; Cleaves, D. 2002. Urbanization's impact on timber harvesting in the south-central United States. Journal of Environmental Management. 64: 65-66.

National Association of State Foresters. 2006. State forestry statistics. http://www.stateforesters.org/node/896 [Date accessed: July 8, 2009].

National Scenic Byways Program. 2010. America's byways: national scenic byways online. http://www.byways.org. [Date accessed: January 4, 2011].

Negra, C.; Sweedo, C.C.; Cavender-Bares, K.; O'Malley, R. 2008. Indicators of carbon storage in U.S. ecosystems: baseline for terrestrial carbon accounting. Journal of Environmental Quality. 37: 1376-1382.

Nowak, D.J.; Walton, J.T.; Dwyer, J.F. [and others]. 2005. The increasing influence of urban environments on U.S. forest management. Journal of Forestry. 103(8): 377–382.

Outdoor Recreation Resources Review Commission. 1962. Outdoor recreation for America. Washington, DC: U.S. Governmentt Printing Office. 246 p.

Outdoor Resources Review Group. 2009. Great outdoors America. http://www.orrgroup.org/documents/July2009_Great-Outdoors-America-report.pdf. [Date accessed: September 30, 2011].

Papanastasis, V.P. 2009. Restoration of degraded grazing lands through grazing management: can it work. Restoration Ecology. 17: 441–445.

President's Commission on Americans Outdoors. 1986. Report and recommendations to the President of the United States. Washington, DC: U.S. Government Printing Office. 210 p.

Price, M.; Moss, L.; Williams, P.W. 1997. Chapter 12: tourism and amenity migration. In: Messerli, B.; Ives, J.D., eds. Mountains of the world: a global priority. New York: The Parthenon Publishing Group: 249-280.

Radeloff, V.C.; Stewart, S.I.; Hawbaker, T.J. [and others]. 2010. Housing growth in and near United States protected areas limits their conservation value. http://www.pnas.org/content/107/2/940.full. [Date accessed: August 23, 2011].

Reeves, M.C.; Mitchell, J.E. (In press). A synoptic review of U.S. rangelands: a technical document supporting the 2010 USDA Forest Service RPA assessment. Gen. Tech. Rep. XXX. Fort Collins, CO: U.S. Department of Agriculture Forest Service, Rocky Mountains Research Station.

Robles, M.D.; Flather, C.H.; Stein, S.M. [and others]. 2008. The geography of private forests that support at-risk species in the conterminous United States. http://www.esajournals.org/doi/pdf/10.1890/070106. [Date accessed: August 16, 2011].

Rudzitis, G.; Johansen, H.E. 1991. How important is wilderness? Results from a United States survey. Environmental Management. 15(2): 227.

Santos, F.I.M. 2010. Modeling the influence of environmental amenities on recent trends in U.S. population migration. Athens, GA: University of Georgia. 45 p. M.S. thesis.

Schlesinger, W.H. 1997. Biogeochemistry: an analysis of global change. New York: Academic Press. 588 p.

Schneider, I.; Winter, P. 1998. Multiple use management preferences by visitors with differing leisure identity salience. Journal of Park and Recreation Administration. 16(4): 22-38.

Schultz, P.W.; Zelezny, L. 2003. Reframing environmental messages to be congruent with American values. Human Ecology Review. 10(2): 126-136.

Schuster, R.; Cordell, H.K.; Phillips, B. 2005. Measurement of direct-use wilderness values: a qualitative study. In: Peden, J.G.; Schuster, R.M., eds. Proceedings of the 2005 northeastern recreation research symposium; Bolton Landing, NY. Gen. Tech. Rep. NE-341. Newtown Square, PA: U.S. Department of Agriculture Forest Service, Northeastern Research Station: 188-195.

Scurlock, J.M.; Hall, D.O. 1998. The global carbon sink: a grassland perspective. Global Change Biology. 4: 229-233.

Smith, W.B. 2009. Forest area. In: Smith, W.B., tech. coord. Forest resources of the United States, 2007. Gen. Tech. Rep. WO-78. Washington, DC: U.S. Department of Agriculture Forest Service, Washington Office: 12-15.

Smith, W.B.; Miles, P.D.; Perry, C.H.; Pugh, S.A. 2009. Forest resources of the United States, 2007. Gen. Tech. Report WO-78. Washington, DC: U.S. Department of Agriculture Forest Service, Washington Office. 336 p.

Stein, S.; Butler, B. 2004. On the frontline: private forests and water resources, FS-790. Wildland Waters. Washington, DC: U.S. Department of Agriculture Forest Service. 24 p.

Stein, S.; McRoberts, R.; Alig, R. [and others]. 2005. Forests on the edge: housing development on America's private forests. Gen. Tech. Rep. PNW-GTR-636. Portland, OR: U.S. Department of Agriculture Forest Service, Pacific Northwest Research Station. 16 p.

Stein, S.M.; McRoberts, R.E.; Mahal, L.G. [and others]. 2009. Private forests, public benefits: increased housing density and other pressures on private forest contributions. Gen. Tech. Rep. PNW-GTR-795. Portland, OR: U.S. Department of Agriculture Forest Service, Pacific Northwest Research Station. 74 p.

Syphard, A.D.; Radeloff, V.C.; Keeley, J.E. [and others]. 2007. Human influence on California fire regimes. Ecological Applications. 17(5): 1388-1402.

Tennessee Valley Authority. [N.d.]. Recreation resources inventory, 2008. Available from: Jerry Fouse, Tennessee Valley Authority, Recreation Manager, 400 W. Summit Hill Drive, WT 11A, Knoxville, TN 37902-1401.

Thorne, S.; Sundquist, D. 2001. New Hampshire's vanishing forests: conversion, fragmentation and parcelization of forests in the granite state. http://forestsociety.org/pdf/vanishing_forests.pdf. [Date accessed: August 16, 2011].

Tkacz, B.; Moody, B.; Castillo, J.V. 2007. Forest health status in North America. Proceedings: impacts of air pollution and climate change on forest ecosystems. The Scientific World Journal. 7(S1): 28-36.

The Trust for Public Land. 2009. City park facts. Available from: Center for City Park Excellence, The Trust for Public Land, 660 Pennsylvania Avenue SE, Suite 401, Washington, DC. 20003.

The Trust for Public Land. 2010. Conservation almanac: federal, state, local & private lands. http://www.conservationalmanac.org. [Date accessed: October 25, 2011].

U.S. Army Corps of Engineers. 2006. Value to the nation, fast facts. http://www.corpsresults.us/recreation/recfastfacts.asp. [Date accessed: February 23, 2009].

U.S. Census Bureau. 2000. Census 2000 U.S. gazetteer files: counties. http://www.census.gov/geo/www/gazetteer/places2k.html#counties. [Date accessed: October 24, 2011].

U.S. Census Bureau. 2002. County business patterns. http://www.census.gov/econ/cbp/download/02_data/index.htm. [Date accessed: August 24, 2009].

U.S. Census Bureau. 2004a. U.S. interim projections by age, sex, race, and Hispanic origin. http://www.census.gov/population/www/projections/usinterimproj/. [Date accessed: August 16, 2011].

U.S. Census Bureau. 2004b. Census of housing, historical census of housing tables. http://www.census.gov/hhes/www/housing/census/historic/vacation.html. [Date accessed: October 26, 2011].

U.S. Census Bureau. 2007a. State and local government finances. In: The statistical abstract of the United States. http://www.census.gov/prod/2006pubs/07statab/stlocgov.pdf. [Date accessed: February 10, 2011].

U.S. Census Bureau. 2007b. County business patterns. http://www.census.gov/econ/cbp/download/07_data/index.htm. [Date accessed: August 24, 2009].

U.S. Census Bureau. 2007c. Census of governments. http://www.census.gov/govs/cog/. [Date accessed: March 31, 2009].

U.S. Census Bureau. 2008. Population estimates—annual estimates of the resident population for counties: April 1, 2000 to July 1, 2008. http://www.census.gov/popest/counties/CO-EST2008-01.html. [Date accessed: September 8, 2009].

U.S. Census Bureau. 2010a. The 2010 statistical abstract, table 346–land and water area of states and other entities: 2008. http://www.census.gov/prod/2009pubs/10statab/geo.pdf. [Date accessed: October 24, 2011].

U.S. Census Bureau. 2010b. The 2010 statistical abstract, table 800. farms—number and acreage: 1990 to 2008. http://www.census.gov/prod/2009pubs/10statab/agricult.pdf. [Date accessed: October 25, 2011].

U.S. Census Bureau. 2011. The 2011 statistical abstract: the national data book. http://www.census.gov/compendia/statab/2011/tables/11s0822.pdf. [Date accessed: August 19, 2011].

U.S. Department of Agriculture (USDA) Forest Service. (In press). Future scenarios and assumptions for the 2010 Resource Planning Act (RPA) assessment. Gen. Tech. Rep. XX. Washington, DC: U.S. Department of Agriculture Forest Service.

USDA Forest Service. 1980. An assessment of the forest and range land situation in the United States. Report FS-345. Washington, DC: U.S. Government Printing Office. 630 p.

USDA Forest Service. 1990. An analysis of the outdoor recreation and wilderness situation in the United States: 1989-2040. Gen. Tech. Rep. RM-189. Fort Collins, CO: Rocky Mountains Forest and Range Experiment Station. 112 p.

USDA Forest Service. 2007. Forest insects and disease conditions in the United States, 2006. http://gis.fs.fed.us/foresthealth/publications/ConditionsReport_06_final.pdf. [Date accessed: October 24, 2011].

USDA Forest Service. 2008. Land areas report as of September 30, 2008. http://www.fs.fed.us/land/staff/lar/2008/lar08index.html. [Date accessed: March 11, 2009].

USDA Forest Service. 2009a. State park inventory study [data]. Shela H. Mou, comp.

USDA Forest Service. 2009b. National survey on recreation and the environment, 2005-2009 [data set]. http://www.srs.fs.usda.gov/trends/Nsre/NSRECert.html. [Date accessed: October 27, 2011].

USDA Forest Service. 2010. Current Forest Data and Maps. Forest Inventory and Analysis National Program. http://www.fia.fs.fed.us/slides/current-data.pdf. [Date accessed: October 25, 2011].

USDA National Agricultural Statistics Service. 2007. Census of agriculture, vol. 1. http://www.agcensus.usda.gov/Publications/2007/Full_Report. [Date accessed: October 25, 2011].

USDA Natural Resources Conservation Service, and Iowa State University Statistical Laboratory. 2000. Summary report: 1997 natural resources inventory http://www.nrcs.usda.gov/Internet/FSE_DOCUMENTS/nrcs143_012094.pdf. [Date accessed: October 24, 2011].

USDA Natural Resources Conservation Service. 2007. National resources inventory 2003, land use. http://www.docstoc.com/docs/6826033/National-Resources-Inventory. [Date accessed: October 24, 2011].

USDA Natural Resources Conservation Service. 2009. Summary Report: 2007 National Resources Inventory. http://www.nrcs.usda.gov/Internet/FSE_DOCUMENTS//stelprdb1041379.pdf. [Date accessed: October 24, 2011].

U.S. Department of Commerce (USDC), National Oceanic and Atmospheric Administration. 2004. List of coastal counties for the bureau of the census statistical abstract series. http://www.census.gov/geo/landview/lv6help/coastal_cty.pdf. [Date accessed: March 27, 2009].

USDC National Oceanic and Atmospheric Administration. 2005. National climatic data center. http://cdo.ncdc.noaa.gov/cgi-bin/climaps/climaps.pl. [Date accessed: August 14, 2009].

U.S. Geological Survey. 2004. Bailey's ecoregions and subregions of the United States. http://nationalatlas.gov/mld/ecoregp.html. [Date accessed: September 2, 2011].

U.S. Geological Survey. 2005a. Federal lands of the United States. http://nationalatlas.gov/mld/fedlanp.html. [Date accessed: October 26, 2011].

U.S. Geological Survey. 2005b. Indian lands of the United States. http://nationalatlas.gov/mld/indlanp.html. [Date accessed: October 26, 2011].

U.S. Department of the Interior, (USDI). 2009. Recreation one-stop initiative: recreation information database. http://www.recreation.gov. [Date accessed: April 3, 2009].

USDI Bureau of Land Management. 2008a. Public land statistics 2008. http://www.blm.gov/public_land_statistics/pls08/index.htm. [Date accessed: June 23, 2009].

USDI Bureau of Land Management. 2008b. Payment in lieu of taxes (PILT), acres by agency. http://www.nbc.gov/pilt/pilt/search.cfm. [Date accessed: April 13, 2009].

USDI Bureau of Reclamation. 2008. Recreation fast facts. http://www.usbr.gov/recreation/facts.html. [Date accessed: February 19, 2009].

USDI Fish and Wildlife Service. 2009. Annual report of lands under the control of the U.S. Fish and Wildlife Service as of September 30, 2008. http://www.fws.gov/refuges/land/pdf/AnnLandsReport_2008.pdf. [Date accessed: June 23, 2009].

USDI Heritage Conservation and Recreation Service. 1979. The third nationwide outdoor recreation plan: the assessment. Washington, DC: U.S. Government Printing Office. 55 p.

USDI National Park Service. 1941. A study of the park and recreation problem of the United States. http://www.nps.gov/history/history/online_books/parks_america/index.htm. [Date accessed: January 28, 2011].

USDI National Park Service. 2008. Listing of acreage by State and county as of 12/31/2008. http://www.nature.nps.gov/stats/acreagemenu.cfm. [Date accessed: February 26, 2009].

United Nations Environment Programme and World Tourism Organization. 2005. Making tourism more sustainable: a guide for policy makers. Paris, France and Madrid, Spain: UNEP and WTO. 209 p.

Walls, M.A.; Darley, S.R.; Siikamäki, J.V. 2009. The state of the great outdoors: America's parks, public lands, and recreation resources. http://www.rff.org/RFF/Documents/RFF-RPT-ORRG-State-of-Outdoors.pdf. [Date accessed: September 30, 2011].

Wear, D.N.; Liu, R.; Foreman, J.M.; Sheffield, R.M. 1999. The effects of population growth on timber management and inventories in Virginia. Forest Ecology and Management. 118: 107-115.

Wear, D.N. 2011. Forecasts of county-level land uses under three future scenarios: a technical document supporting the Forest Service 2010 RPA Assessment. Gen. Tech. Rep. SRS–141. Asheville, NC: U.S. Department of Agriculture Forest Service, Southern Research Station. 41 p.

Weinberg, A.; Larson, C. 2008. Forestland for sale: challenges and opportunities for conservation over the next ten years. Open Space Institute/Conservation Research Program Report. New York: Open Space Institute, Inc. 19 p.

White, E.M.; Alig, R.J.; Stein, S.M. 2010. Socio-economic changes and forestland development: commonalities and distinctions between the eastern and western USA. Journal of Forestry. 1087: 329-337.

White, E.M.; Morzillo, A.T.; Alig, R.J. 2009. Past and projected rural land conversion in the U.S. at State, regional, and national levels. Landscape and Urban Planning. 89: 37-48.

Wilderness Institute. 2009. Wilderness database [data]. Missoula, MT: University of Montana, College of Forestry and Conservation.

Wilderness Net. [N.d.]. U.S. Public Law 88-577, The Wilderness Act of September 3, 1964, 78 Stat. 890. http://www.wilderness.net/index.cfm?fuse=NWPS&sec=legisAct&error=404. [Date accessed: August 16, 2011].

Wildlife Management Institute (WMI). 1997. Organization, authority, and programs of State fish and wildlife agencies. Washington, DC: Wildlife Management Institute. 164 p.

Williams, D.R.; Watson, A.E. 2007. Wilderness values: perspectives from the non-economic social science. In: Watson, A.; Sproull, J.; Dean, L., comps. Science and stewardship to protect and sustain wilderness values: eighth World Wilderness Congress symposium. RMRS-P-49. Fort Collins, CO: U.S. Department of Agriculture Forest Service, Rocky Mountains Research Station: 123-133.

Winter, P.L. 2008. Pacific Southwest Research Station and Region 5 sustainable operations survey report. http://www.fs.fed.us/psw/publications/documents/psw_misc8083.pdf. [Date accessed: September 7, 2011].

Winter, P.L.; Chavez, D.J. 2008. Wildland recreationists' natural resource management priorities and preferences: a connection to environmental identity. In: Chavez, D.J.; Winter, P.L.; Absher, J.D., eds. Recreation visitor research: studies of diversity. Gen. Tech. Rep. PSW-GTR-210. Albany, CA: U.S. Department of Agriculture Forest Service, Pacific Southwest Research Station: 163-174.

Zarnoch, S.J.; Cordell, H.K.; Betz, C.J.; Langner, L. 2010. Projecting county-level populations under three future scenarios: a technical document supporting the Forest Service 2010 RPA Assessment. e-Gen. Tech. Rep. SRS–128. Asheville, NC: U.S. Department of Agriculture Forest Service, Southern Research Station. 8 p.

The Forest Service, United States Department of Agriculture (USDA), is dedicated to the principle of multiple use management of the Nation's forest resources for sustained yields of wood, water, forage, wildlife, and recreation. Through forestry research, cooperation with the States and private forest owners, and management of the National Forests and National Grasslands, it strives—as directed by Congress—to provide increasingly greater service to a growing Nation.

The USDA prohibits discrimination in all its programs and activities on the basis of race, color, national origin, age, disability, and where applicable, sex, marital status, familial status, parental status, religion, sexual orientation, genetic information, political beliefs, reprisal, or because all or part of an individual's income is derived from any public assistance program. (Not all prohibited bases apply to all programs.) Persons with disabilities who require alternative means for communication of program information (Braille, large print, audiotape, etc.) should contact USDA's TARGET Center at (202) 720-2600 (voice and TDD).

To file a complaint of discrimination, write to USDA, Director, Office of Civil Rights, 1400 Independence Avenue, SW, Washington, D.C. 20250-9410, or call (800) 795-3272 (voice) or (202) 720-6382 (TDD). USDA is an equal opportunity provider and employer.

Cordell, H. Ken; Betz, Carter J.; and Zarnoch, Stanley J. 2013. Recreation and protected land resources in the United States: a technical document supporting the Forest Service 2010 RPA Assessment. Gen. Tech. Rep. SRS-169. Asheville, NC: U.S. Department of Agriculture Forest Service, Southern Research Station. 198 p.

This report provides an overview of the public and private land and water resources of the United States. Described is use of natural and developed land as recreation resources with an emphasis on nature-based recreation. Also described is land protection through conservation organizations and public funding programs, with an emphasis on protecting private land through funding for purchase or for conservation easements. Outdoor recreation resources include land, water, snow and ice, scenery, developed sites, facilities, and user services. Protected land resources range from farm lands to remote wilderness, but mostly are the undeveloped lands in the United States with various forms of protection status.

The total U.S. land area is 2.43 billion acres, which contains 169 million acres of water, and consists of a diversity of land use and cover types. The United States loses about 2 million acres of forest, farm, and open space each year. In attempting to conserve such lands, land trusts and governments have instituted programs to obtain easements or purchase the land outright. The Federal Government holds in trust about 640 million acres of land (30 percent of the country's total land area). This includes national parks, national forests, national wildlife refuges, and other Federal agency ownerships. These lands, along with State and local government lands are important recreation resources serving the public interest. Private lands and recreation businesses are also important recreation resources. Projections to 2060 of per capita area of public and private land and water show a steady downward trend across all regions of the United States.

Keywords: Land conservation, private land, public land, recreation resources, trends and forecasts.

How do you rate this publication?

Scan this code to submit your feedback or go to www.srs.fs.usda.gov/pubeval

You may request additional copies of this publication by email at pubrequest@fs.fed.us. Number of copies is limited to two per person.

USDA

United States Department of Agriculture

Forest Service

RPA

Southern Research Station

General Technical Report SRS-169

January 2013

www.ingramcontent.com/pod-product-compliance
Lightning Source LLC
Chambersburg PA
CBHW080246290526
45790CB00005B/1716